CROQUIS POP 2

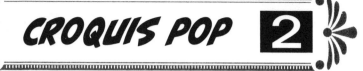

Writer KwangHyun SEO
Artist JinHo Ko

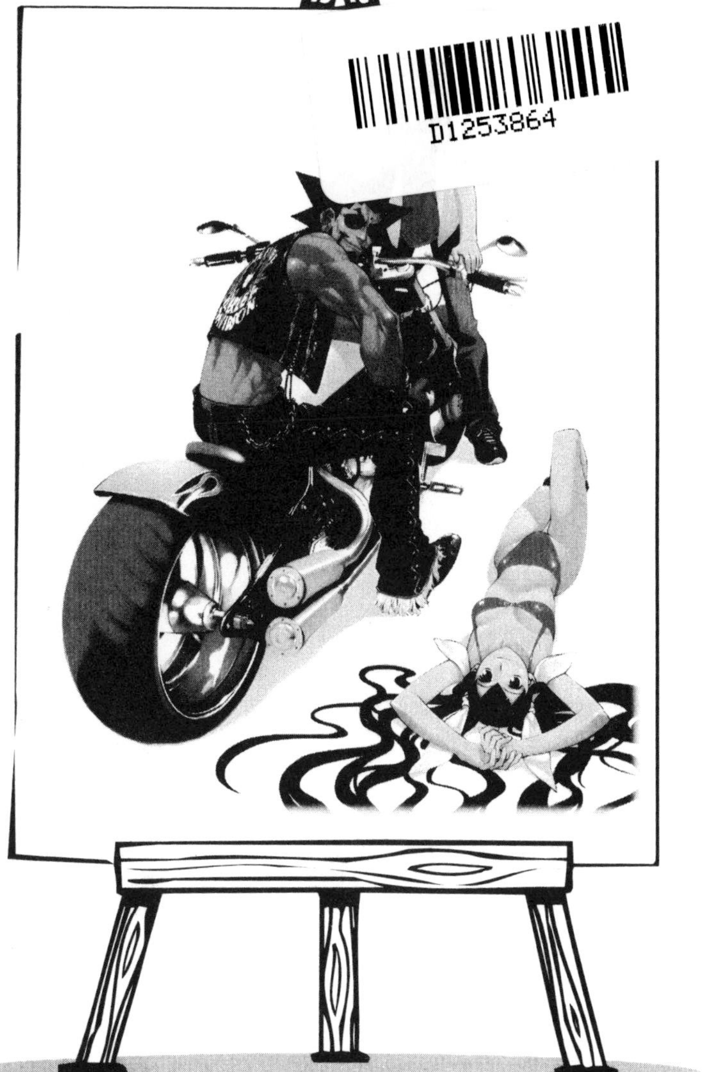

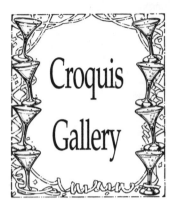

Croquis
Gallery

DIRECTOR/
JinHo KO

STORY/
KwangHyun SEO

STAFF/
JaeHyun SONG
KyungSoo JEON
InSun CHO

SPECIAL THANKS TO
HyunSook JUNG,
JungYun KIM, DongIl
KIM, KiSam KIM,
GyuMin KIM, YunChul
KIM, AND JuJin LEE.

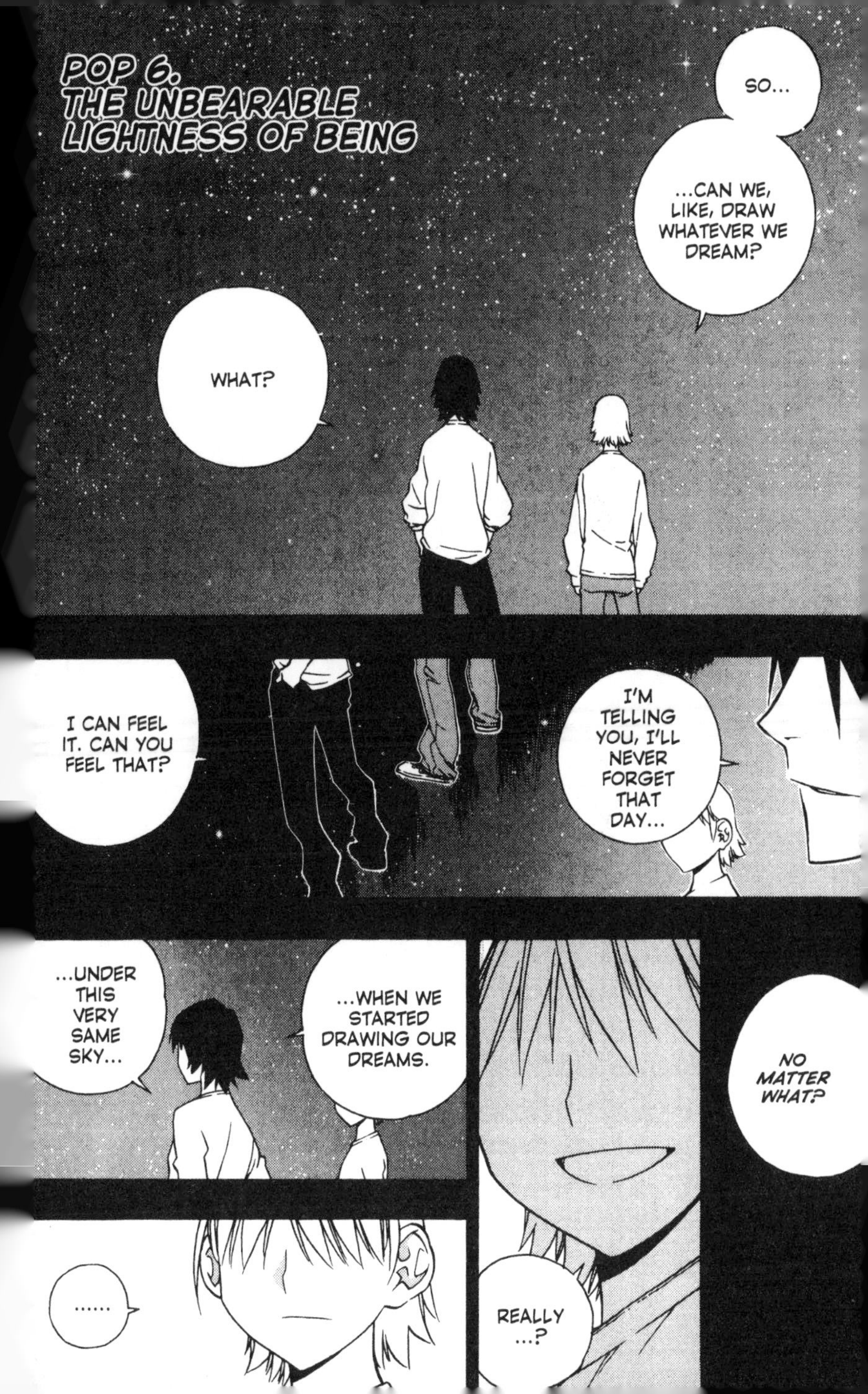
POP 6.
THE UNBEARABLE LIGHTNESS OF BEING
SO...
...CAN WE, LIKE, DRAW WHATEVER WE DREAM?
WHAT?
I CAN FEEL IT. CAN YOU FEEL THAT?
I'M TELLING YOU, I'LL NEVER FORGET THAT DAY...
...UNDER THIS VERY SAME SKY...
...WHEN WE STARTED DRAWING OUR DREAMS.
......
NO MATTER WHAT?
REALLY ...?

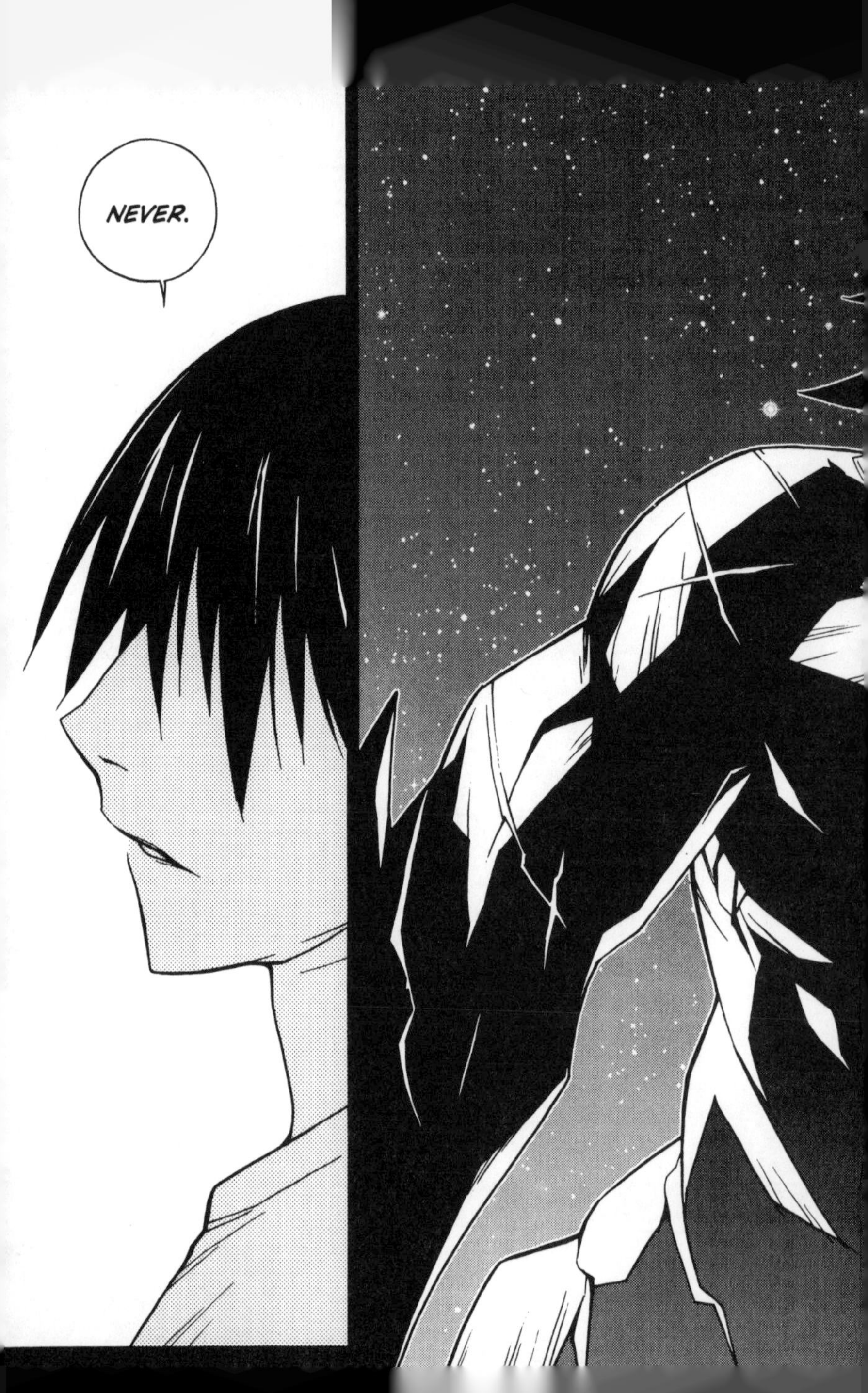
NEVER.

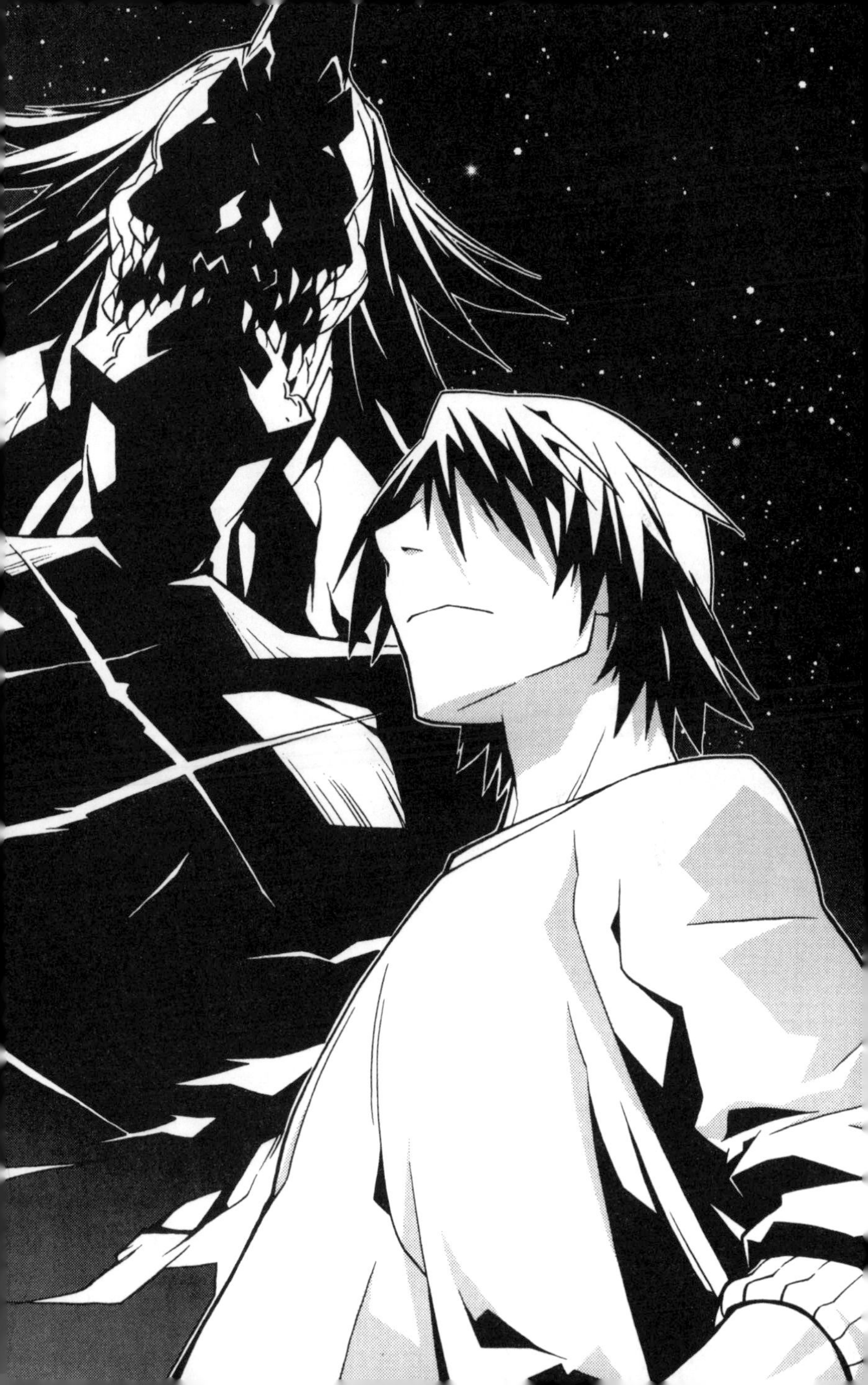

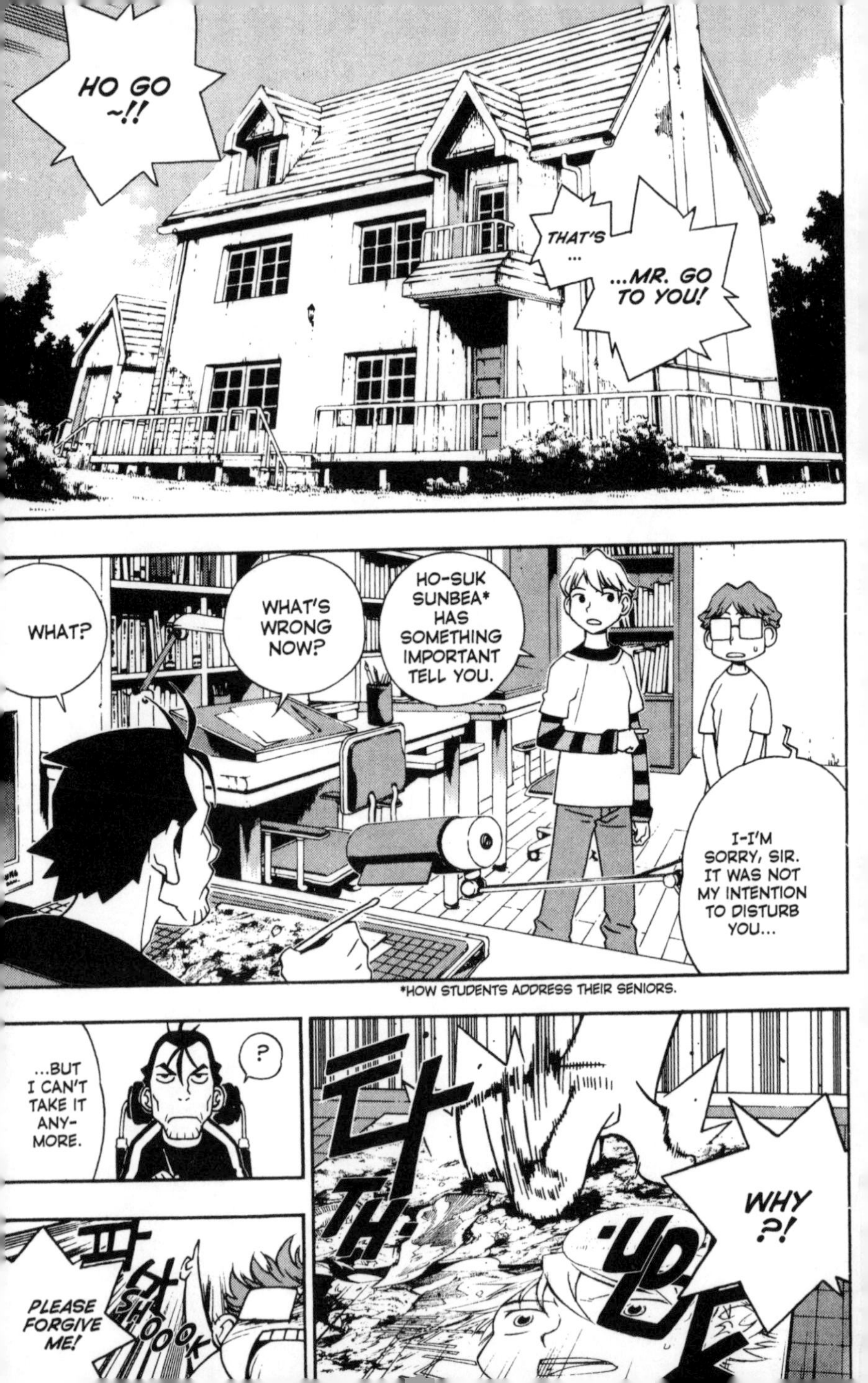
HO GO ~!!
THAT'S ...
...MR. GO TO YOU!
WHAT?
WHAT'S WRONG NOW?
HO-SUK SUNBEA* HAS SOMETHING IMPORTANT TELL YOU.
I-I'M SORRY, SIR. IT WAS NOT MY INTENTION TO DISTURB YOU...
*HOW STUDENTS ADDRESS THEIR SENIORS.
...BUT I CAN'T TAKE IT ANYMORE.
?
SHOOK
PLEASE FORGIVE ME!
TH-UD
WHY ?!

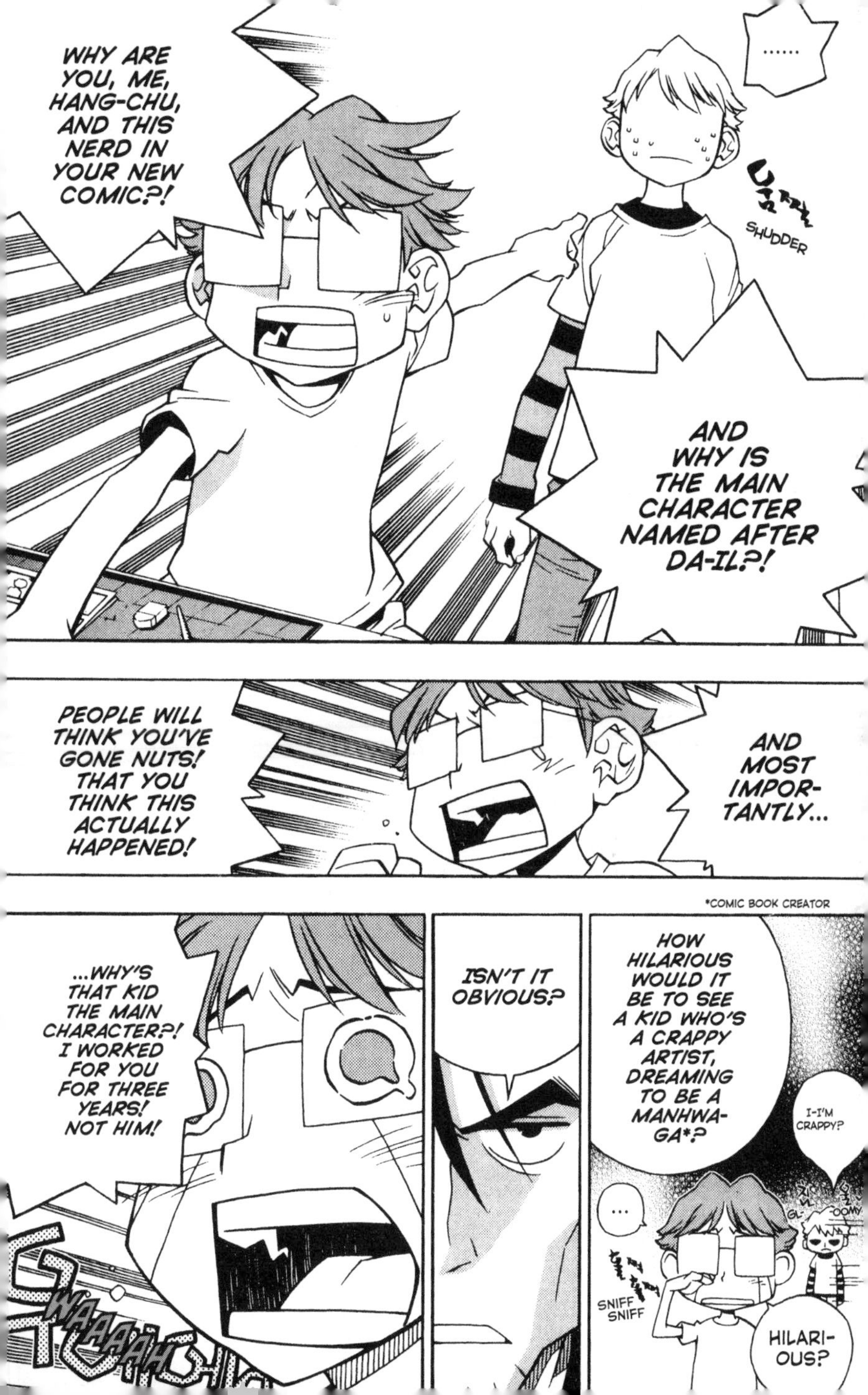
WHY ARE YOU, ME, HANG-CHU, AND THIS NERD IN YOUR NEW COMIC?!
......
SHUDDER
AND WHY IS THE MAIN CHARACTER NAMED AFTER DA-IL?!
PEOPLE WILL THINK YOU'VE GONE NUTS! THAT YOU THINK THIS ACTUALLY HAPPENED!
AND MOST IMPOR-TANTLY...
*COMIC BOOK CREATOR
...WHY'S THAT KID THE MAIN CHARACTER?! I WORKED FOR YOU FOR THREE YEARS! NOT HIM!
WAAAAH
ISN'T IT OBVIOUS?
HOW HILARIOUS WOULD IT BE TO SEE A KID WHO'S A CRAPPY ARTIST, DREAMING TO BE A MANHWA-GA*?
I-I'M CRAPPY?
...
GL-OOMY
SNIFF SNIFF
HILARI-OUS?

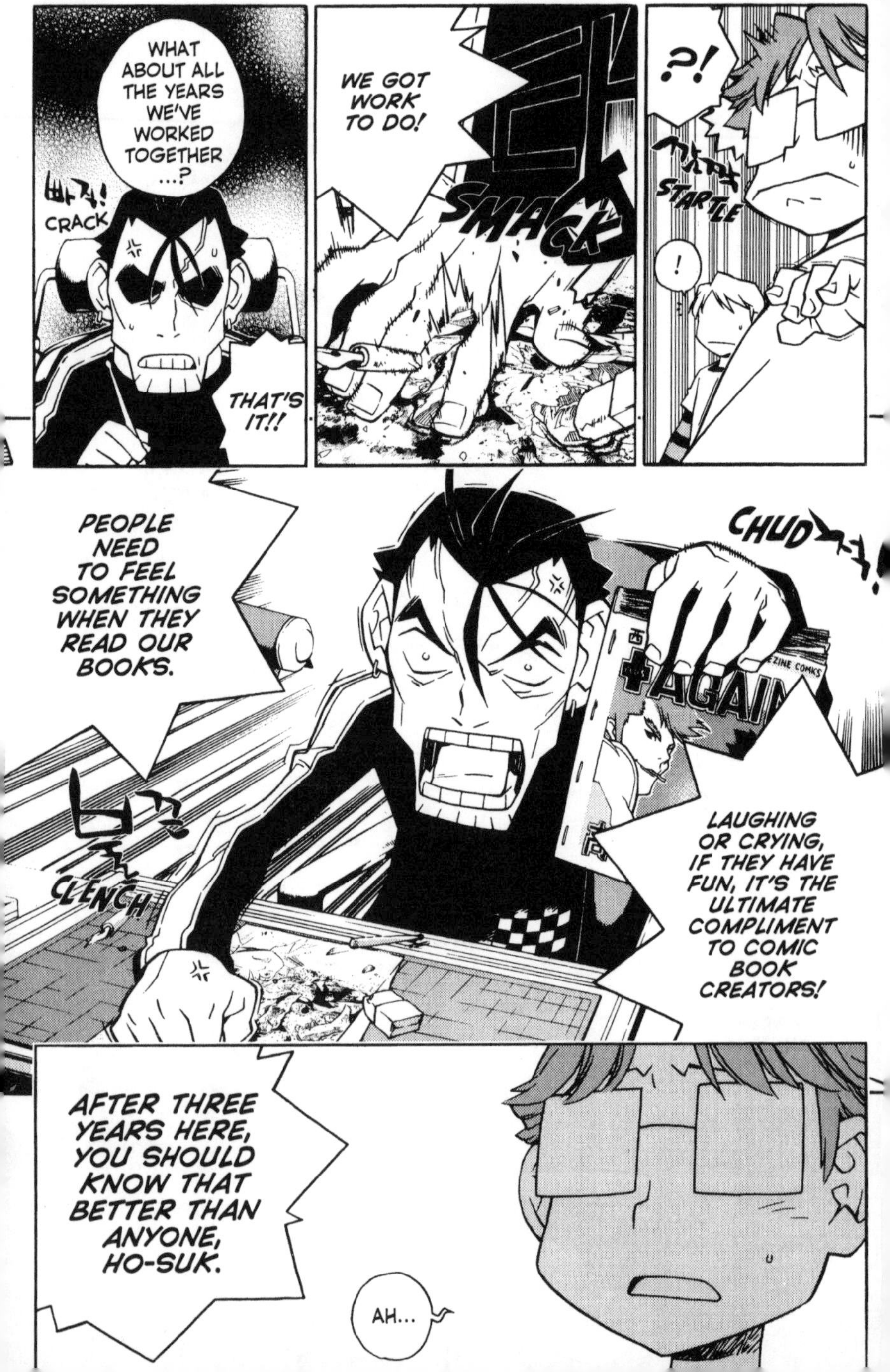
WHAT ABOUT ALL THE YEARS WE'VE WORKED TOGETHER ...?
빠직! CRACK
THAT'S IT!!
WE GOT WORK TO DO!
SMACK
?!
STARTLE
!
PEOPLE NEED TO FEEL SOMETHING WHEN THEY READ OUR BOOKS.
CHUD
+AGAIN
CLENCH
LAUGHING OR CRYING, IF THEY HAVE FUN, IT'S THE ULTIMATE COMPLIMENT TO COMIC BOOK CREATORS!
AFTER THREE YEARS HERE, YOU SHOULD KNOW THAT BETTER THAN ANYONE, HO-SUK.
AH...

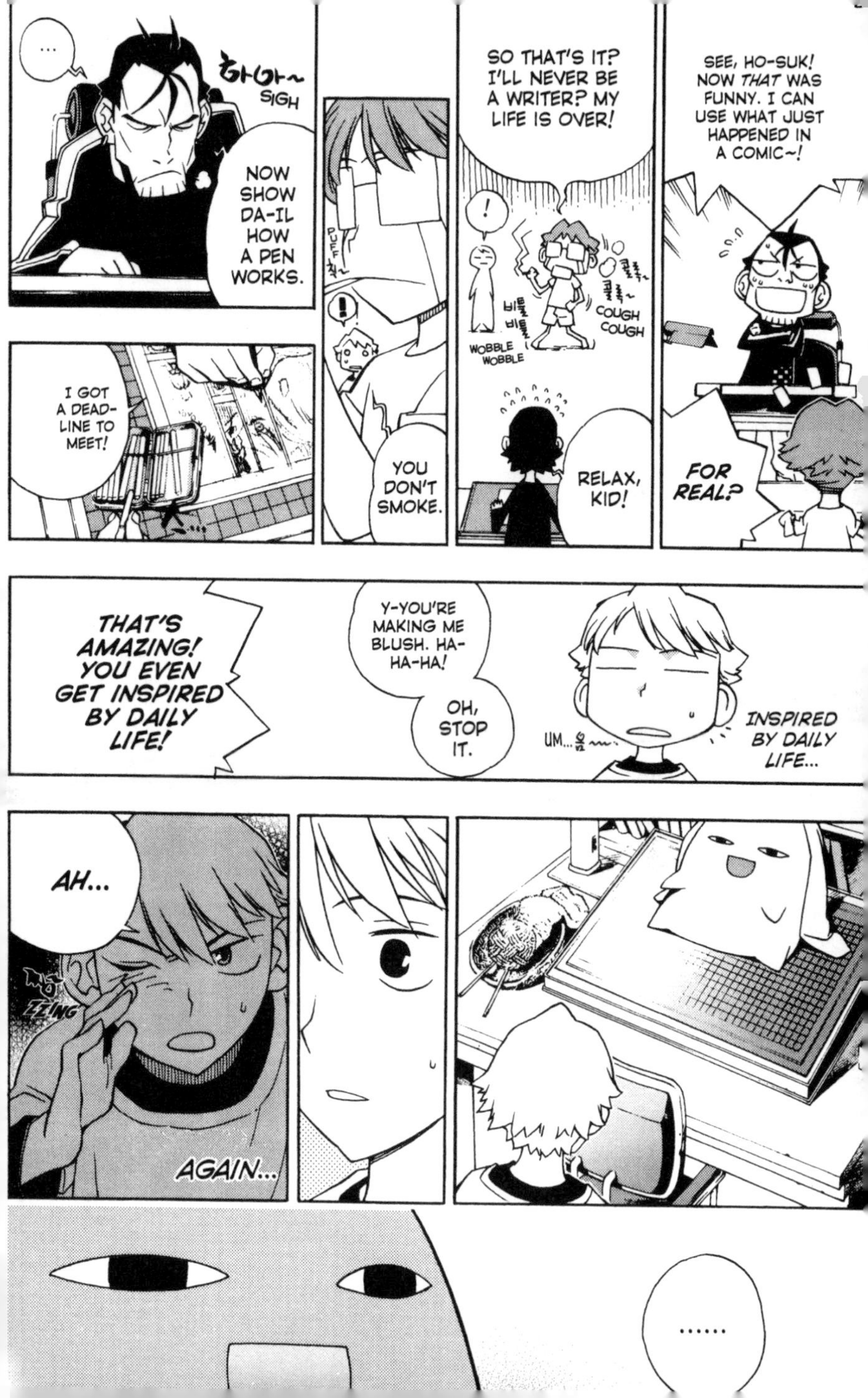
...
하아~
SIGH
NOW SHOW DA-IL HOW A PEN WORKS.
I GOT A DEAD-LINE TO MEET!
...
PUFF
!
YOU DON'T SMOKE.
SO THAT'S IT? I'LL NEVER BE A WRITER? MY LIFE IS OVER!
!
WOBBLE WOBBLE
COUGH COUGH
RELAX, KID!
SEE, HO-SUK! NOW *THAT* WAS FUNNY. I CAN USE WHAT JUST HAPPENED IN A COMIC~!
FOR REAL?
THAT'S AMAZING! YOU EVEN GET INSPIRED BY DAILY LIFE!
Y-YOU'RE MAKING ME BLUSH. HA-HA-HA!
OH, STOP IT.
UM...
INSPIRED BY DAILY LIFE...
AH...
ZZING
AGAIN...
......

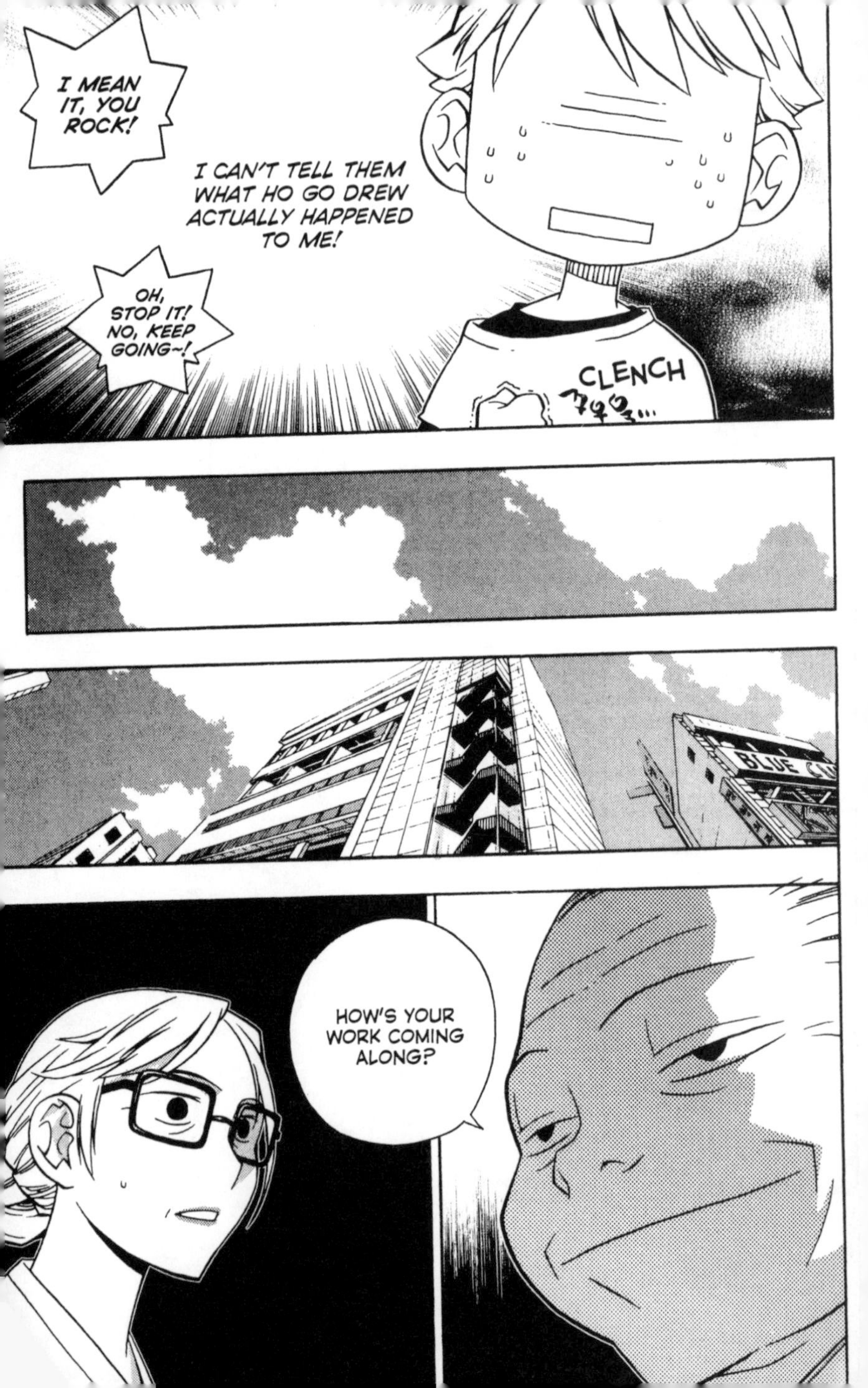
I MEAN IT, YOU ROCK!
I CAN'T TELL THEM WHAT HO GO DREW ACTUALLY HAPPENED TO ME!
OH, STOP IT! NO, KEEP GOING~!
CLENCH
BLUE
HOW'S YOUR WORK COMING ALONG?

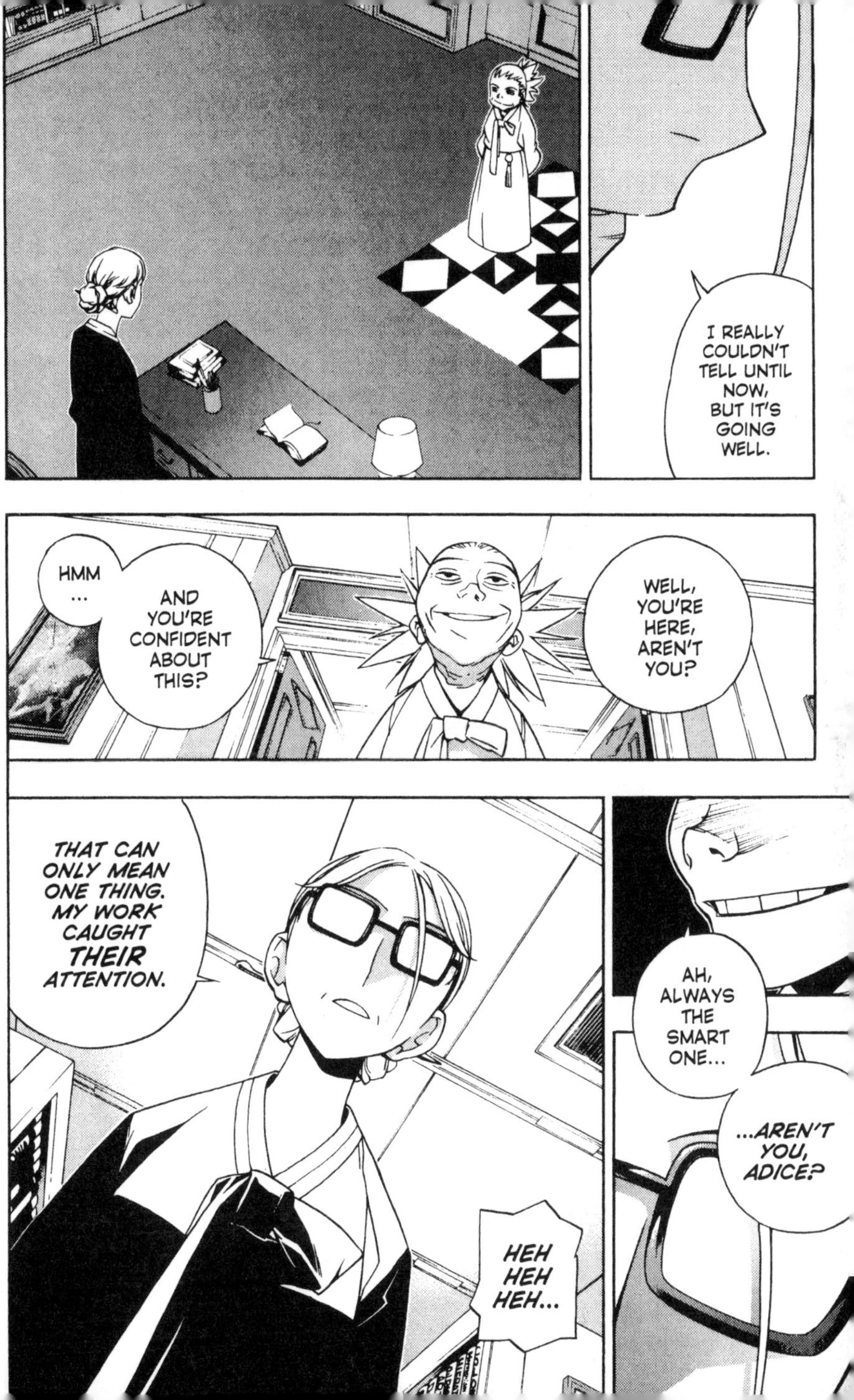
I REALLY COULDN'T TELL UNTIL NOW, BUT IT'S GOING WELL.
HMM ...
AND YOU'RE CONFIDENT ABOUT THIS?
WELL, YOU'RE HERE, AREN'T YOU?
THAT CAN ONLY MEAN ONE THING. MY WORK CAUGHT THEIR ATTENTION.
HEH HEH HEH...
AH, ALWAYS THE SMART ONE...
...AREN'T YOU, ADICE?

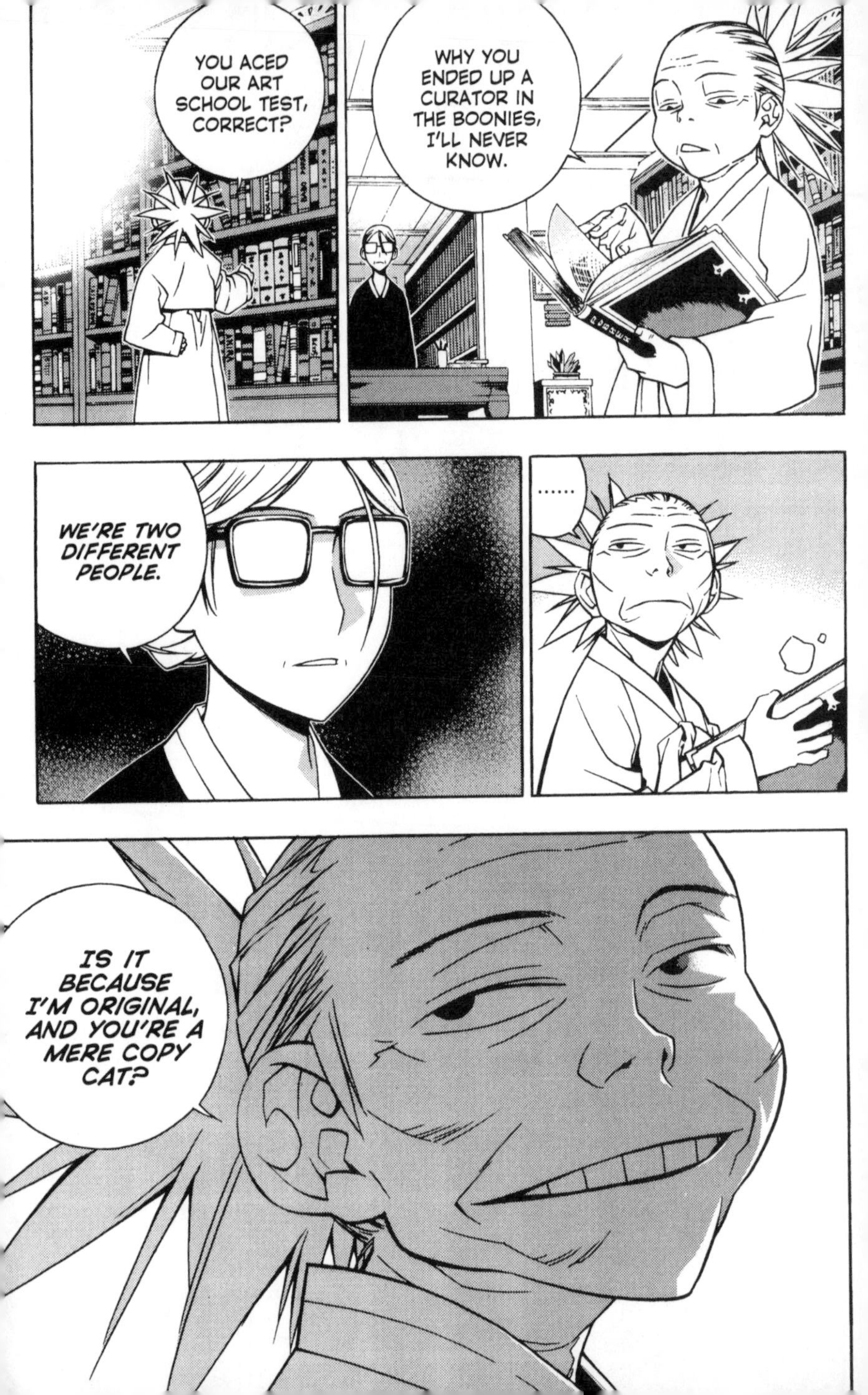
YOU ACED OUR ART SCHOOL TEST, CORRECT?
WHY YOU ENDED UP A CURATOR IN THE BOONIES, I'LL NEVER KNOW.
WE'RE TWO DIFFERENT PEOPLE.
......
IS IT BECAUSE I'M ORIGINAL, AND YOU'RE A MERE COPY CAT?

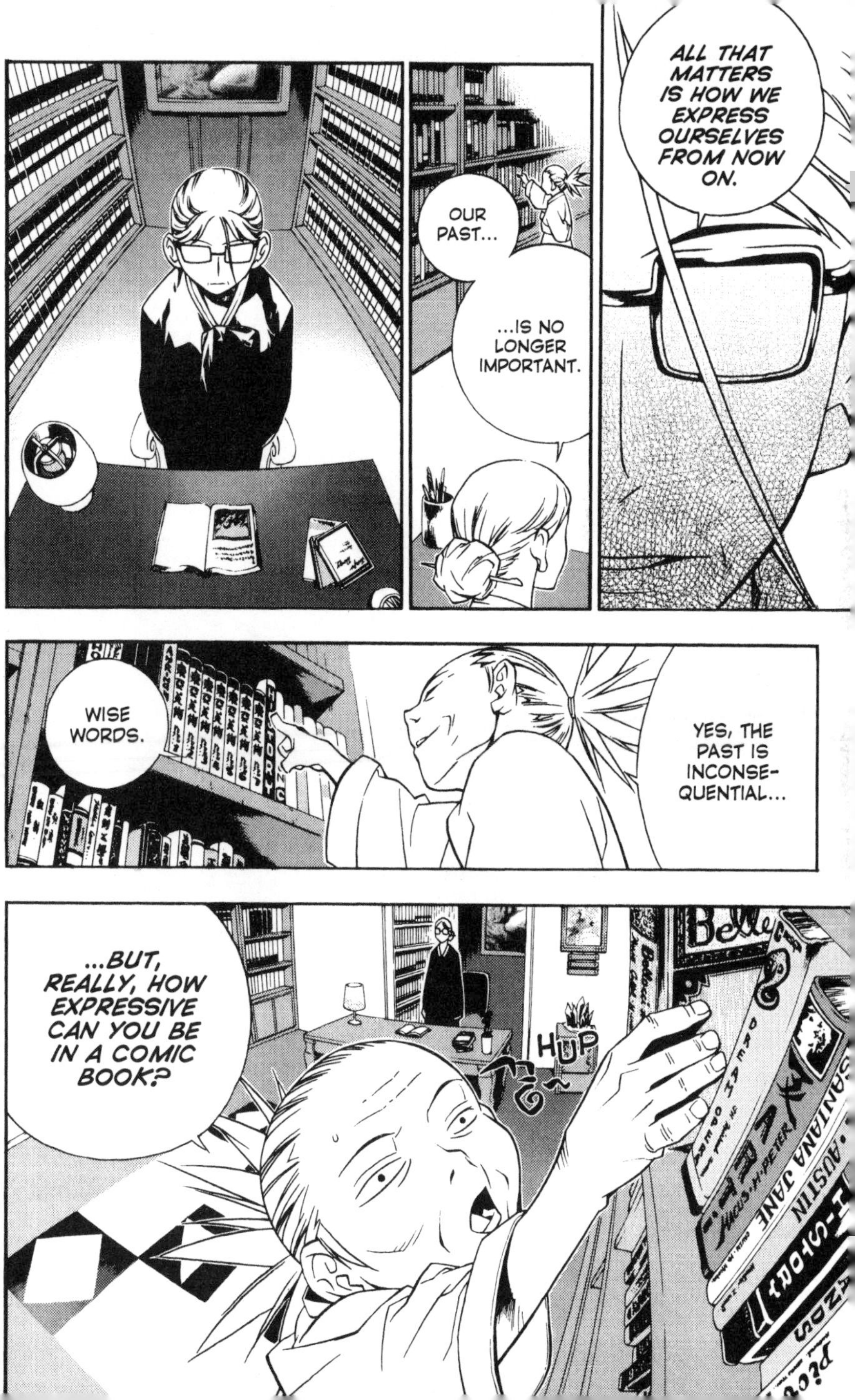
OUR PAST...
...IS NO LONGER IMPORTANT.
ALL THAT MATTERS IS HOW WE EXPRESS OURSELVES FROM NOW ON.
WISE WORDS.
YES, THE PAST IS INCONSE-QUENTIAL...
...BUT, REALLY, HOW EXPRESSIVE CAN YOU BE IN A COMIC BOOK?
HUP

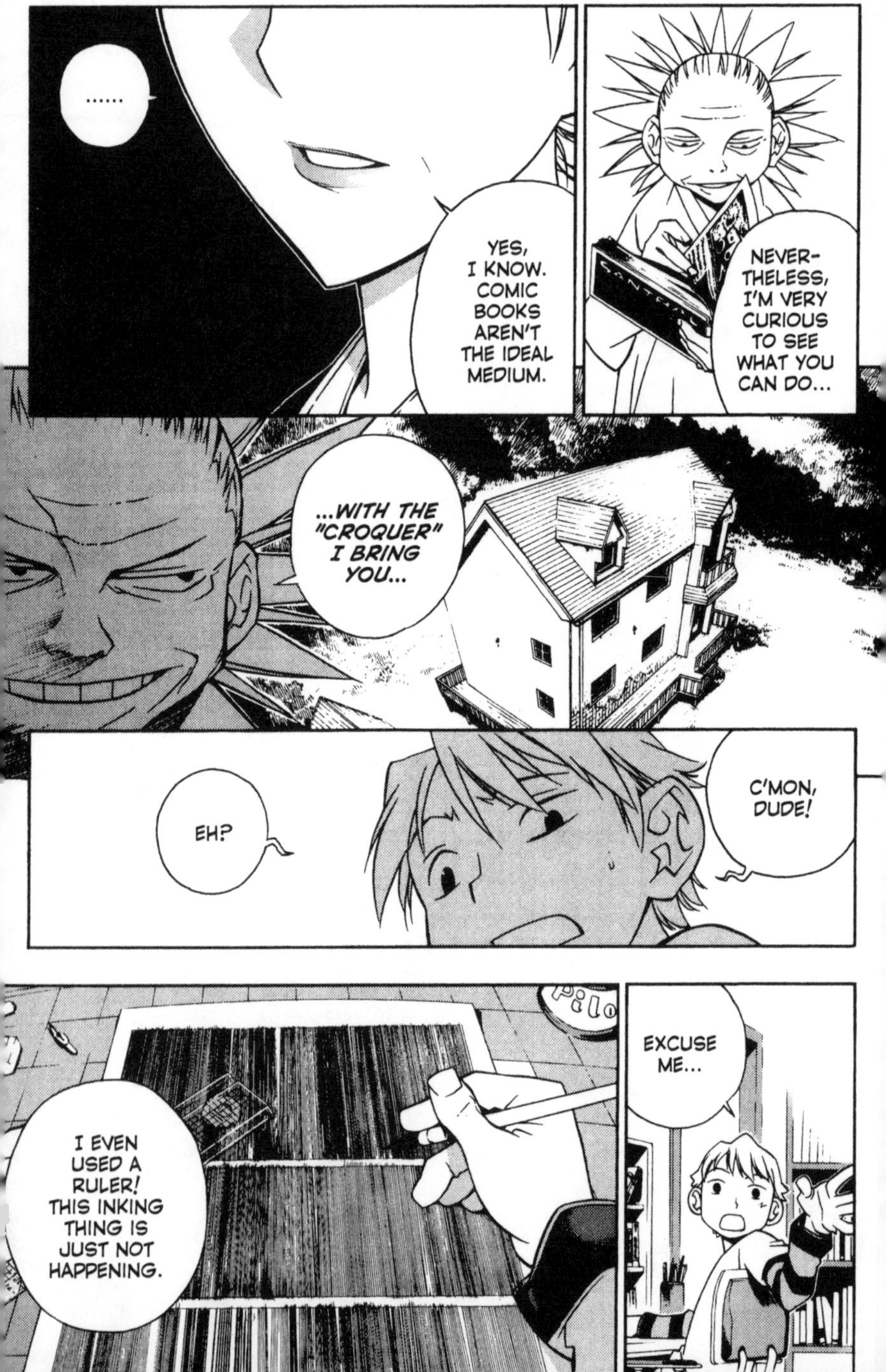
......
YES, I KNOW. COMIC BOOKS AREN'T THE IDEAL MEDIUM.
NEVER-THELESS, I'M VERY CURIOUS TO SEE WHAT YOU CAN DO...
...WITH THE "CROQUER" I BRING YOU...
EH?
C'MON, DUDE!
I EVEN USED A RULER! THIS INKING THING IS JUST NOT HAPPENING.
EXCUSE ME...

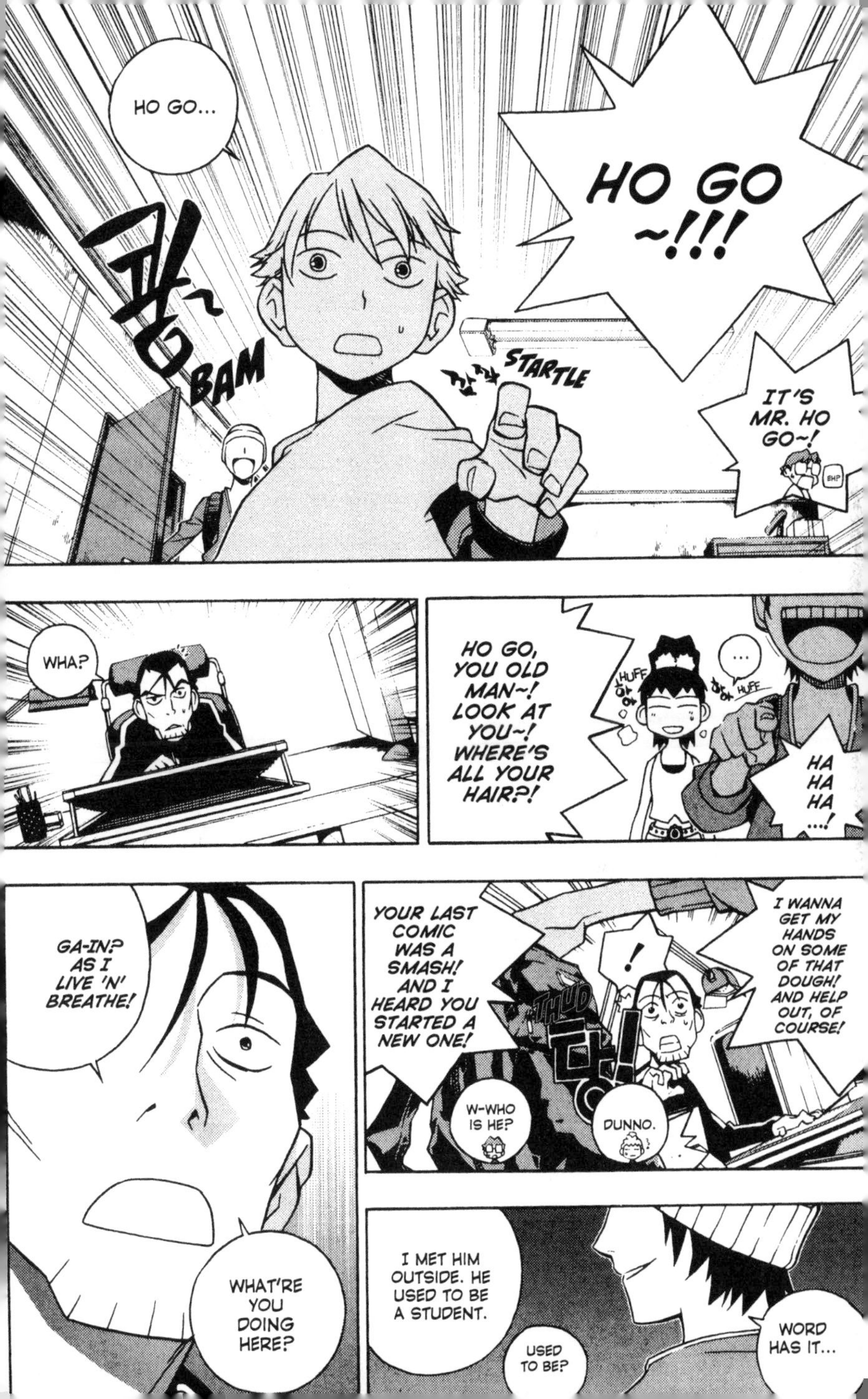
HO GO...
HO GO ~!!!
BAM
STARTLE
IT'S MR. HO GO~!
EHP
WHA?
HO GO, YOU OLD MAN~! LOOK AT YOU~! WHERE'S ALL YOUR HAIR?!
HUFF
...
HUFF
HA HA HA ...!
GA-IN? AS I LIVE 'N' BREATHE!
WHAT'RE YOU DOING HERE?
YOUR LAST COMIC WAS A SMASH! AND I HEARD YOU STARTED A NEW ONE!
!
THUD
I WANNA GET MY HANDS ON SOME OF THAT DOUGH! AND HELP OUT, OF COURSE!
W-WHO IS HE?
DUNNO.
I MET HIM OUTSIDE. HE USED TO BE A STUDENT.
USED TO BE?
WORD HAS IT...

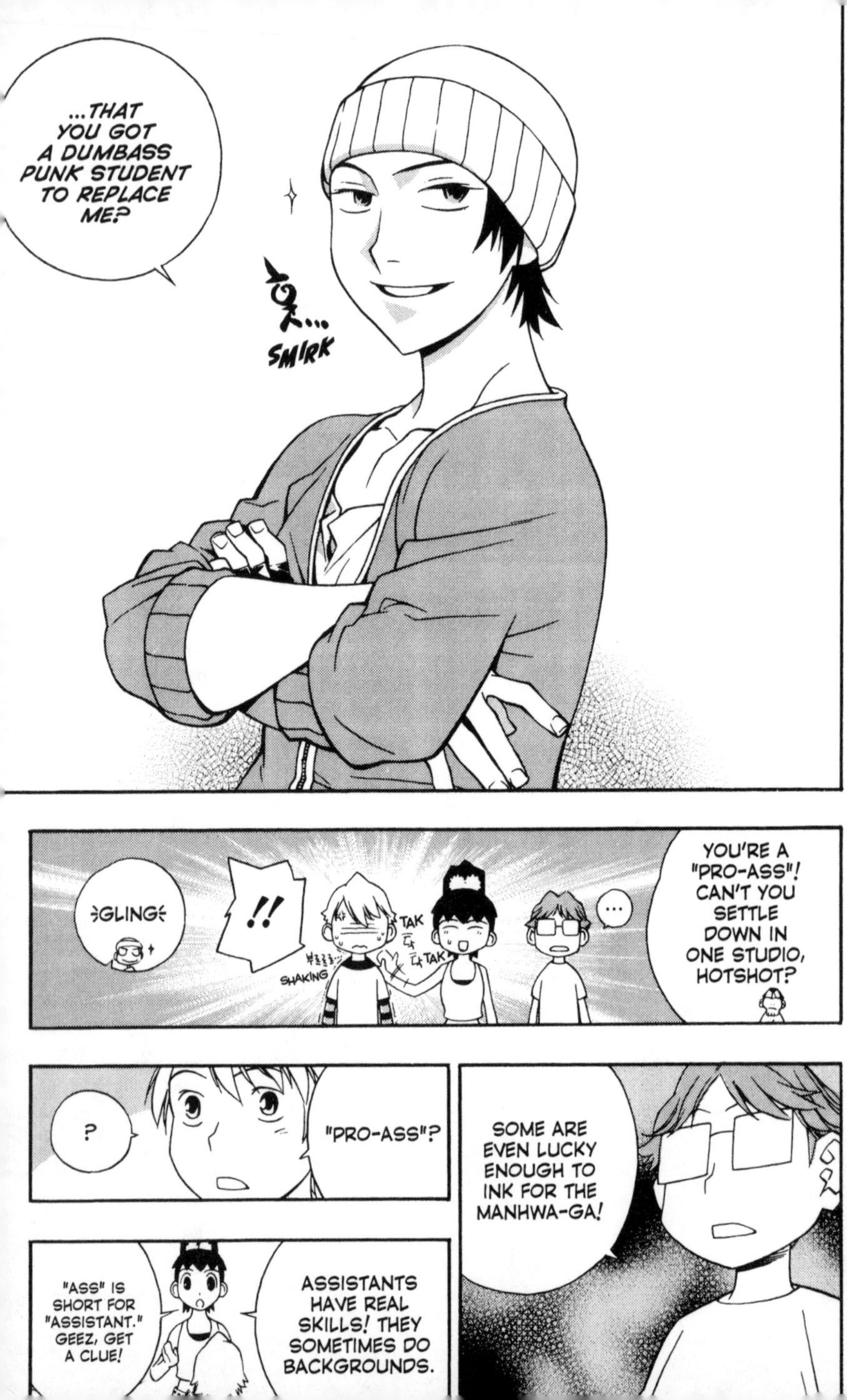
...THAT YOU GOT A DUMBASS PUNK STUDENT TO REPLACE ME?
SMIRK
GLING
!!
SHAKING
TAK
TAK
...
YOU'RE A "PRO-ASS"! CAN'T YOU SETTLE DOWN IN ONE STUDIO, HOTSHOT?
?
"PRO-ASS"?
"ASS" IS SHORT FOR "ASSISTANT." GEEZ, GET A CLUE!
ASSISTANTS HAVE REAL SKILLS! THEY SOMETIMES DO BACKGROUNDS.
SOME ARE EVEN LUCKY ENOUGH TO INK FOR THE MANHWA-GA!

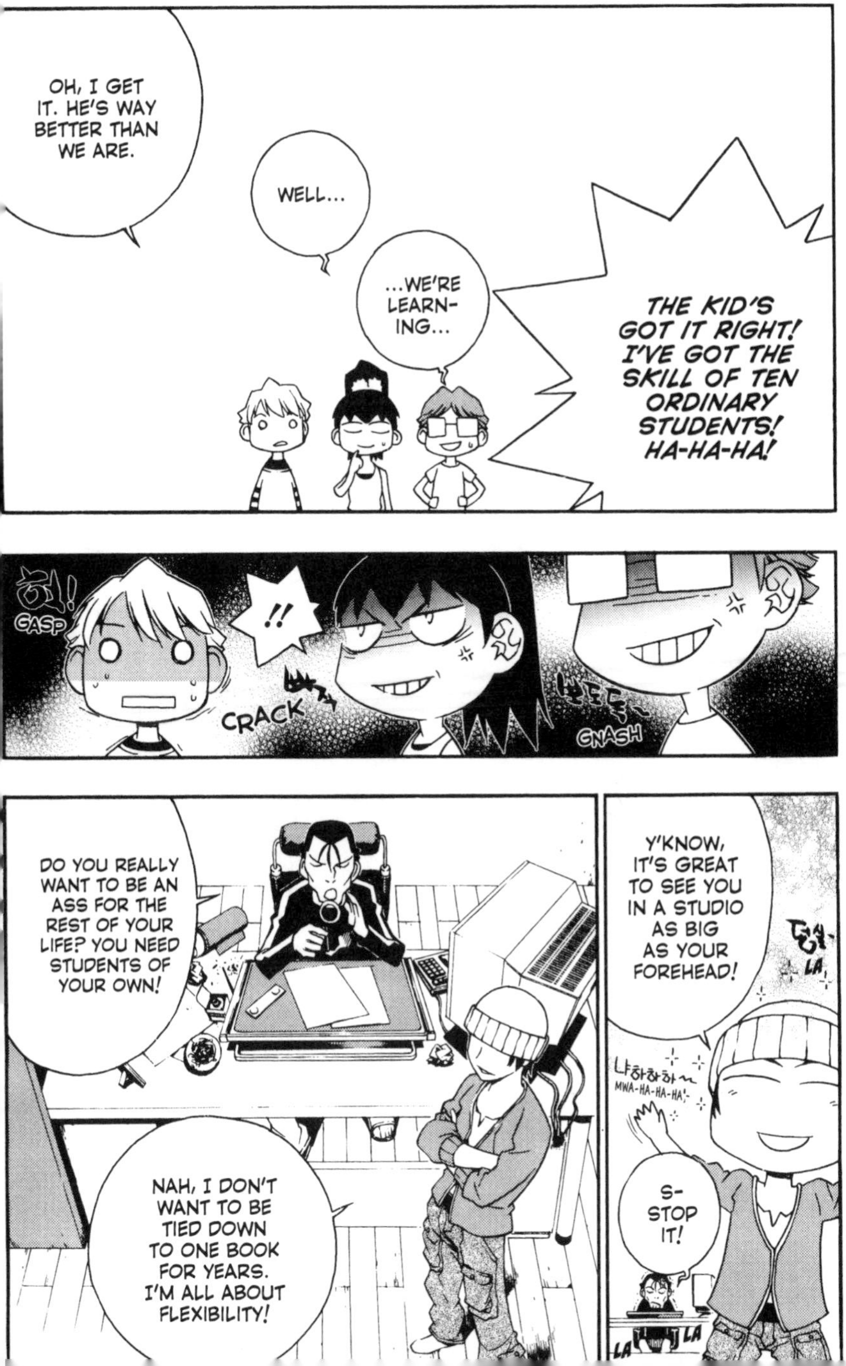
OH, I GET IT. HE'S WAY BETTER THAN WE ARE.
WELL...
...WE'RE LEARN-ING...
THE KID'S GOT IT RIGHT! I'VE GOT THE SKILL OF TEN ORDINARY STUDENTS! HA-HA-HA!
헉!
GASP
!!
CRACK
GNASH
DO YOU REALLY WANT TO BE AN ASS FOR THE REST OF YOUR LIFE? YOU NEED STUDENTS OF YOUR OWN!
NAH, I DON'T WANT TO BE TIED DOWN TO ONE BOOK FOR YEARS. I'M ALL ABOUT FLEXIBILITY!
Y'KNOW, IT'S GREAT TO SEE YOU IN A STUDIO AS BIG AS YOUR FOREHEAD!
LA
MWA-HA-HA-HA
S-STOP IT!
LA
LA

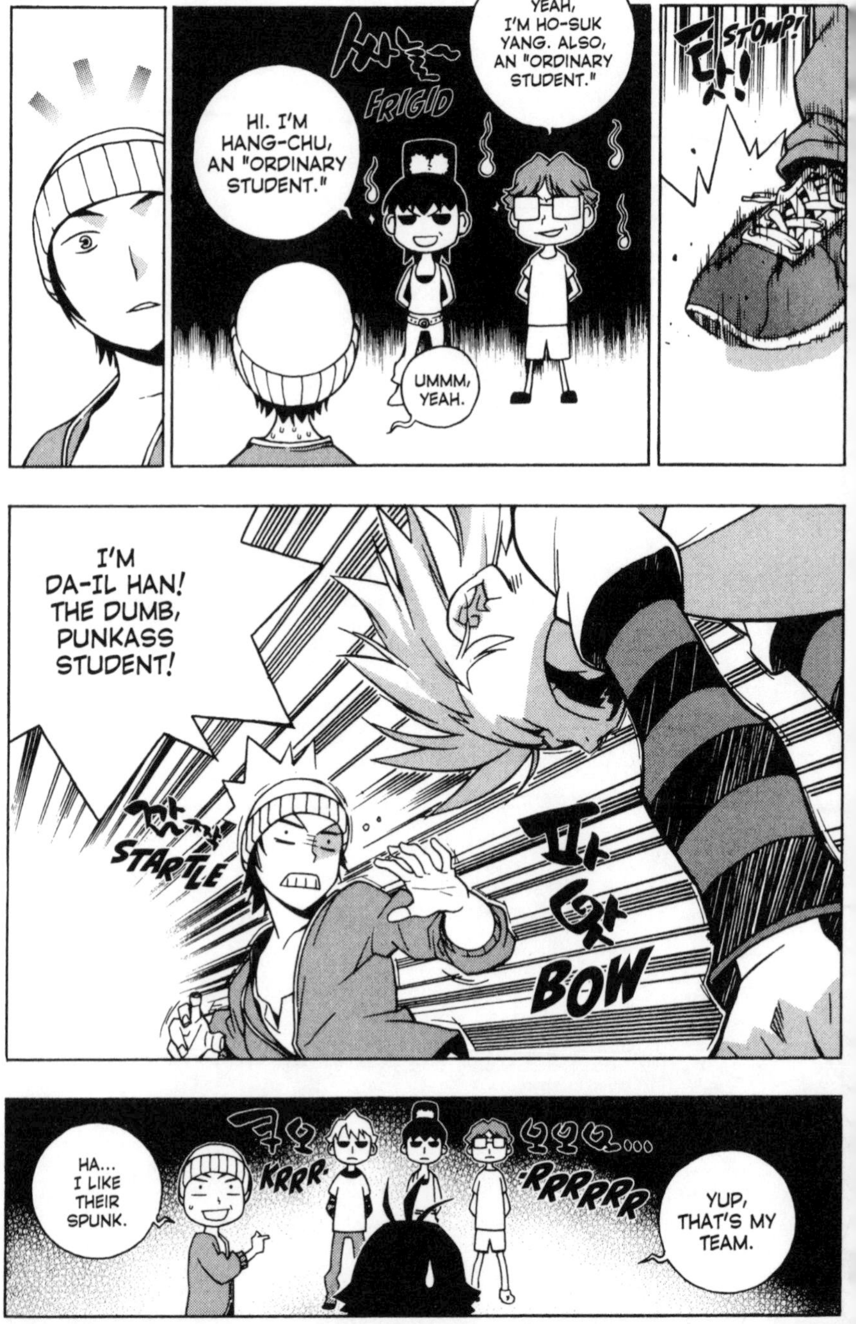
FRIGID
HI. I'M HANG-CHU, AN "ORDINARY STUDENT."
YEAH, I'M HO-SUK YANG. ALSO, AN "ORDINARY STUDENT."
UMMM, YEAH.
STOMP!
I'M DA-IL HAN! THE DUMB, PUNKASS STUDENT!
STARTLE
BOW
HA... I LIKE THEIR SPUNK.
KRRR-
-RRRRRR
YUP, THAT'S MY TEAM.

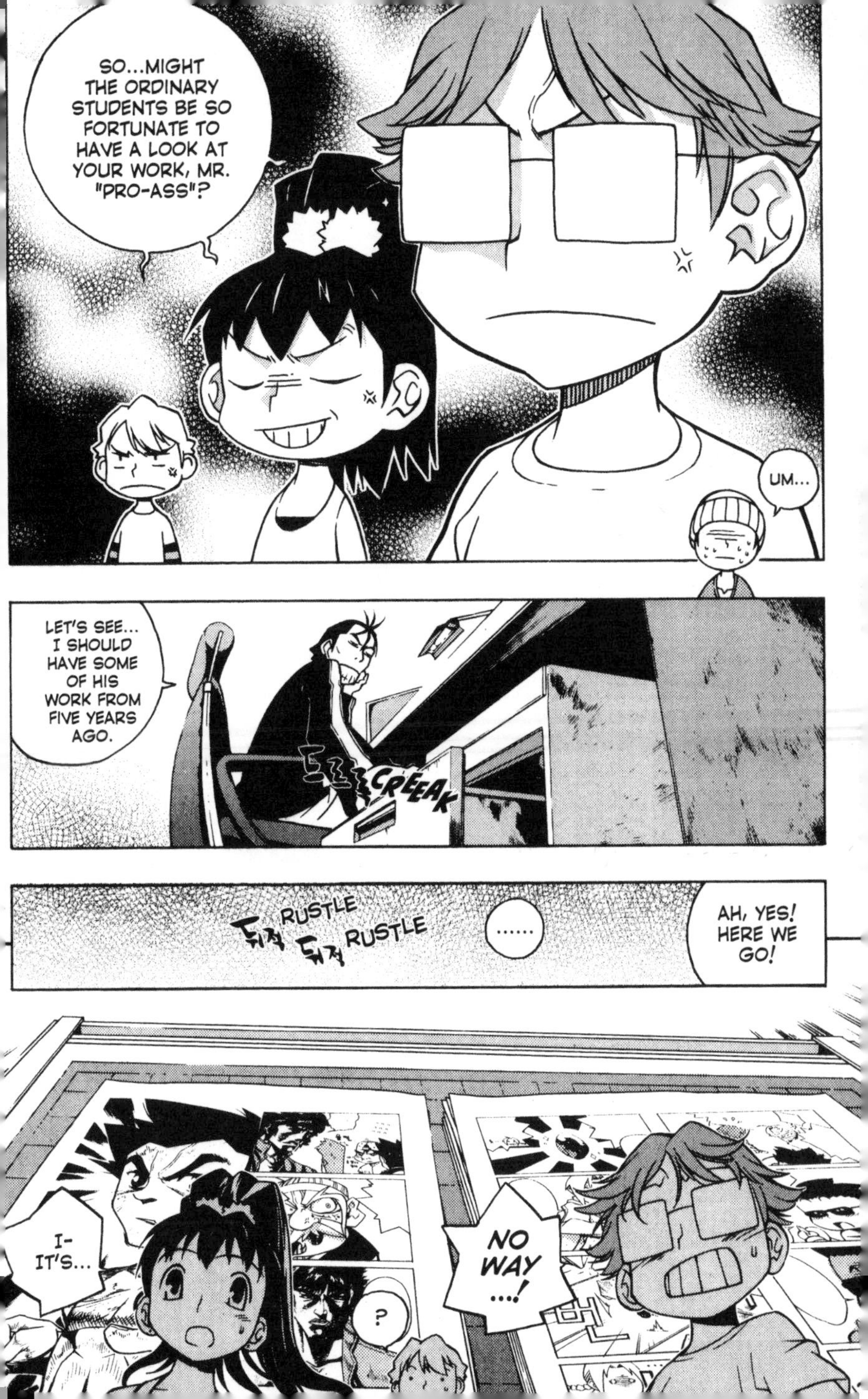
SO...MIGHT THE ORDINARY STUDENTS BE SO FORTUNATE TO HAVE A LOOK AT YOUR WORK, MR. "PRO-ASS"?
UM...
LET'S SEE... I SHOULD HAVE SOME OF HIS WORK FROM FIVE YEARS AGO.
CREEAK
RUSTLE
RUSTLE
......
AH, YES! HERE WE GO!
I- IT'S...
?
NO WAY ....!

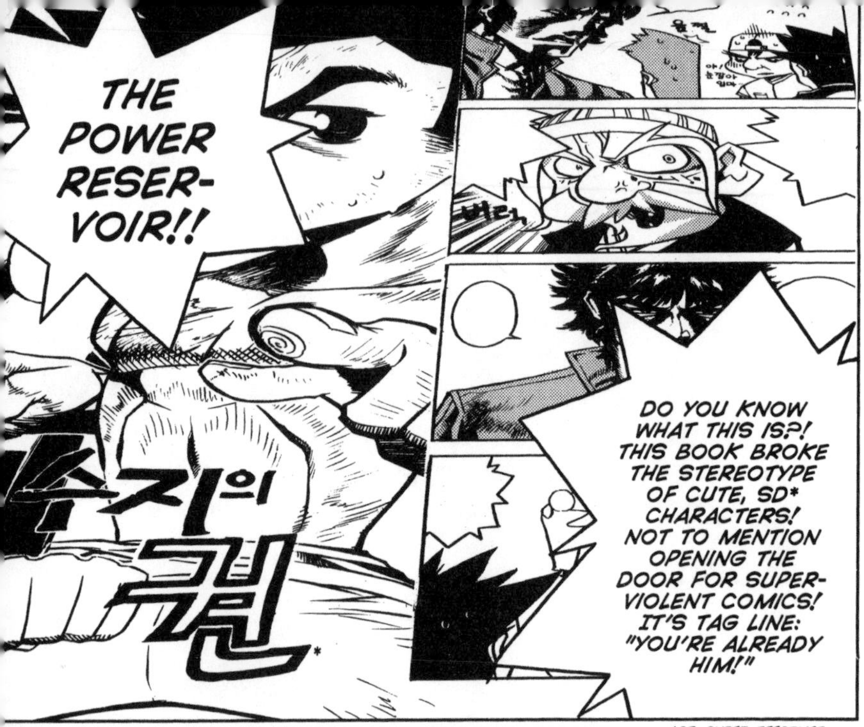
THE POWER RESER-VOIR!!
수지의 권*
울컥
버럭
DO YOU KNOW WHAT THIS IS?! THIS BOOK BROKE THE STEREOTYPE OF CUTE, SD* CHARACTERS! NOT TO MENTION OPENING THE DOOR FOR SUPER-VIOLENT COMICS! IT'S TAG LINE: "YOU'RE ALREADY HIM!"

*THE POWER RESERVOIR

*SD: SUPER-DEFORMED

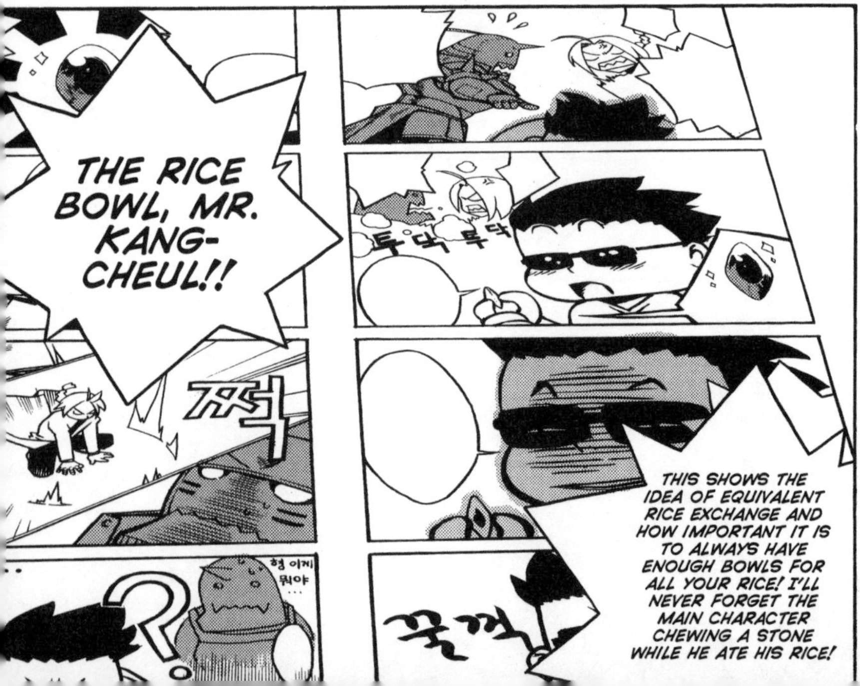
THE RICE BOWL, MR. KANG-CHEUL!!
쩍
형 이게 뭐야 ...
투닥 투닥
THIS SHOWS THE IDEA OF EQUIVALENT RICE EXCHANGE AND HOW IMPORTANT IT IS TO ALWAYS HAVE ENOUGH BOWLS FOR ALL YOUR RICE! I'LL NEVER FORGET THE MAIN CHARACTER CHEWING A STONE WHILE HE ATE HIS RICE!

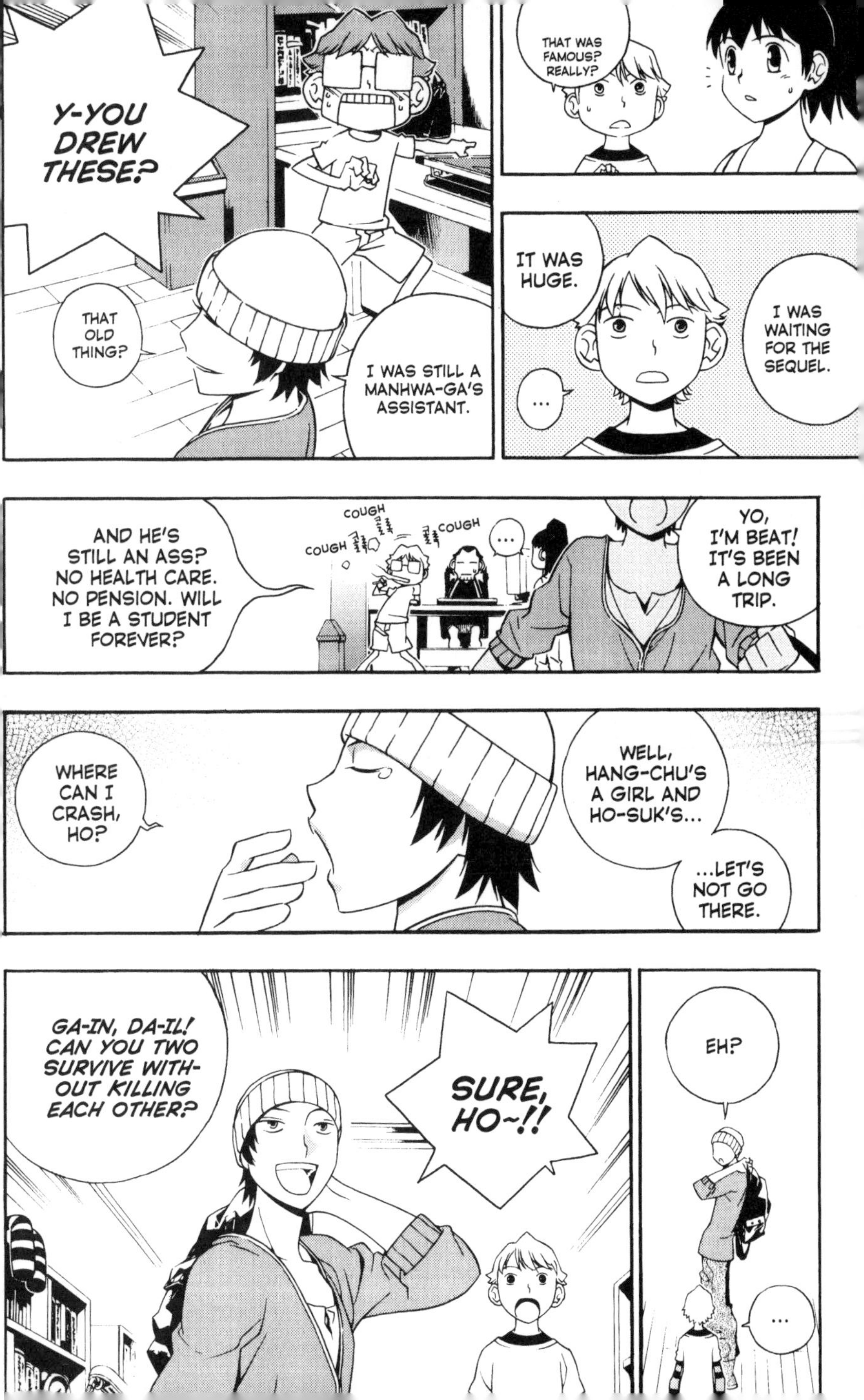
Y-YOU DREW THESE?
THAT OLD THING?
I WAS STILL A MANHWA-GA'S ASSISTANT.
THAT WAS FAMOUS? REALLY?
IT WAS HUGE.
...
I WAS WAITING FOR THE SEQUEL.
AND HE'S STILL AN ASS? NO HEALTH CARE. NO PENSION. WILL I BE A STUDENT FOREVER?
COUGH
COUGH
COUGH
...
YO, I'M BEAT! IT'S BEEN A LONG TRIP.
WHERE CAN I CRASH, HO?
WELL, HANG-CHU'S A GIRL AND HO-SUK'S...
...LET'S NOT GO THERE.
GA-IN, DA-IL! CAN YOU TWO SURVIVE WITH-OUT KILLING EACH OTHER?
SURE, HO~!!
EH?
...

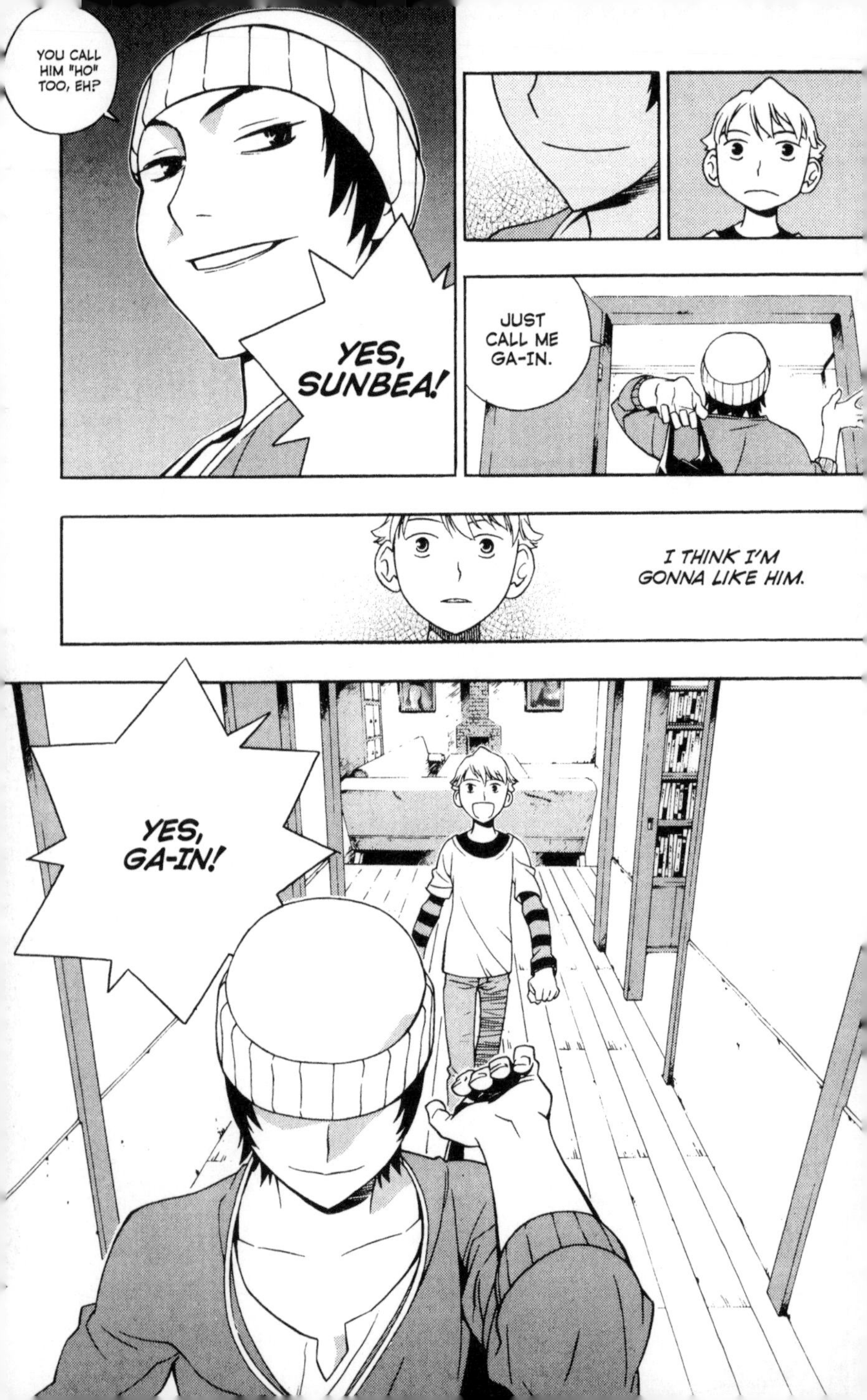
YOU CALL HIM "HO" TOO, EH?
YES, SUNBEA!
JUST CALL ME GA-IN.
I THINK I'M GONNA LIKE HIM.
YES, GA-IN!

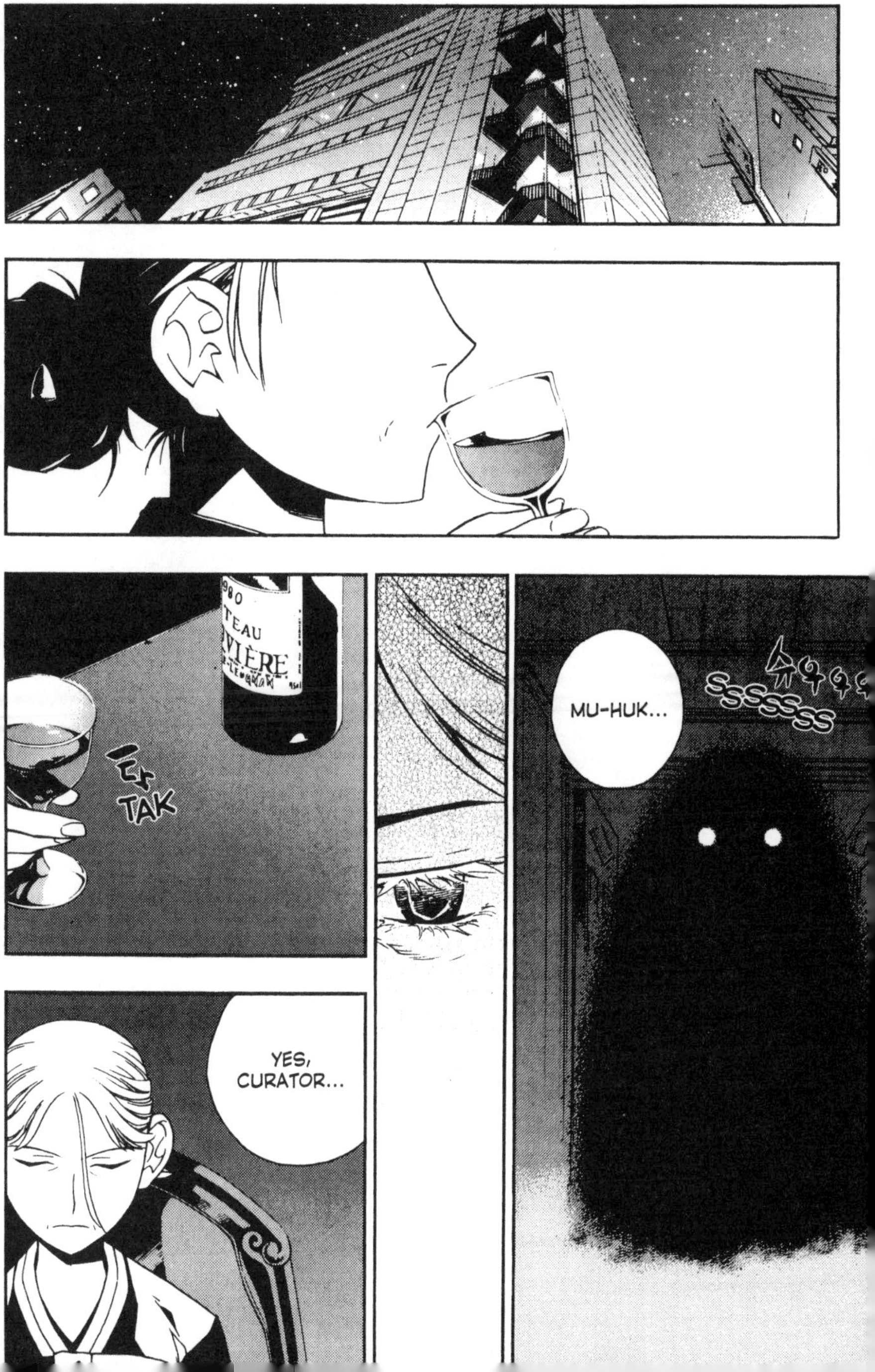

TAK
YES, CURATOR...
MU-HUK...
SSSSSSS

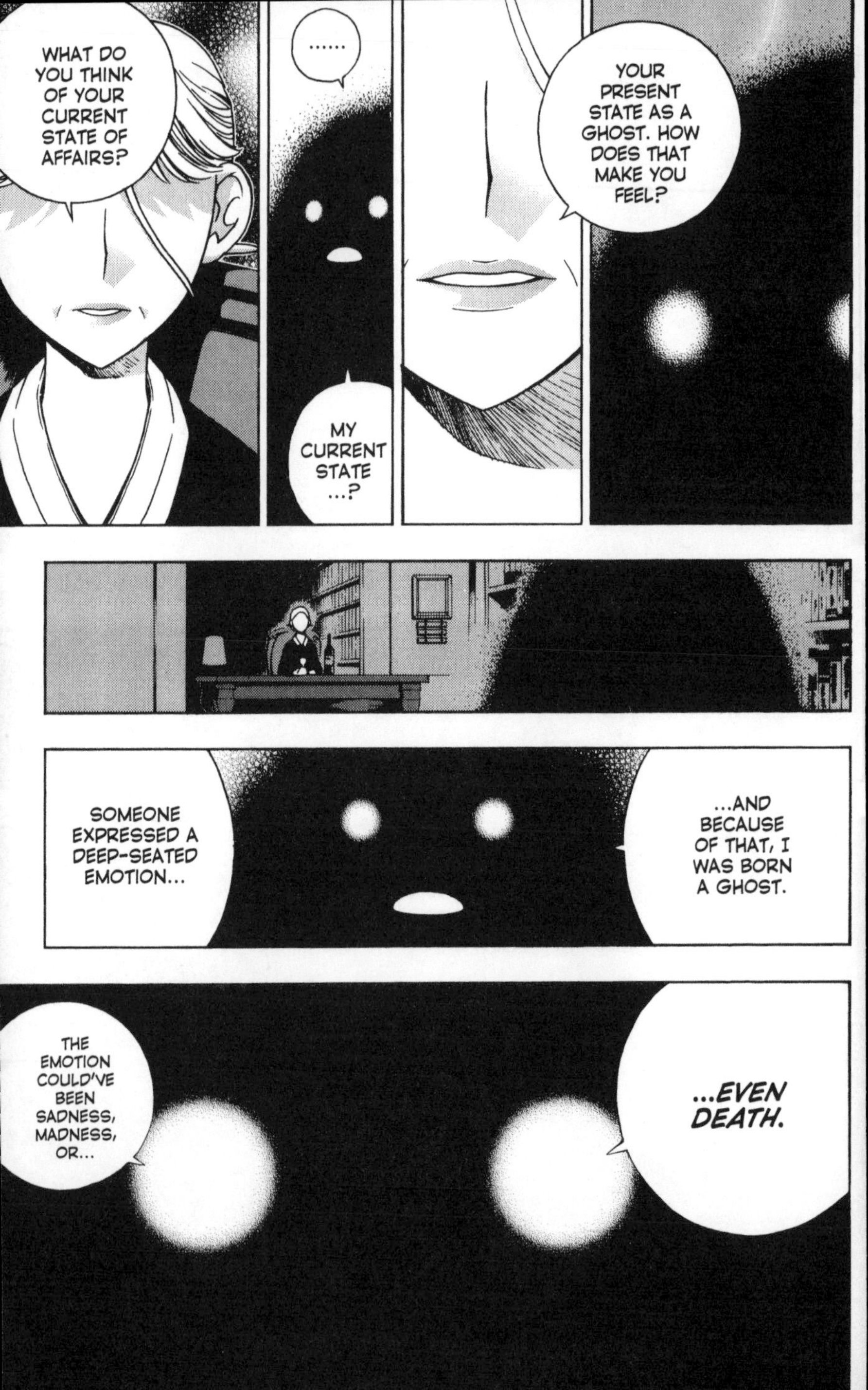
WHAT DO YOU THINK OF YOUR CURRENT STATE OF AFFAIRS?
......
MY CURRENT STATE ...?
YOUR PRESENT STATE AS A GHOST. HOW DOES THAT MAKE YOU FEEL?
SOMEONE EXPRESSED A DEEP-SEATED EMOTION...
...AND BECAUSE OF THAT, I WAS BORN A GHOST.
THE EMOTION COULD'VE BEEN SADNESS, MADNESS, OR...
...EVEN DEATH.

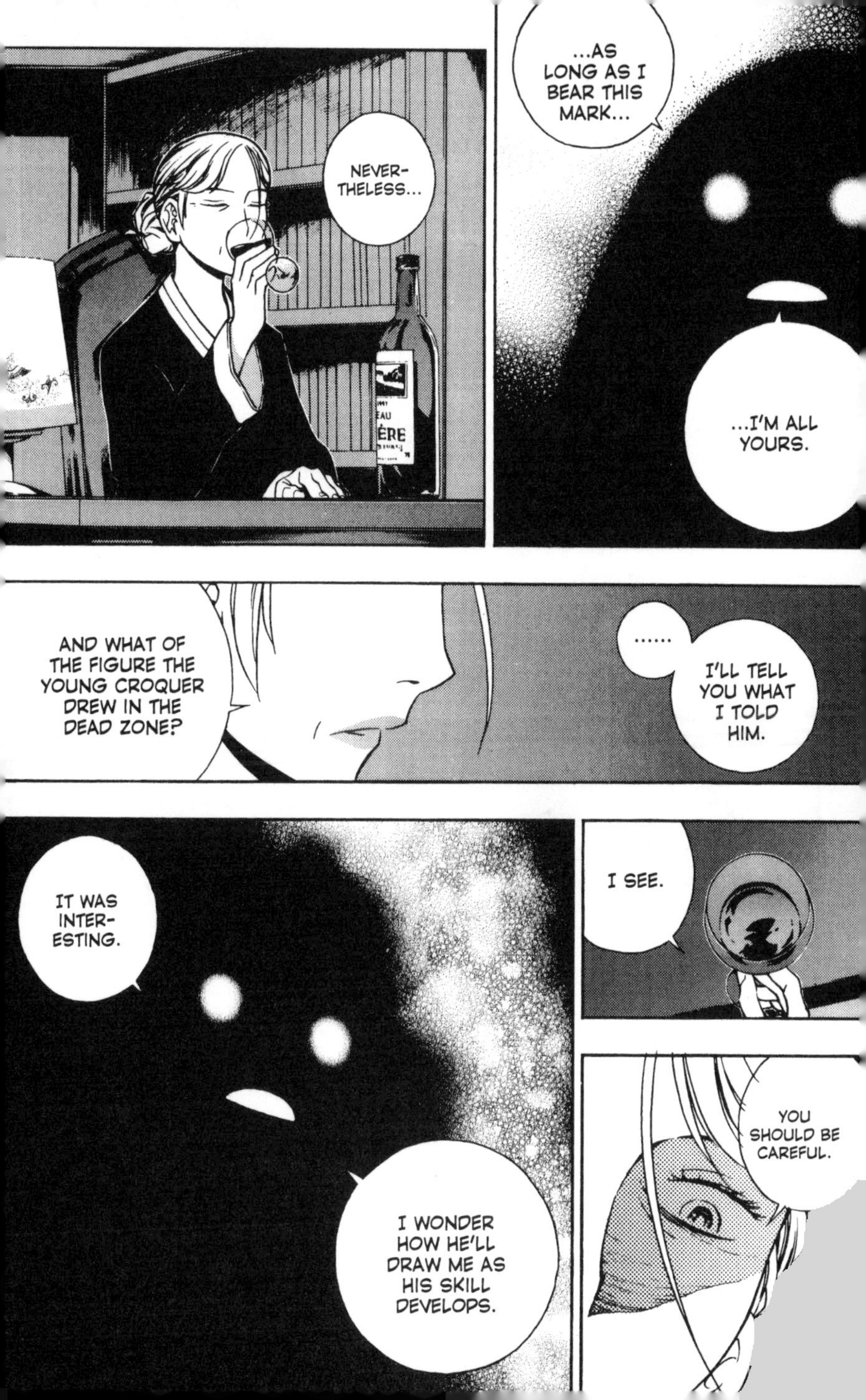
NEVER-THELESS...
...AS LONG AS I BEAR THIS MARK...
...I'M ALL YOURS.
AND WHAT OF THE FIGURE THE YOUNG CROQUER DREW IN THE DEAD ZONE?
......
I'LL TELL YOU WHAT I TOLD HIM.
IT WAS INTER-ESTING.
I WONDER HOW HE'LL DRAW ME AS HIS SKILL DEVELOPS.
I SEE.
YOU SHOULD BE CAREFUL.

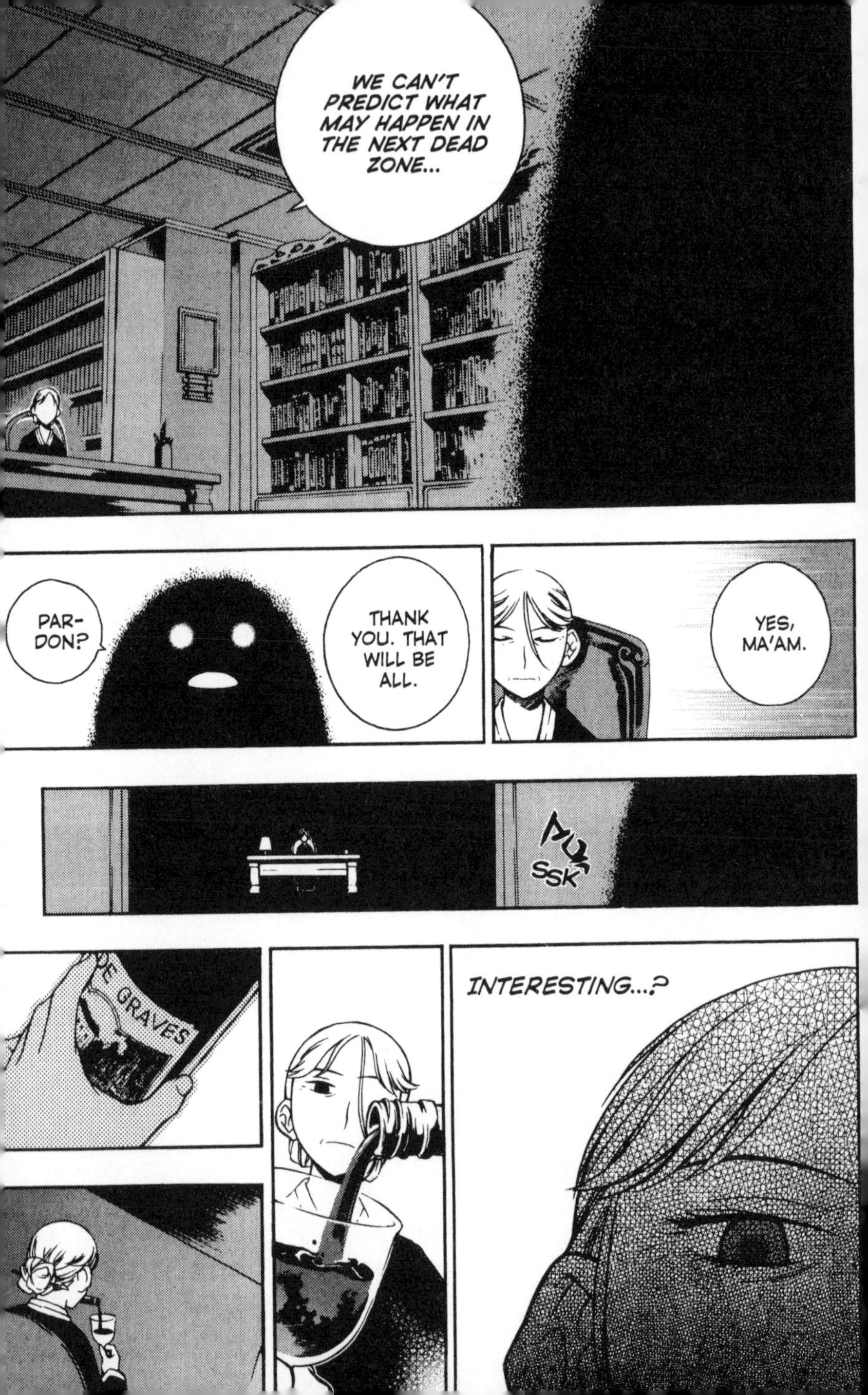

WE CAN'T PREDICT WHAT MAY HAPPEN IN THE NEXT DEAD ZONE...
PAR-DON?
THANK YOU. THAT WILL BE ALL.
YES, MA'AM.
SSK
E GRAVES
INTERESTING...?

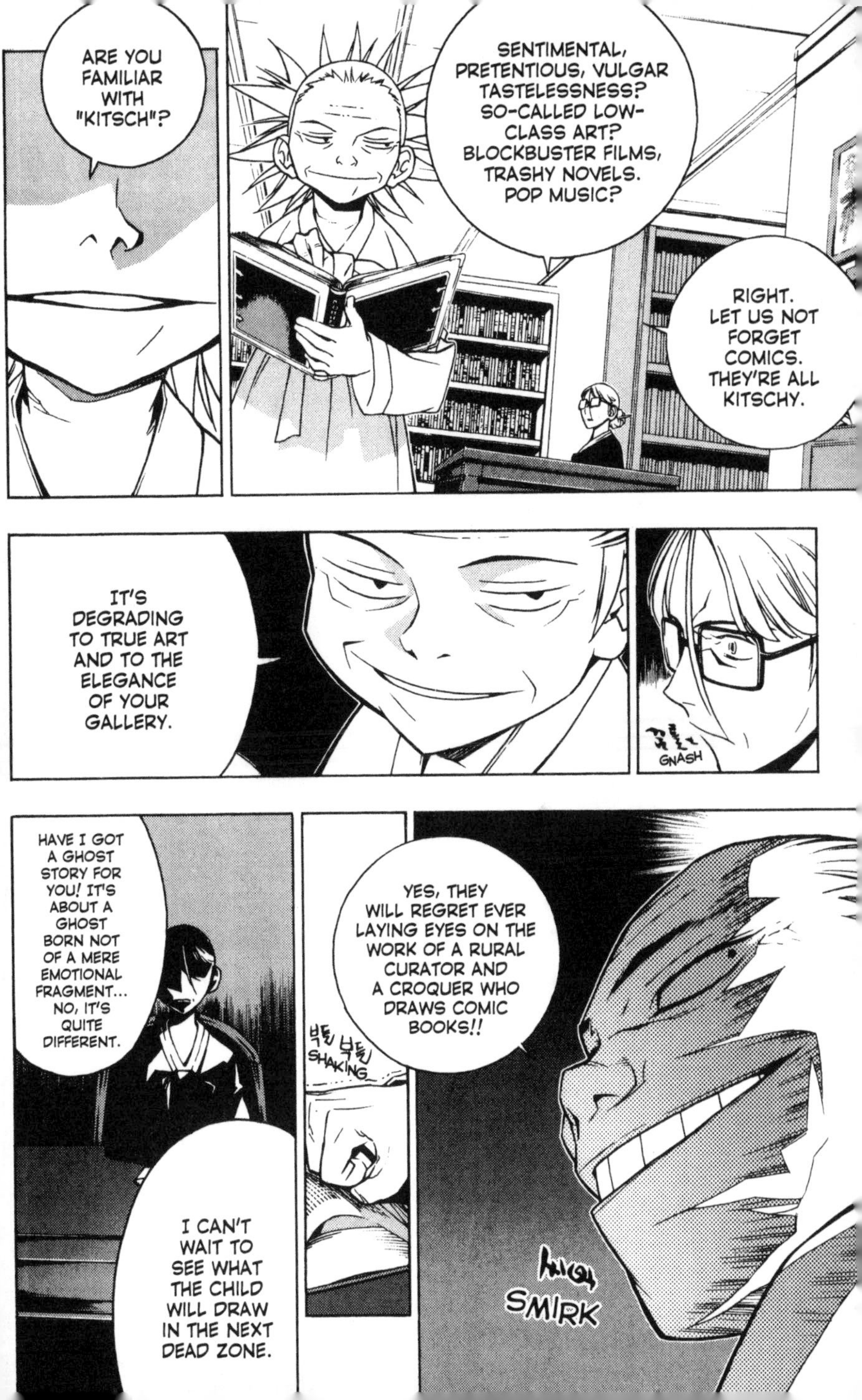
ARE YOU FAMILIAR WITH "KITSCH"?
SENTIMENTAL, PRETENTIOUS, VULGAR TASTELESSNESS? SO-CALLED LOW-CLASS ART? BLOCKBUSTER FILMS, TRASHY NOVELS. POP MUSIC?
RIGHT. LET US NOT FORGET COMICS. THEY'RE ALL KITSCHY.
IT'S DEGRADING TO TRUE ART AND TO THE ELEGANCE OF YOUR GALLERY.
GNASH
HAVE I GOT A GHOST STORY FOR YOU! IT'S ABOUT A GHOST BORN NOT OF A MERE EMOTIONAL FRAGMENT... NO, IT'S QUITE DIFFERENT.
I CAN'T WAIT TO SEE WHAT THE CHILD WILL DRAW IN THE NEXT DEAD ZONE.
YES, THEY WILL REGRET EVER LAYING EYES ON THE WORK OF A RURAL CURATOR AND A CROQUER WHO DRAWS COMIC BOOKS!!
SHAKING
SMIRK

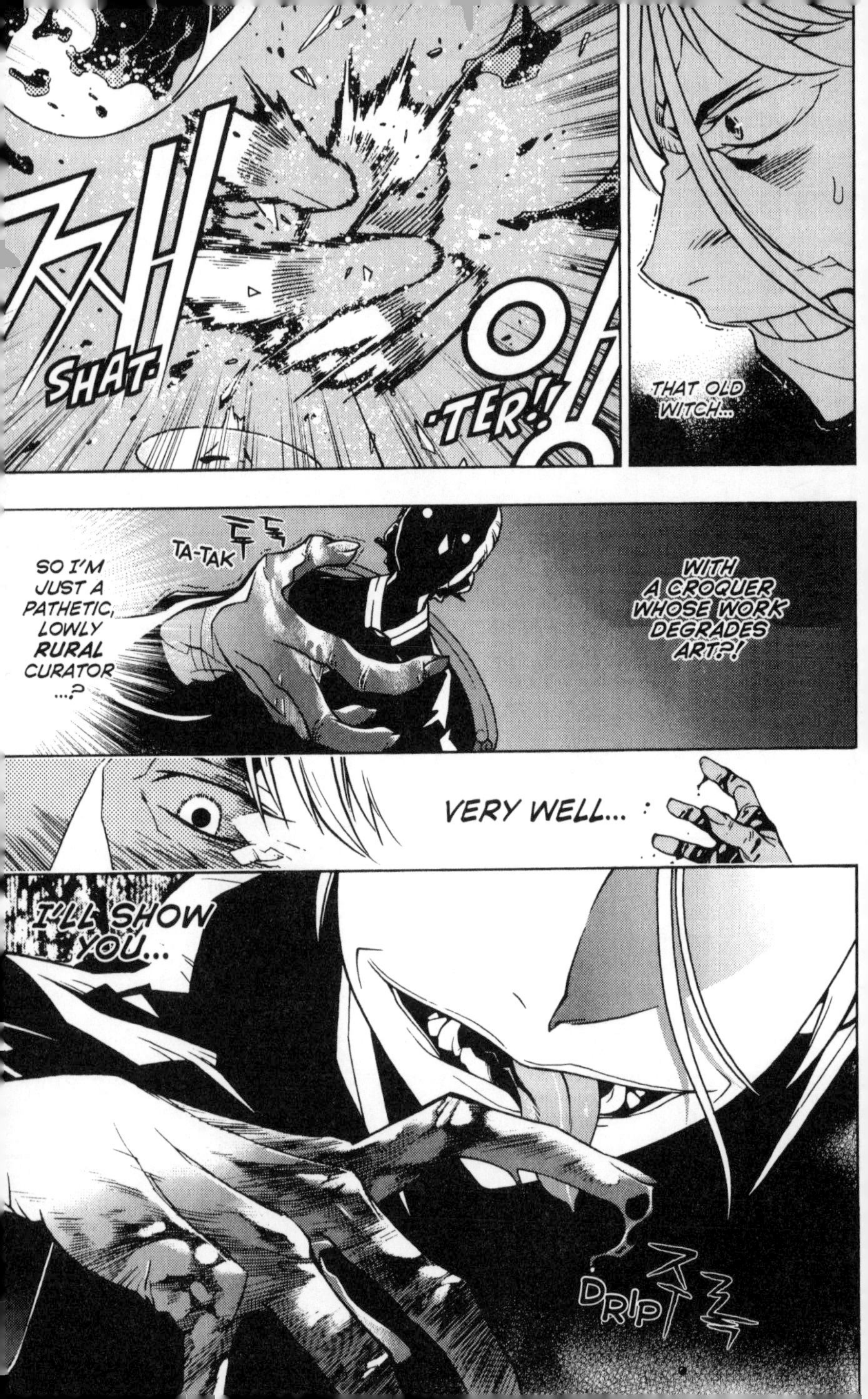
SHAT-
-TER!!
THAT OLD WITCH...
SO I'M JUST A PATHETIC, LOWLY RURAL CURATOR ...?
TA-TAK
WITH A CROQUER WHOSE WORK DEGRADES ART?!
VERY WELL...
I'LL SHOW YOU...
DRIP

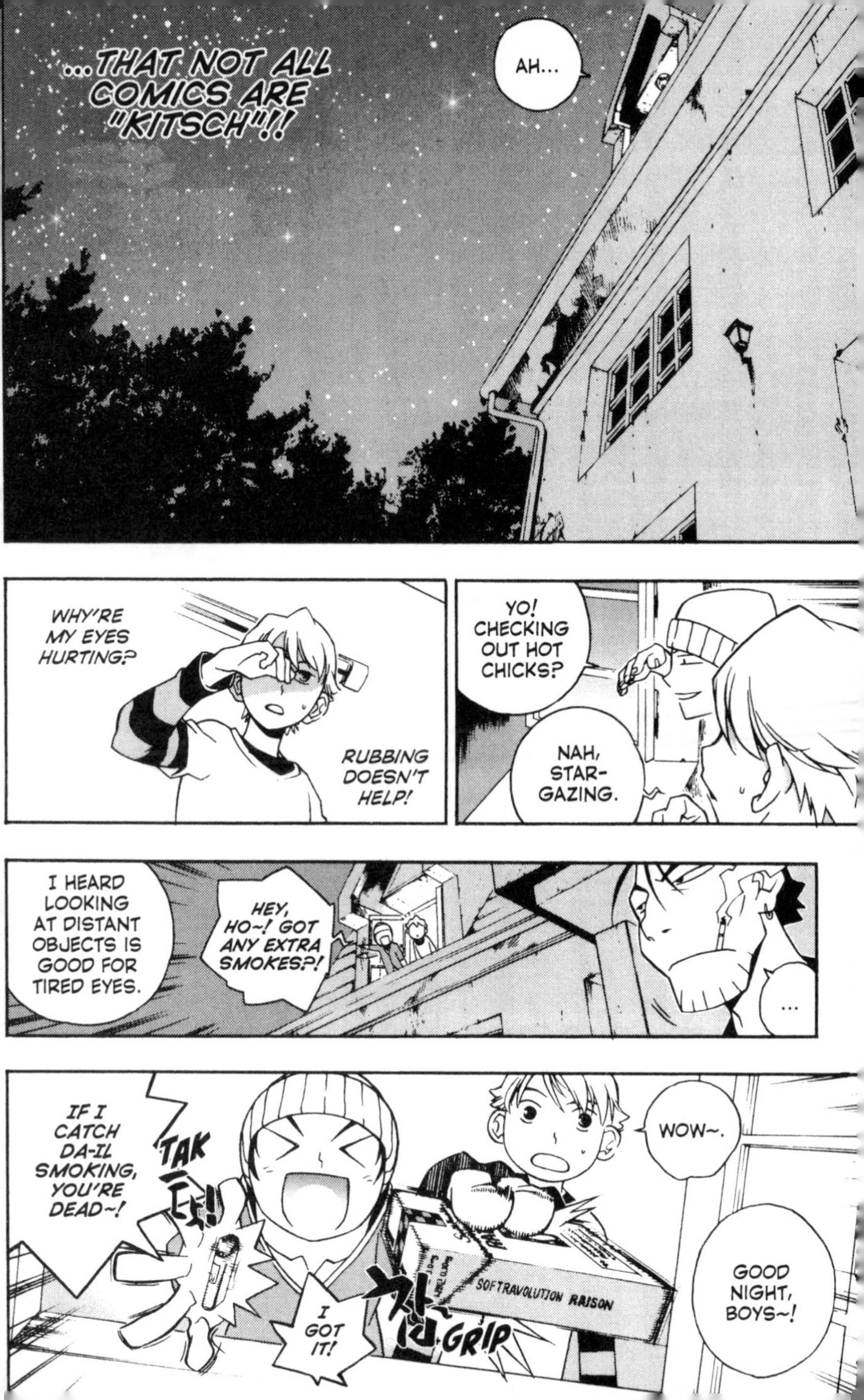
...THAT NOT ALL COMICS ARE "KITSCH"!!
AH...
WHY'RE MY EYES HURTING?
RUBBING DOESN'T HELP!
YO! CHECKING OUT HOT CHICKS?
NAH, STAR-GAZING.
I HEARD LOOKING AT DISTANT OBJECTS IS GOOD FOR TIRED EYES.
HEY, HO~! GOT ANY EXTRA SMOKES?!
...
IF I CATCH DA-IL SMOKING, YOU'RE DEAD~!
TAK
I GOT IT!
GRIP
SOFTRAVOLUTION RAISON
WOW~.
GOOD NIGHT, BOYS~!

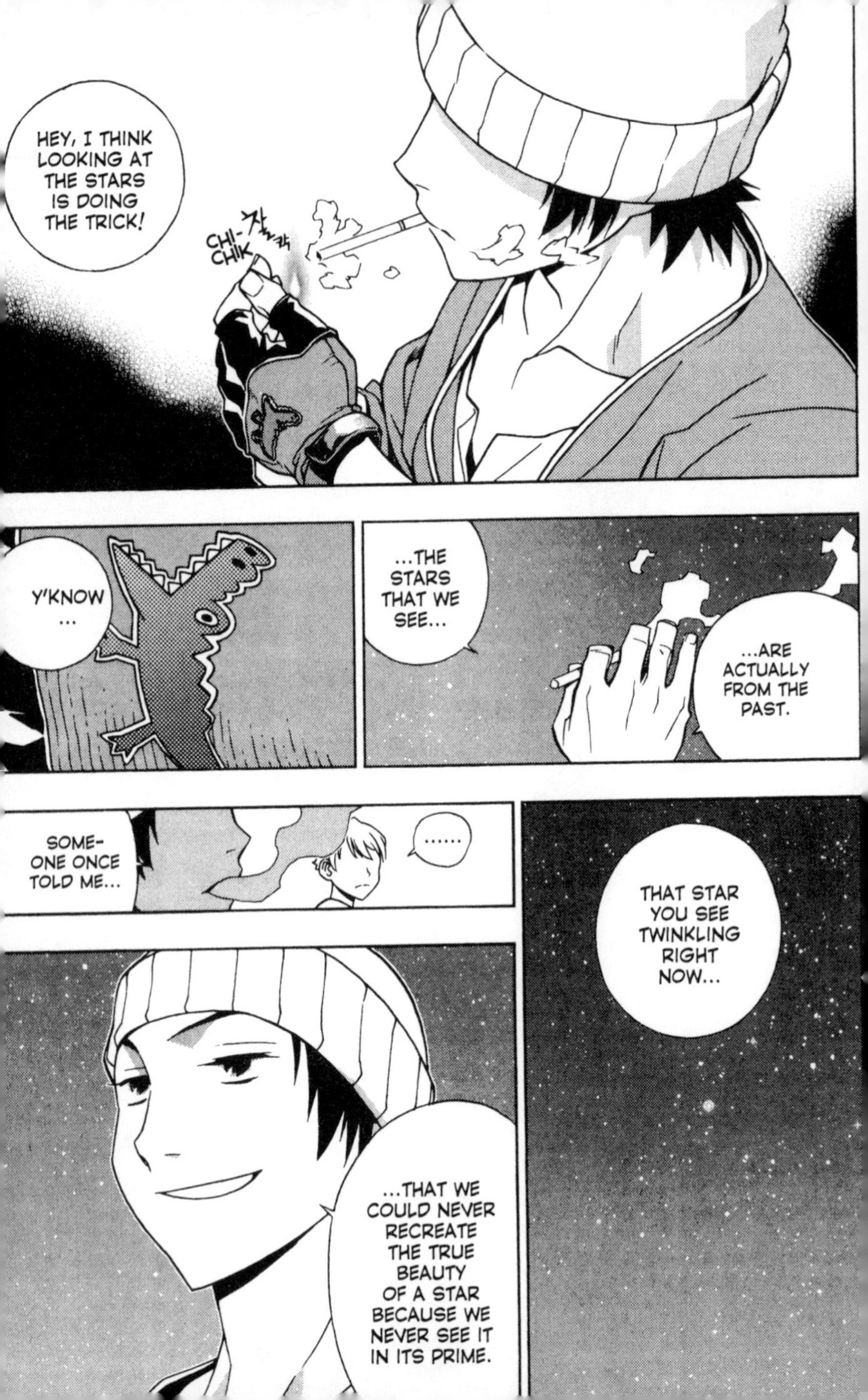
HEY, I THINK LOOKING AT THE STARS IS DOING THE TRICK!
CHI-CHIK
Y'KNOW ...
...THE STARS THAT WE SEE...
...ARE ACTUALLY FROM THE PAST.
SOME-ONE ONCE TOLD ME...
......
THAT STAR YOU SEE TWINKLING RIGHT NOW...
...THAT WE COULD NEVER RECREATE THE TRUE BEAUTY OF A STAR BECAUSE WE NEVER SEE IT IN ITS PRIME.

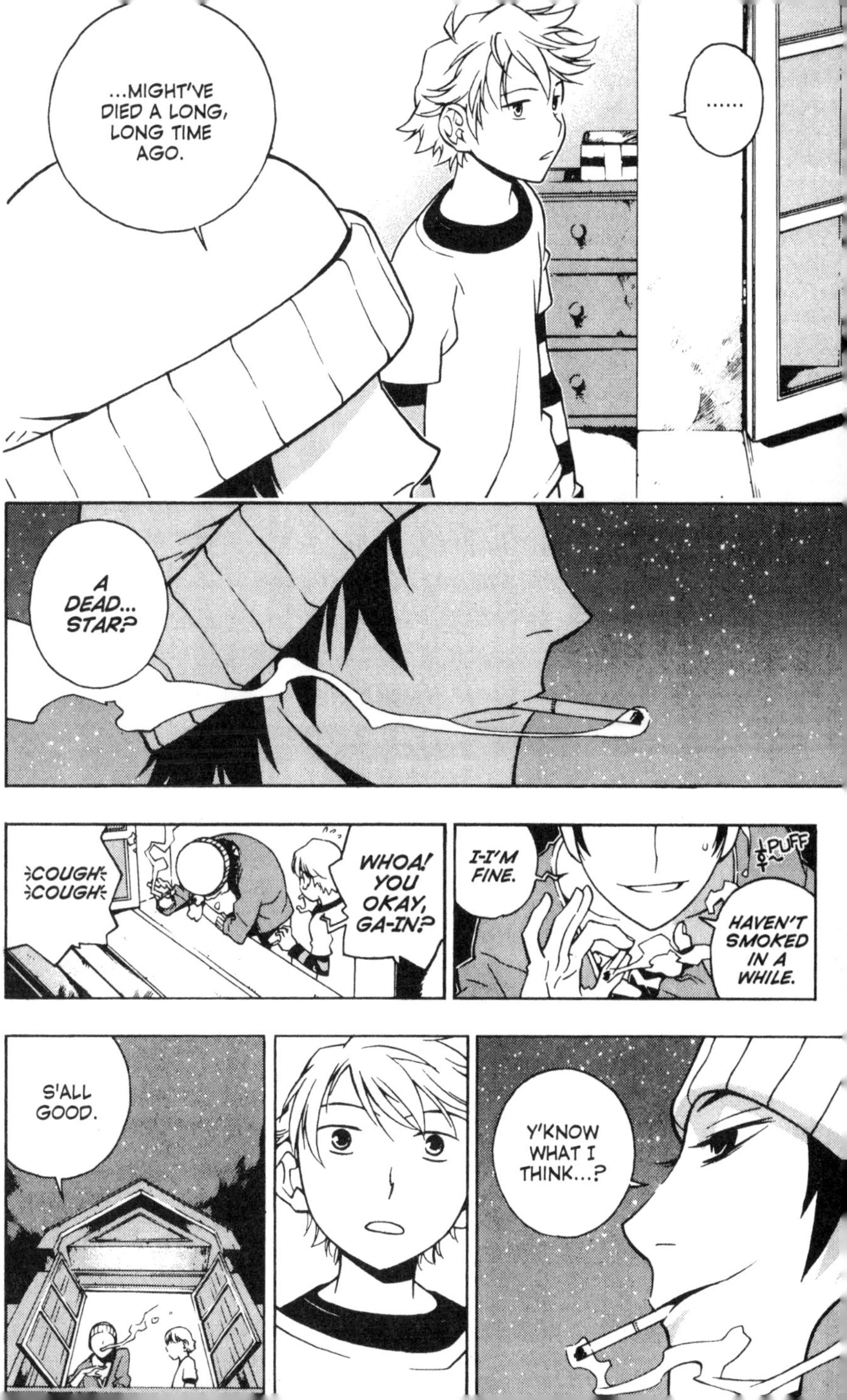
...MIGHT'VE DIED A LONG, LONG TIME AGO.
......
A DEAD... STAR?
COUGH COUGH
WHOA! YOU OKAY, GA-IN?
I-I'M FINE.
PUFF
HAVEN'T SMOKED IN A WHILE.
S'ALL GOOD.
Y'KNOW WHAT I THINK...?

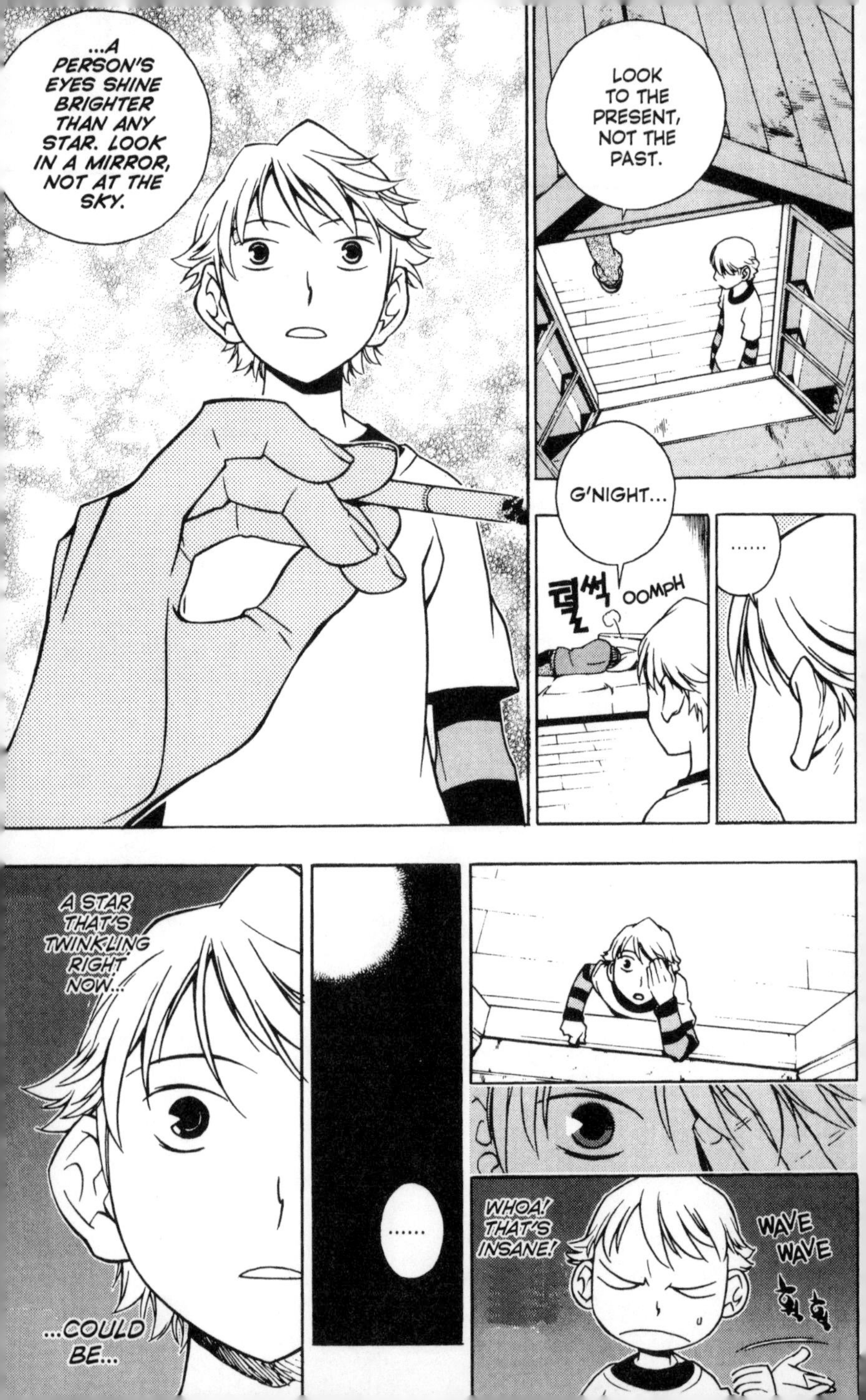
...A PERSON'S EYES SHINE BRIGHTER THAN ANY STAR. LOOK IN A MIRROR, NOT AT THE SKY.
LOOK TO THE PRESENT, NOT THE PAST.
G'NIGHT...
털썩 OOMPH
......
A STAR THAT'S TWINKLING RIGHT NOW...
...COULD BE...
......
WHOA! THAT'S INSANE!
WAVE WAVE

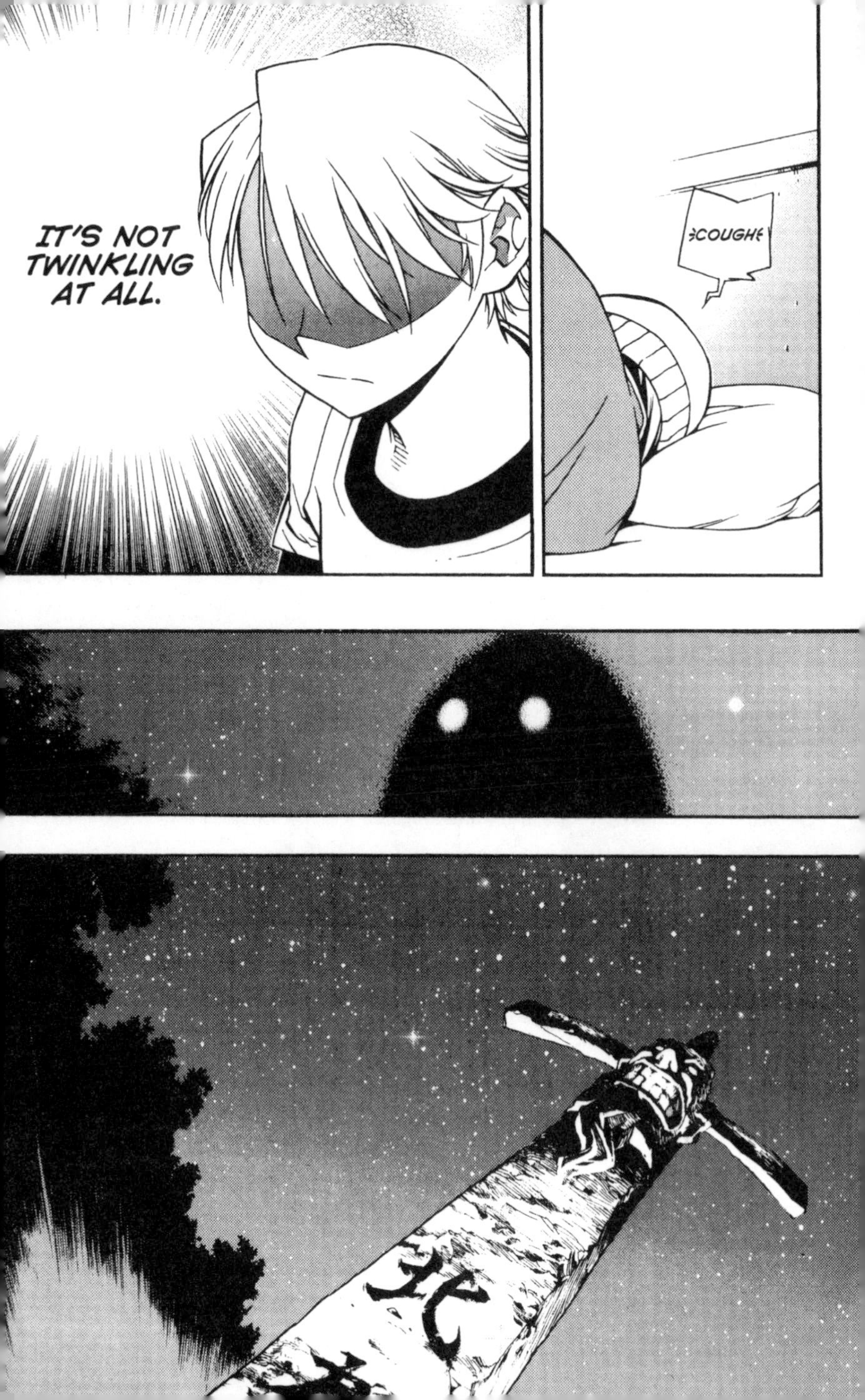
IT'S NOT TWINKLING AT ALL.
COUGH

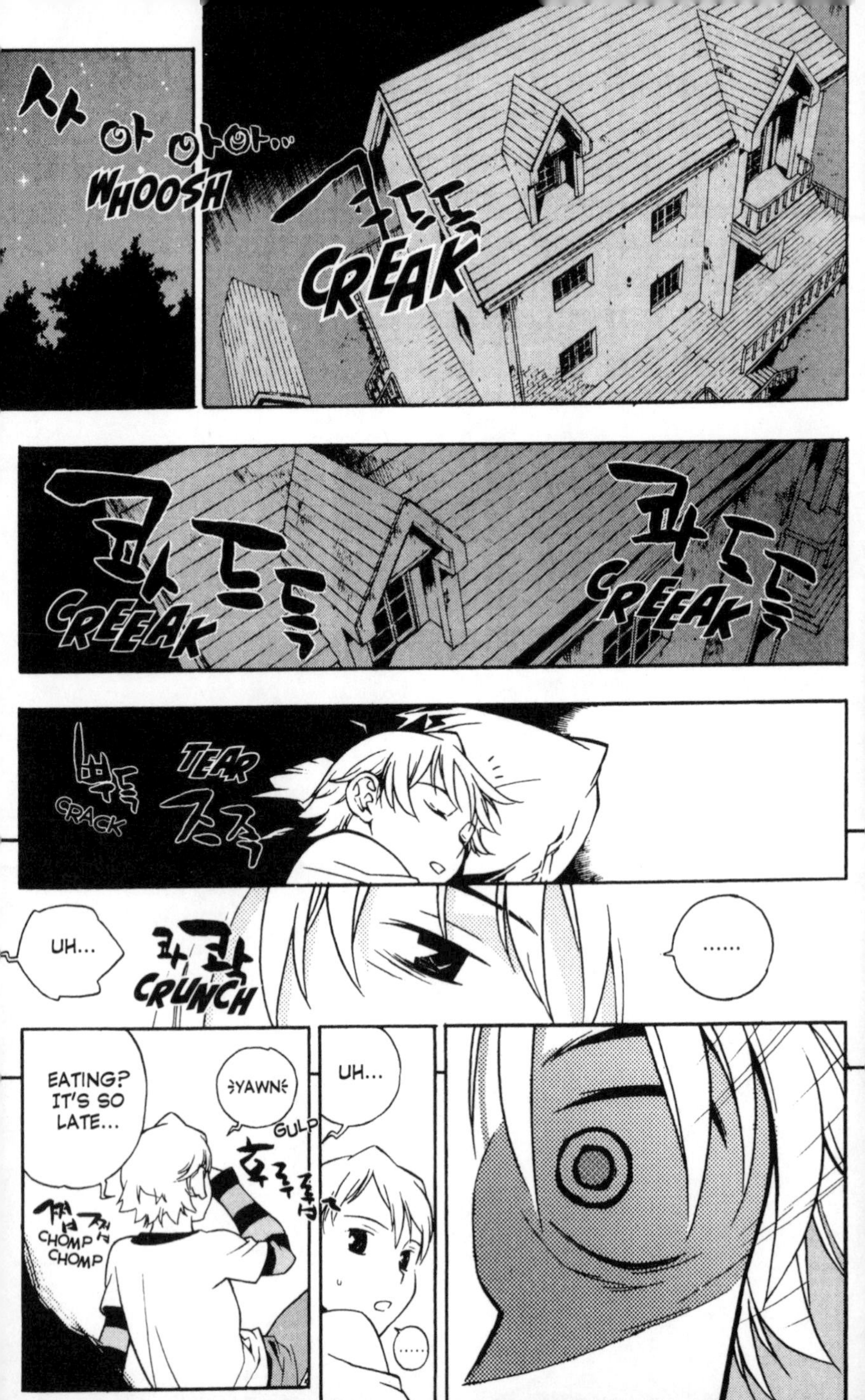
WHOOSH
CREAK
CREEAK
CREEAK
CRACK
TEAR
UH...
CRUNCH
......
EATING? IT'S SO LATE...
CHOMP CHOMP
YAWN
GULP
UH...
......

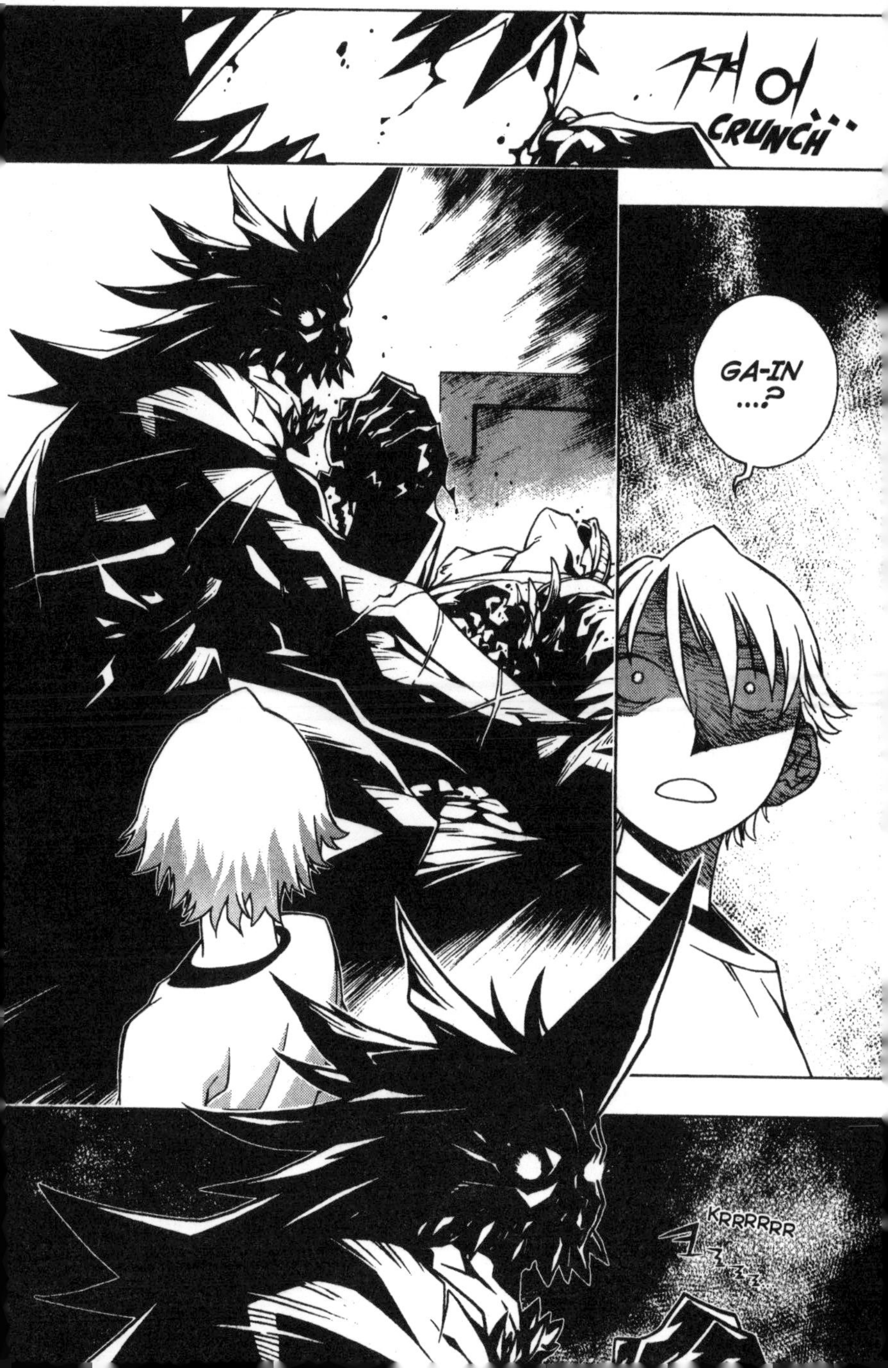
깨어
CRUNCH...
GA-IN ...?
KRRRRRR

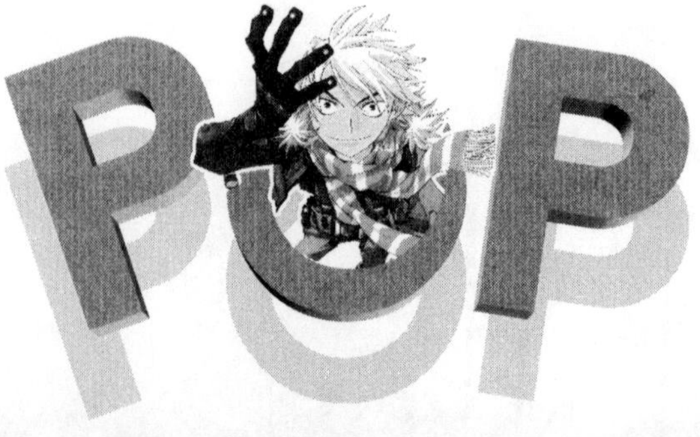
POP

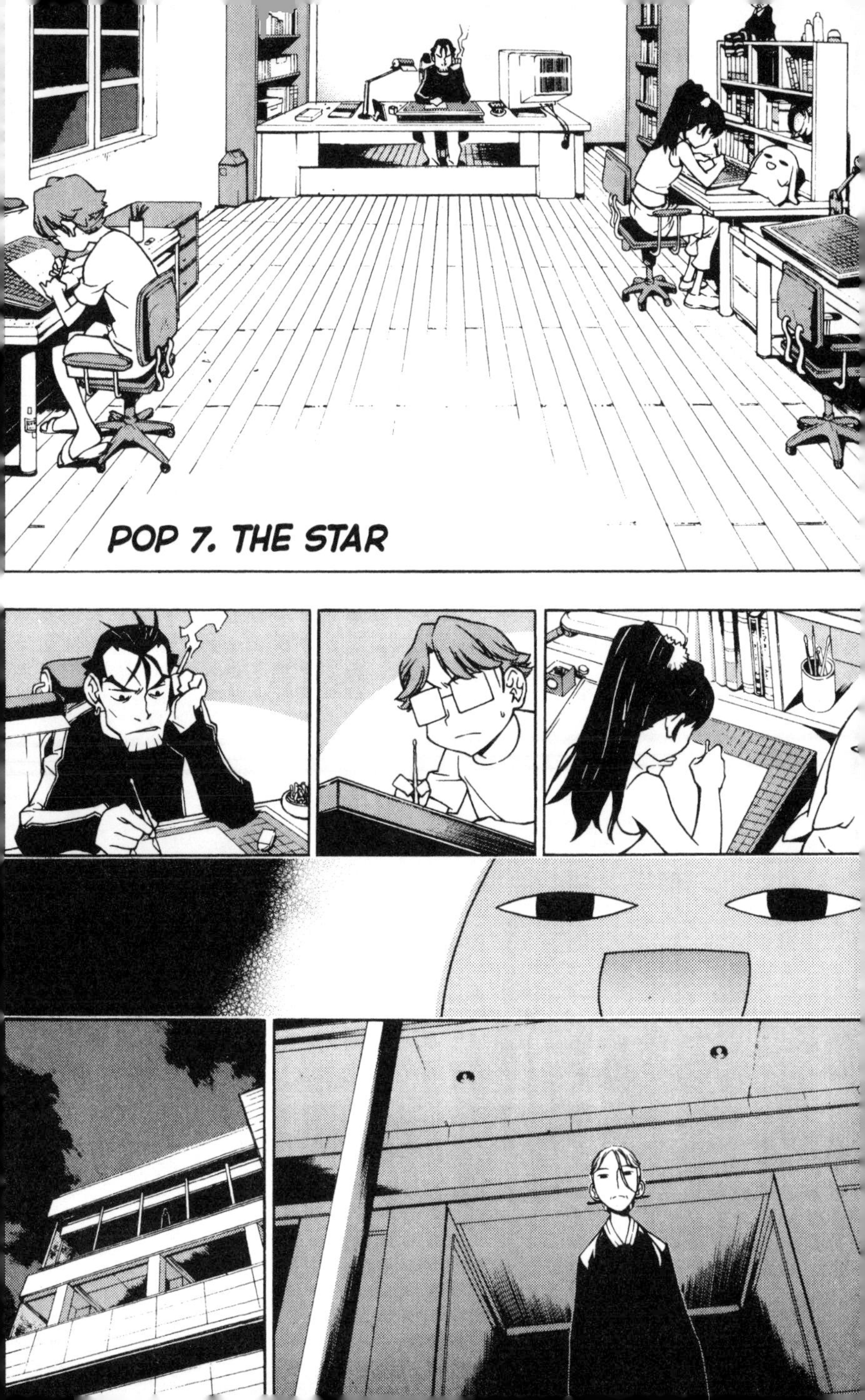
POP 7. THE STAR

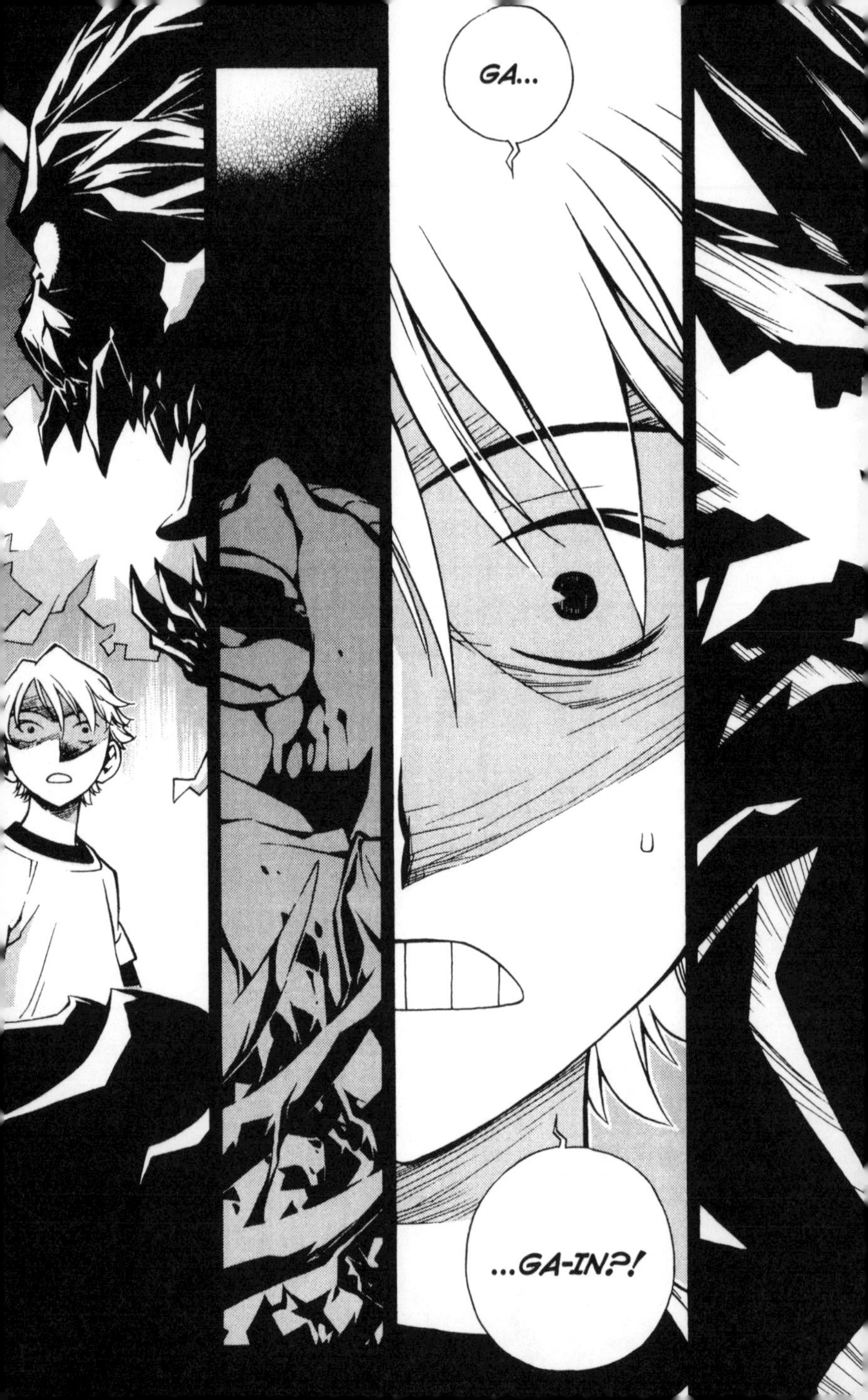
GA...
...GA-IN?!

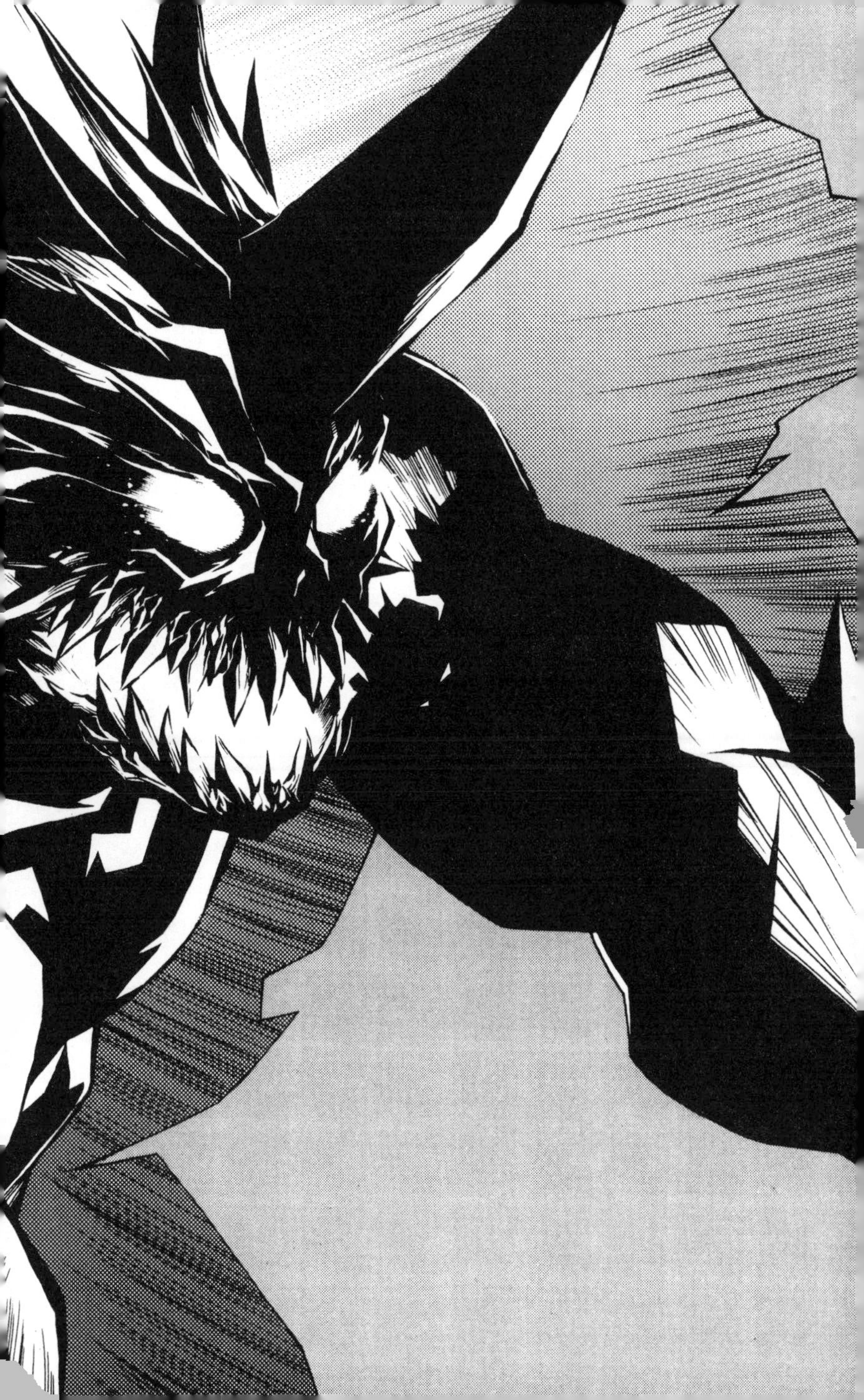

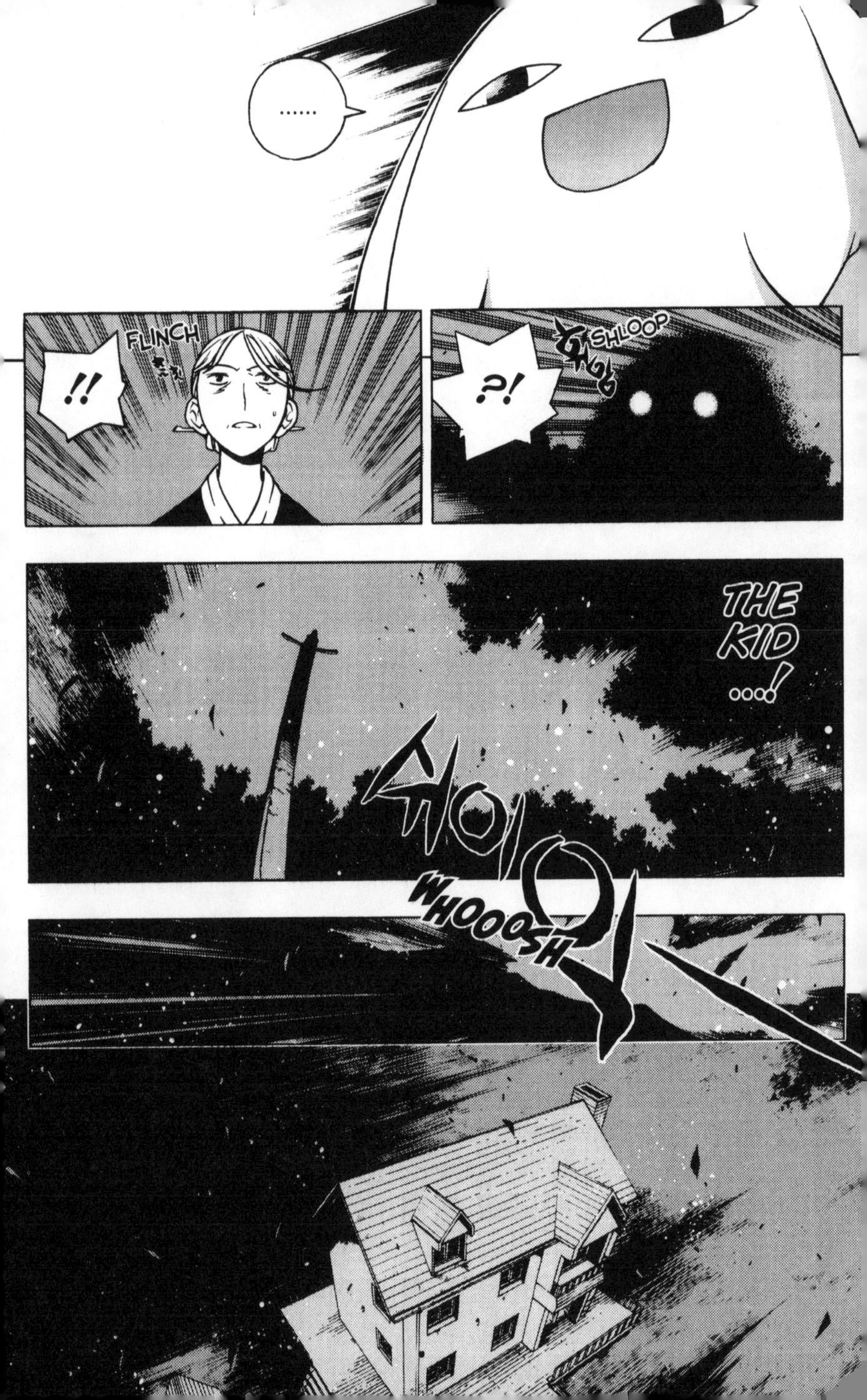

......
FLINCH
!!
SHLOOP
?!
THE KID ...!
WHOOOSH

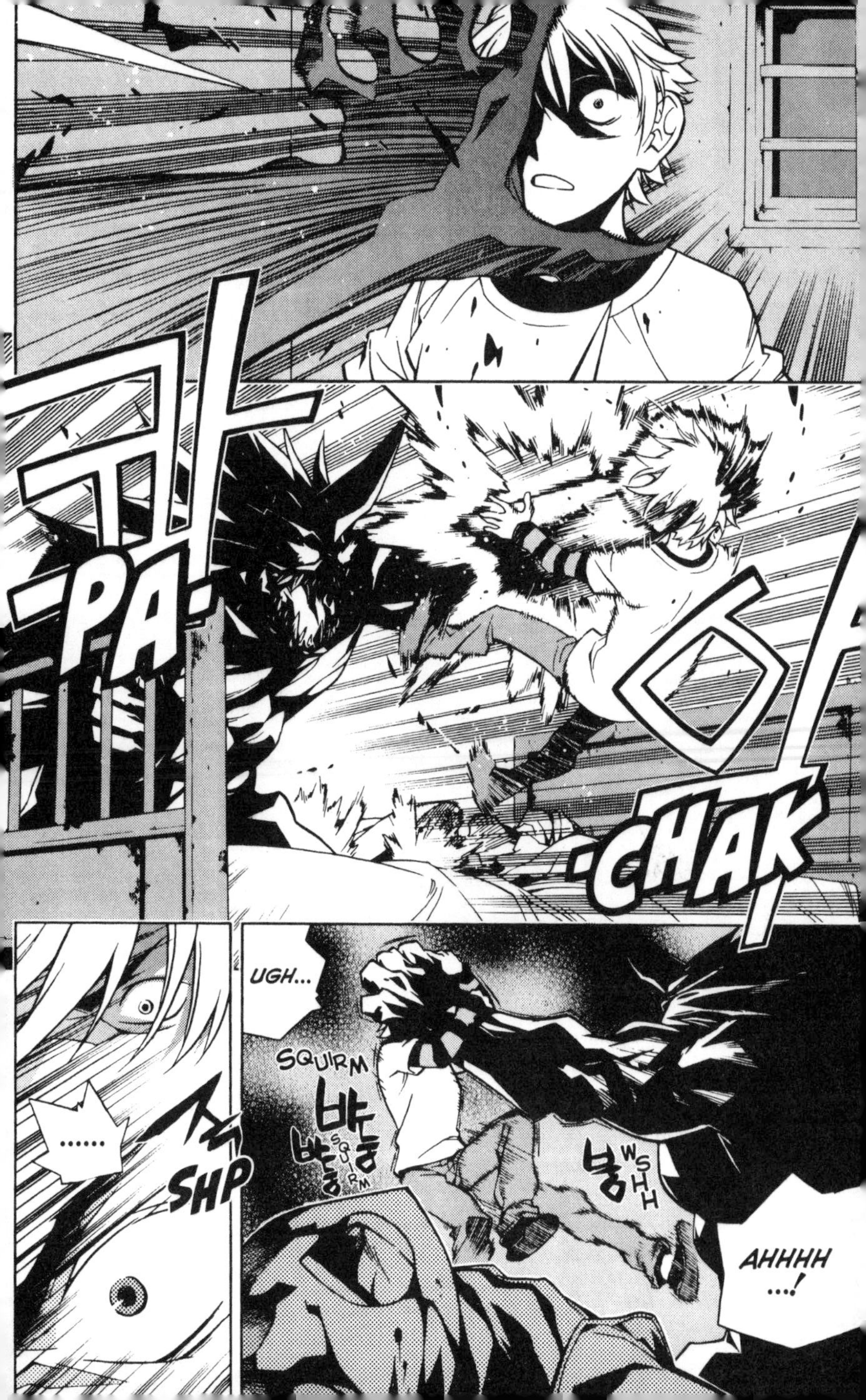

-PA-
-CHAK
......
SHP
UGH...
SQUIRM
SQUIRM
WSHH
AHHHH ...!

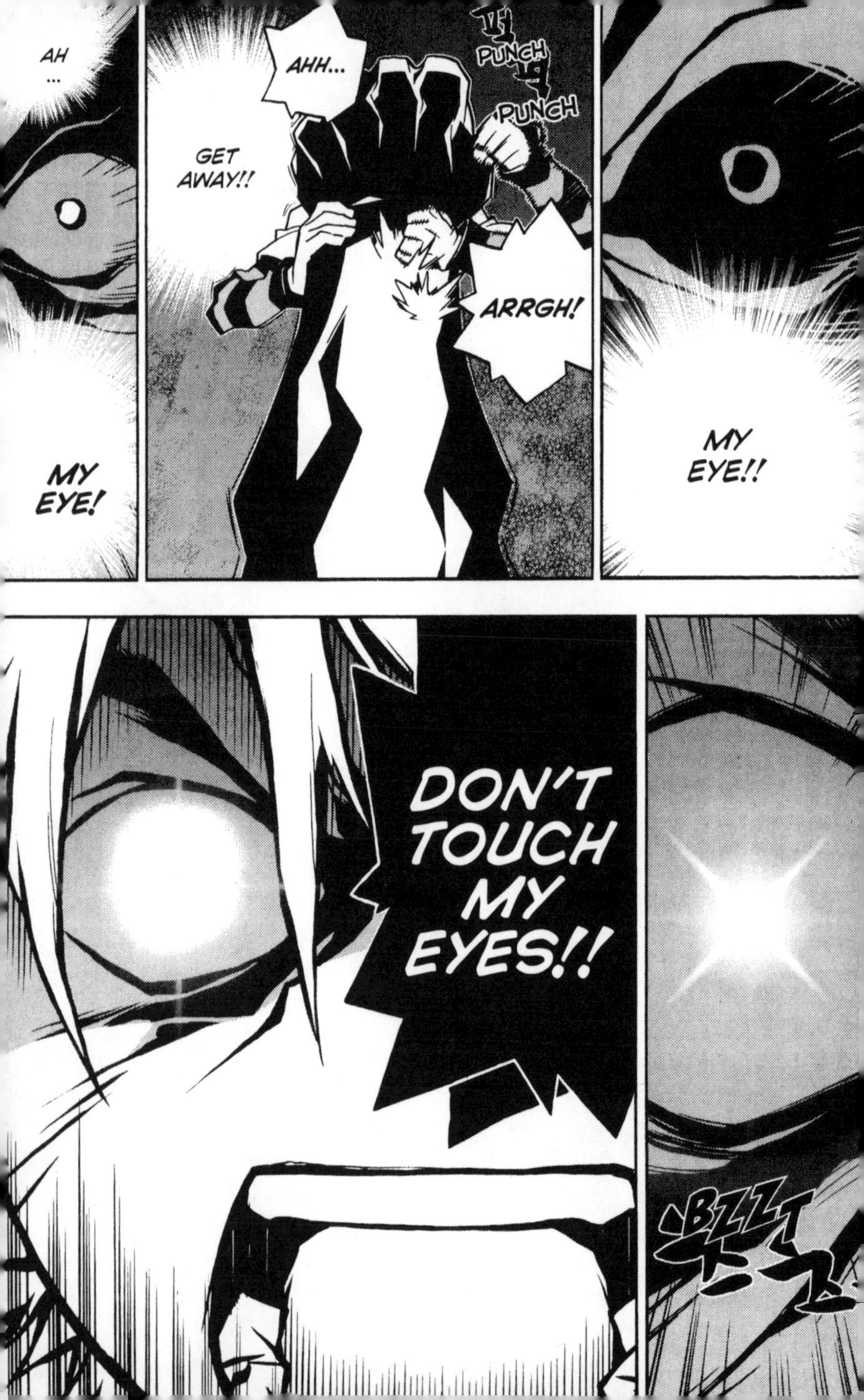
AH ...
MY EYE!
AHH...
GET AWAY!!
PUNCH
PUNCH
ARRGH!
MY EYE!!
DON'T TOUCH MY EYES!!
BZZT

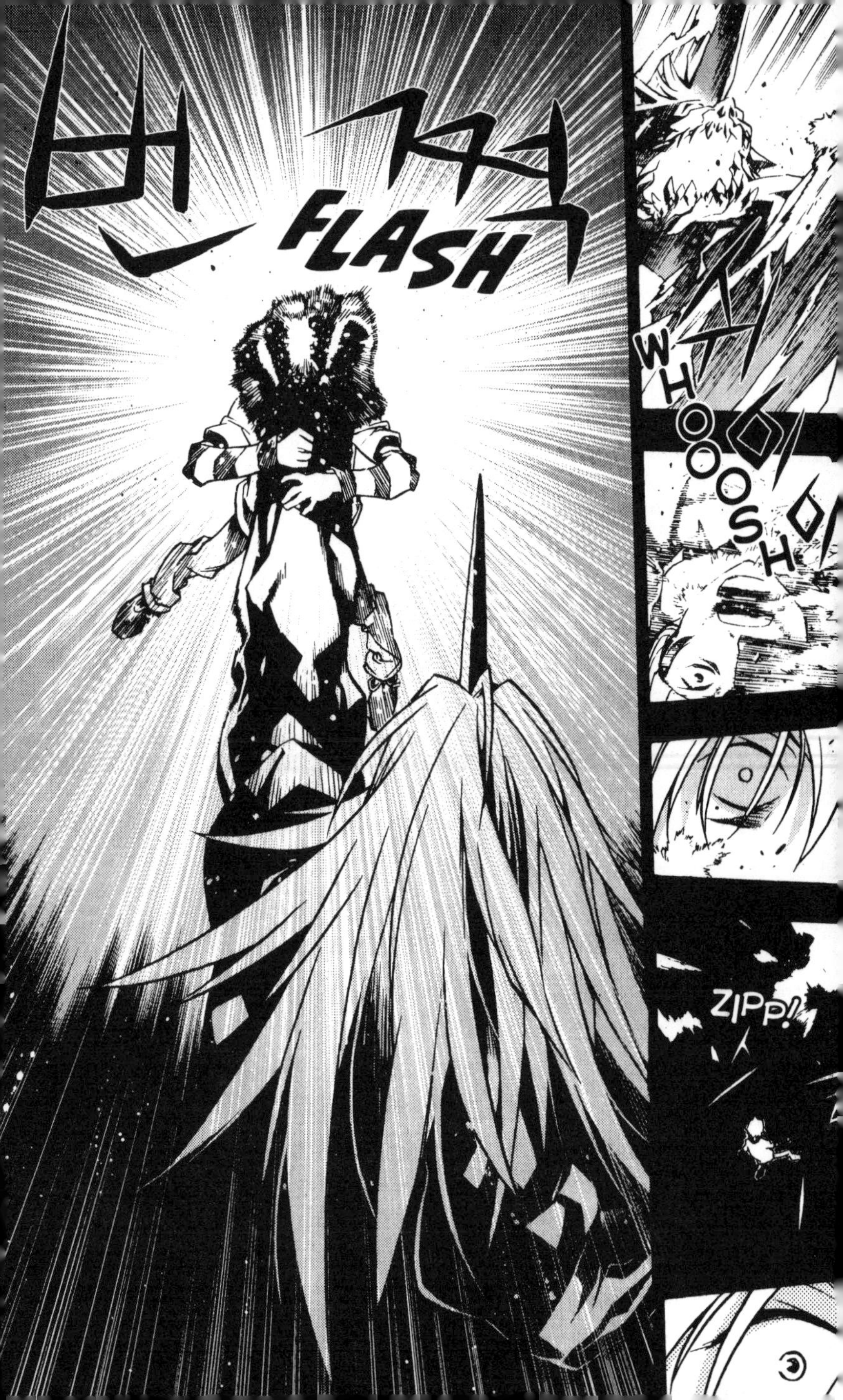
번쩍
FLASH
WHOOOSH
ZIPP!

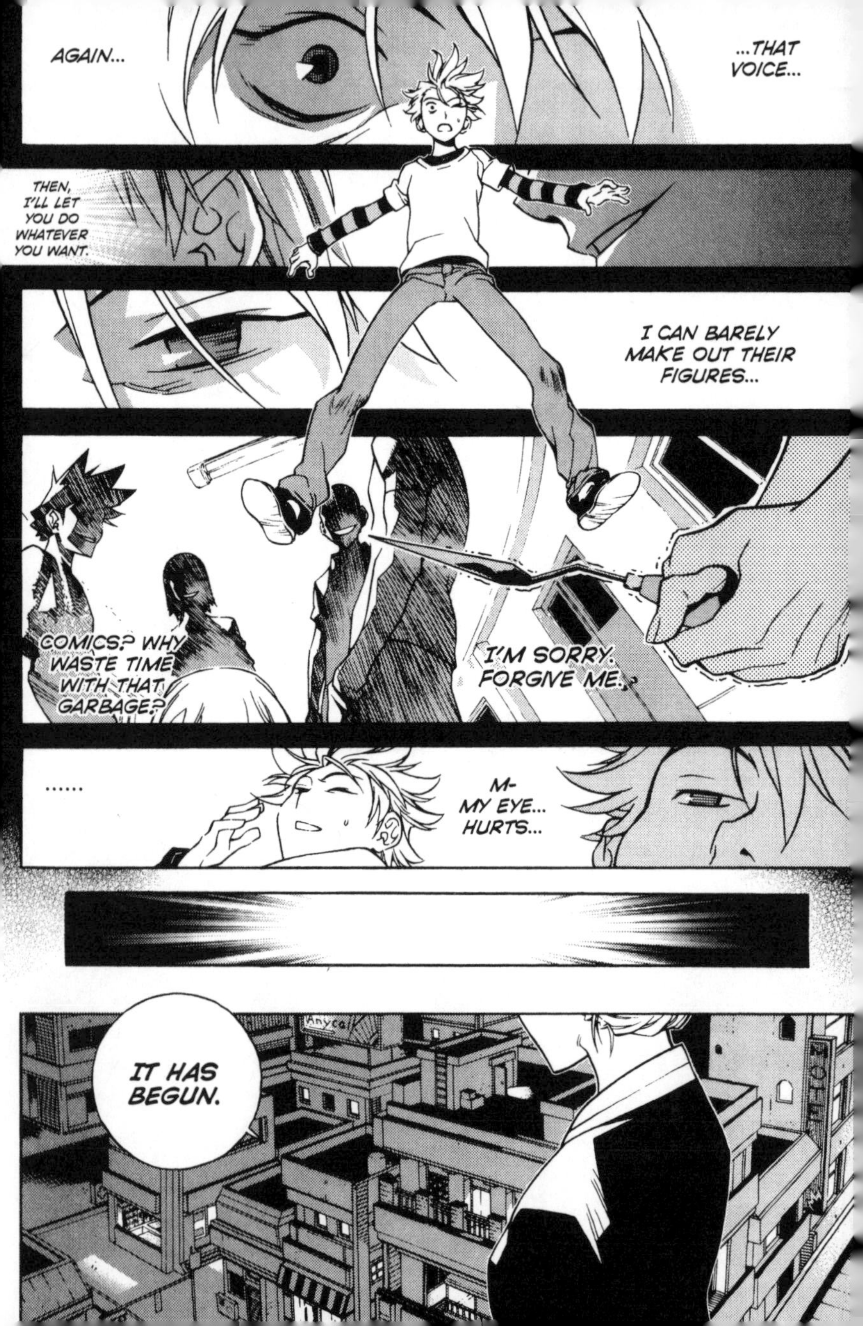
AGAIN...
...THAT VOICE...
THEN, I'LL LET YOU DO WHATEVER YOU WANT.
I CAN BARELY MAKE OUT THEIR FIGURES...
COMICS? WHY WASTE TIME WITH THAT GARBAGE?
I'M SORRY. FORGIVE ME...
......
M- MY EYE... HURTS...
IT HAS BEGUN.

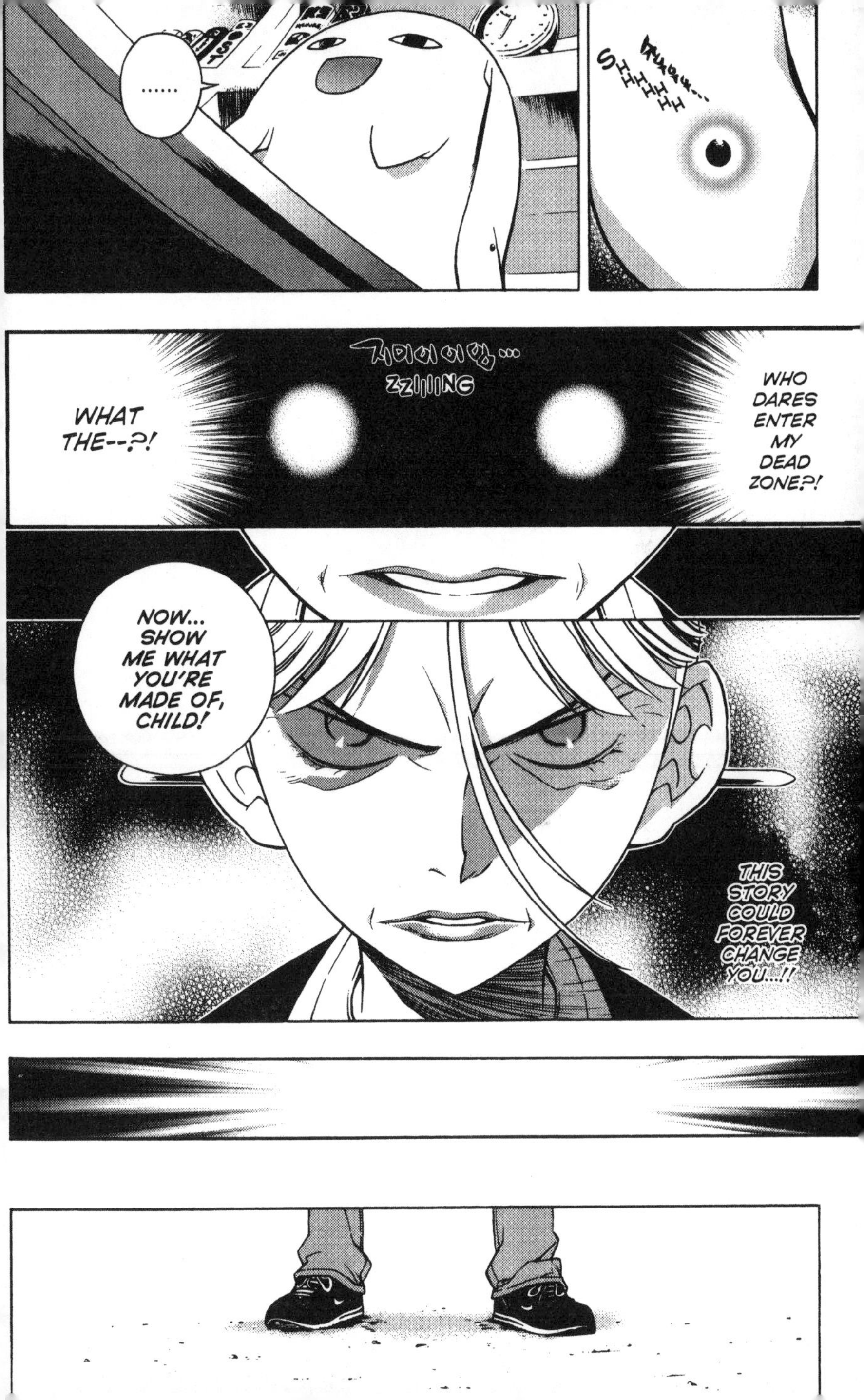

......
SHHHHHHH
지이이이잉...
ZZIIIING
WHAT THE--?!
WHO DARES ENTER MY DEAD ZONE?!
NOW... SHOW ME WHAT YOU'RE MADE OF, CHILD!
THIS STORY COULD FOREVER CHANGE YOU...!!

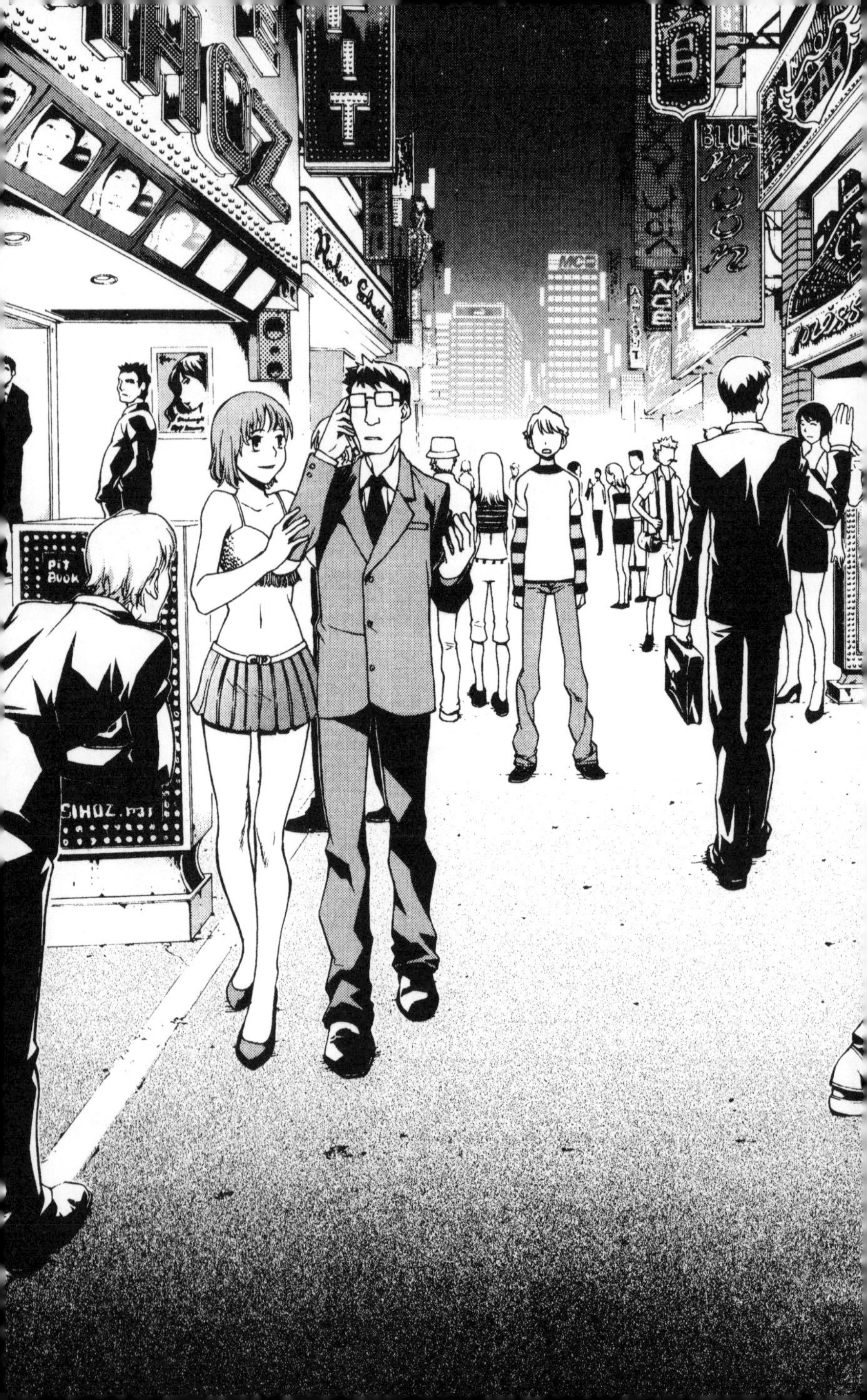
PIT
PIT
BOOK
BLUE

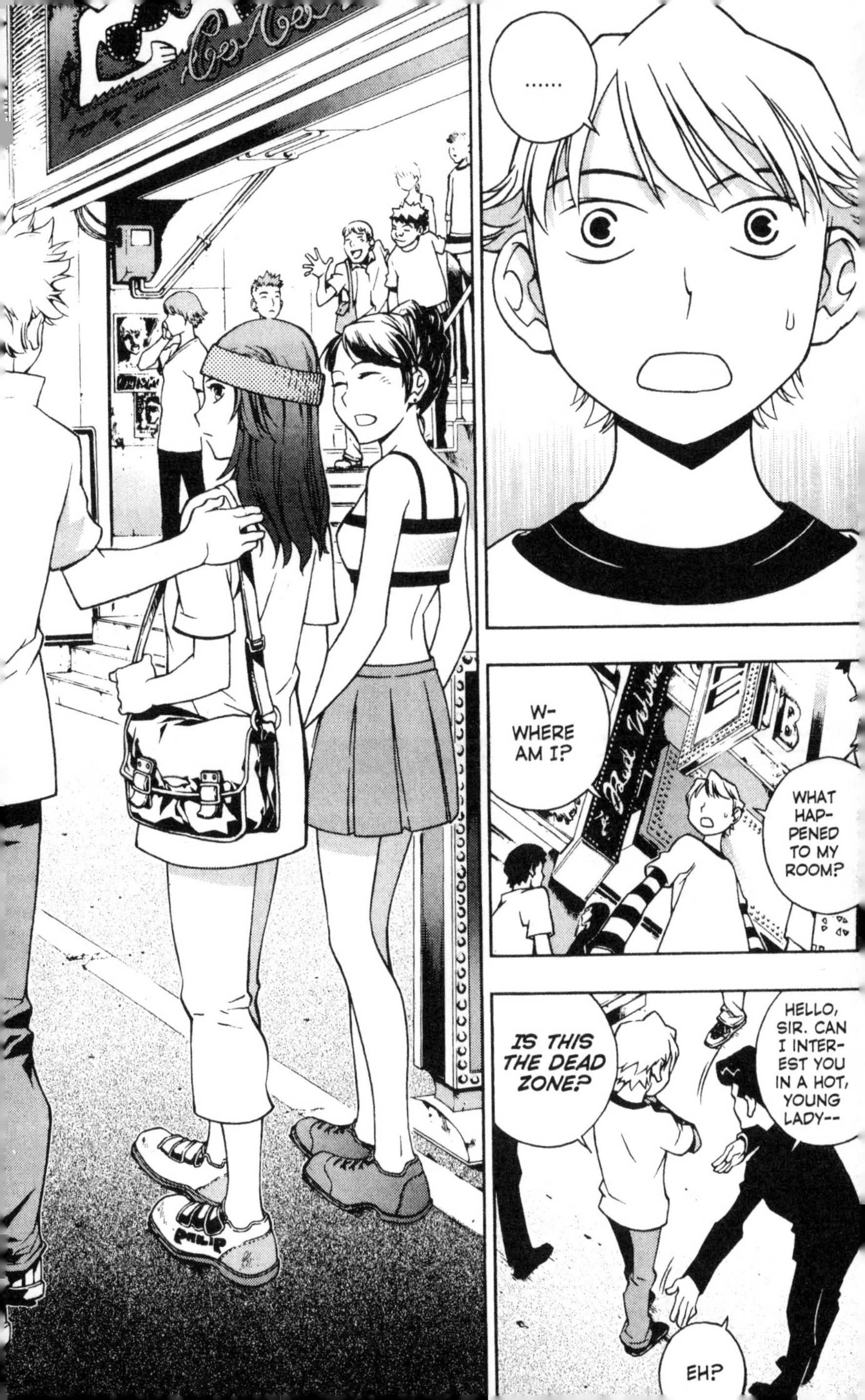
......
W-WHERE AM I?
WHAT HAPPENED TO MY ROOM?
IS THIS THE DEAD ZONE?
HELLO, SIR. CAN I INTEREST YOU IN A HOT, YOUNG LADY--
EH?

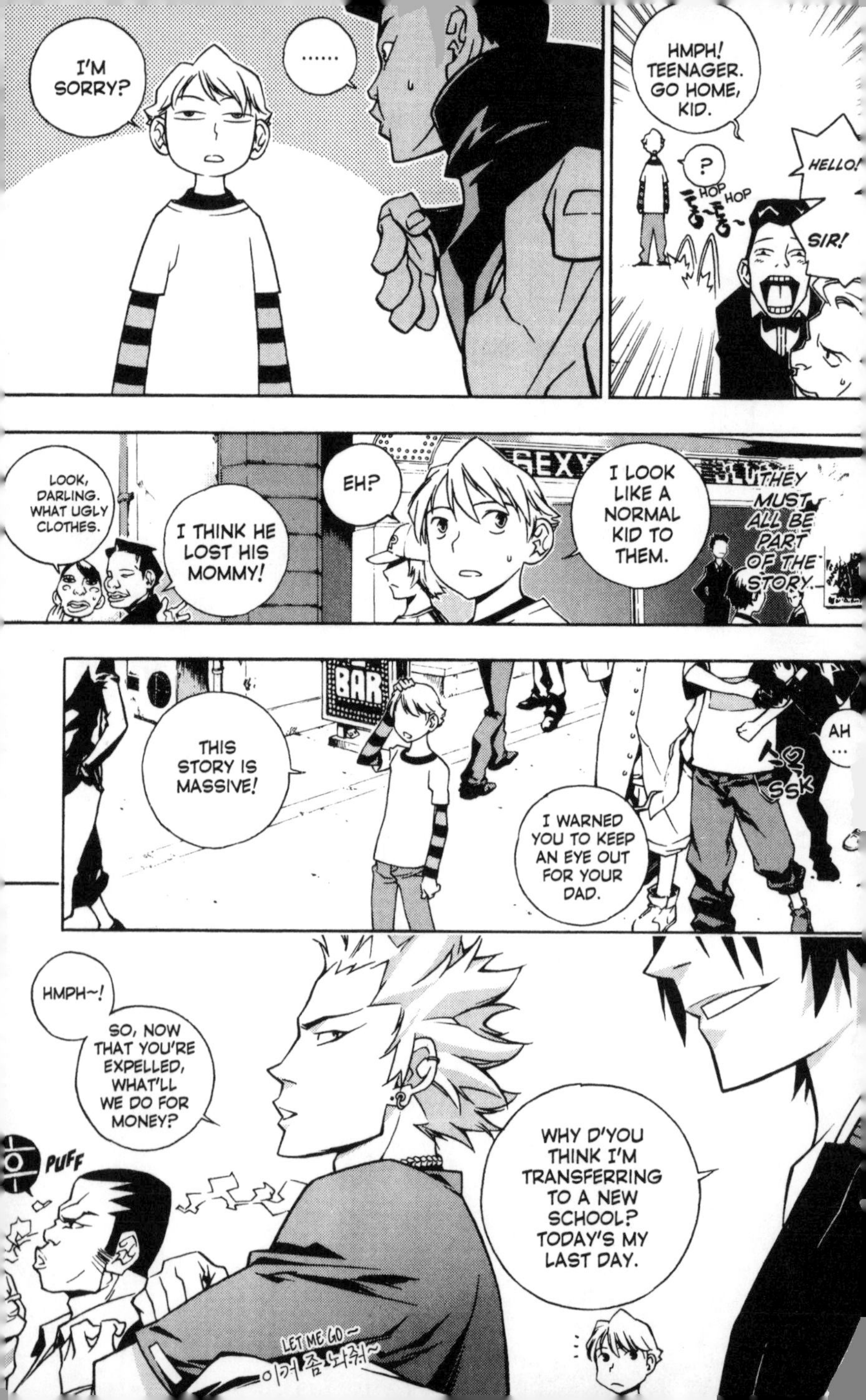
I'M SORRY?
......
HMPH! TEENAGER. GO HOME, KID.
?
HOP HOP
HELLO!
SIR!
LOOK, DARLING. WHAT UGLY CLOTHES.
I THINK HE LOST HIS MOMMY!
EH?
SEXY
I LOOK LIKE A NORMAL KID TO THEM.
THEY MUST ALL BE PART OF THE STORY.
BAR
THIS STORY IS MASSIVE!
I WARNED YOU TO KEEP AN EYE OUT FOR YOUR DAD.
AH ...
SSK
HMPH~!
SO, NOW THAT YOU'RE EXPELLED, WHAT'LL WE DO FOR MONEY?
PUFF
WHY D'YOU THINK I'M TRANSFERRING TO A NEW SCHOOL? TODAY'S MY LAST DAY.
LET ME GO ~
이거 좀 놔줘~

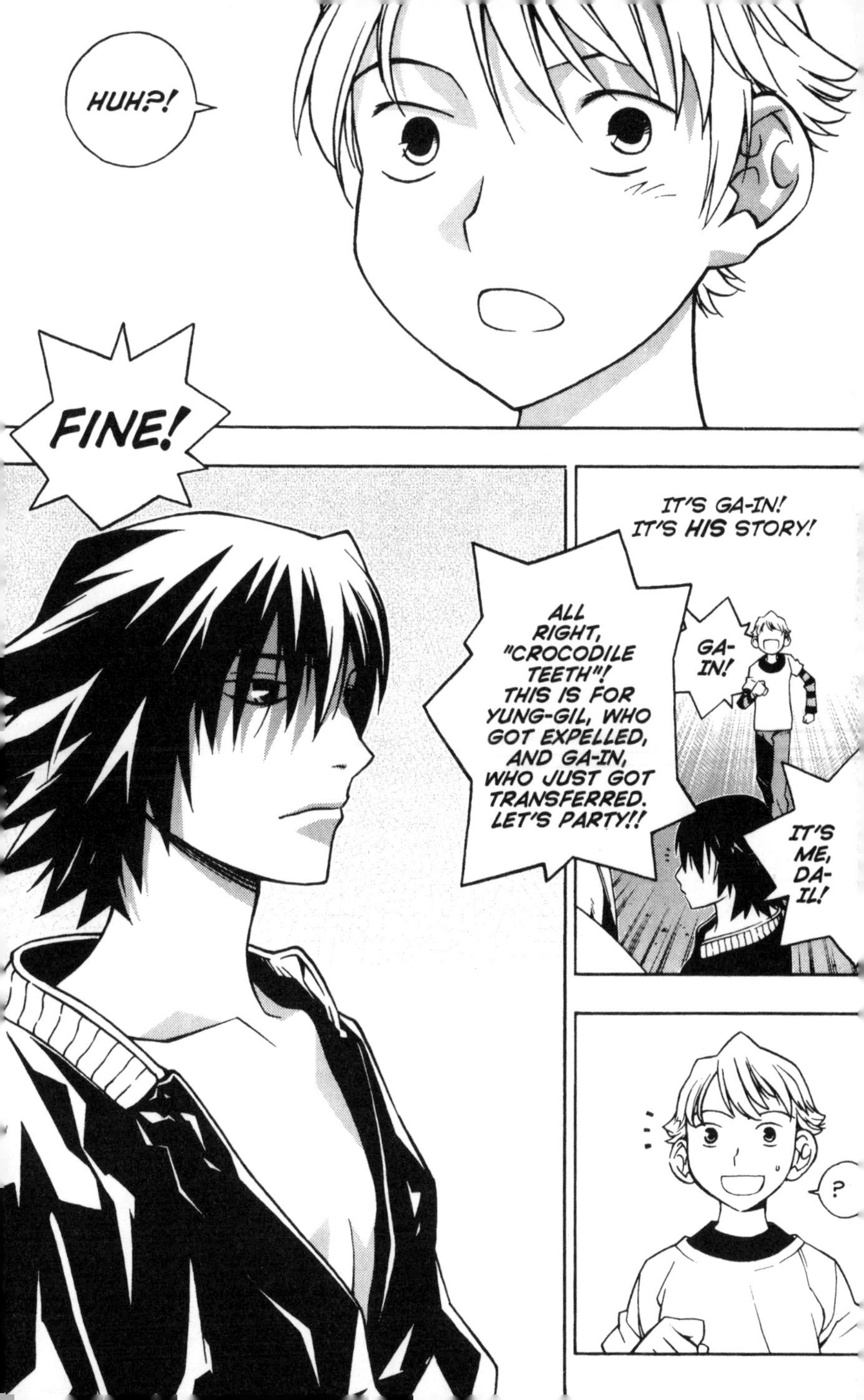
HUH?!
FINE!
ALL RIGHT, "CROCODILE TEETH"! THIS IS FOR YUNG-GIL, WHO GOT EXPELLED, AND GA-IN, WHO JUST GOT TRANSFERRED. LET'S PARTY!!
IT'S GA-IN! IT'S HIS STORY!
GA-IN!
IT'S ME, DA-IL!
?

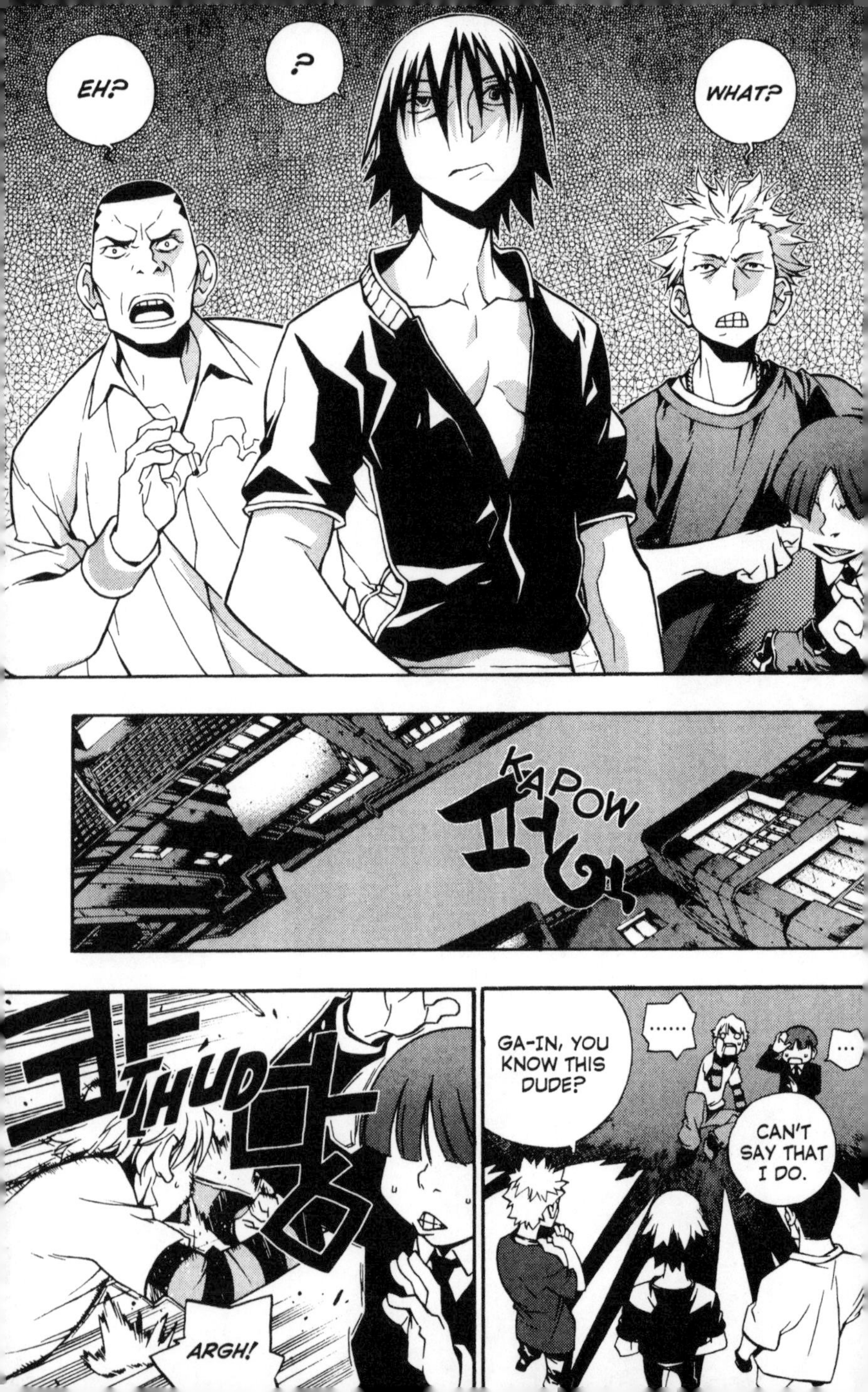
EH?
?
WHAT?
KAPOW
THUD
ARGH!
GA-IN, YOU KNOW THIS DUDE?
......
...
CAN'T SAY THAT I DO.

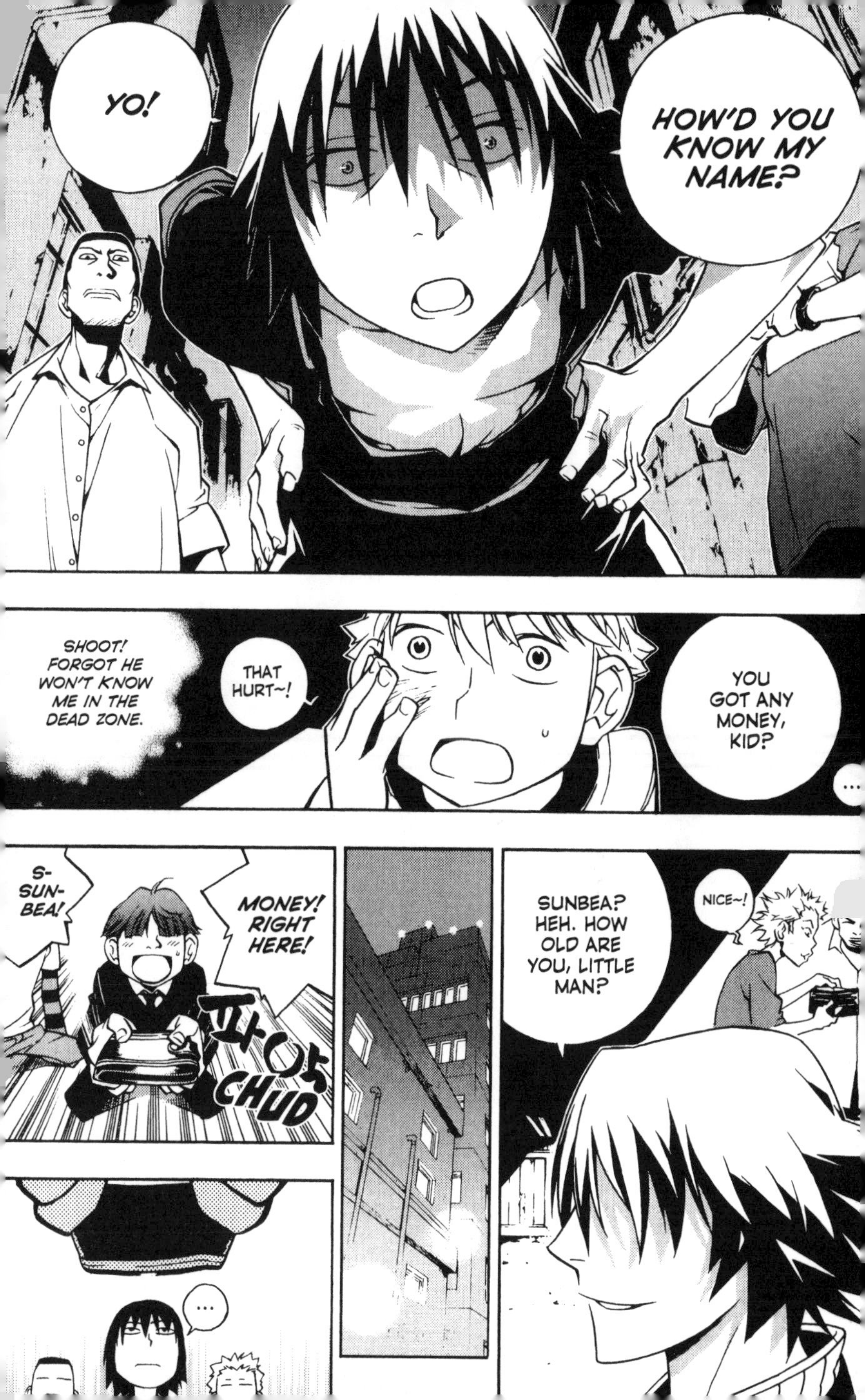
YO!
HOW'D YOU KNOW MY NAME?
SHOOT! FORGOT HE WON'T KNOW ME IN THE DEAD ZONE.
THAT HURT~!
YOU GOT ANY MONEY, KID?
...
S-SUNBEA!
MONEY! RIGHT HERE!
CHUD
SUNBEA? HEH. HOW OLD ARE YOU, LITTLE MAN?
NICE~!
...

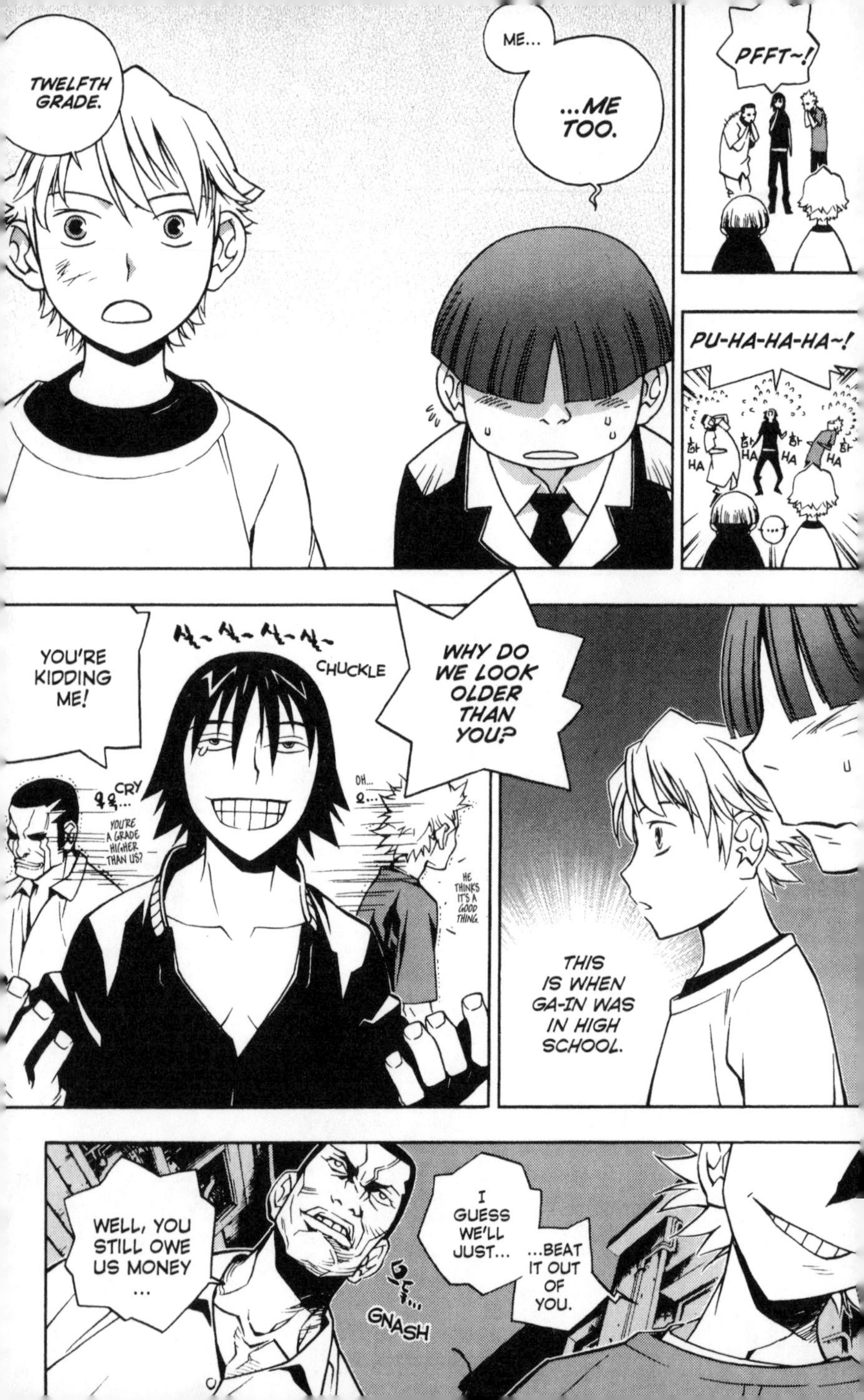
TWELFTH GRADE.
ME...
...ME TOO.
PFFT~!
PU-HA-HA-HA~!
HA
HA
HA
HA
YOU'RE KIDDING ME!
CHUCKLE
WHY DO WE LOOK OLDER THAN YOU?
CRY
YOU'RE A GRADE HIGHER THAN US?
OH...
HE THINKS IT'S A GOOD THING.
THIS IS WHEN GA-IN WAS IN HIGH SCHOOL.
WELL, YOU STILL OWE US MONEY ...
GNASH
I GUESS WE'LL JUST...
...BEAT IT OUT OF YOU.

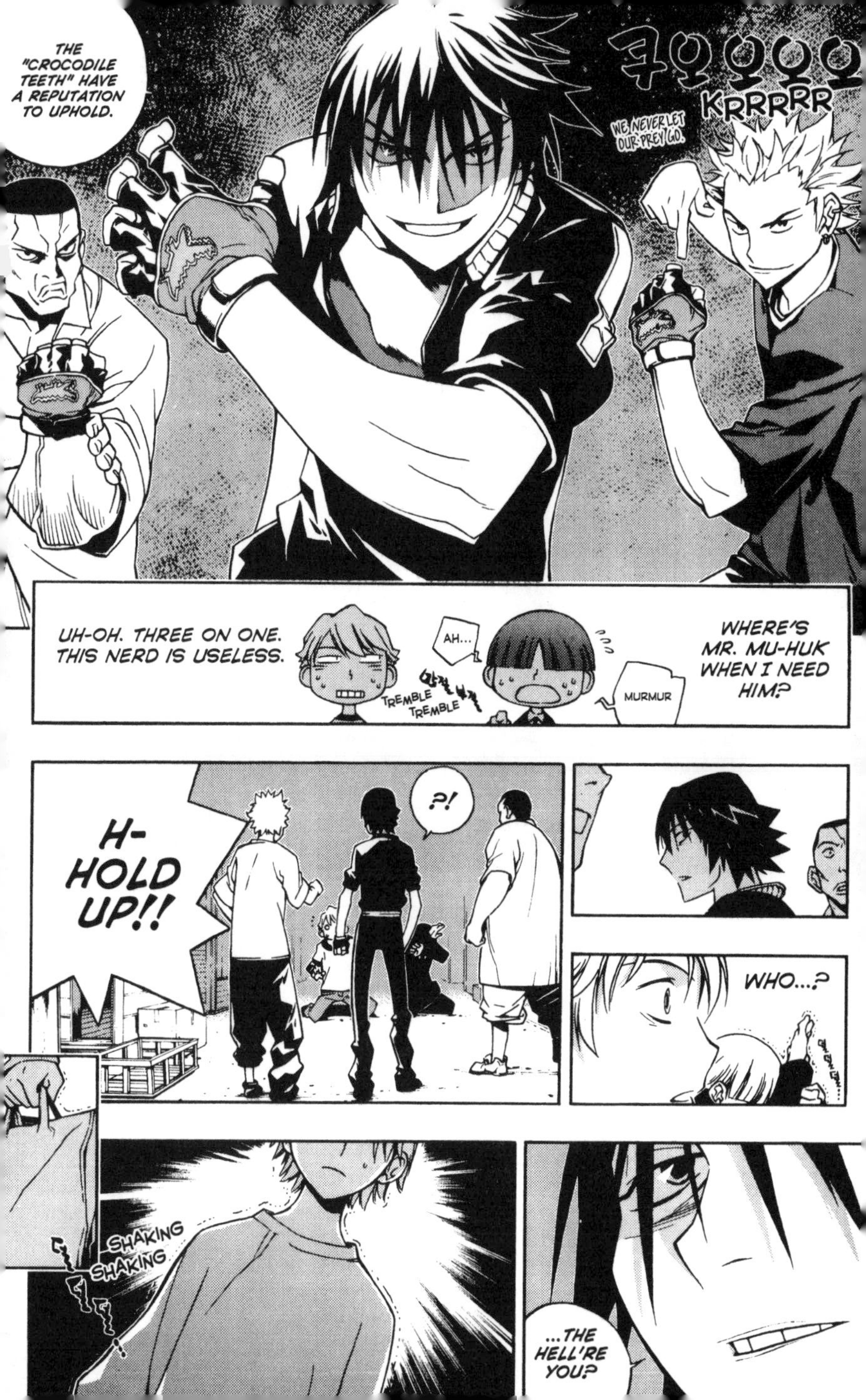
THE "CROCODILE TEETH" HAVE A REPUTATION TO UPHOLD.
WE NEVER LET OUR PREY GO.
크오오오오
KRRRRR
UH-OH. THREE ON ONE. THIS NERD IS USELESS.
AH...
TREMBLE TREMBLE
MURMUR
WHERE'S MR. MU-HUK WHEN I NEED HIM?
H-HOLD UP!!
?!
WHO...?
SHAKING SHAKING
...THE HELL'RE YOU?

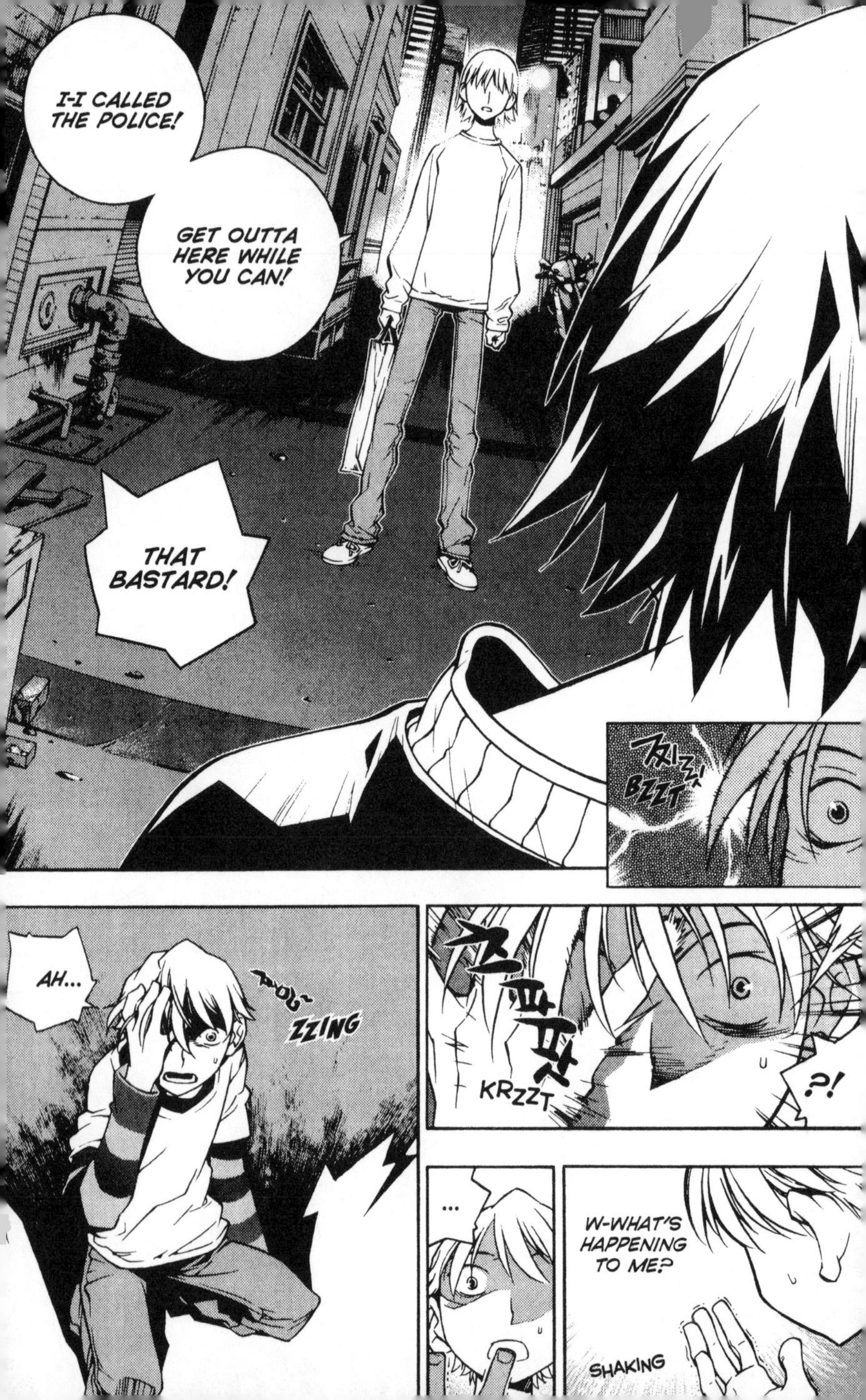
I-I CALLED THE POLICE!
GET OUTTA HERE WHILE YOU CAN!
THAT BASTARD!
BZZT
AH...
ZZING
KRZZT
?!
...
W-WHAT'S HAPPENING TO ME?
SHAKING

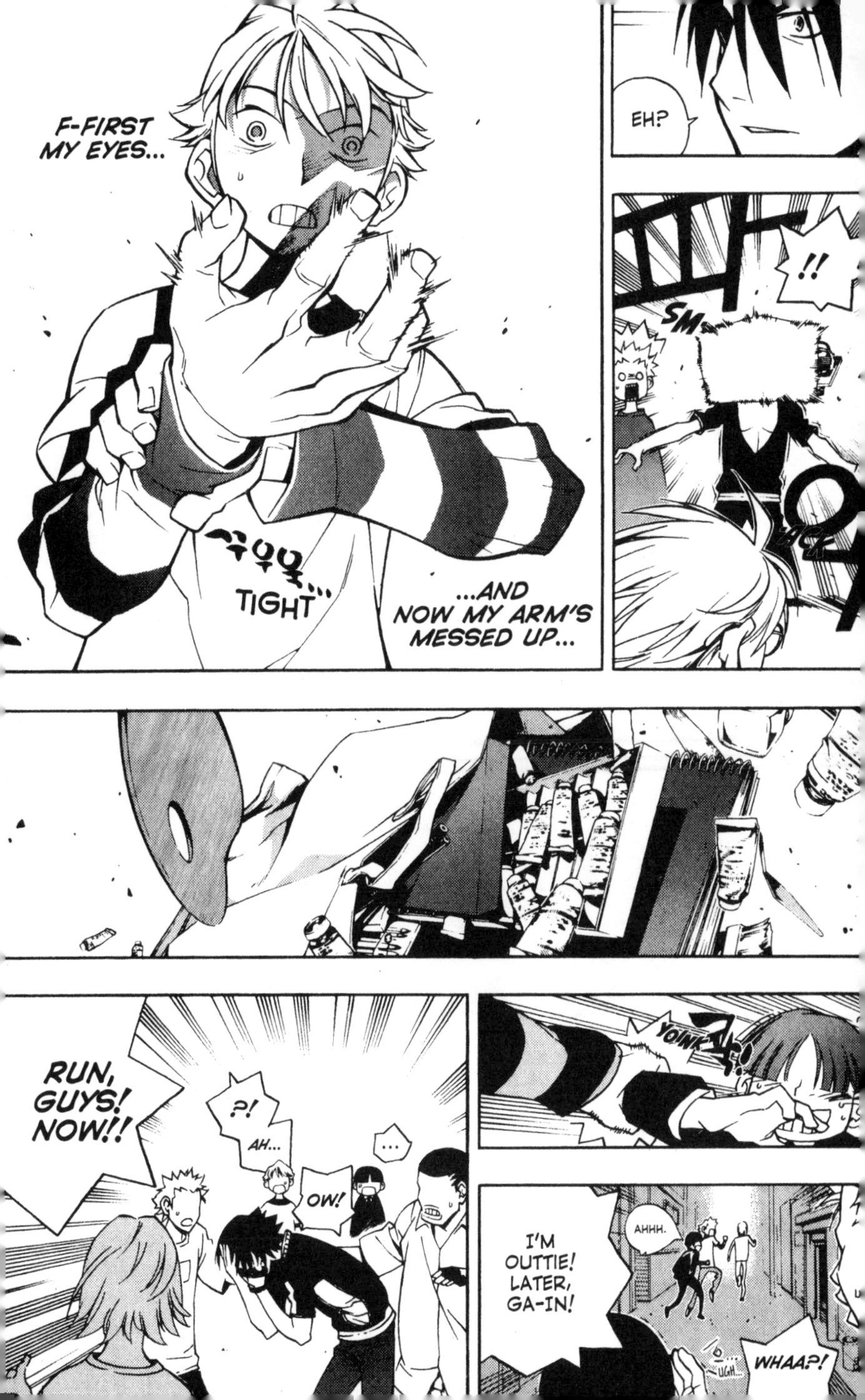
F-FIRST MY EYES...
꽈우욱...
TIGHT
...AND NOW MY ARM'S MESSED UP...
EH?
!!
SM
ACK
RUN, GUYS! NOW!!
?!
AH...
...
OW!
YOINK
AHHH.
I'M OUTTIE! LATER, GA-IN!
UGH...
WHAA?!

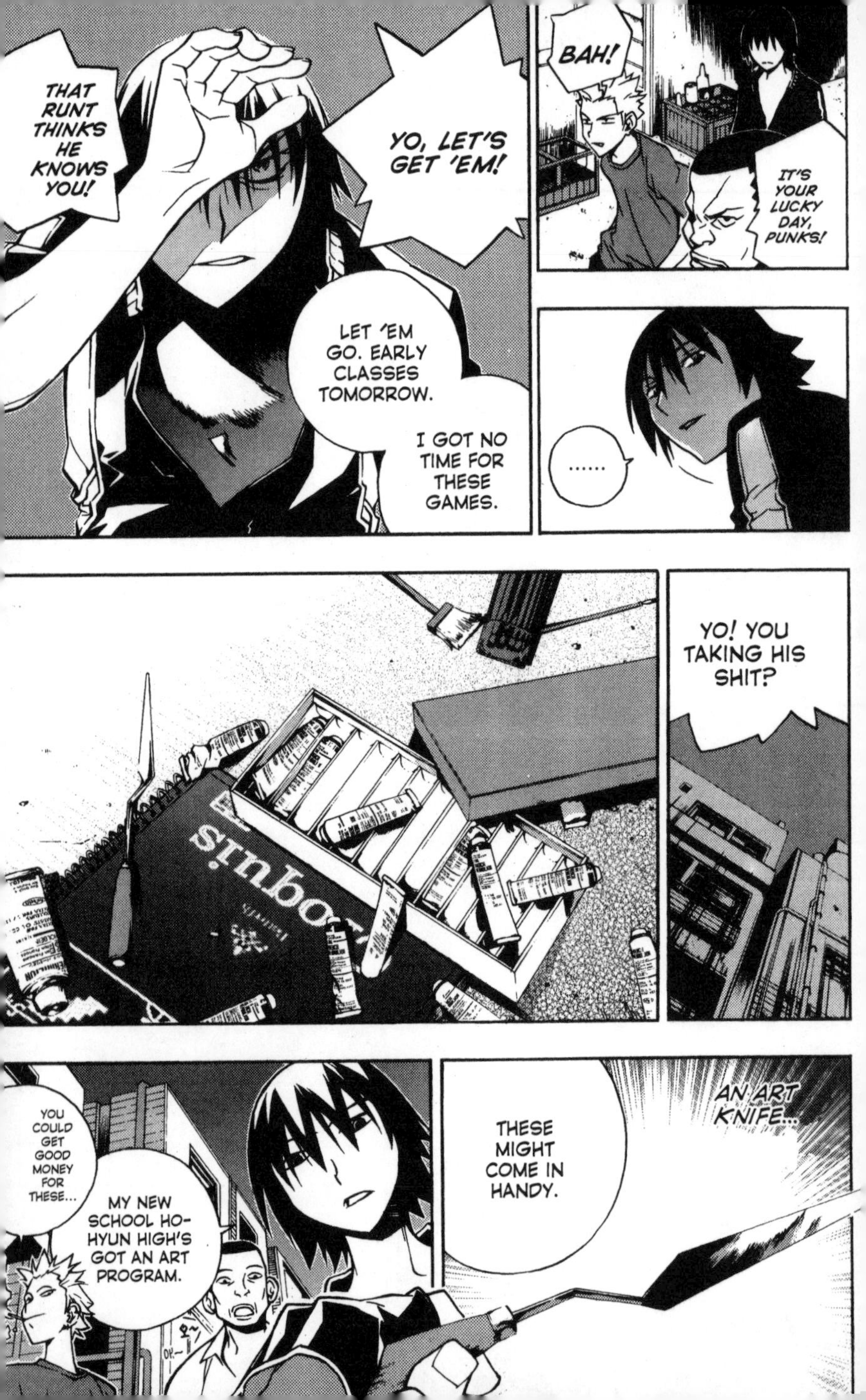
THAT RUNT THINKS HE KNOWS YOU!
YO, LET'S GET 'EM!
LET 'EM GO. EARLY CLASSES TOMORROW.
I GOT NO TIME FOR THESE GAMES.
BAH!
IT'S YOUR LUCKY DAY, PUNKS!
......
YO! YOU TAKING HIS SHIT?
YOU COULD GET GOOD MONEY FOR THESE...
MY NEW SCHOOL HO-HYUN HIGH'S GOT AN ART PROGRAM.
THESE MIGHT COME IN HANDY.
AN ART KNIFE...

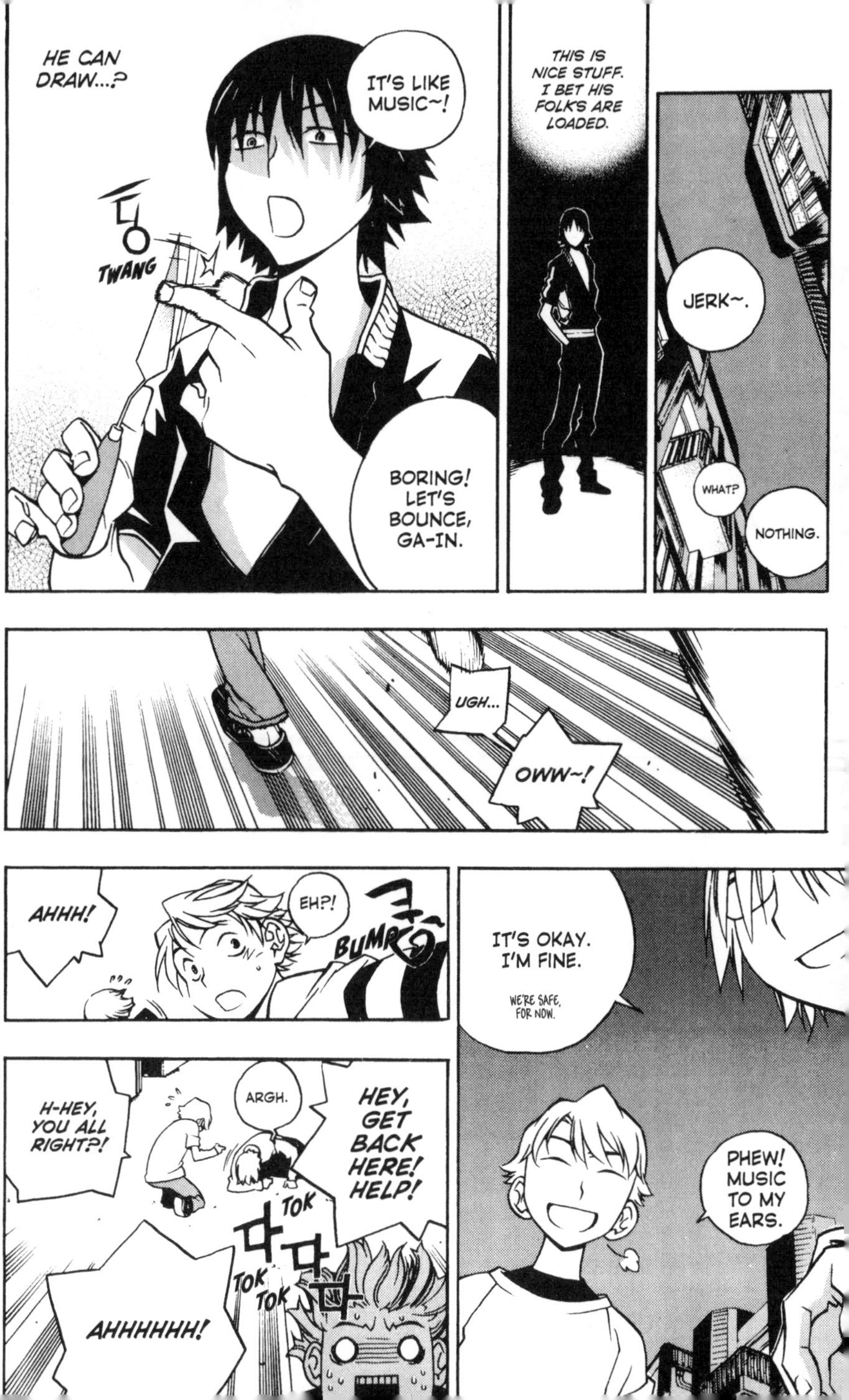
HE CAN DRAW...?
IT'S LIKE MUSIC~!
TWANG
BORING! LET'S BOUNCE, GA-IN.
THIS IS NICE STUFF. I BET HIS FOLKS ARE LOADED.
JERK~.
WHAT?
NOTHING.
UGH...
OWW~!
AHHH!
EH?!
BUMP
H-HEY, YOU ALL RIGHT?!
ARGH.
HEY, GET BACK HERE! HELP!
TOK
TOK
TOK
AHHHHHH!
IT'S OKAY. I'M FINE.
WE'RE SAFE, FOR NOW.
PHEW! MUSIC TO MY EARS.

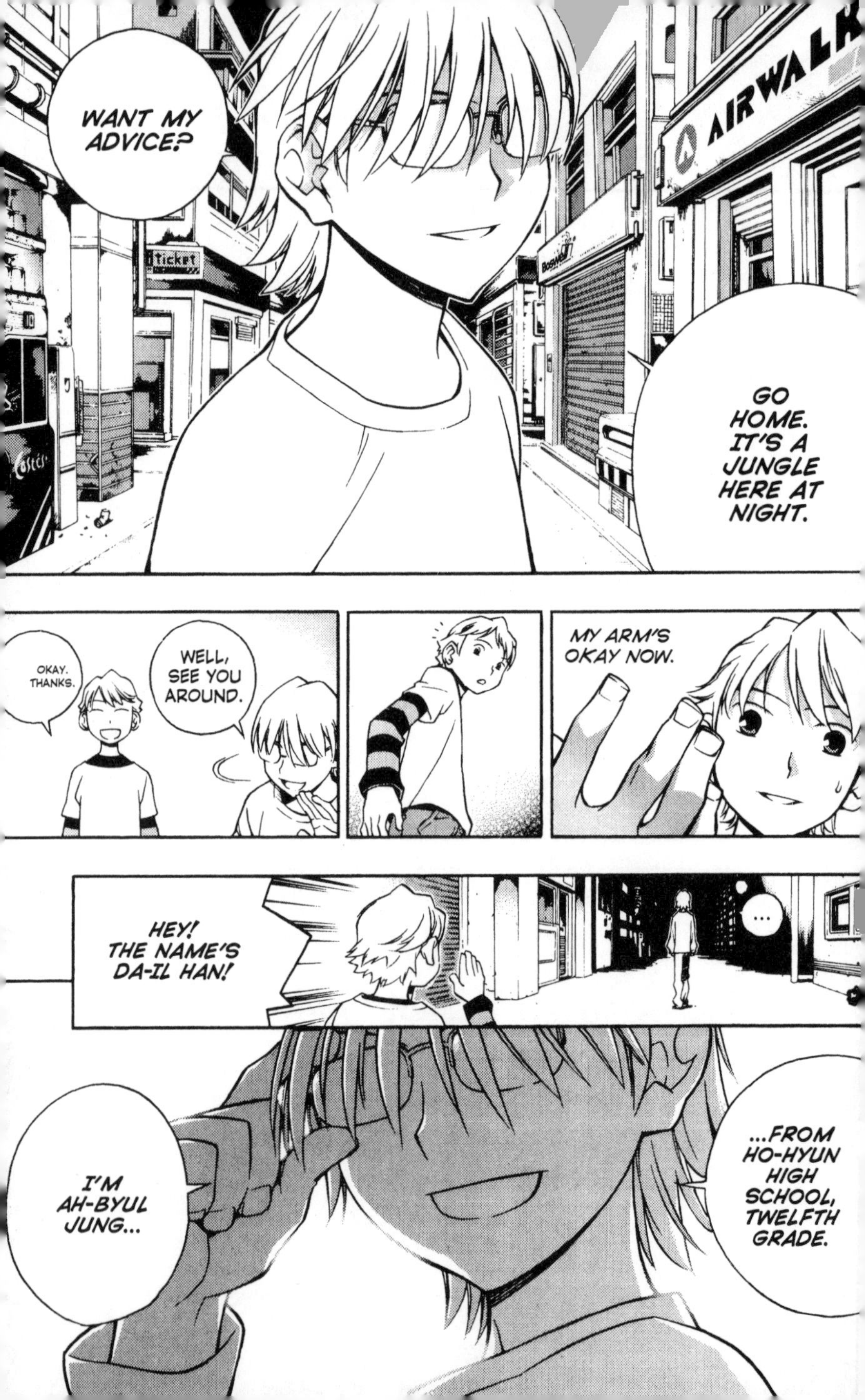
WANT MY ADVICE?
AIRWALK
Ticket
GO HOME. IT'S A JUNGLE HERE AT NIGHT.
OKAY. THANKS.
WELL, SEE YOU AROUND.
MY ARM'S OKAY NOW.
HEY! THE NAME'S DA-IL HAN!
...
I'M AH-BYUL JUNG...
...FROM HO-HYUN HIGH SCHOOL, TWELFTH GRADE.

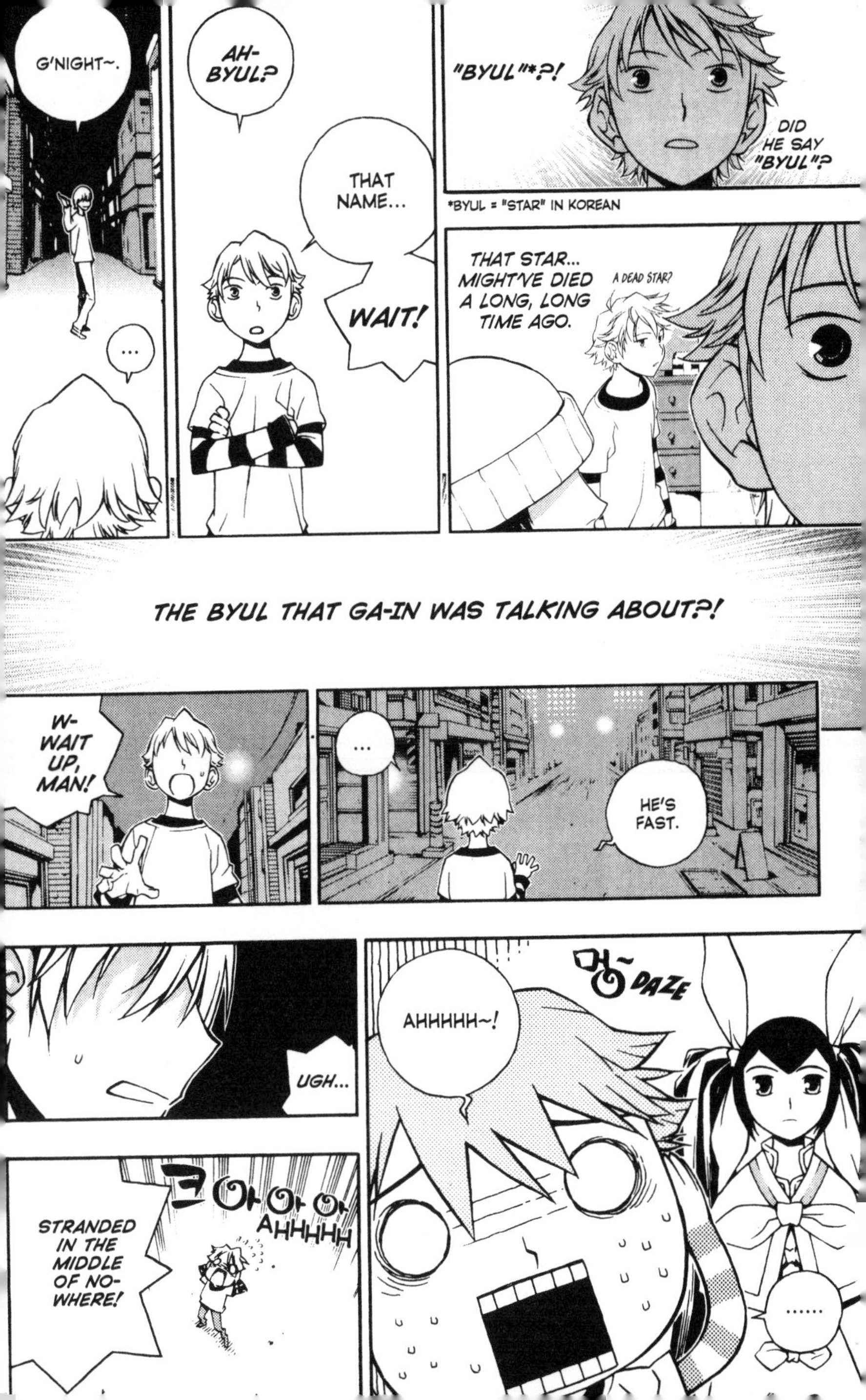

G'NIGHT~.
...
AH-BYUL?
THAT NAME...
WAIT!
"BYUL"*?!
DID HE SAY "BYUL"?
*BYUL = "STAR" IN KOREAN
THAT STAR... MIGHT'VE DIED A LONG, LONG TIME AGO.
A DEAD STAR?
THE BYUL THAT GA-IN WAS TALKING ABOUT?!
W-WAIT UP, MAN!
...
HE'S FAST.
UGH...
STRANDED IN THE MIDDLE OF NO-WHERE!
크아아아
AHHHHH
멍~
DAZE
AHHHHH~!
....

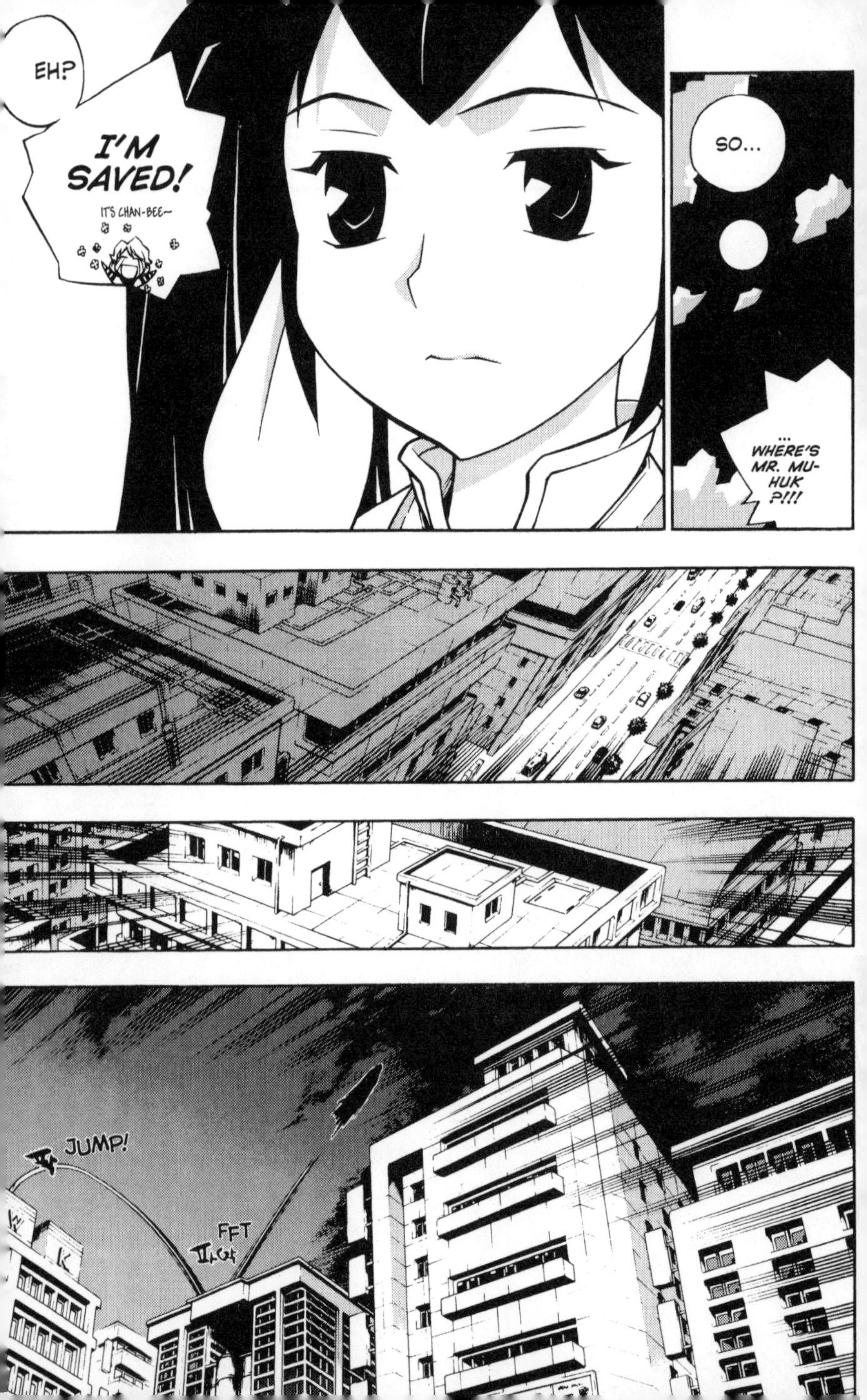
EH?
I'M SAVED!
IT'S CHAN-BEE~
SO...
... WHERE'S MR. MU-HUK ?!!!
JUMP!
FFT

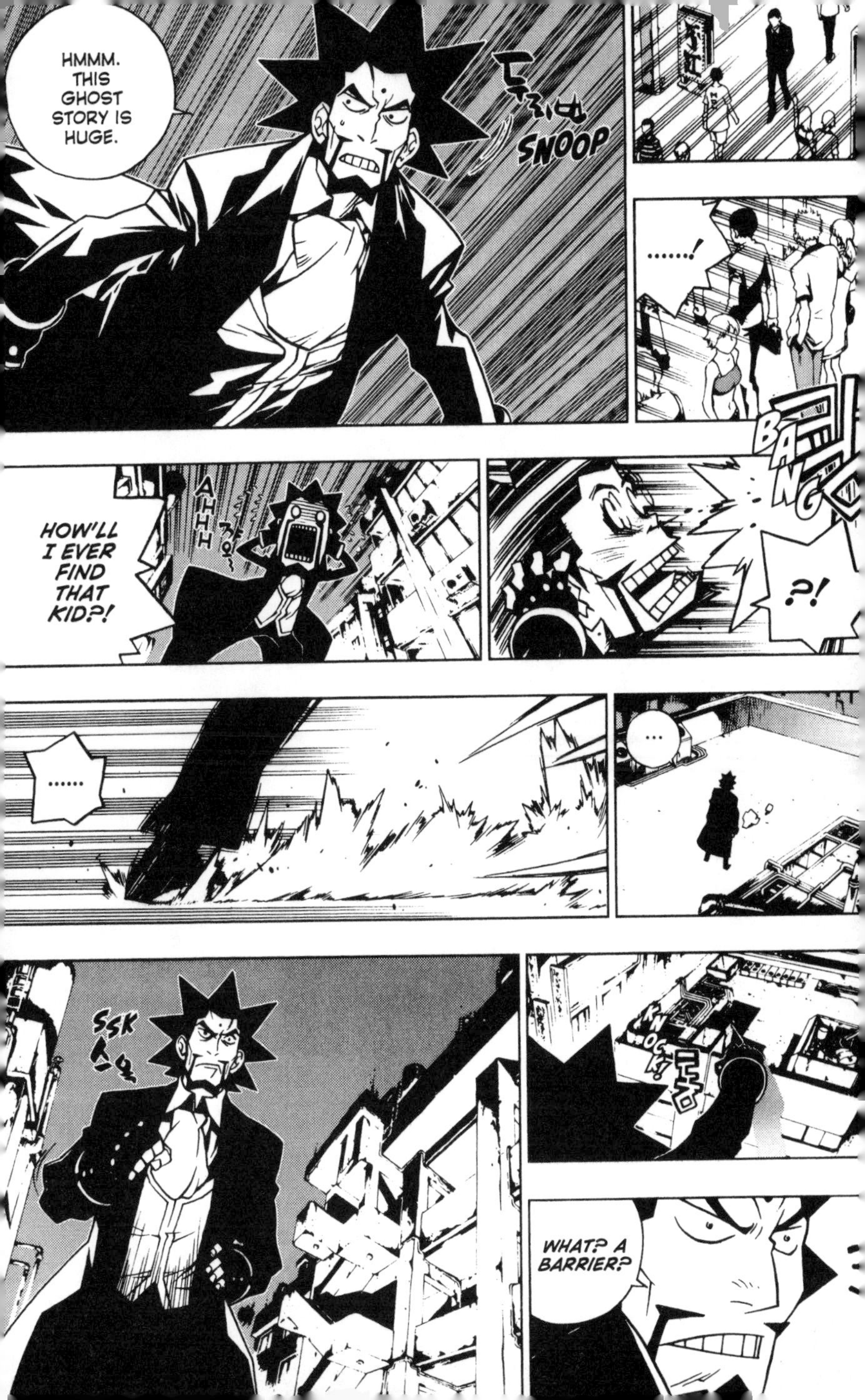
HMMM. THIS GHOST STORY IS HUGE.
SNOOP
......!
AHHH
HOW'LL I EVER FIND THAT KID?!
BANG
?!
......
...
SSK
KNOCK!
WHAT? A BARRIER?

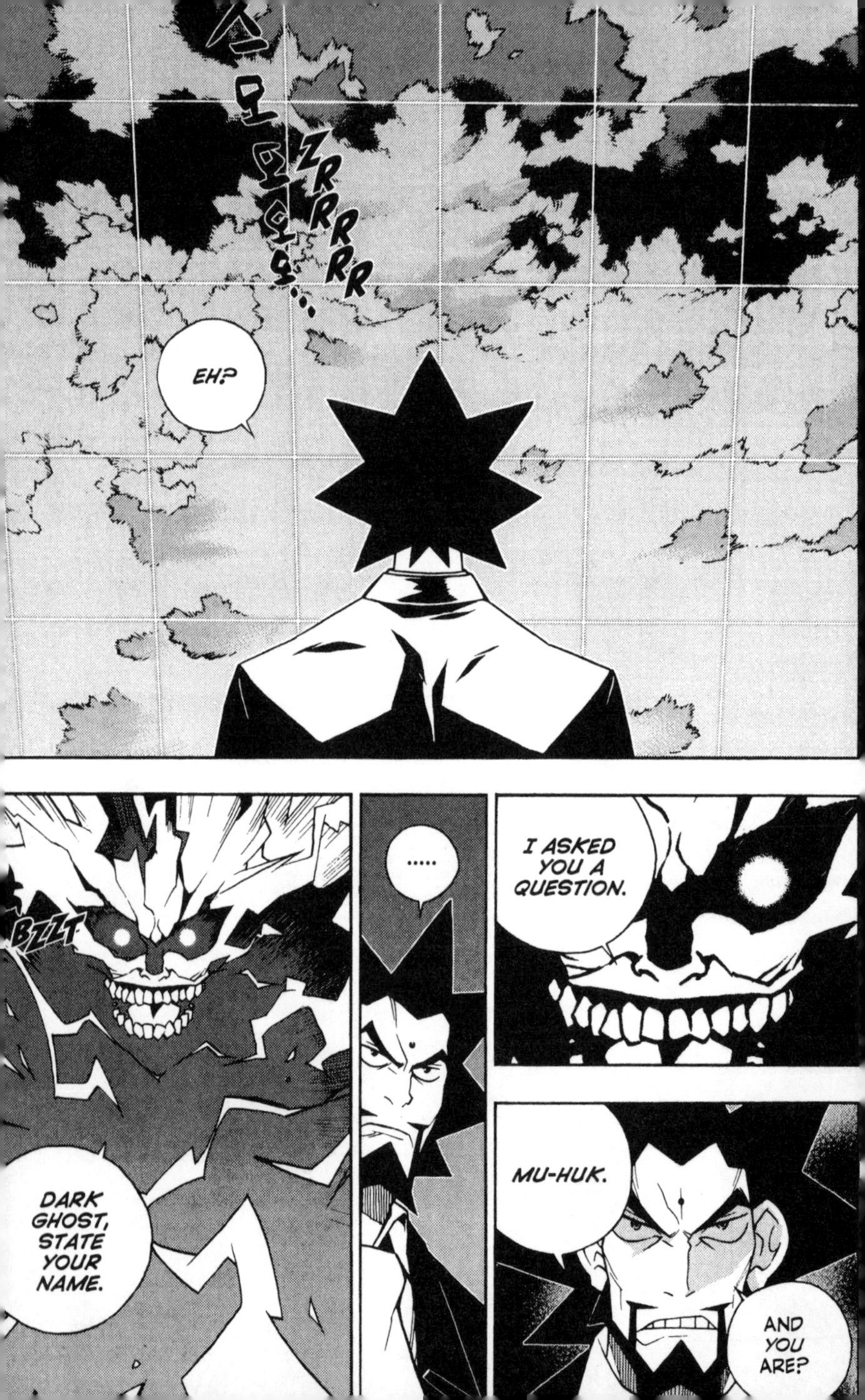
ZRRRRR
EH?
BZZT
DARK GHOST, STATE YOUR NAME.
......
I ASKED YOU A QUESTION.
MU-HUK.
AND YOU ARE?

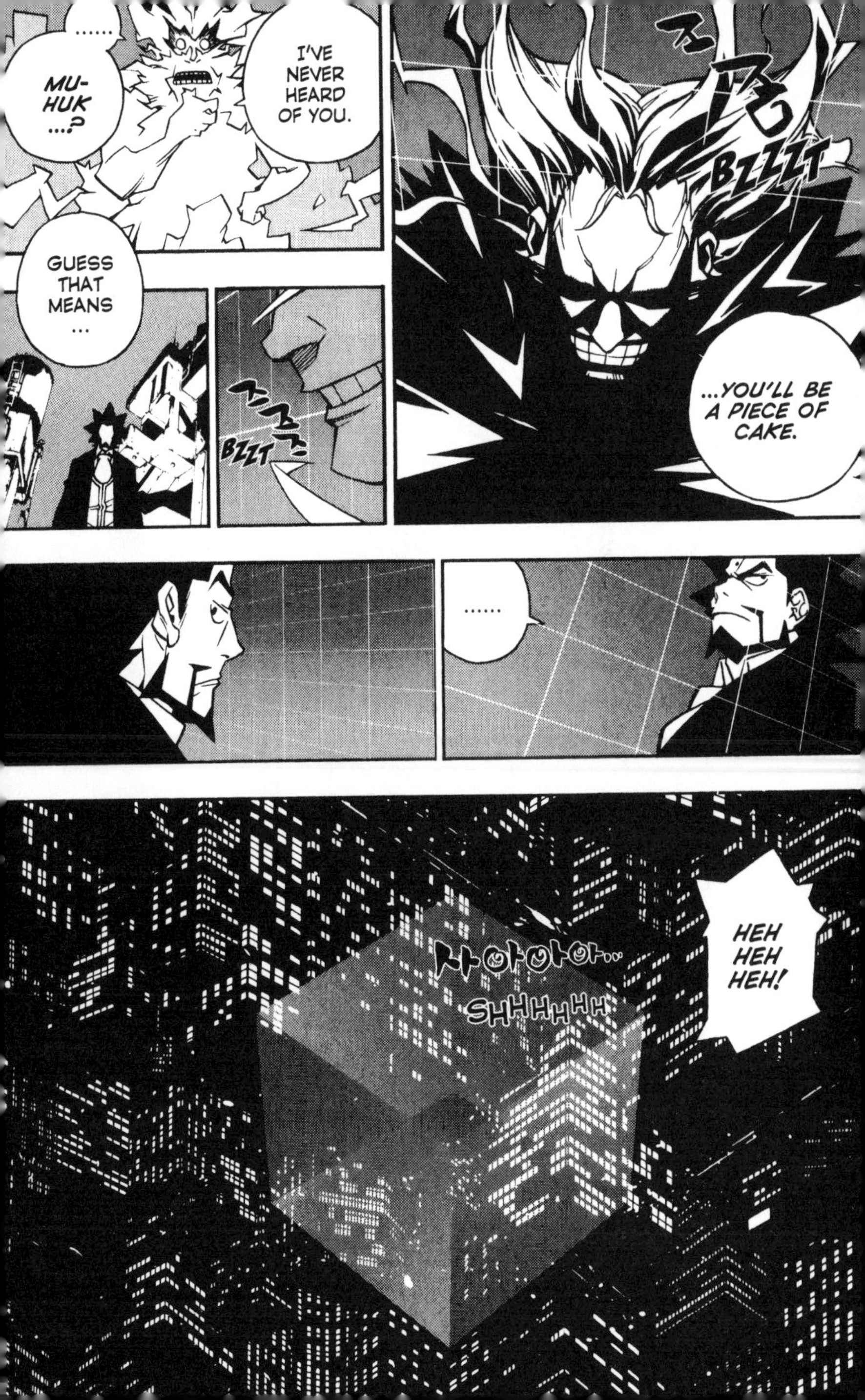
......
MU-HUK ...?
I'VE NEVER HEARD OF YOU.
GUESS THAT MEANS ...
BZZT
BZZZT
...YOU'LL BE A PIECE OF CAKE.
......
SHHHHHH
HEH HEH HEH!

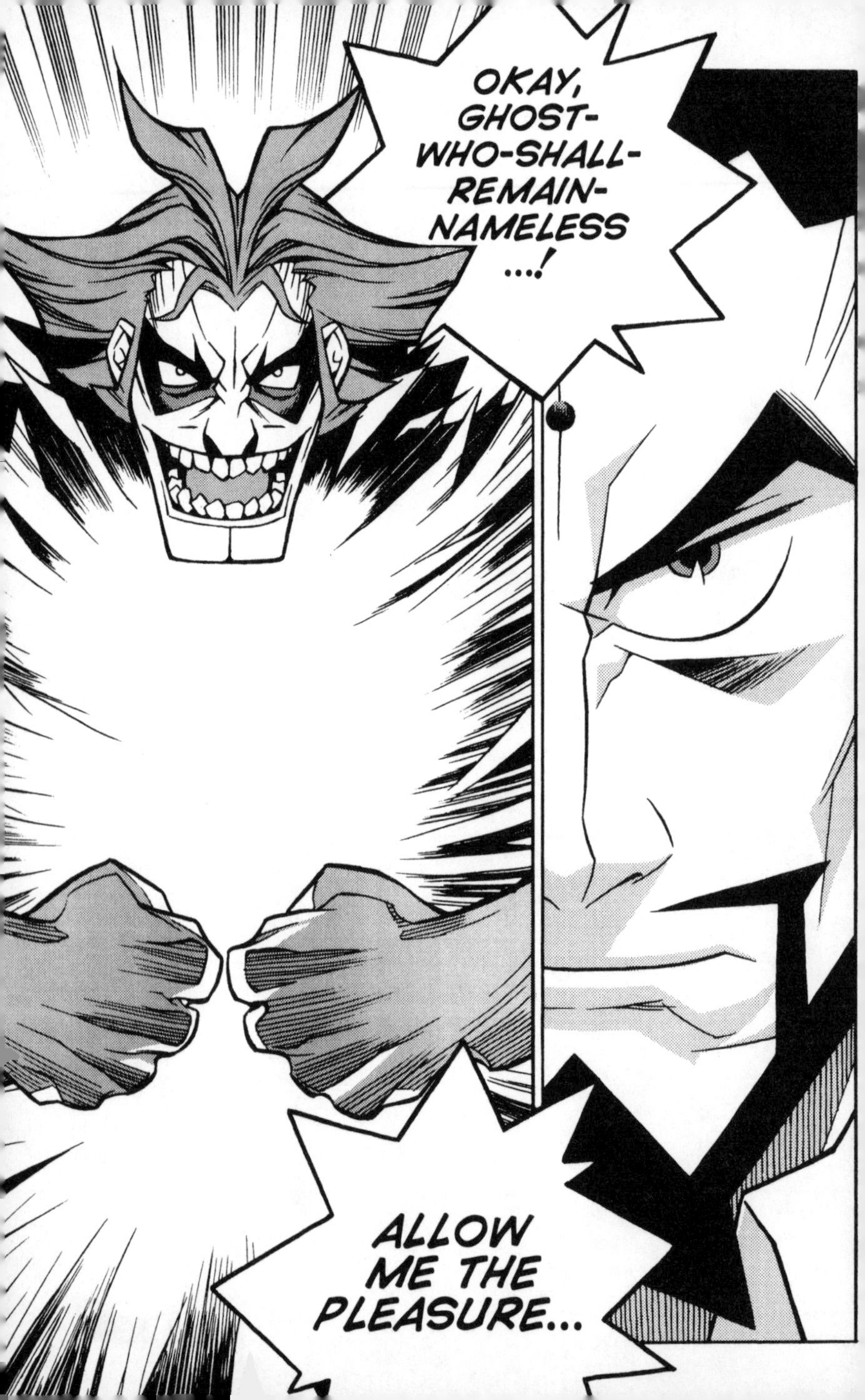
OKAY, GHOST-WHO-SHALL-REMAIN-NAMELESS ...!
ALLOW ME THE PLEASURE...

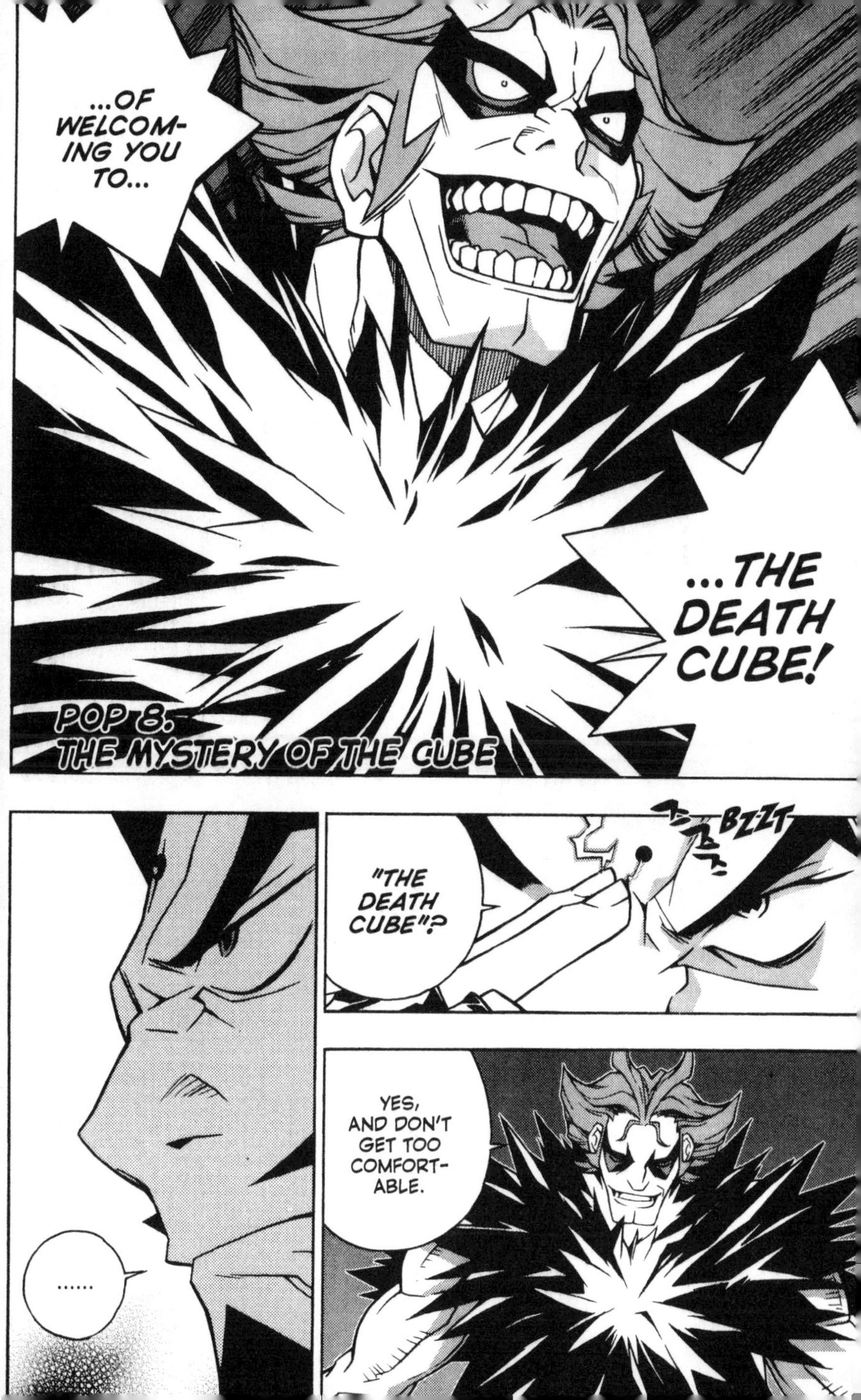
...OF WELCOMING YOU TO...
...THE DEATH CUBE!
POP 8. THE MYSTERY OF THE CUBE
......
"THE DEATH CUBE"?
BZZZT
YES, AND DON'T GET TOO COMFORTABLE.

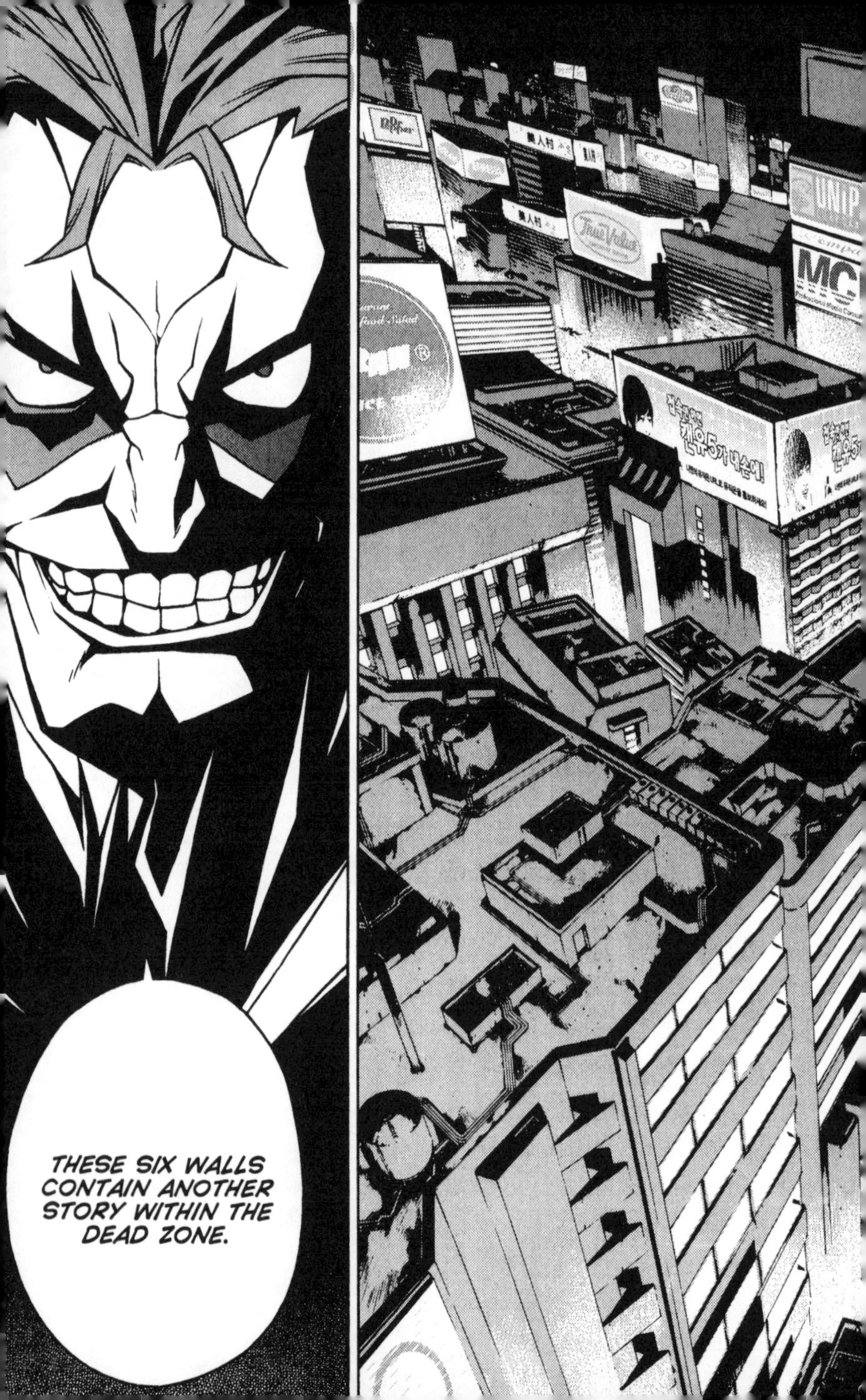
THESE SIX WALLS CONTAIN ANOTHER STORY WITHIN THE DEAD ZONE.
美人村
True Value
UNIP
MC

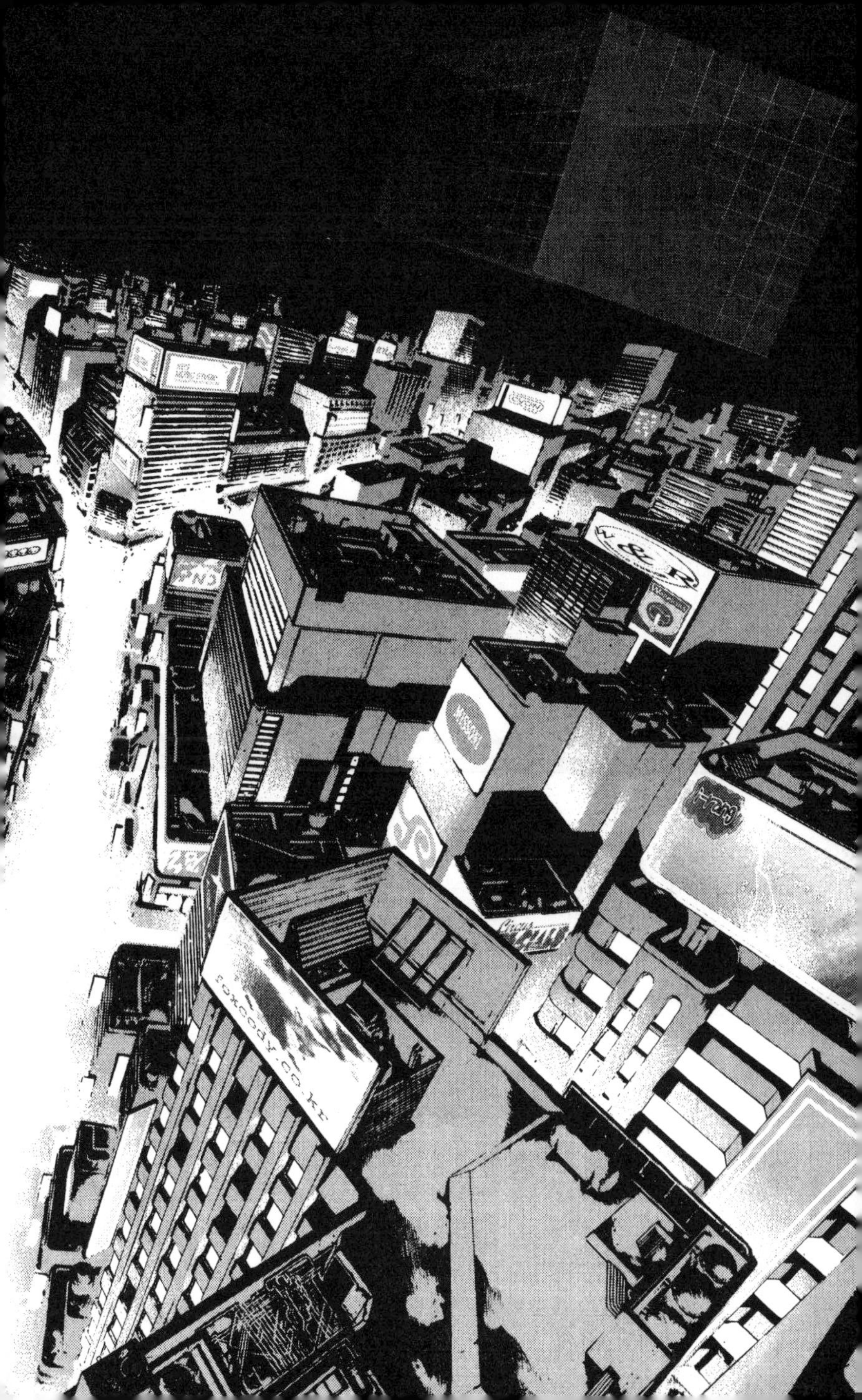
W & R
foxcody.co.kr

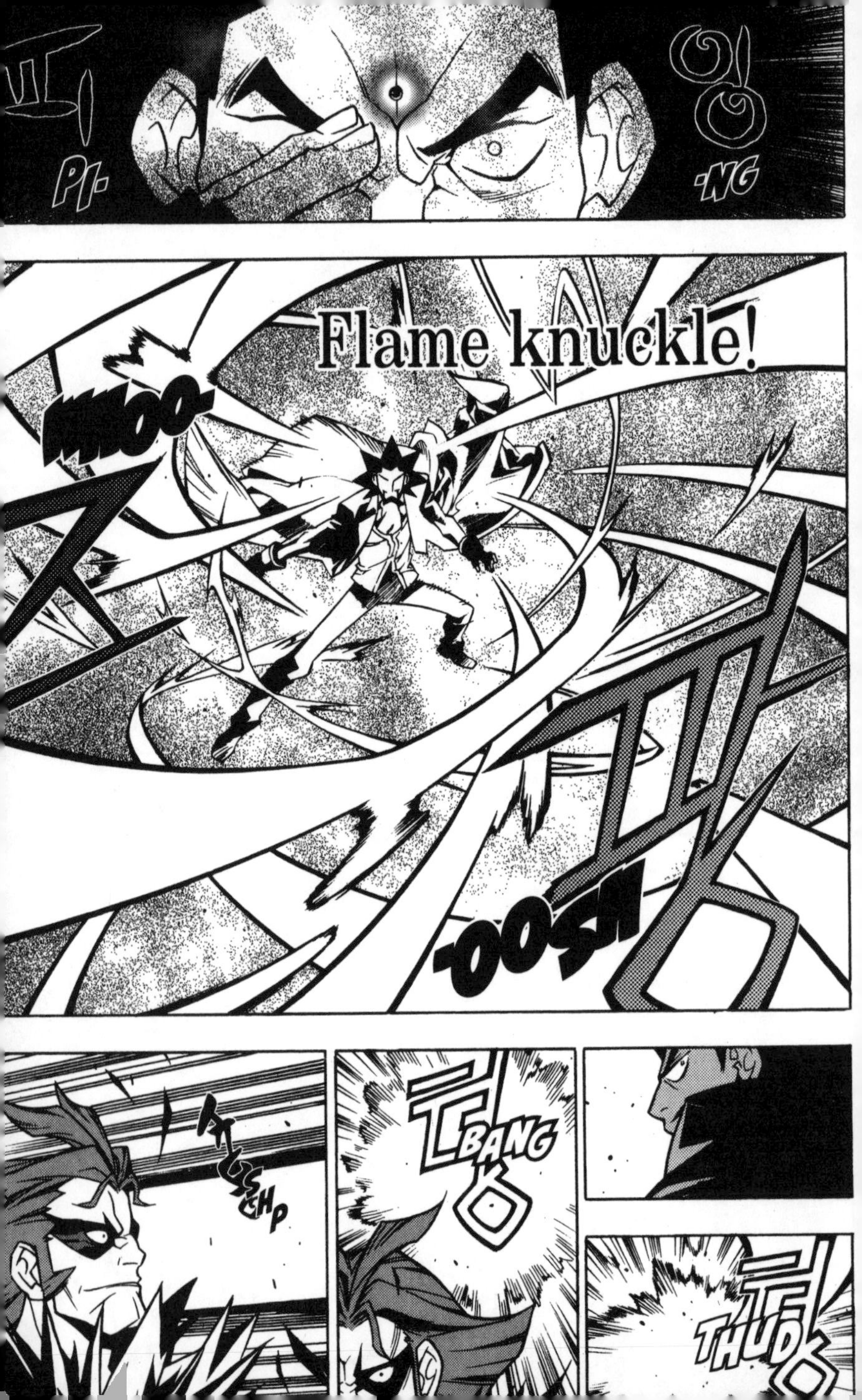

PI-
-NG
WHOO-
Flame knuckle!
-OOSH
KLUSCHP
BANG
THUD

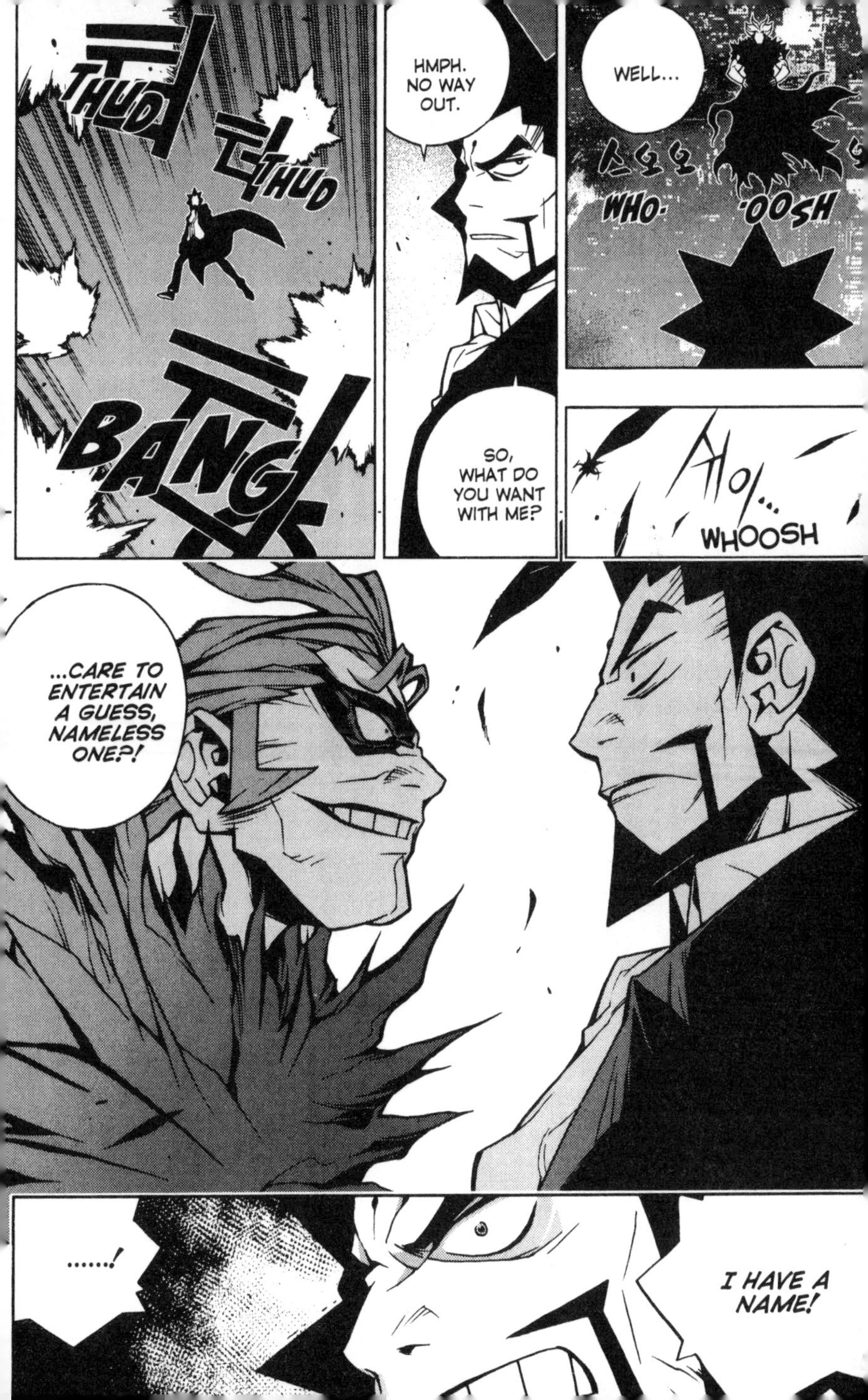
THUD
THUD
BANG
HMPH. NO WAY OUT.
SO, WHAT DO YOU WANT WITH ME?
WELL...
WHO- -OOSH
WHOOSH
...CARE TO ENTERTAIN A GUESS, NAMELESS ONE?!
......!
I HAVE A NAME!

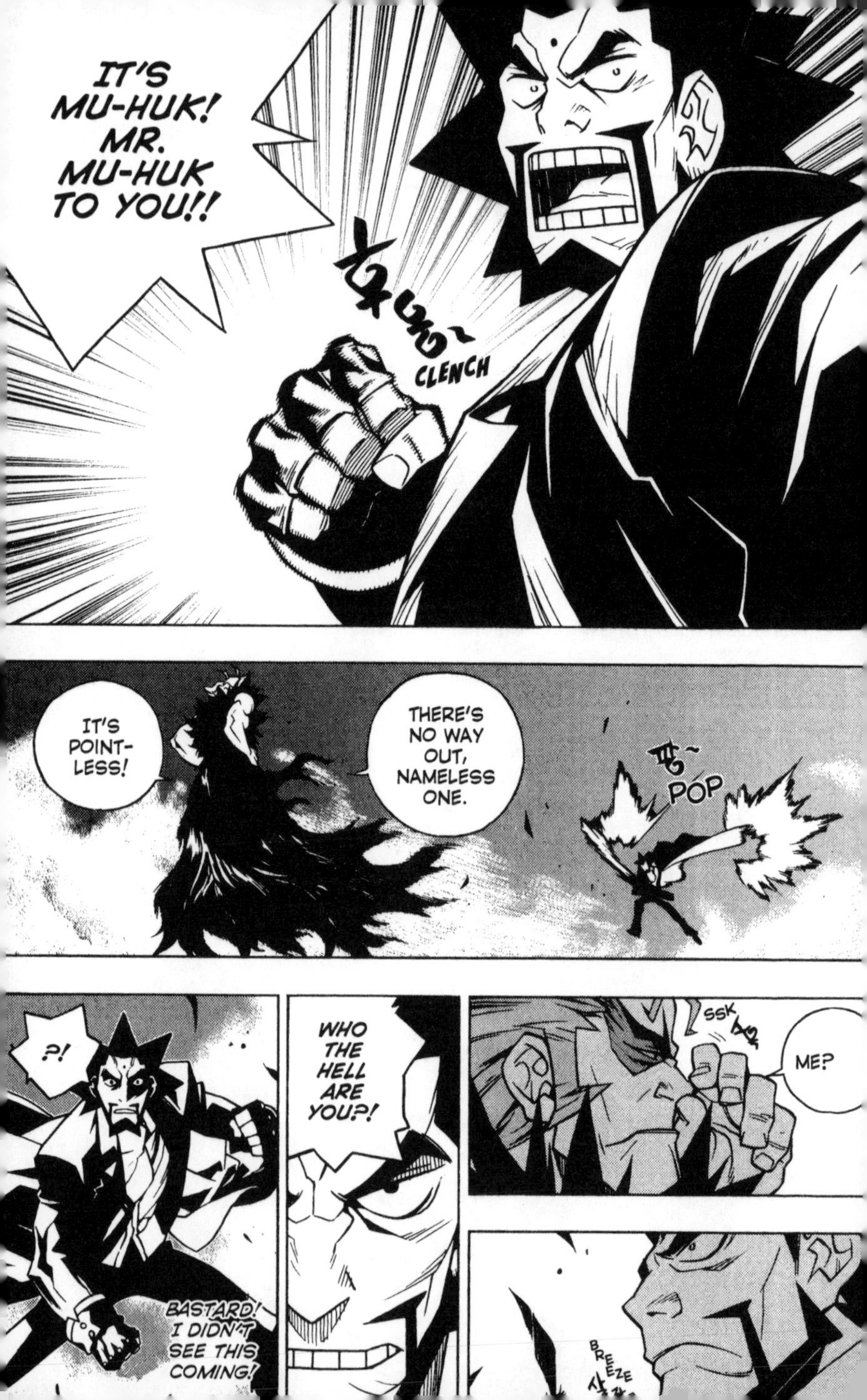
IT'S MU-HUK! MR. MU-HUK TO YOU!!
CLENCH
IT'S POINT-LESS!
THERE'S NO WAY OUT, NAMELESS ONE.
POP
?!
BASTARD! I DIDN'T SEE THIS COMING!
WHO THE HELL ARE YOU?!
SSK
ME?
BREEZE

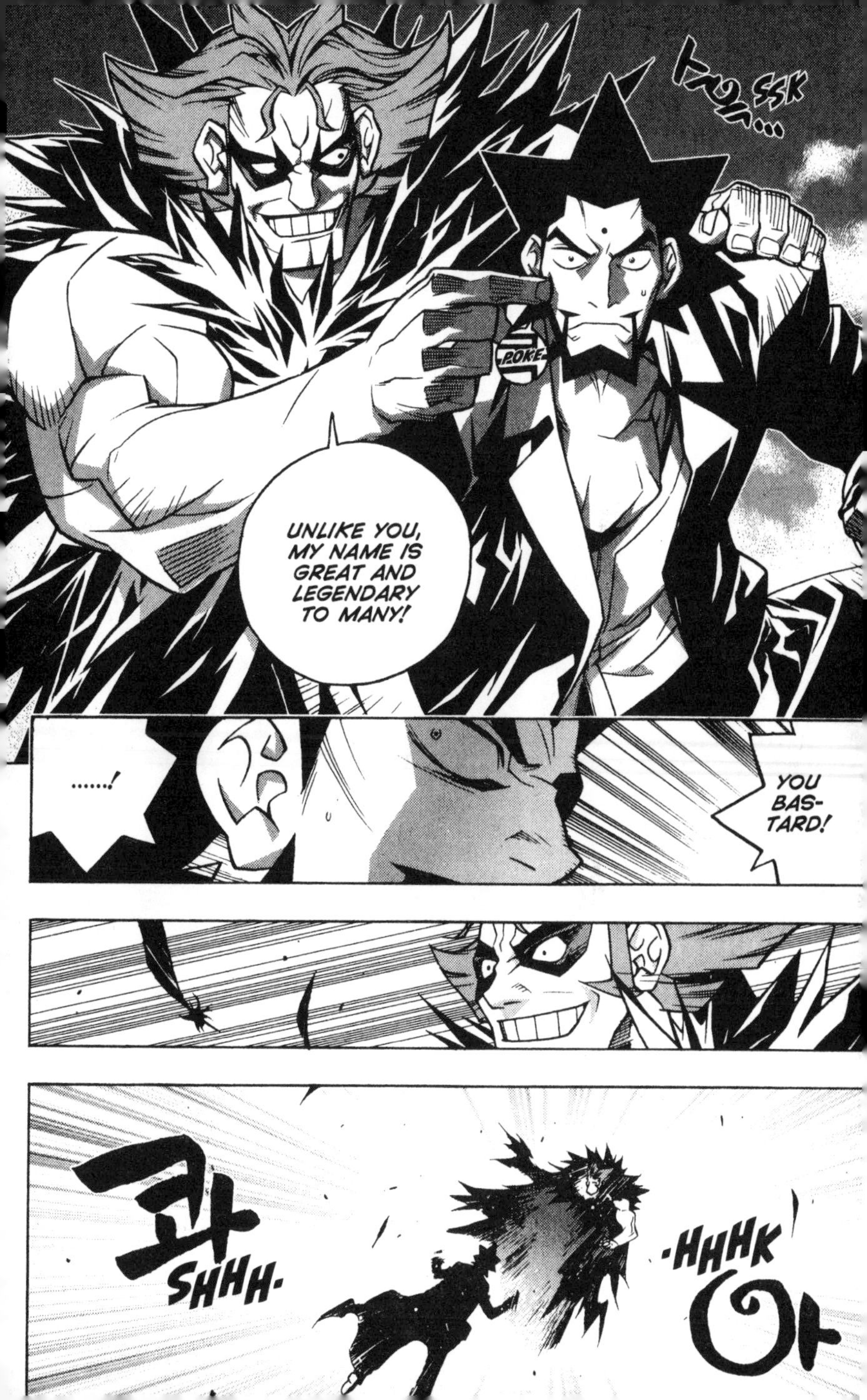

SSK...
POKE
UNLIKE YOU, MY NAME IS GREAT AND LEGENDARY TO MANY!
......!
YOU BAS-TARD!
SHHH-
-HHHK

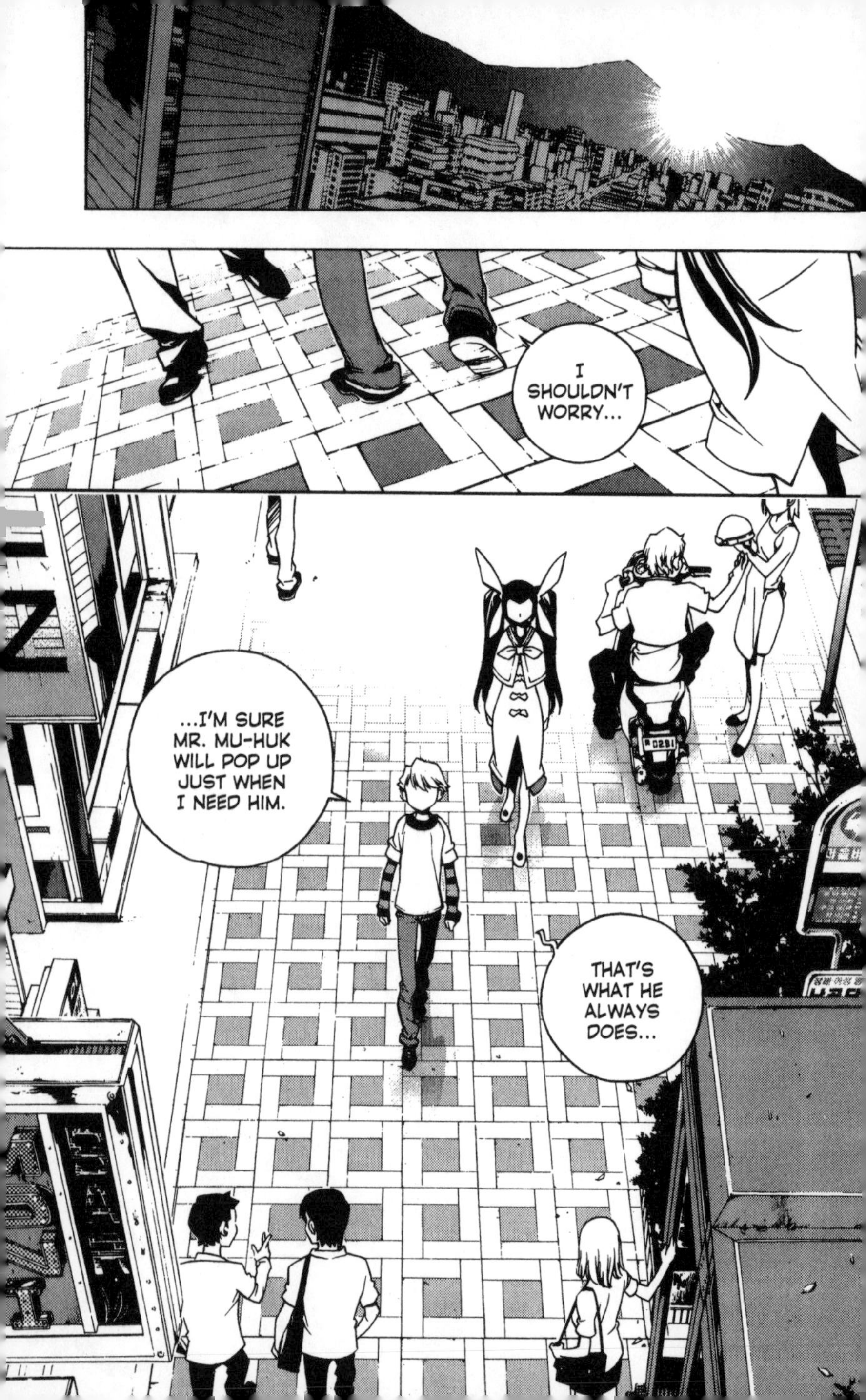
I SHOULDN'T WORRY...
...I'M SURE MR. MU-HUK WILL POP UP JUST WHEN I NEED HIM.
THAT'S WHAT HE ALWAYS DOES...

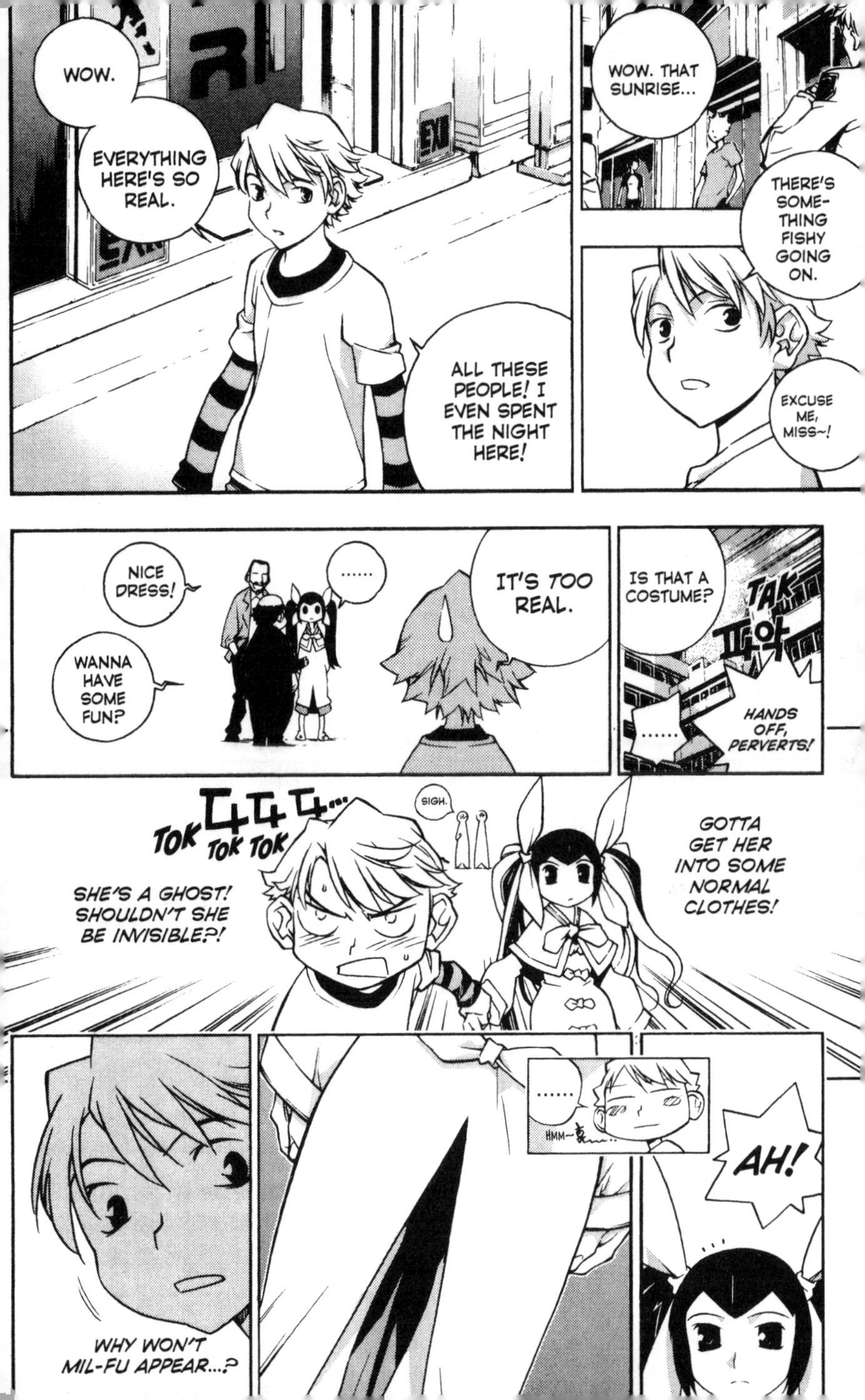
WOW.
EVERYTHING HERE'S SO REAL.
ALL THESE PEOPLE! I EVEN SPENT THE NIGHT HERE!
WOW. THAT SUNRISE...
THERE'S SOME-THING FISHY GOING ON.
EXCUSE ME, MISS~!
NICE DRESS!
WANNA HAVE SOME FUN?
......
IT'S TOO REAL.
IS THAT A COSTUME?
TAK
......
HANDS OFF, PERVERTS!
TOK TOK TOK
SIGH.
SHE'S A GHOST! SHOULDN'T SHE BE INVISIBLE?!
GOTTA GET HER INTO SOME NORMAL CLOTHES!
WHY WON'T MIL-FU APPEAR...?
......
HMM~
AH!

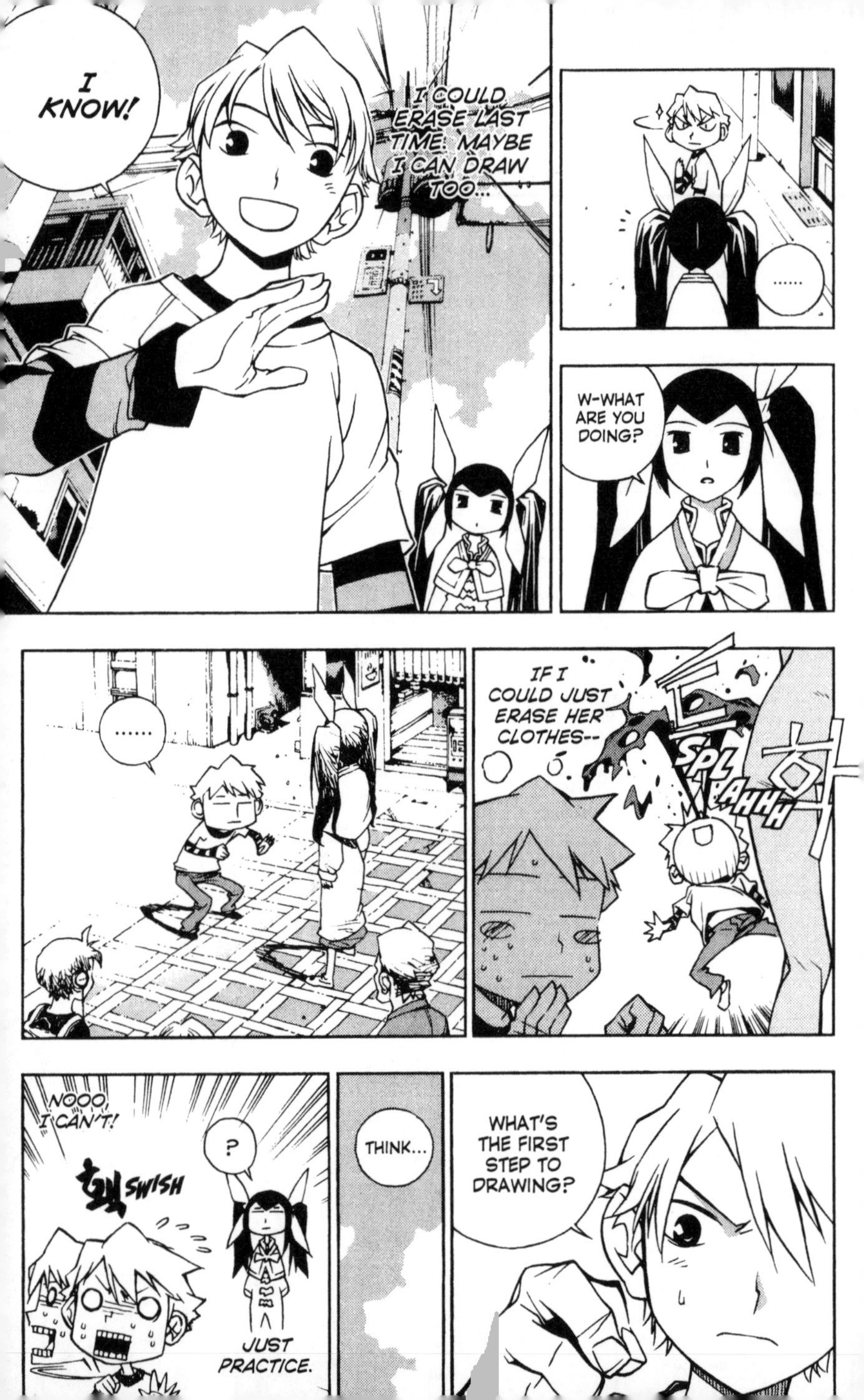
I KNOW!
I COULD ERASE LAST TIME. MAYBE I CAN DRAW TOO...
......
W-WHAT ARE YOU DOING?
......
IF I COULD JUST ERASE HER CLOTHES--
SPLAHHH
NOOO, I CAN'T!
SWISH
?
JUST PRACTICE.
THINK...
WHAT'S THE FIRST STEP TO DRAWING?

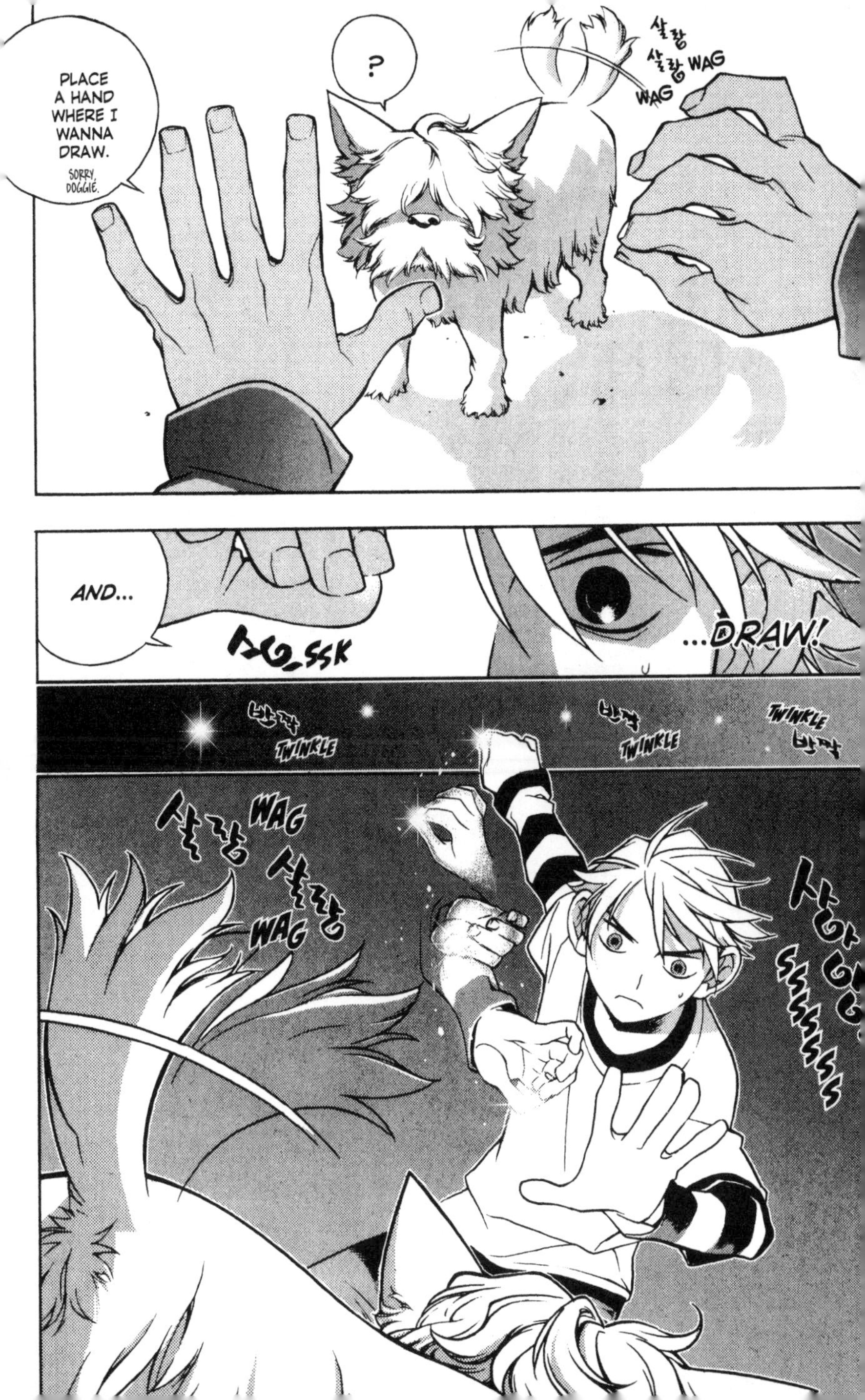
PLACE A HAND WHERE I WANNA DRAW.
SORRY, DOGGIE.
?
살랑 살랑 WAG WAG
AND...
SSK
...DRAW!
반짝 TWINKLE
반짝 TWINKLE
TWINKLE 반짝
살랑 WAG 살랑 WAG

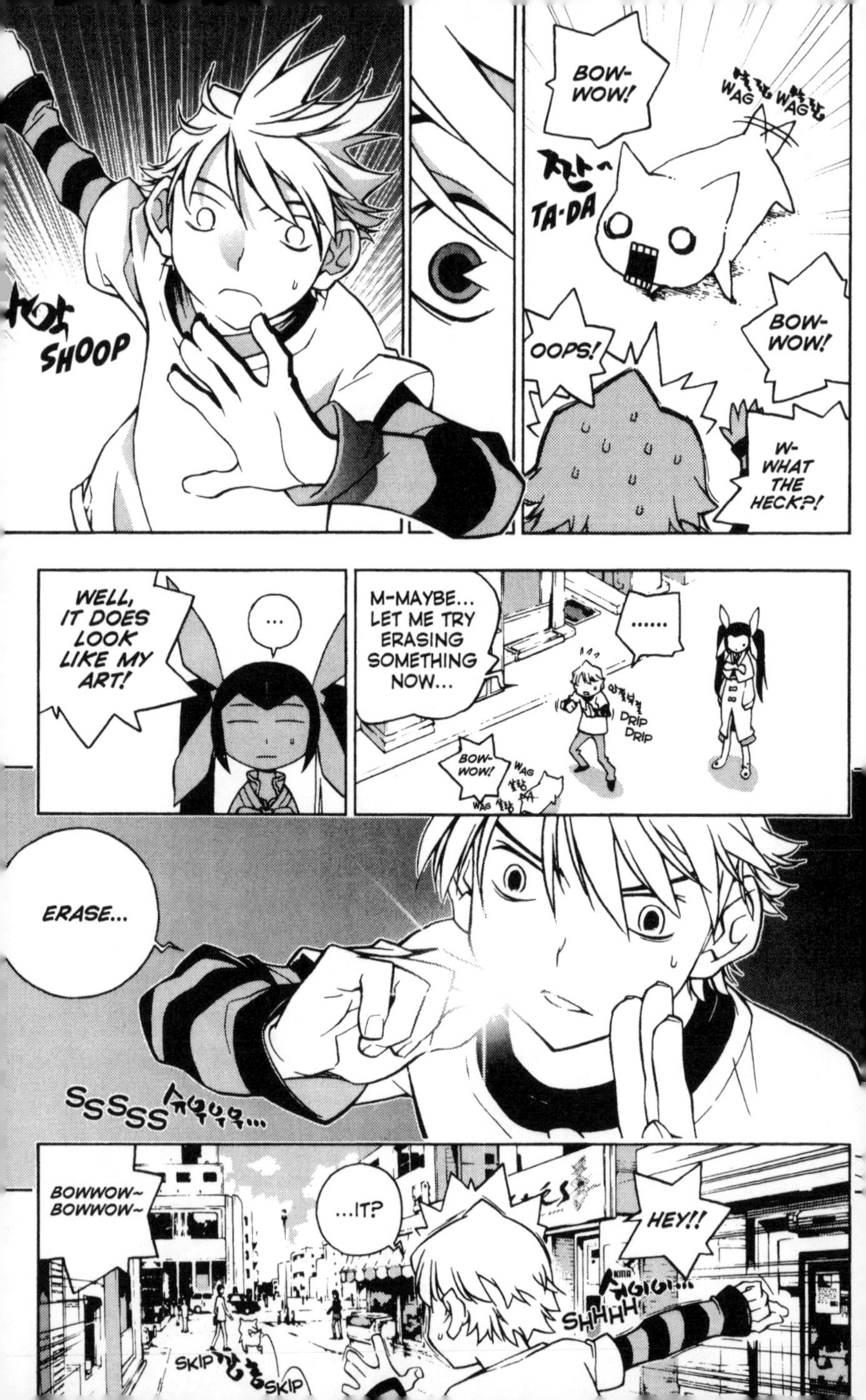

SHOOP
BOW-WOW!
WAG WAG
TA-DA
OOPS!
BOW-WOW!
W-WHAT THE HECK?!
WELL, IT DOES LOOK LIKE MY ART!
...
M-MAYBE... LET ME TRY ERASING SOMETHING NOW...
......
DRIP DRIP
BOW-WOW!
WAG WAG
ERASE...
SSSSS
BOWWOW~ BOWWOW~
...IT?
HEY!!
SHHHH
SKIP SKIP

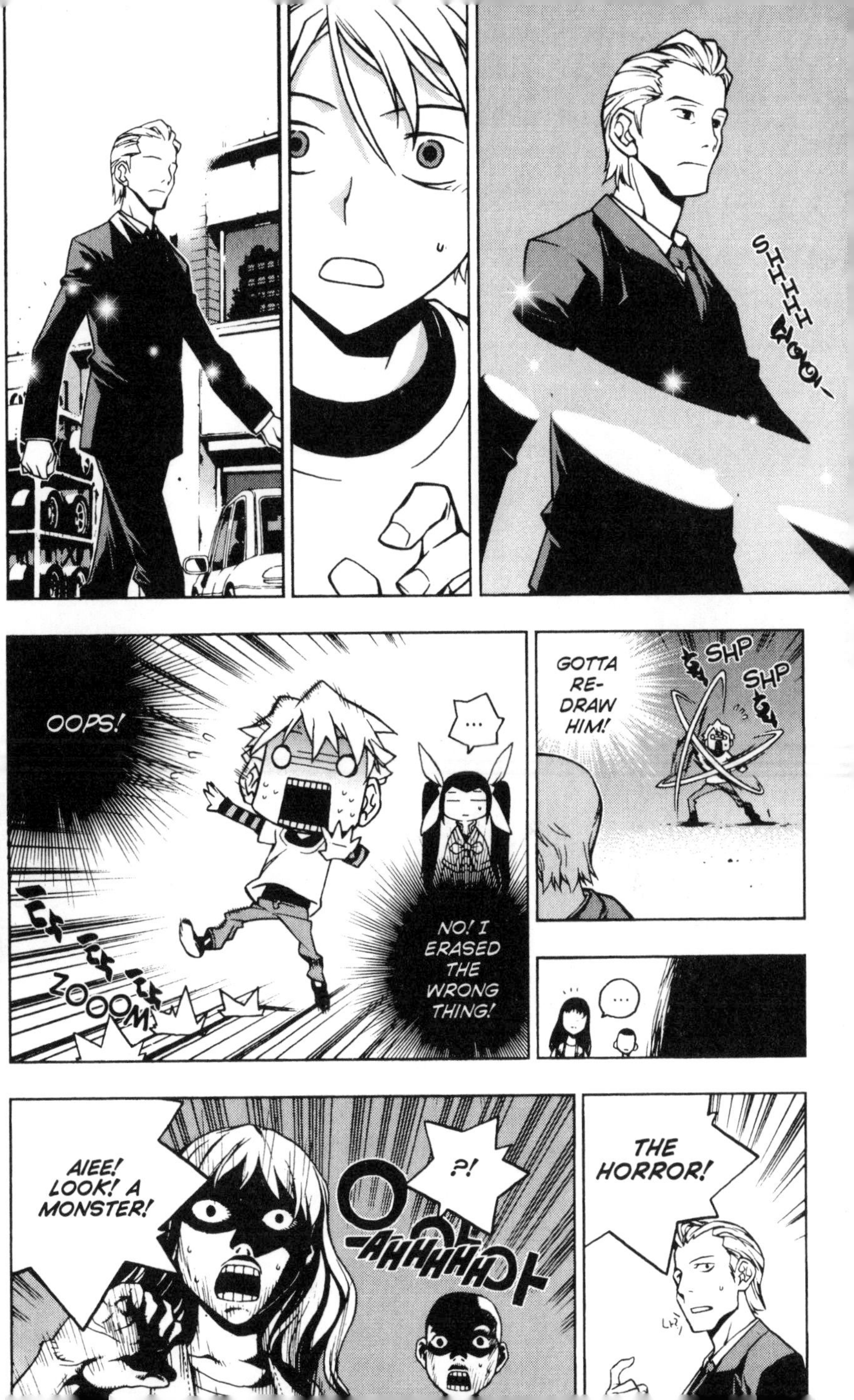
SHIIIIIING
OOPS!
...
NO! I ERASED THE WRONG THING!
ZOOOM
GOTTA RE-DRAW HIM!
SHP
SHP
...
AIEE! LOOK! A MONSTER!
?!
-AHHHHH!
THE HORROR!

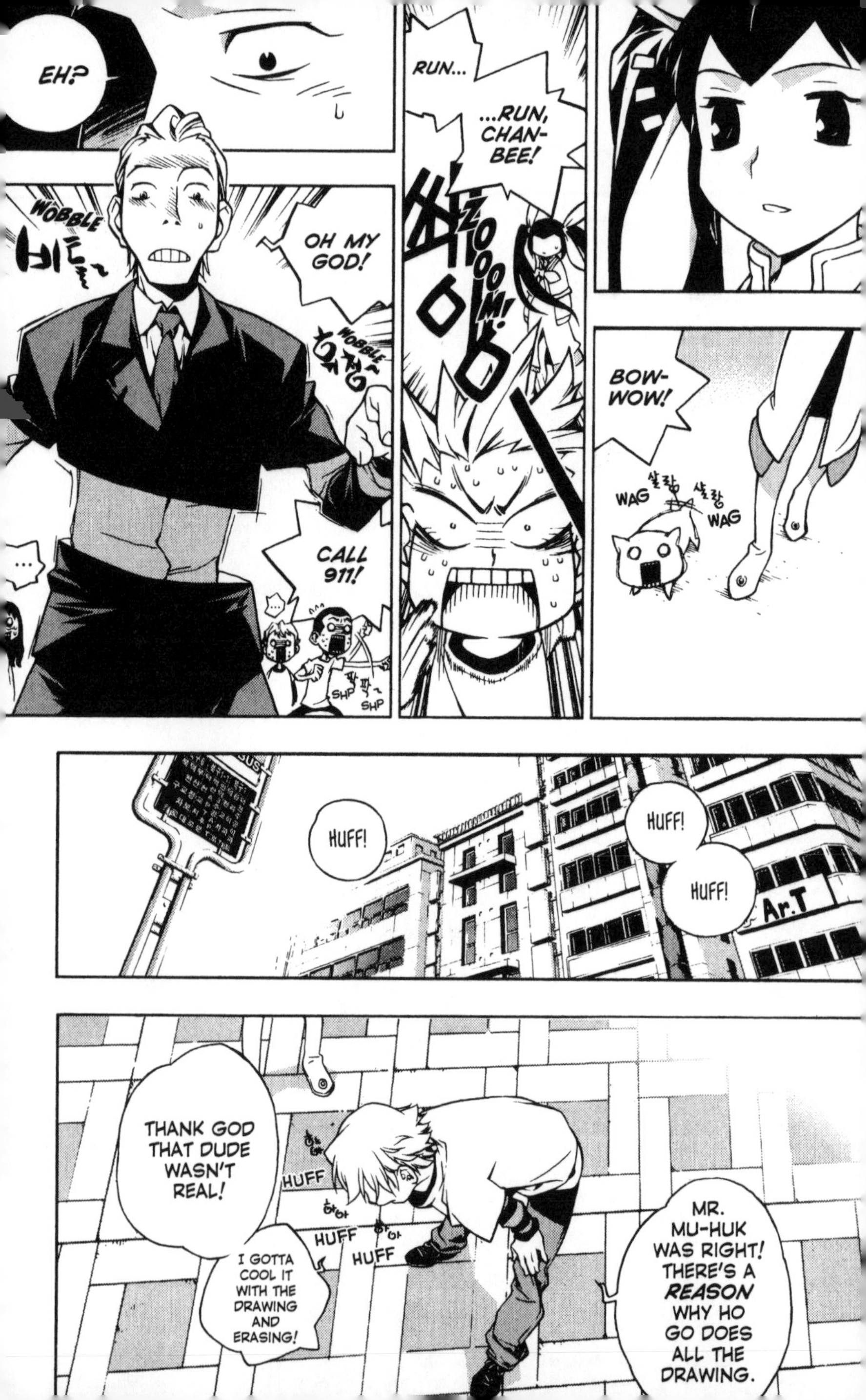
EH?
WOBBLE
OH MY GOD!
WOBBLE
...
CALL 911!
...
SHP SHP
RUN...
...RUN, CHAN-BEE!
ZOOOOM!
BOW-WOW!
WAG 살랑 살랑 WAG
HUFF!
HUFF!
HUFF!
THANK GOD THAT DUDE WASN'T REAL!
HUFF
HUFF
HUFF
I GOTTA COOL IT WITH THE DRAWING AND ERASING!
MR. MU-HUK WAS RIGHT! THERE'S A *REASON* WHY HO GO DOES ALL THE DRAWING.

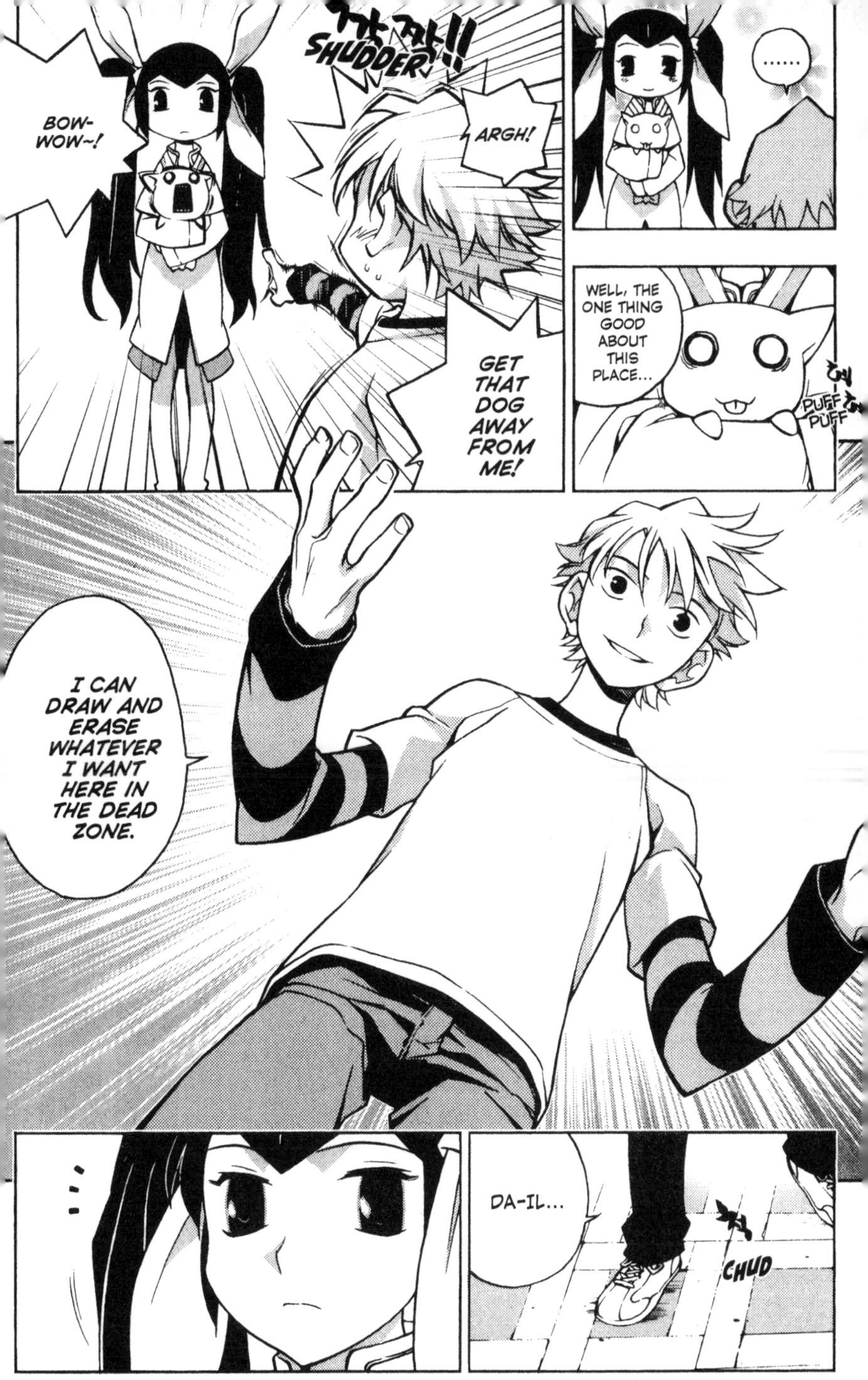
BOW-WOW~!
SHUDDER!!
ARGH!
GET THAT DOG AWAY FROM ME!
......
WELL, THE ONE THING GOOD ABOUT THIS PLACE...
PUFF PUFF
I CAN DRAW AND ERASE WHATEVER I WANT HERE IN THE DEAD ZONE.
...
DA-IL...
CHUD

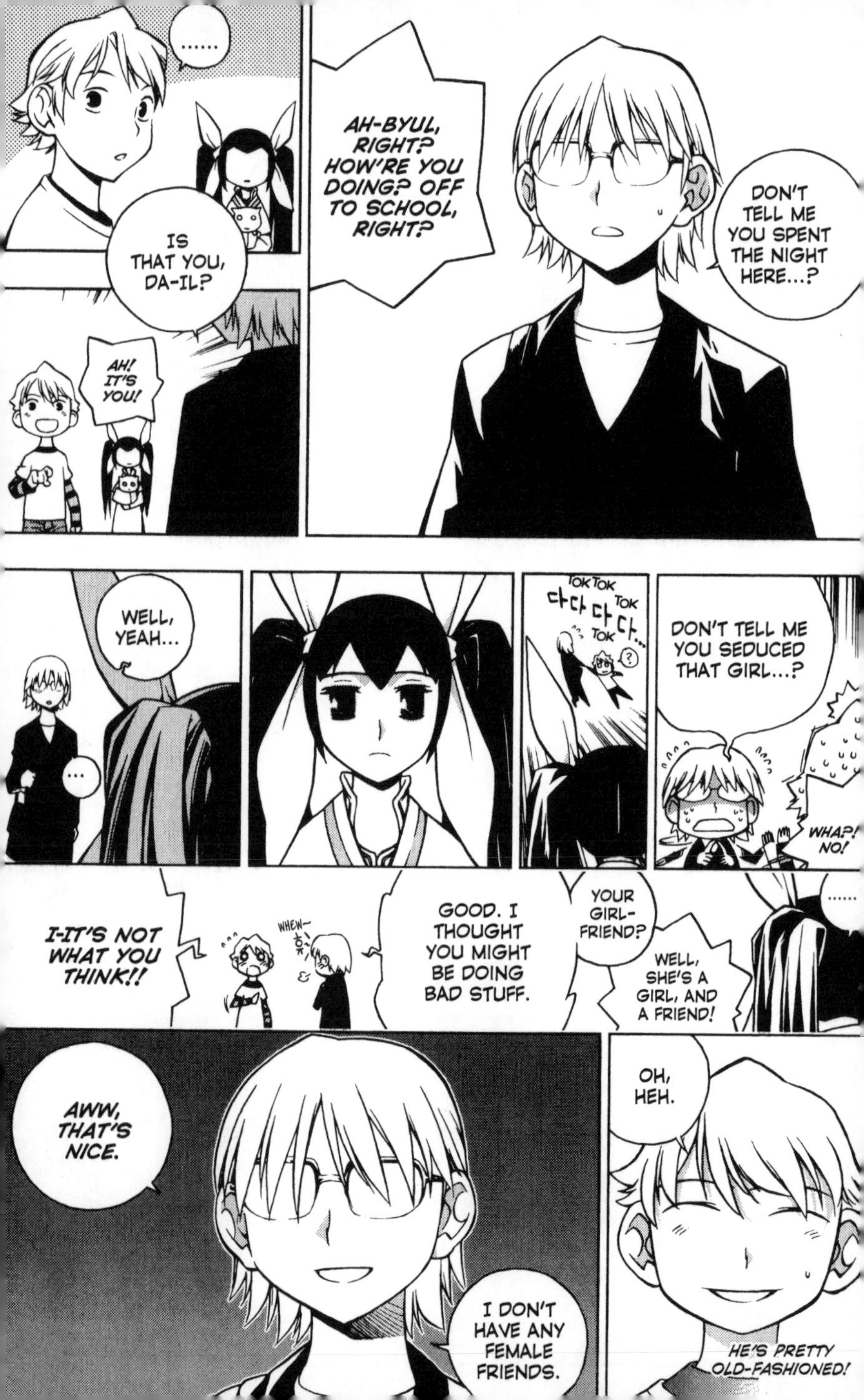
......
IS THAT YOU, DA-IL?
AH! IT'S YOU!
AH-BYUL, RIGHT? HOW'RE YOU DOING? OFF TO SCHOOL, RIGHT?
DON'T TELL ME YOU SPENT THE NIGHT HERE...?
WELL, YEAH...
...
TOK TOK TOK TOK
다다 다다...
DON'T TELL ME YOU SEDUCED THAT GIRL...?
WHA?! NO!
I-IT'S NOT WHAT YOU THINK!!
WHEW~
GOOD. I THOUGHT YOU MIGHT BE DOING BAD STUFF.
YOUR GIRL-FRIEND?
WELL, SHE'S A GIRL, AND A FRIEND!
......
AWW, THAT'S NICE.
I DON'T HAVE ANY FEMALE FRIENDS.
OH, HEH.
HE'S PRETTY OLD-FASHIONED!

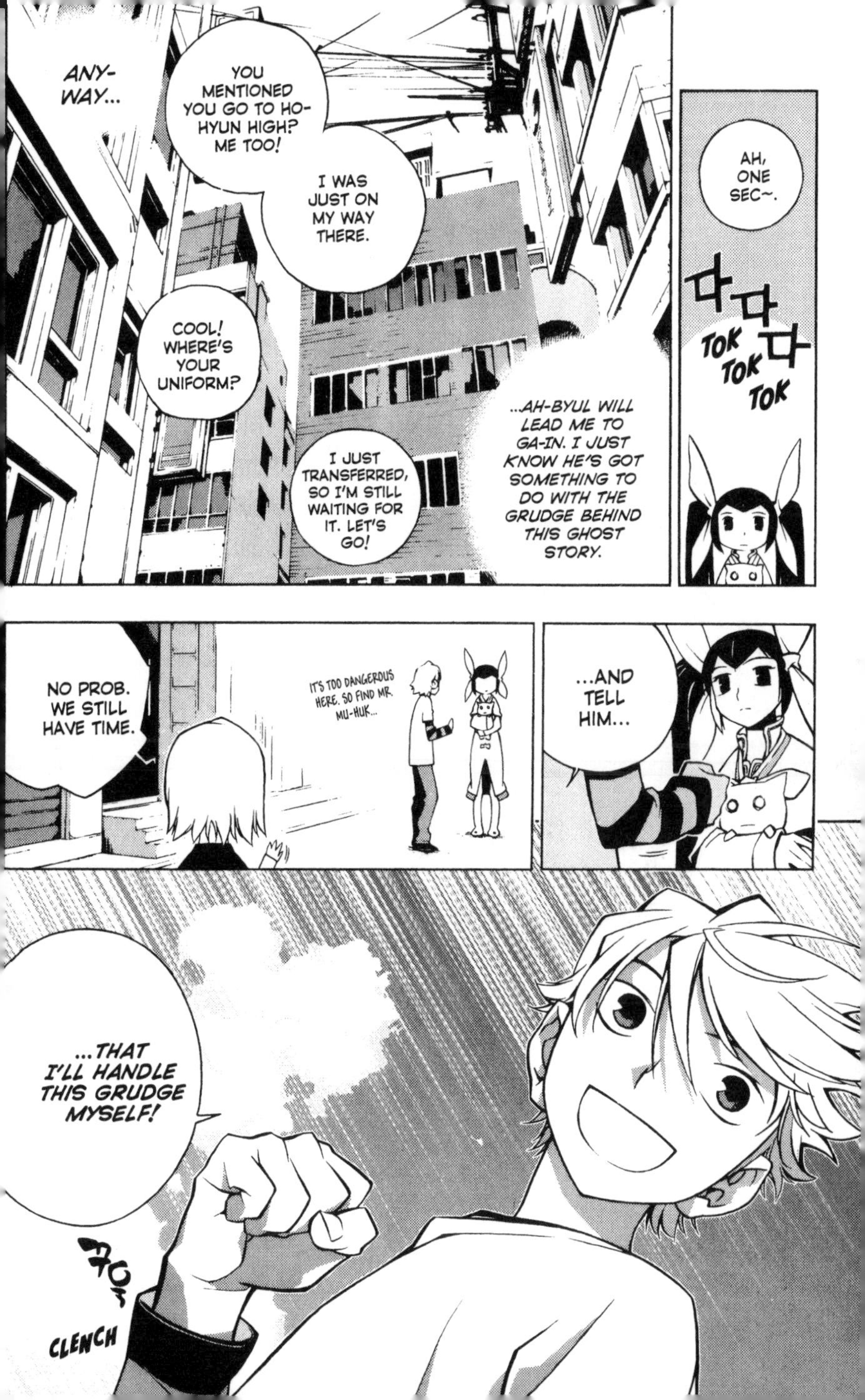
ANY-WAY...
YOU MENTIONED YOU GO TO HO-HYUN HIGH? ME TOO!
I WAS JUST ON MY WAY THERE.
COOL! WHERE'S YOUR UNIFORM?
I JUST TRANSFERRED, SO I'M STILL WAITING FOR IT. LET'S GO!
...AH-BYUL WILL LEAD ME TO GA-IN. I JUST KNOW HE'S GOT SOMETHING TO DO WITH THE GRUDGE BEHIND THIS GHOST STORY.
AH, ONE SEC~.
TOK TOK TOK
NO PROB. WE STILL HAVE TIME.
IT'S TOO DANGEROUS HERE. SO FIND MR. MU-HUK...
...AND TELL HIM...
...THAT I'LL HANDLE THIS GRUDGE MYSELF!
CLENCH

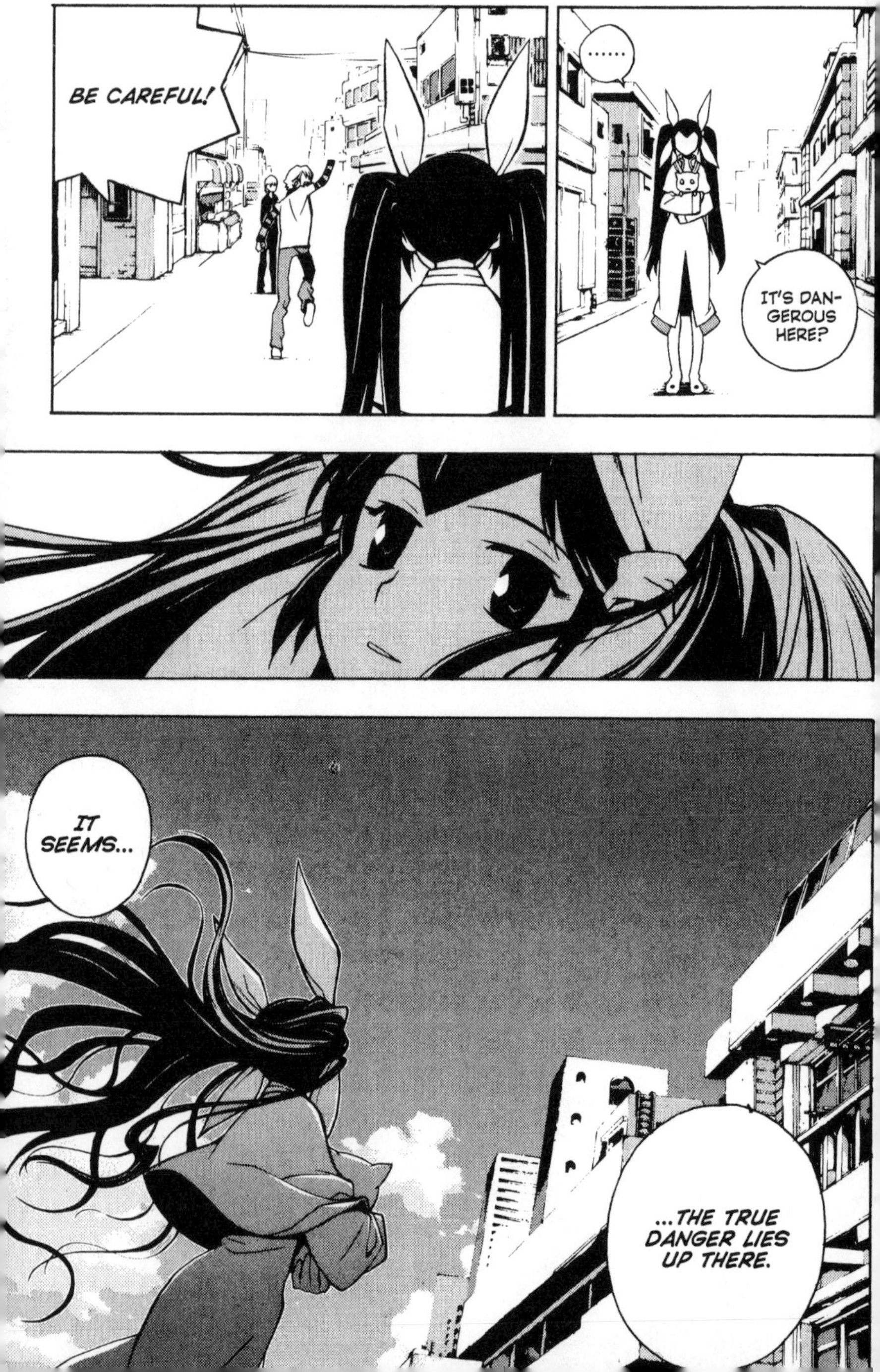
BE CAREFUL!
....
IT'S DAN-GEROUS HERE?
IT SEEMS...
...THE TRUE DANGER LIES UP THERE.

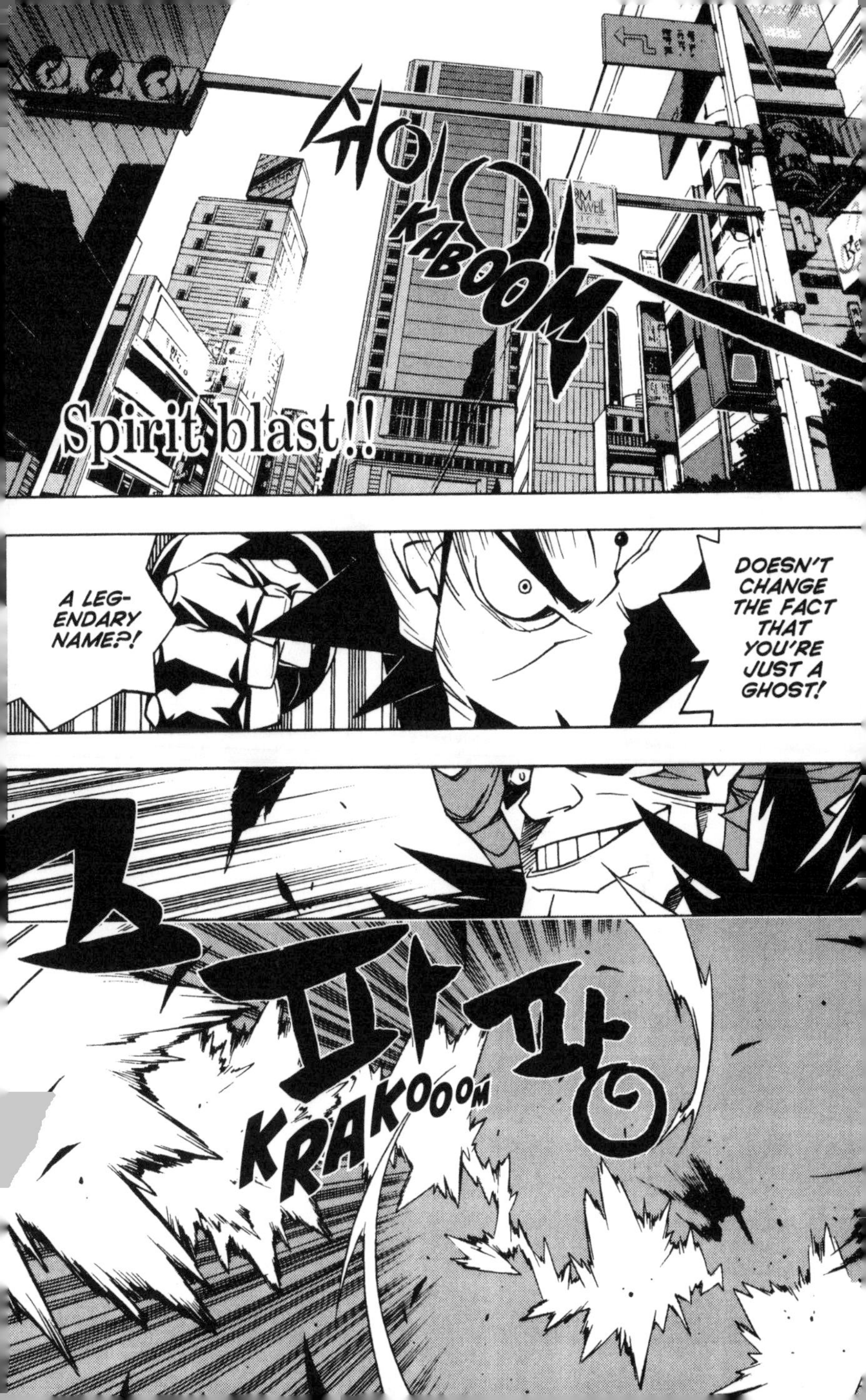
KABOOM
Spirit blast!!
A LEG-ENDARY NAME?!
DOESN'T CHANGE THE FACT THAT YOU'RE JUST A GHOST!
KRAKOOOM

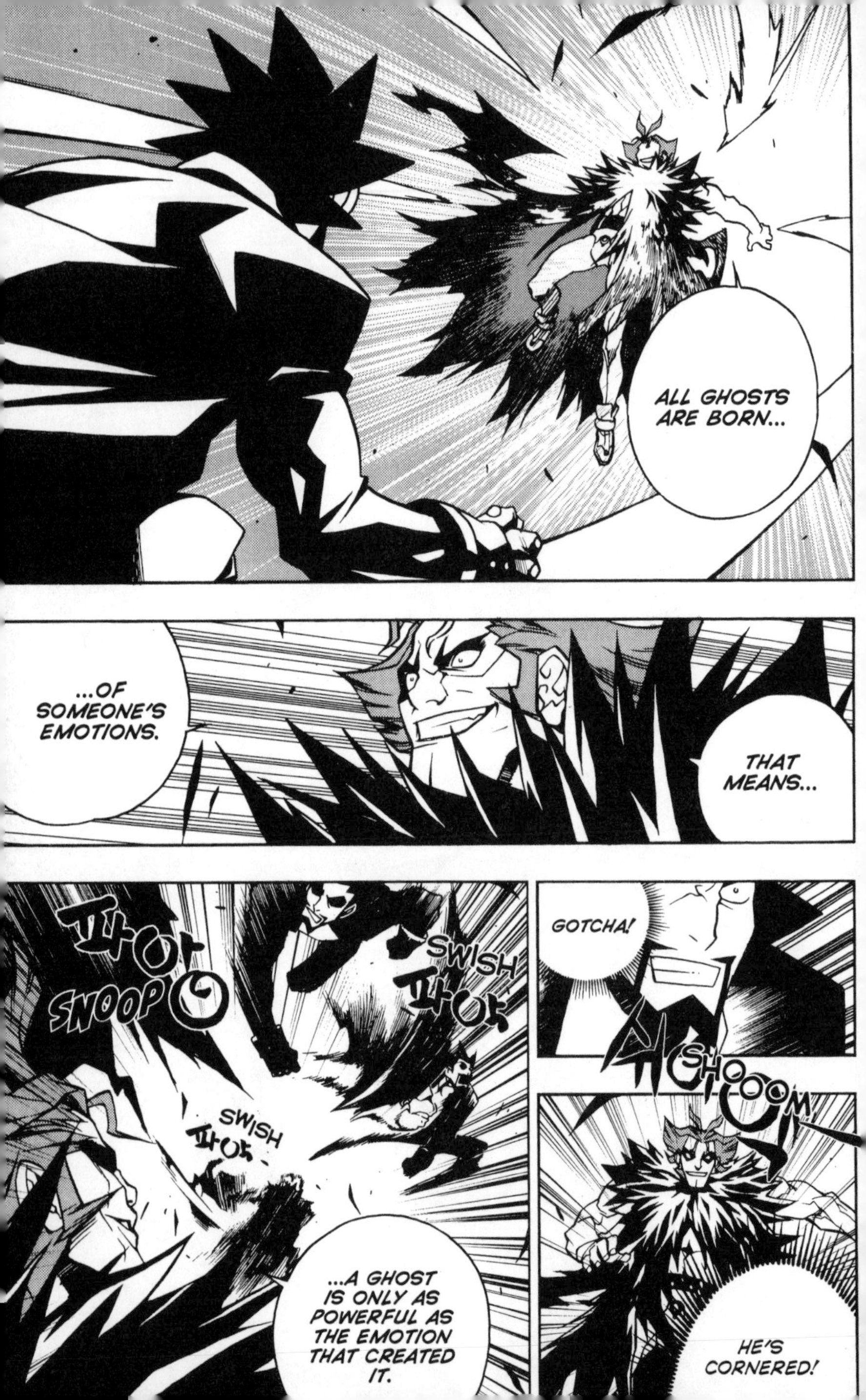
ALL GHOSTS ARE BORN...
...OF SOMEONE'S EMOTIONS.
THAT MEANS...
SNOOP
SWISH
SWISH
...A GHOST IS ONLY AS POWERFUL AS THE EMOTION THAT CREATED IT.
GOTCHA!
SHOOOOM
HE'S CORNERED!

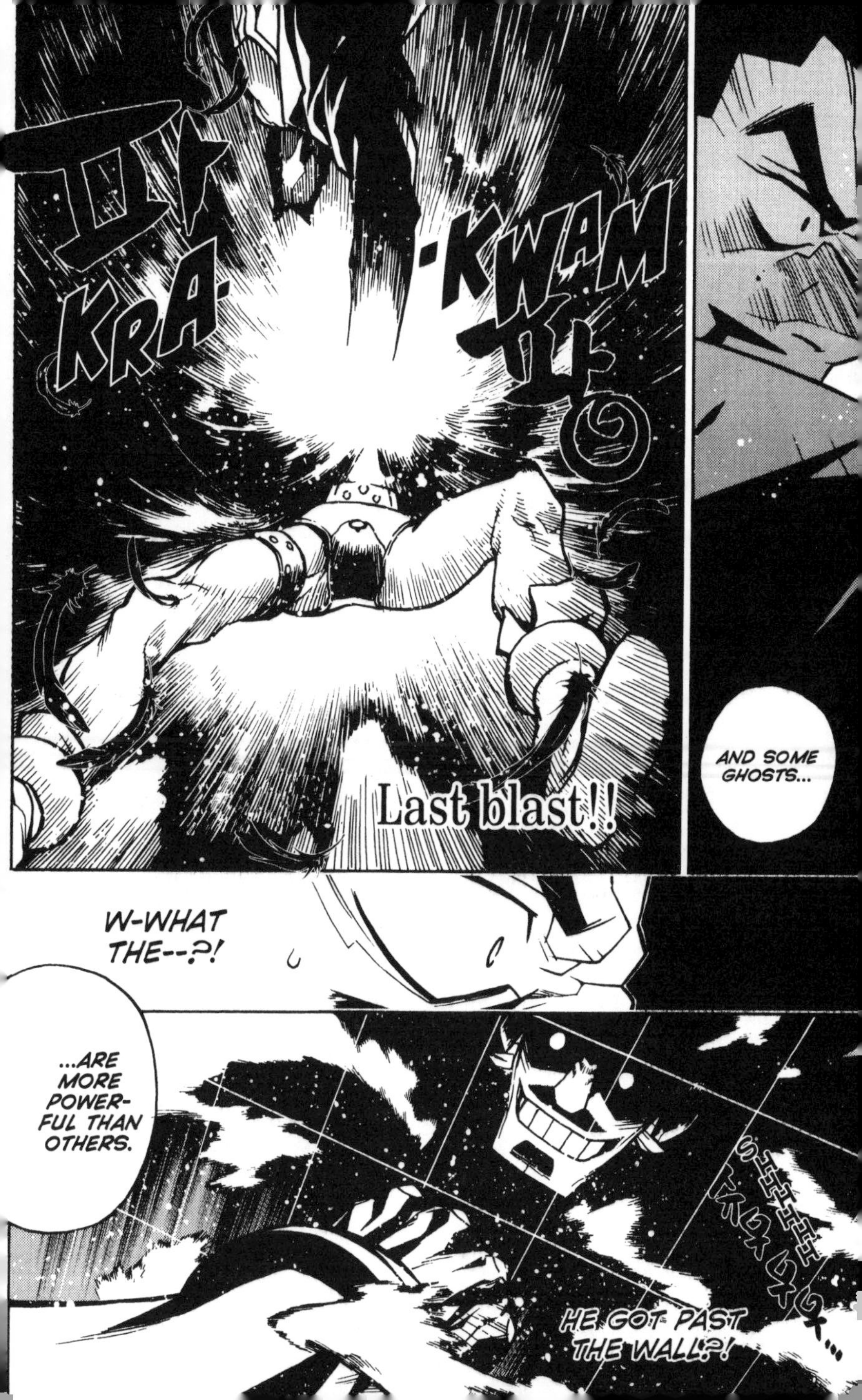
KRA-KWAM
Last blast!!
AND SOME GHOSTS...
W-WHAT THE--?!
...ARE MORE POWER-FUL THAN OTHERS.
HE GOT PAST THE WALL?!

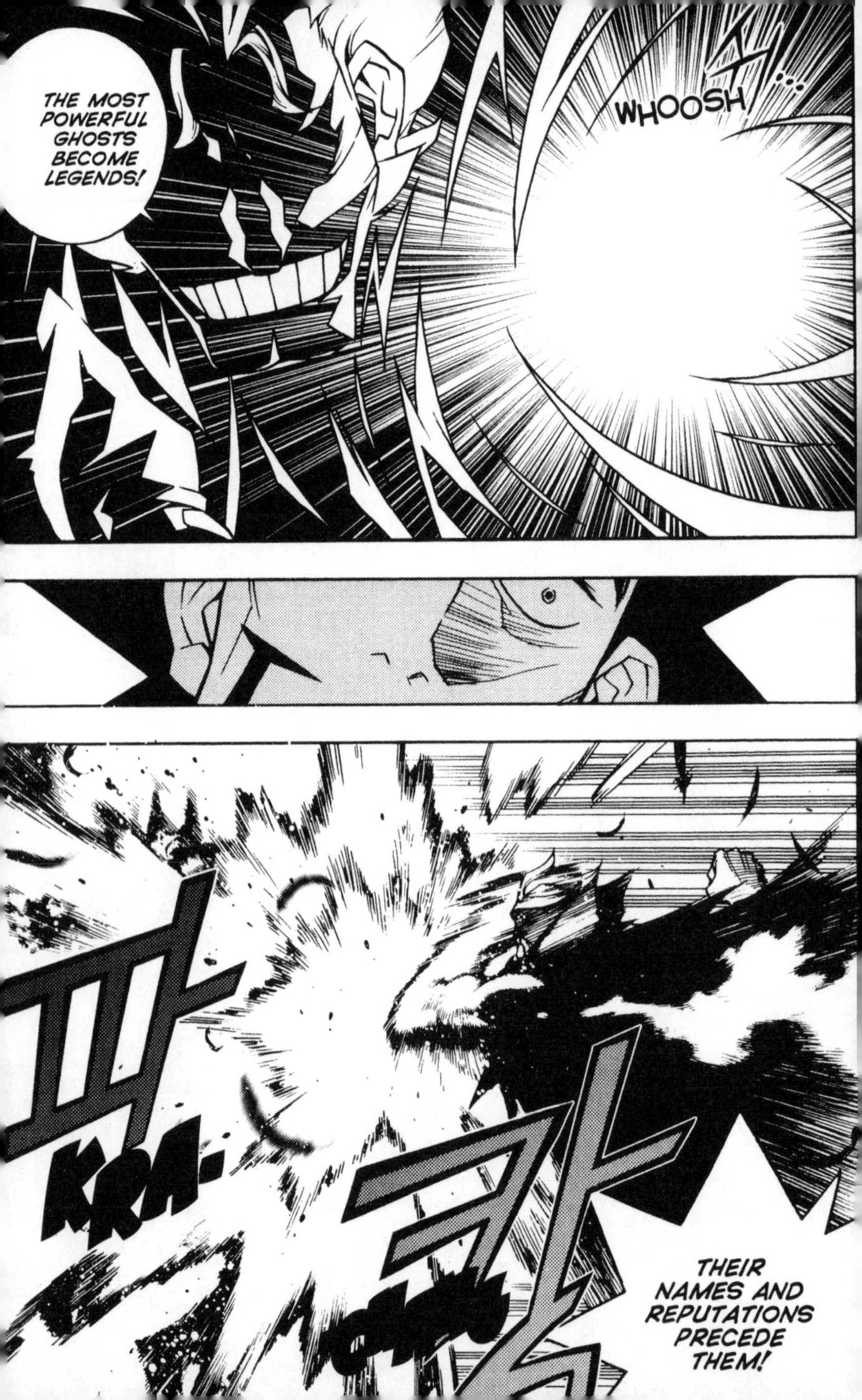
THE MOST POWERFUL GHOSTS BECOME LEGENDS!
WHOOSH
KRA-
THEIR NAMES AND REPUTATIONS PRECEDE THEM!

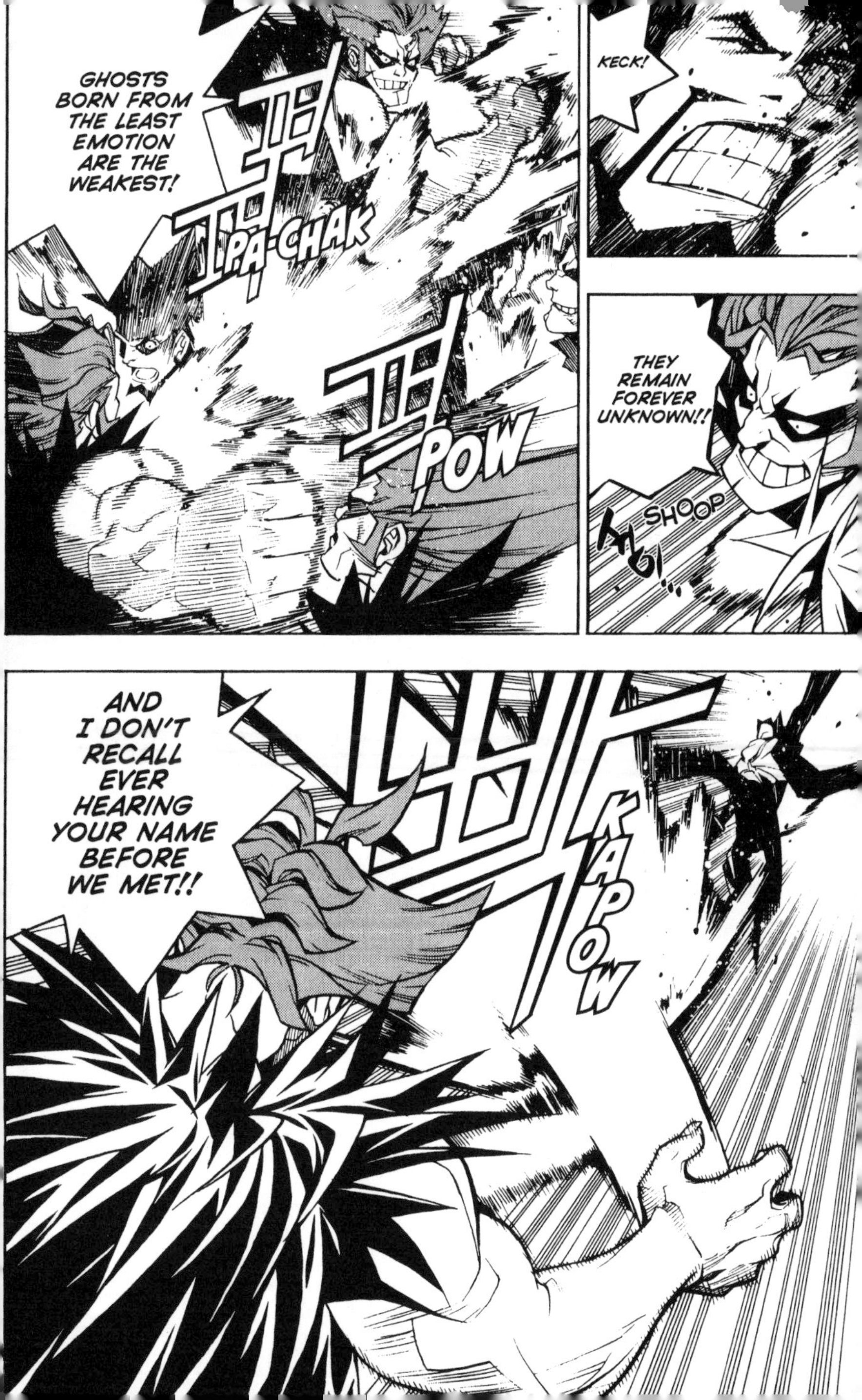
GHOSTS BORN FROM THE LEAST EMOTION ARE THE WEAKEST!
PA-CHAK
POW
KECK!
THEY REMAIN FOREVER UNKNOWN!!
SHOOP
AND I DON'T RECALL EVER HEARING YOUR NAME BEFORE WE MET!!
KAPOW

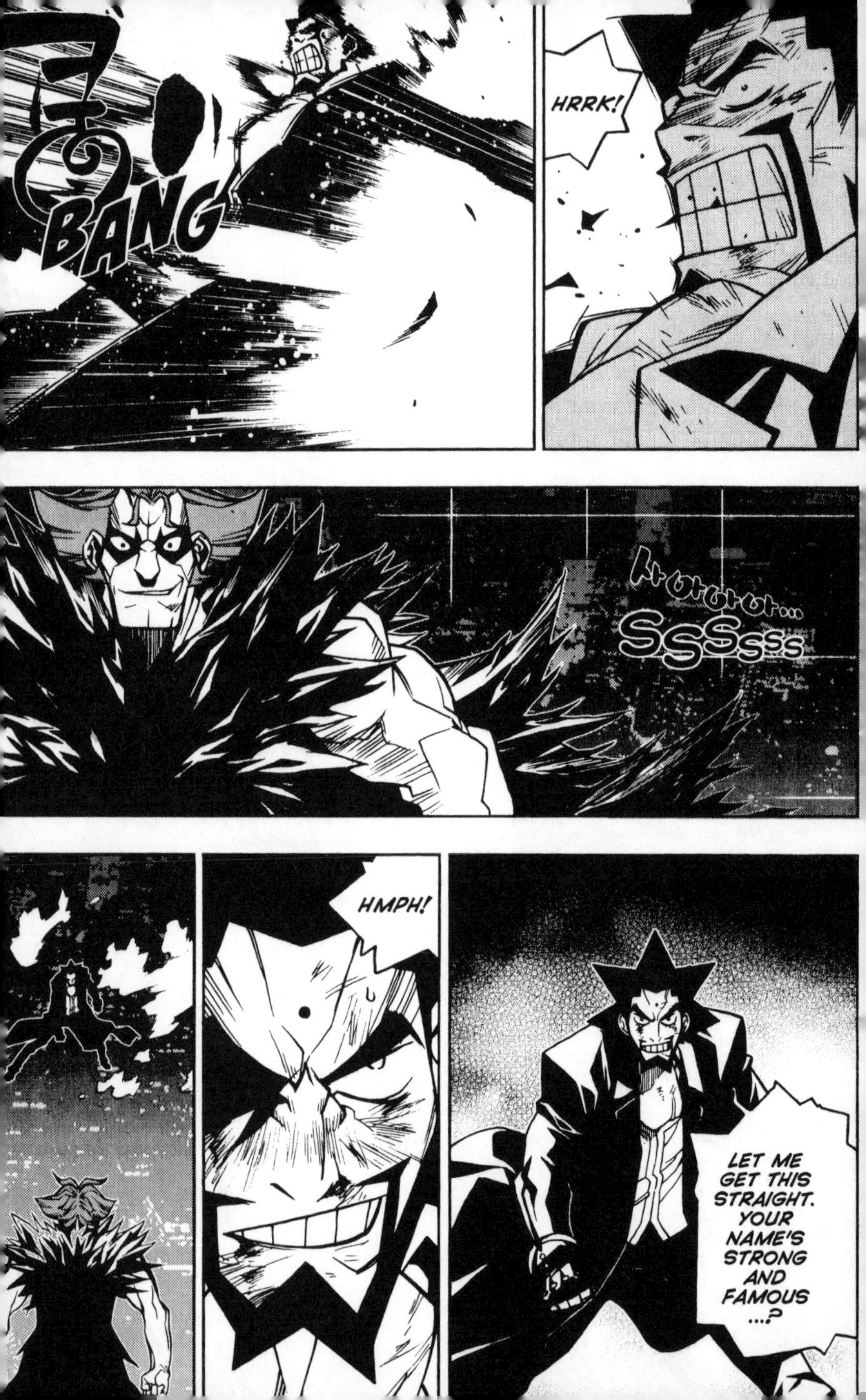
BANG
HRRK!
SSSsss
HMPH!
LET ME GET THIS STRAIGHT. YOUR NAME'S STRONG AND FAMOUS ...?

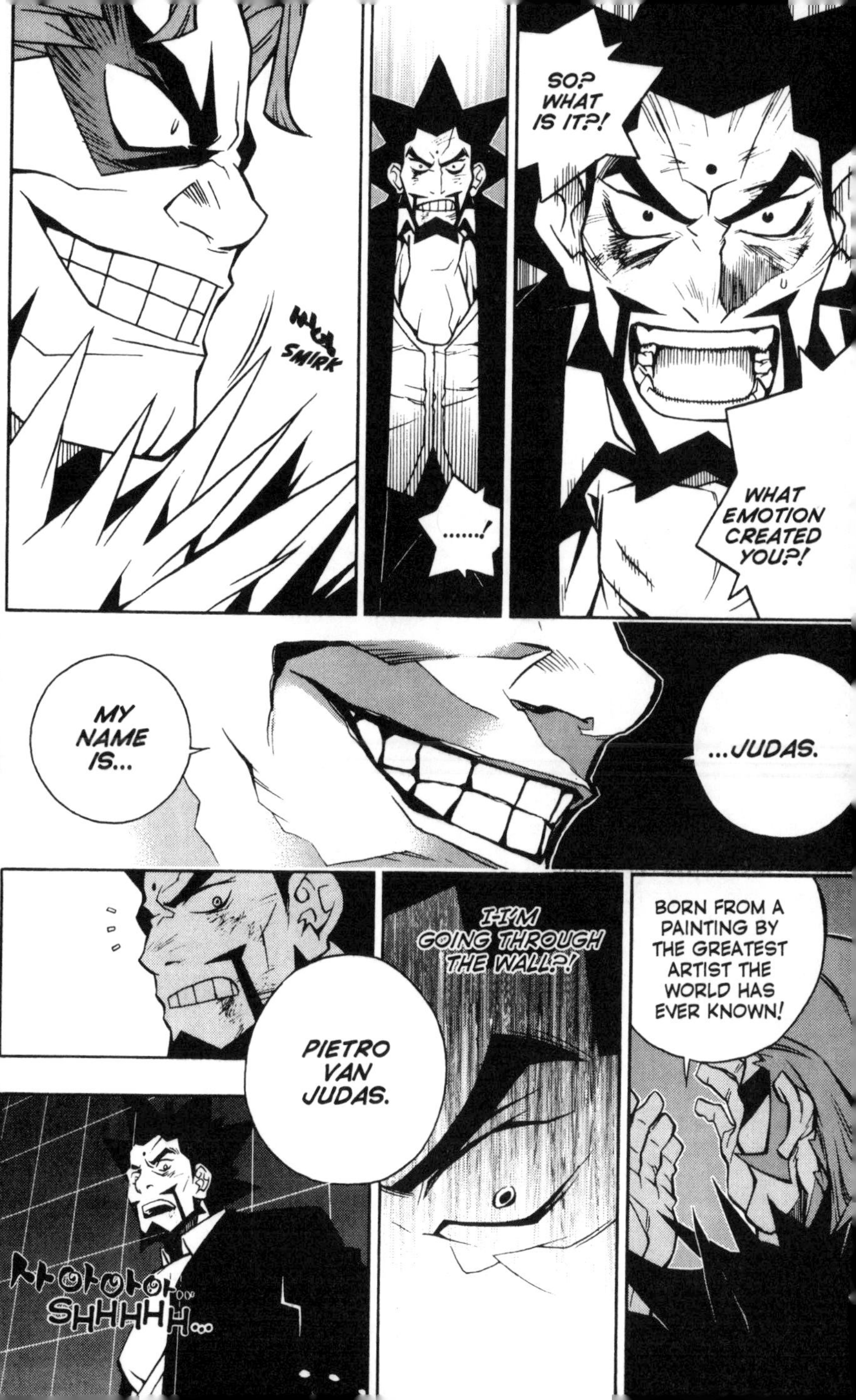
SMIRK
......!
SO? WHAT IS IT?!
WHAT EMOTION CREATED YOU?!
MY NAME IS...
...JUDAS.
PIETRO VAN JUDAS.
사아아아...
SHHHHH...
I-I'M GOING THROUGH THE WALL?!
BORN FROM A PAINTING BY THE GREATEST ARTIST THE WORLD HAS EVER KNOWN!

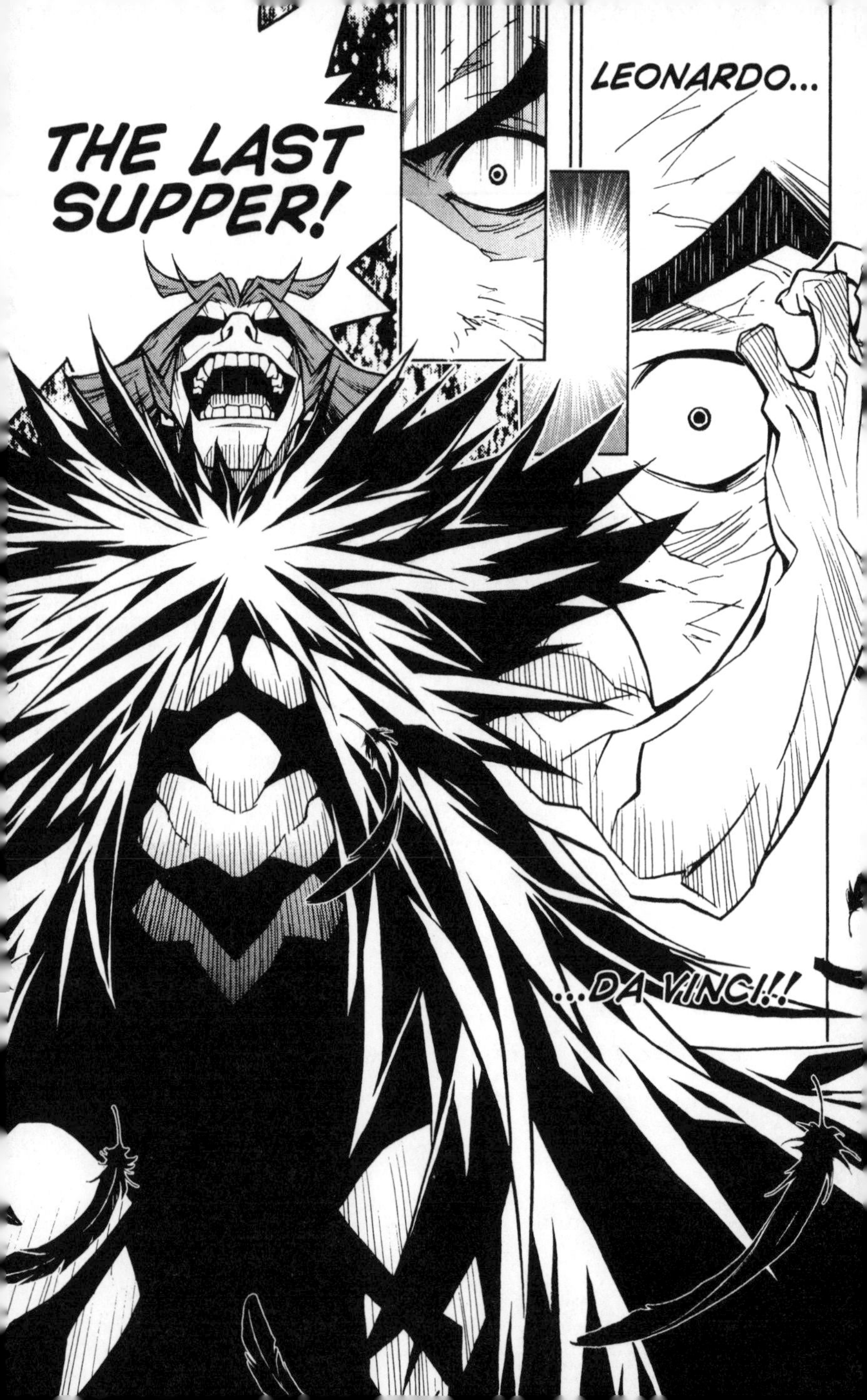
THE LAST SUPPER!
LEONARDO...
...DA VINCI!!

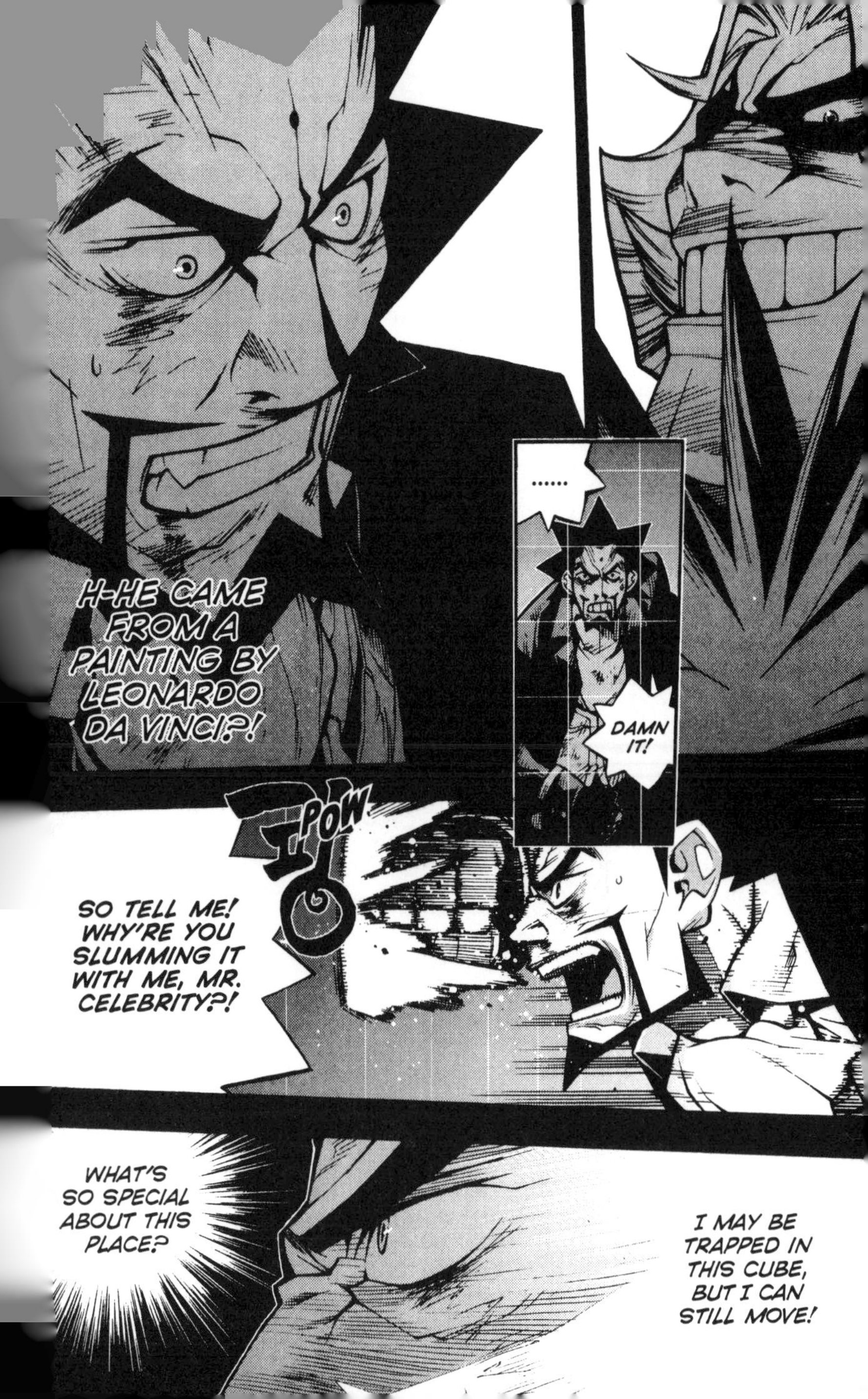
H-HE CAME FROM A PAINTING BY LEONARDO DA VINCI?!
......
DAMN IT!
POW
SO TELL ME! WHY'RE YOU SLUMMING IT WITH ME, MR. CELEBRITY?!
WHAT'S SO SPECIAL ABOUT THIS PLACE?
I MAY BE TRAPPED IN THIS CUBE, BUT I CAN STILL MOVE!

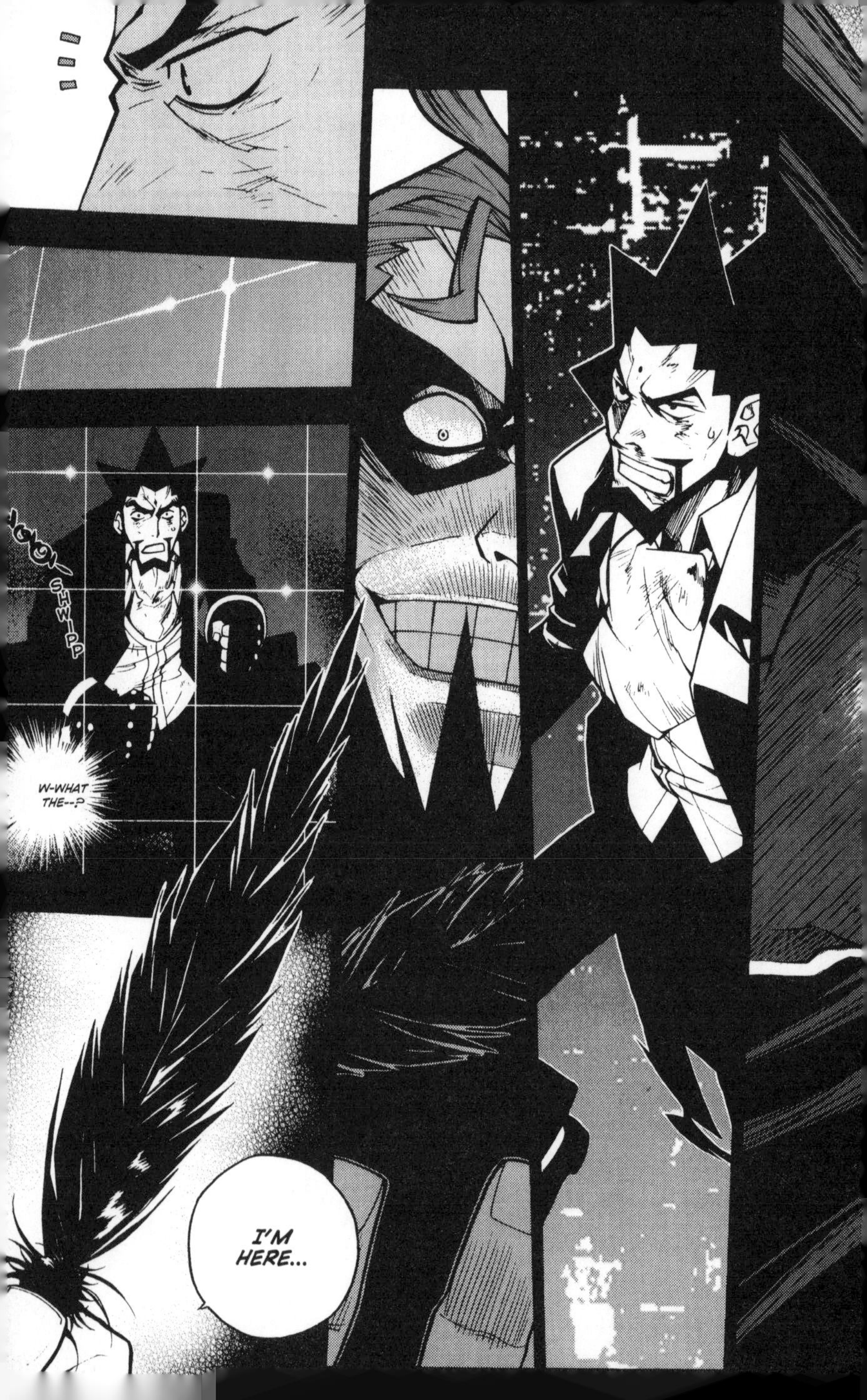
...
SHWIPP
W-WHAT THE--?
I'M HERE...

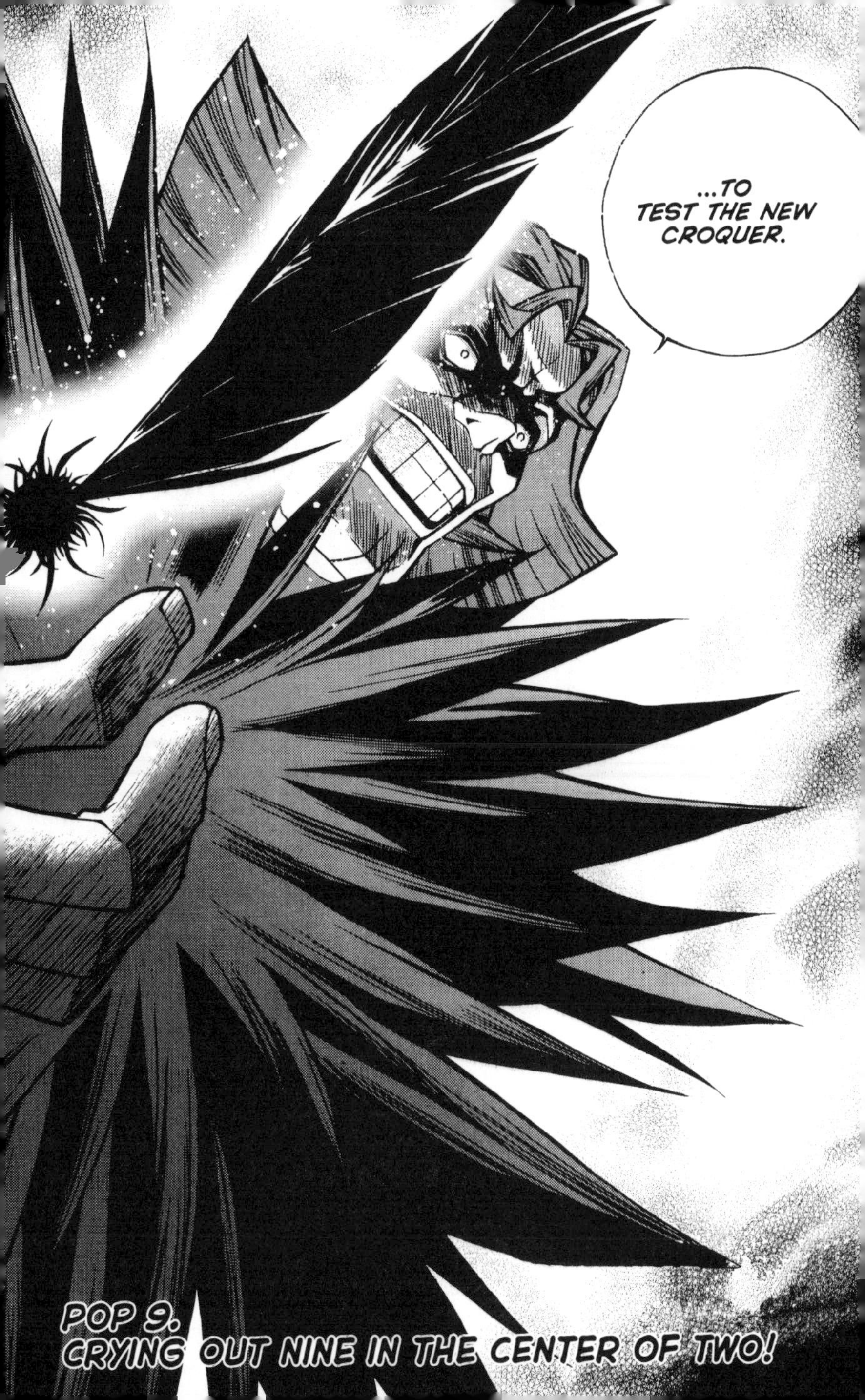
...TO TEST THE NEW CROQUER.
POP 9.
CRYING OUT NINE IN THE CENTER OF TWO!

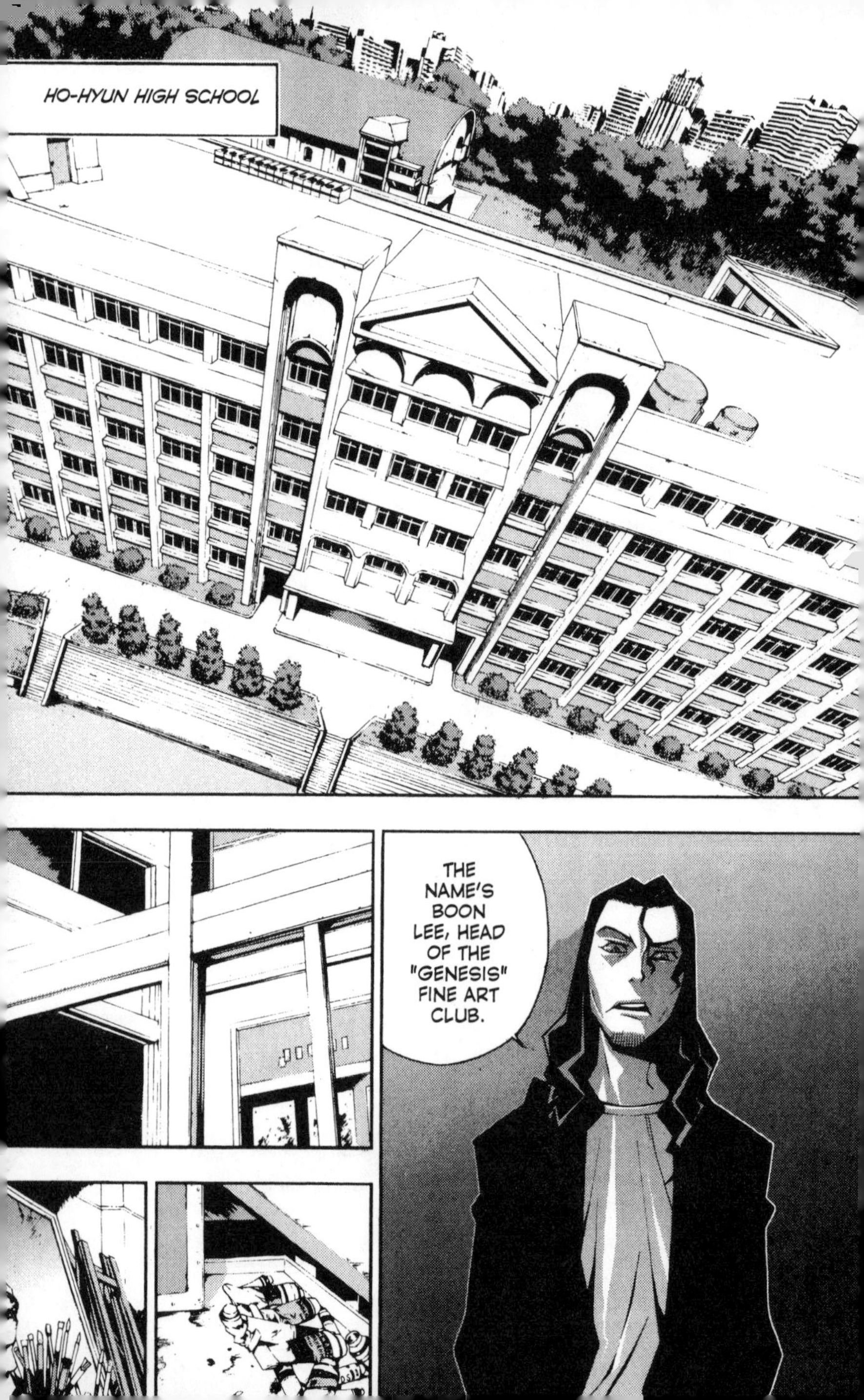
HO-HYUN HIGH SCHOOL
THE NAME'S BOON LEE, HEAD OF THE "GENESIS" FINE ART CLUB.

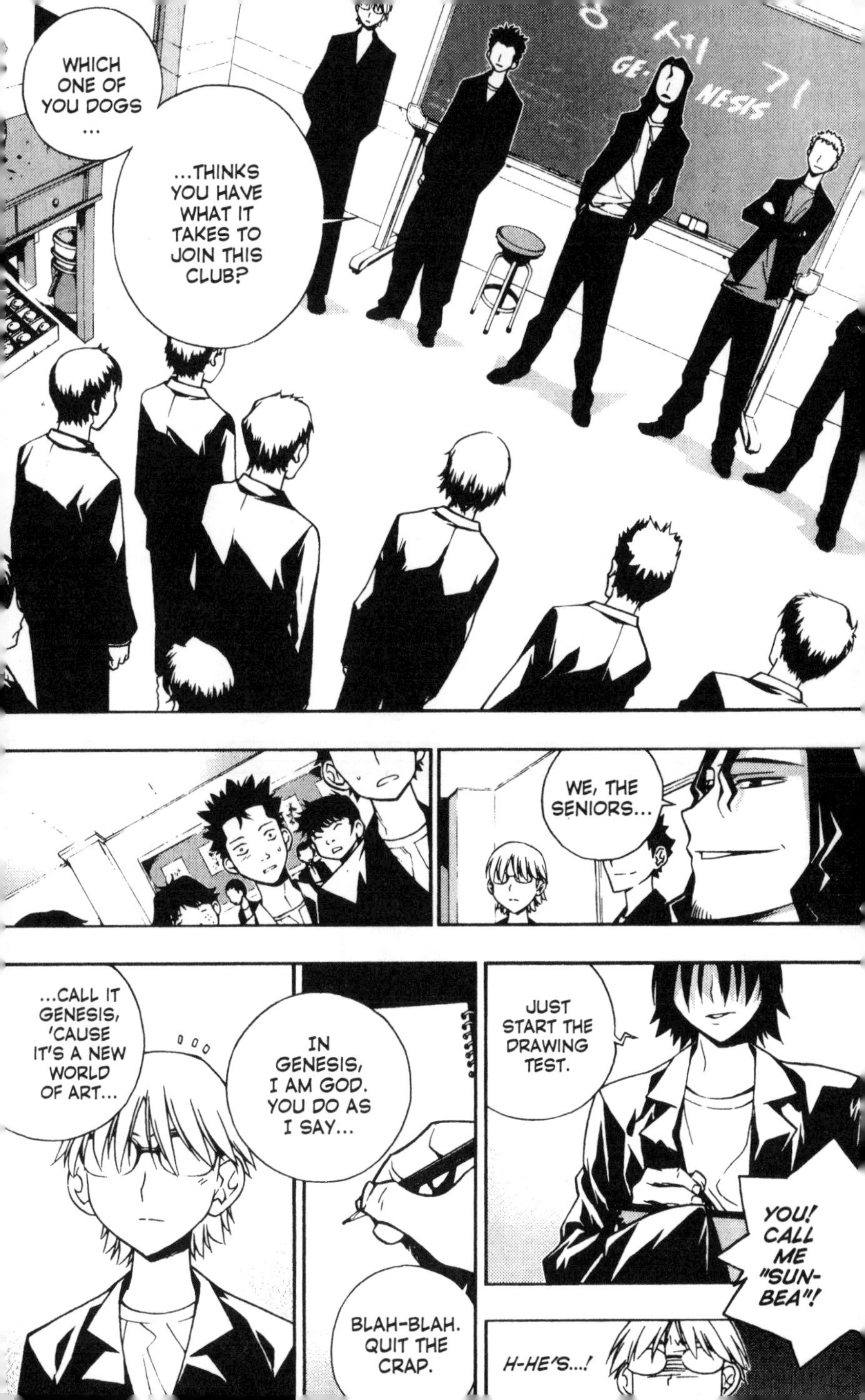
WHICH ONE OF YOU DOGS ...
...THINKS YOU HAVE WHAT IT TAKES TO JOIN THIS CLUB?
GE- NESIS
WE, THE SENIORS...
...CALL IT GENESIS, 'CAUSE IT'S A NEW WORLD OF ART...
IN GENESIS, I AM GOD. YOU DO AS I SAY...
BLAH-BLAH. QUIT THE CRAP.
JUST START THE DRAWING TEST.
YOU! CALL ME "SUN-BEA"!
H-HE'S...!

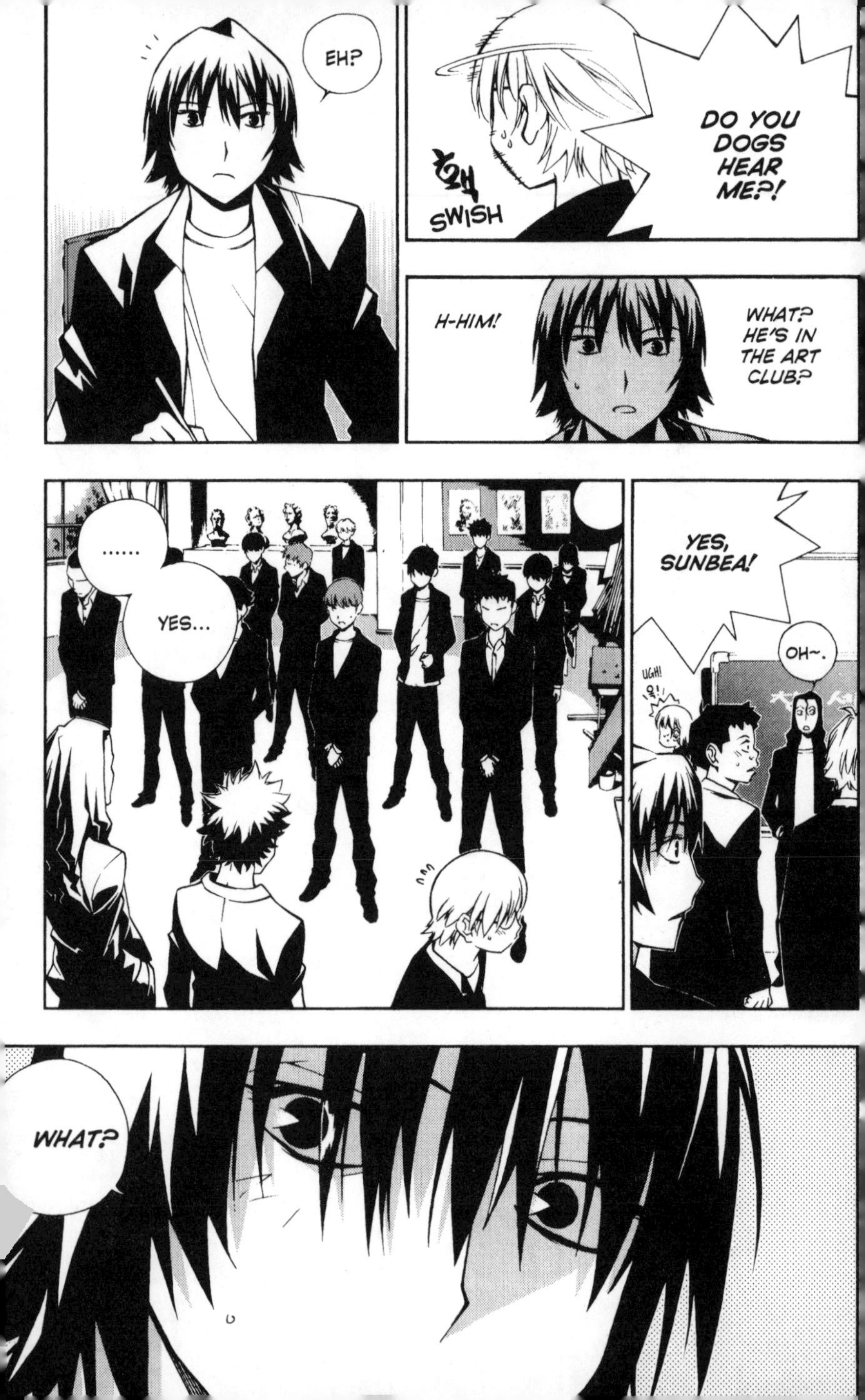
EH?
DO YOU DOGS HEAR ME?!
SWISH
H-HIM!
WHAT? HE'S IN THE ART CLUB?
......
YES...
YES, SUNBEA!
UGH!
OH~.
WHAT?

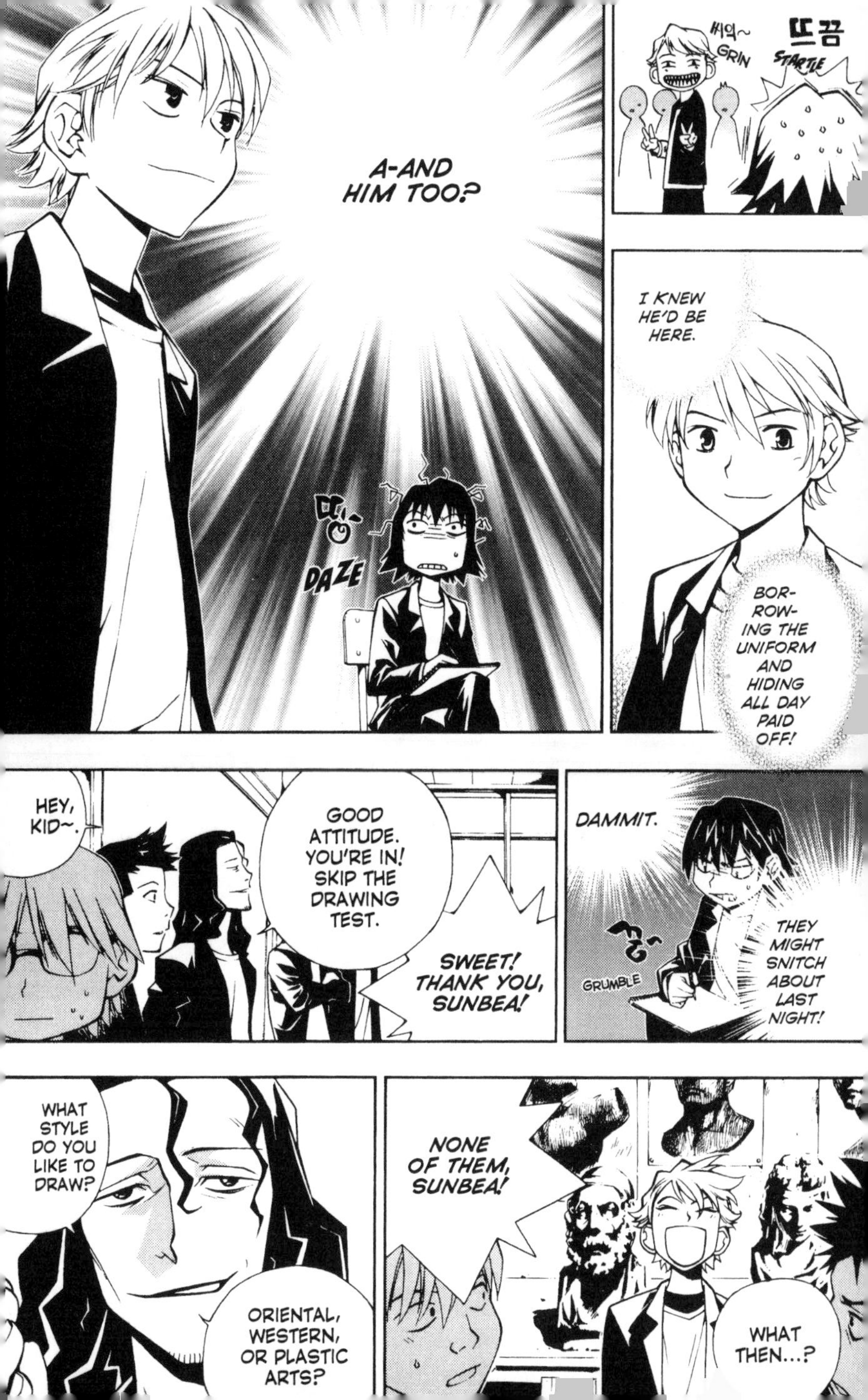

A-AND HIM TOO?
멍
DAZE
씨익~
GRIN
뜨끔
STARTLE
I KNEW HE'D BE HERE.
BOR-ROW-ING THE UNIFORM AND HIDING ALL DAY PAID OFF!
HEY, KID~.
GOOD ATTITUDE. YOU'RE IN! SKIP THE DRAWING TEST.
SWEET! THANK YOU, SUNBEA!
DAMMIT.
끙
GRUMBLE
THEY MIGHT SNITCH ABOUT LAST NIGHT!
WHAT STYLE DO YOU LIKE TO DRAW?
ORIENTAL, WESTERN, OR PLASTIC ARTS?
NONE OF THEM, SUNBEA!
WHAT THEN...?

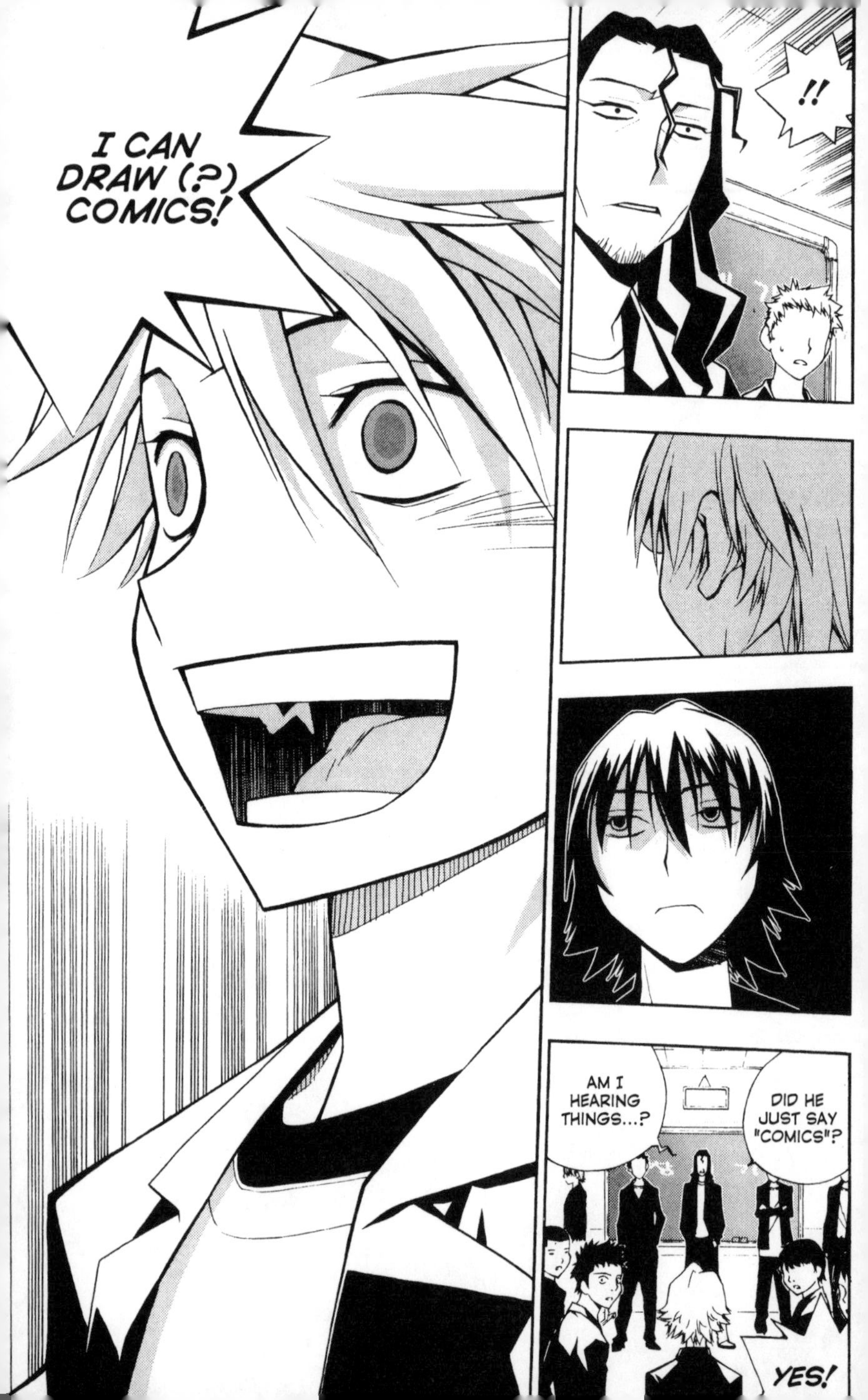
I CAN DRAW (?) COMICS!
!!
AM I HEARING THINGS...?
DID HE JUST SAY "COMICS"?
YES!

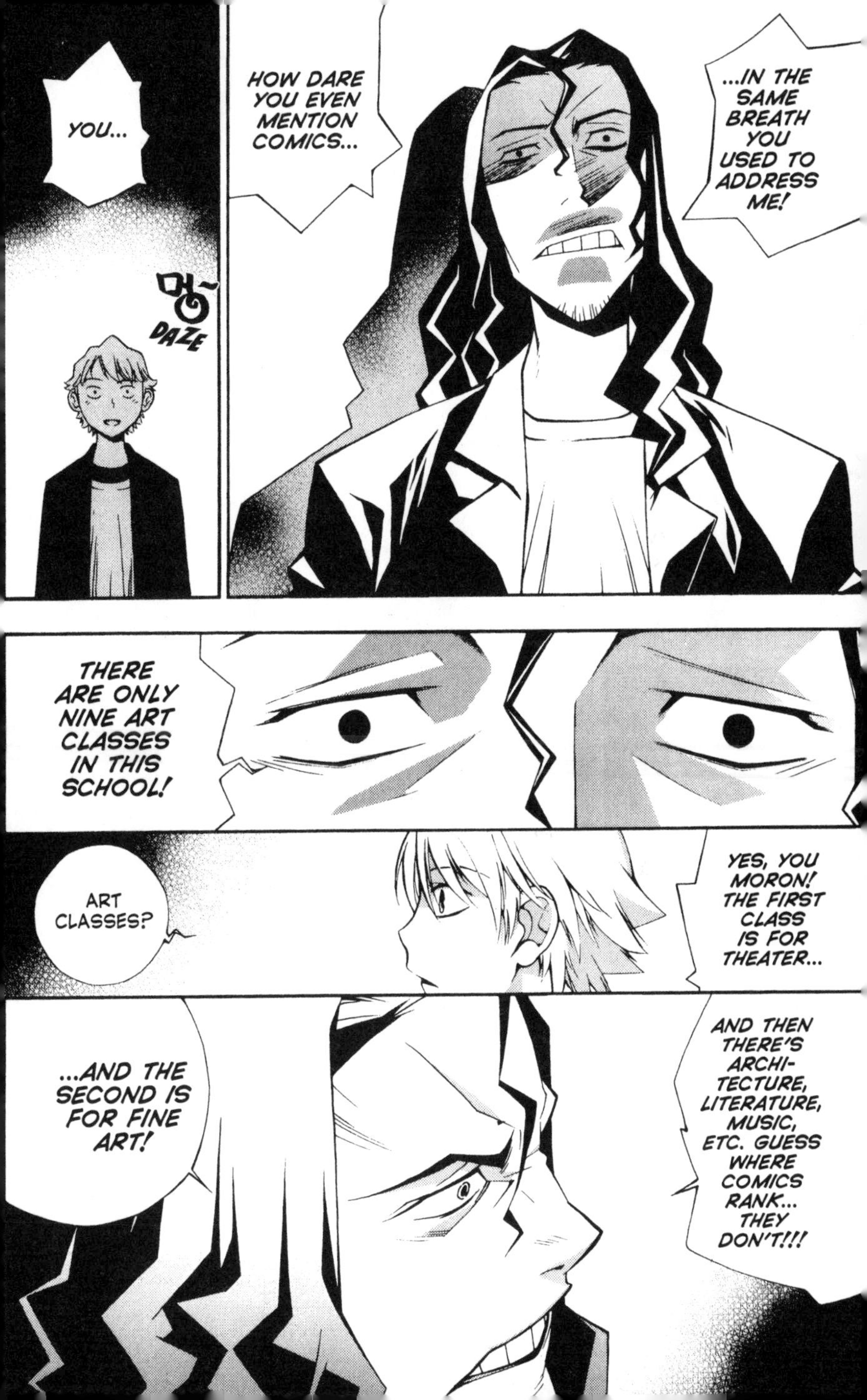
YOU...
DAZE
HOW DARE YOU EVEN MENTION COMICS...
...IN THE SAME BREATH YOU USED TO ADDRESS ME!
THERE ARE ONLY NINE ART CLASSES IN THIS SCHOOL!
ART CLASSES?
YES, YOU MORON! THE FIRST CLASS IS FOR THEATER...
...AND THE SECOND IS FOR FINE ART!
AND THEN THERE'S ARCHI-TECTURE, LITERATURE, MUSIC, ETC. GUESS WHERE COMICS RANK... THEY DON'T!!!

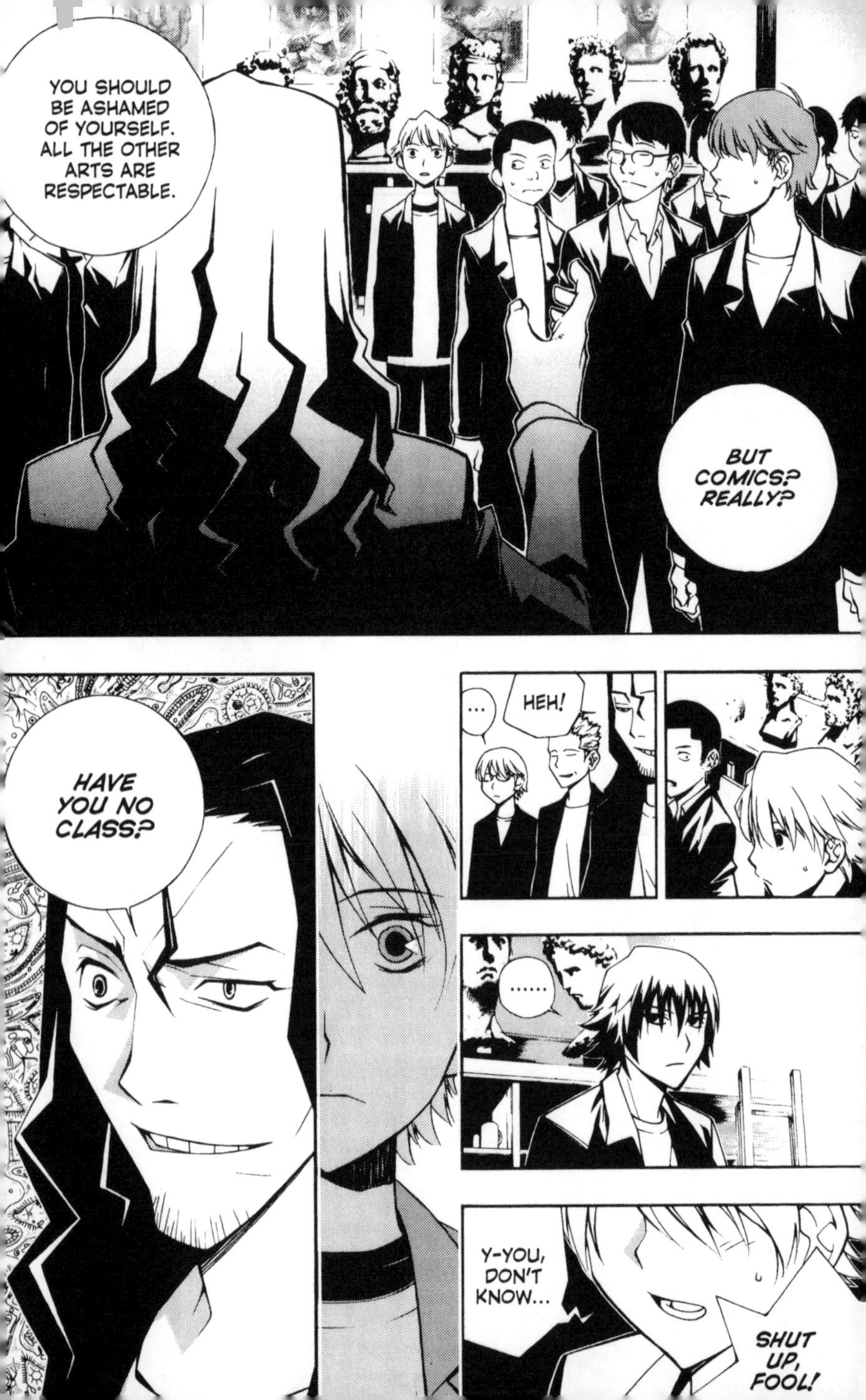
YOU SHOULD BE ASHAMED OF YOURSELF. ALL THE OTHER ARTS ARE RESPECTABLE.
BUT COMICS? REALLY?
HAVE YOU NO CLASS?
...
HEH!
......
Y-YOU, DON'T KNOW...
SHUT UP, FOOL!

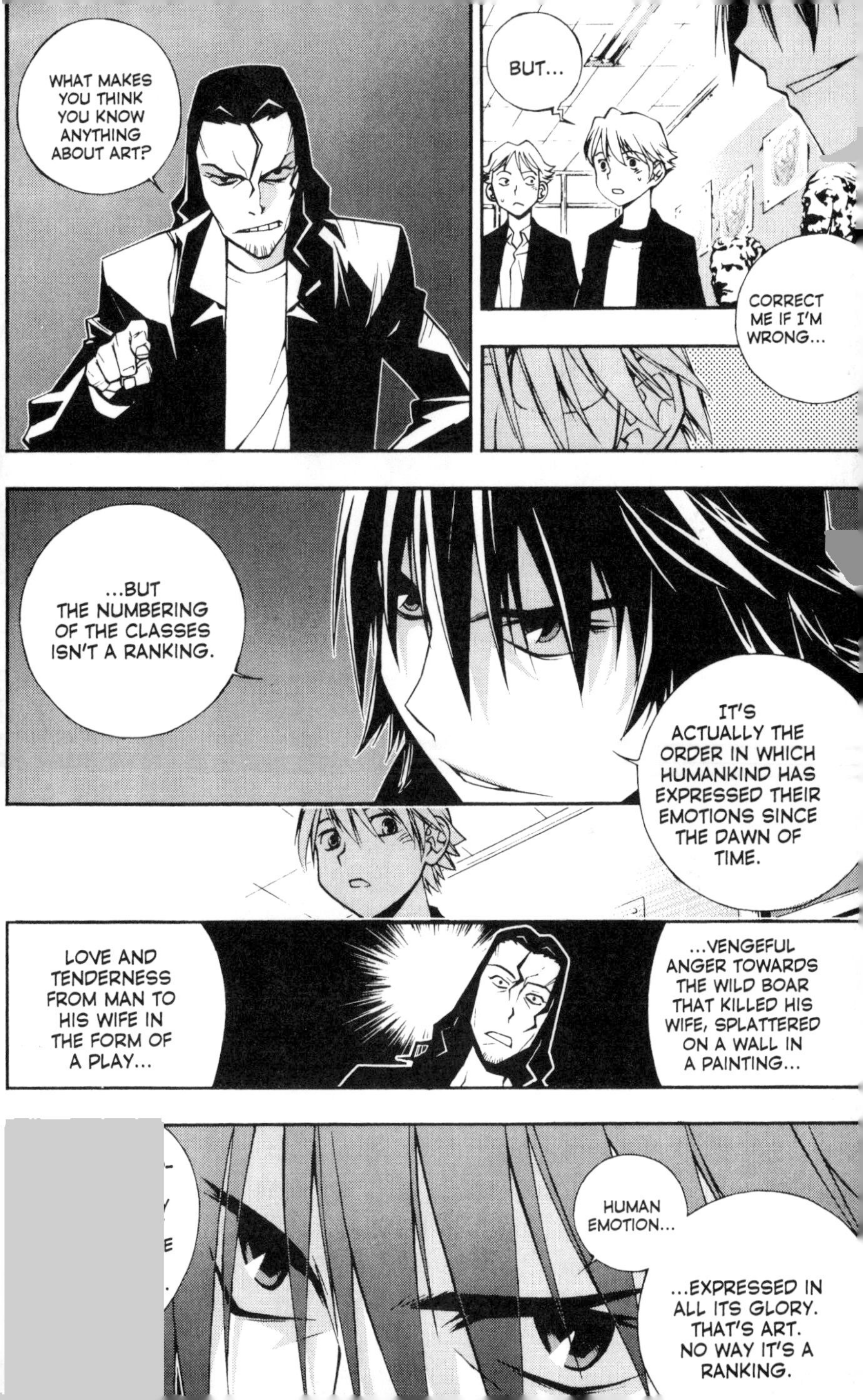
WHAT MAKES YOU THINK YOU KNOW ANYTHING ABOUT ART?
BUT...
CORRECT ME IF I'M WRONG...
...BUT THE NUMBERING OF THE CLASSES ISN'T A RANKING.
IT'S ACTUALLY THE ORDER IN WHICH HUMANKIND HAS EXPRESSED THEIR EMOTIONS SINCE THE DAWN OF TIME.
LOVE AND TENDERNESS FROM MAN TO HIS WIFE IN THE FORM OF A PLAY...
...VENGEFUL ANGER TOWARDS THE WILD BOAR THAT KILLED HIS WIFE, SPLATTERED ON A WALL IN A PAINTING...
HUMAN EMOTION...
...EXPRESSED IN ALL ITS GLORY. THAT'S ART. NO WAY IT'S A RANKING.

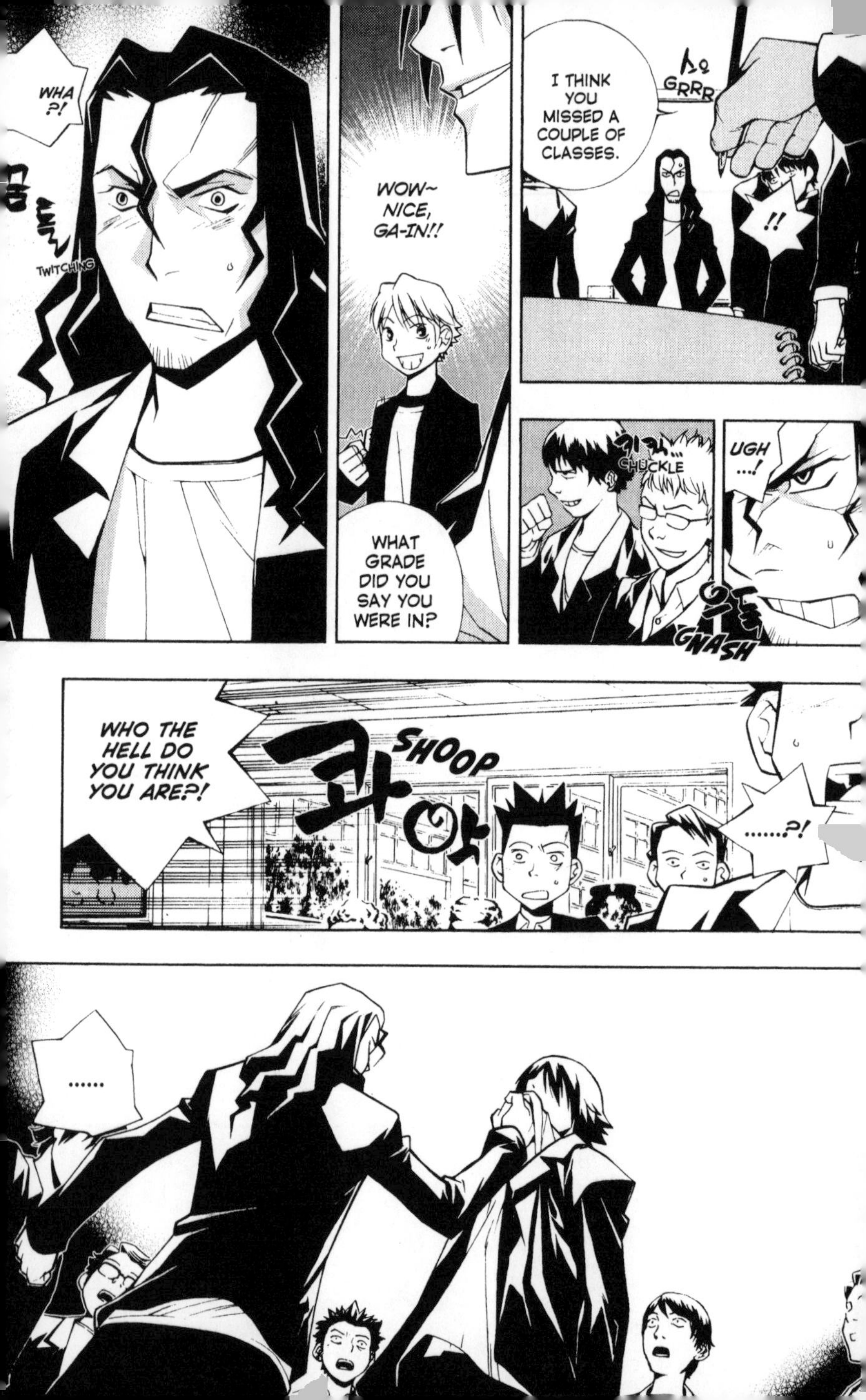
WHA ?!
TWITCHING
WOW~ NICE, GA-IN!!
WHAT GRADE DID YOU SAY YOU WERE IN?
I THINK YOU MISSED A COUPLE OF CLASSES.
GRRR
!!
CHUCKLE
UGH ...!
GNASH
WHO THE HELL DO YOU THINK YOU ARE?!
SHOOP
......?!
......

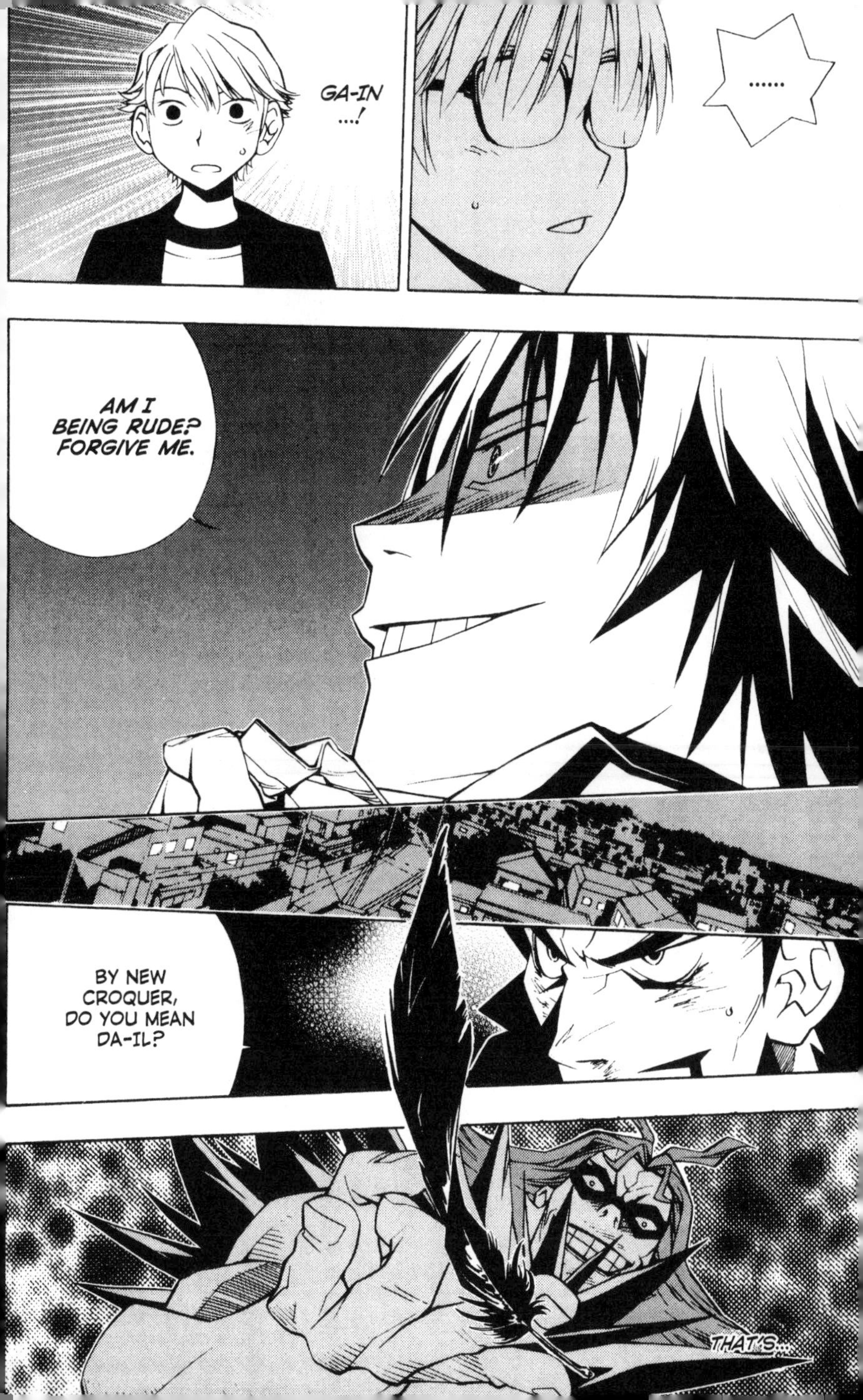
GA-IN ...!
......
AM I BEING RUDE? FORGIVE ME.
BY NEW CROQUER, DO YOU MEAN DA-IL?
THAT'S...

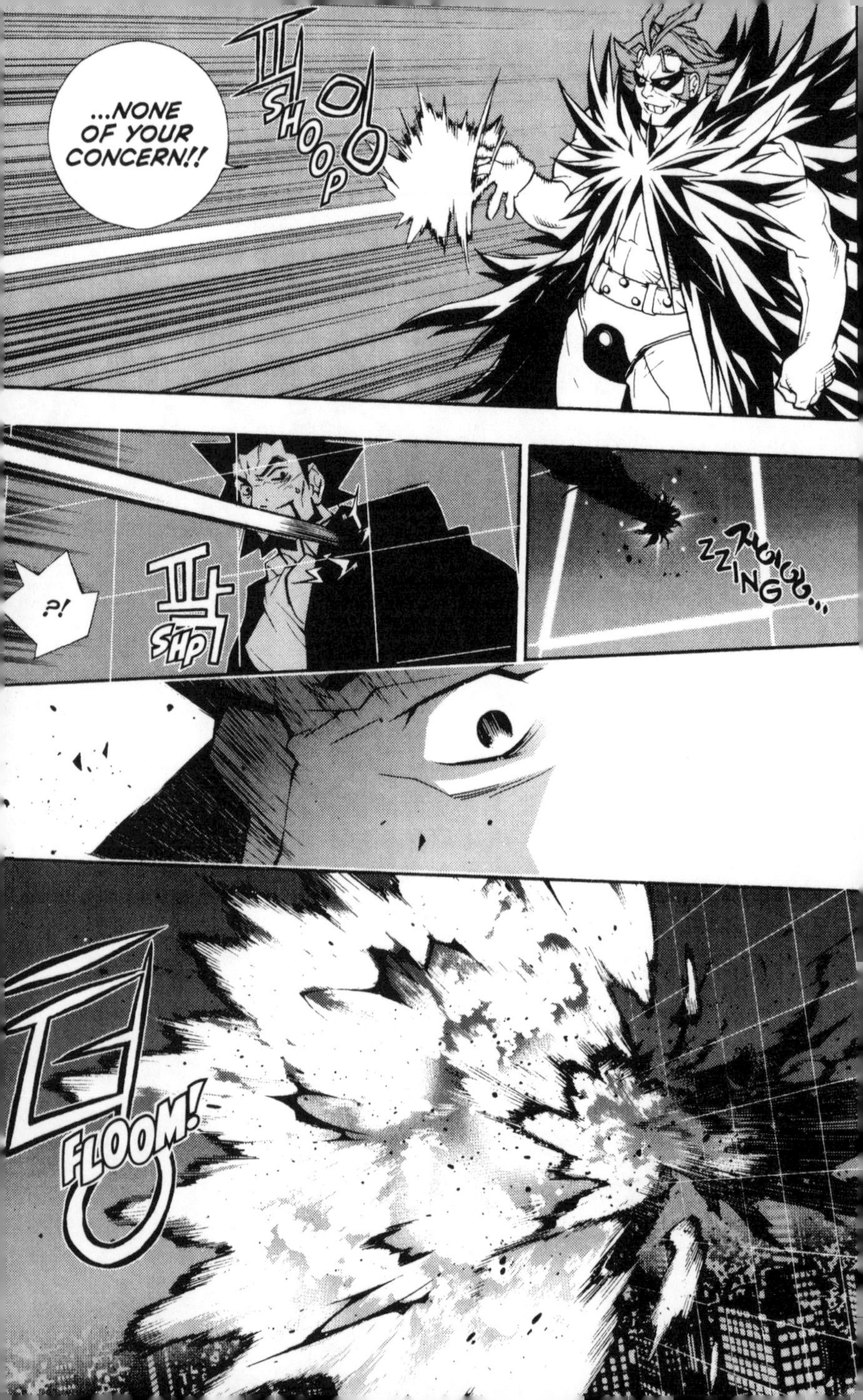
...NONE OF YOUR CONCERN!!
SHOOP
?!
SHP
ZZING...
FLOOM!

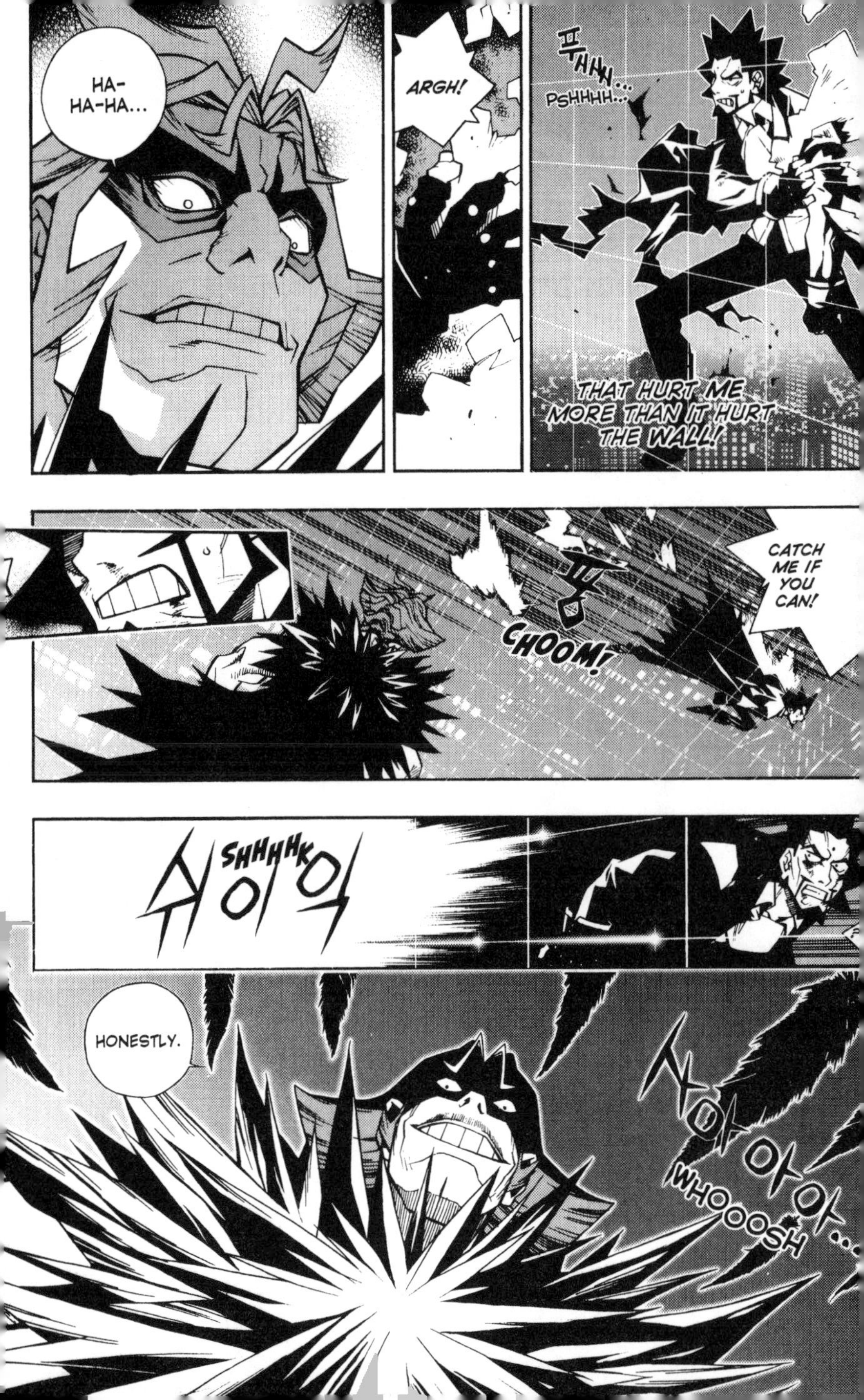
HA-HA-HA...
ARGH!
TTHHH... PSHHHH...
THAT HURT ME MORE THAN IT HURT THE WALL!
CHOOM!
CATCH ME IF YOU CAN!
SHHHHK
HONESTLY.
WHOOOSH

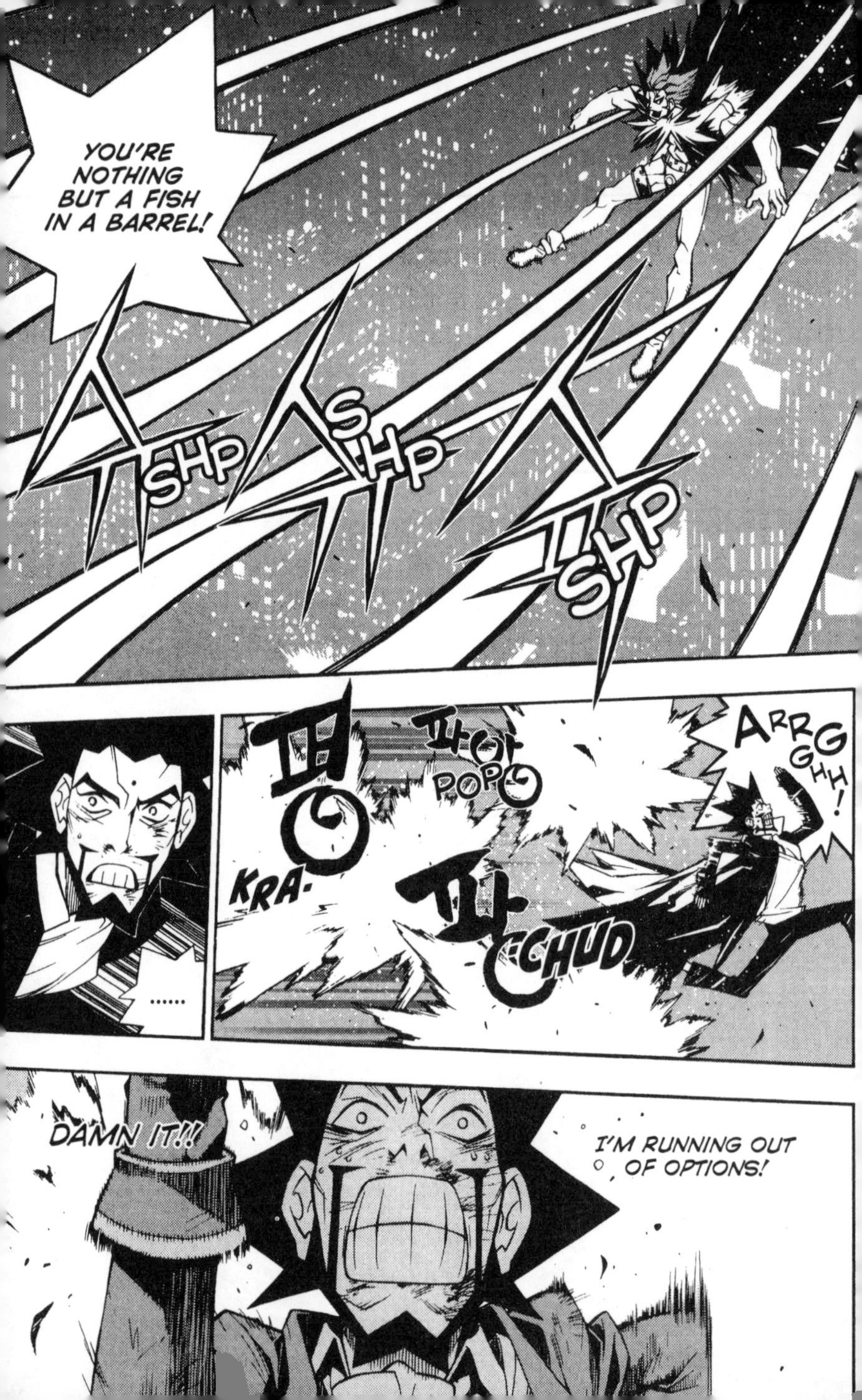
YOU'RE NOTHING BUT A FISH IN A BARREL!
SHP
SHP
SHP
......
POPO
ARRGGHH!
KRA-
-CHUD
DAMN IT!!
I'M RUNNING OUT OF OPTIONS!

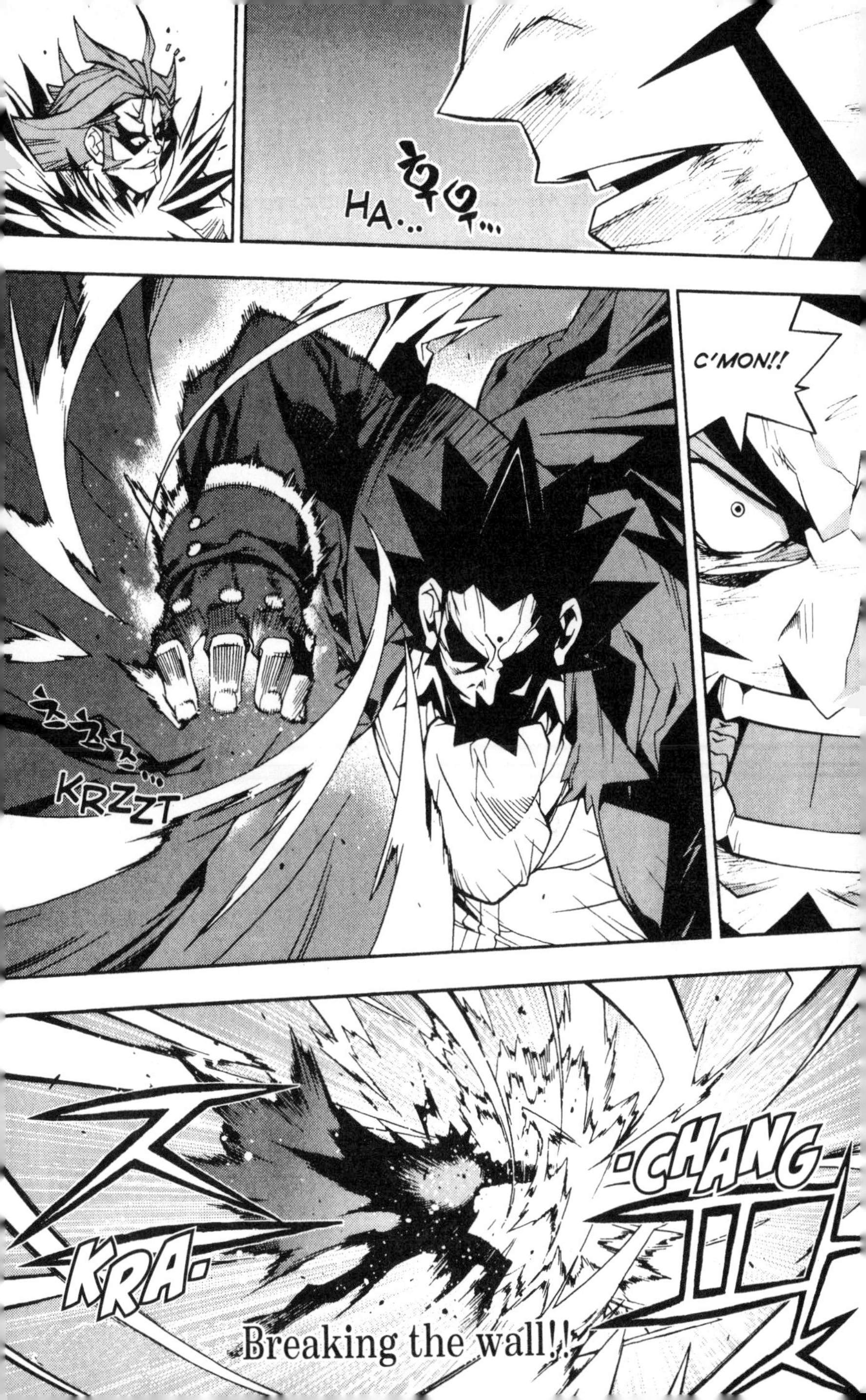
HA...
KRZZT
C'MON!!
KRA-
-CHANG
Breaking the wall!!

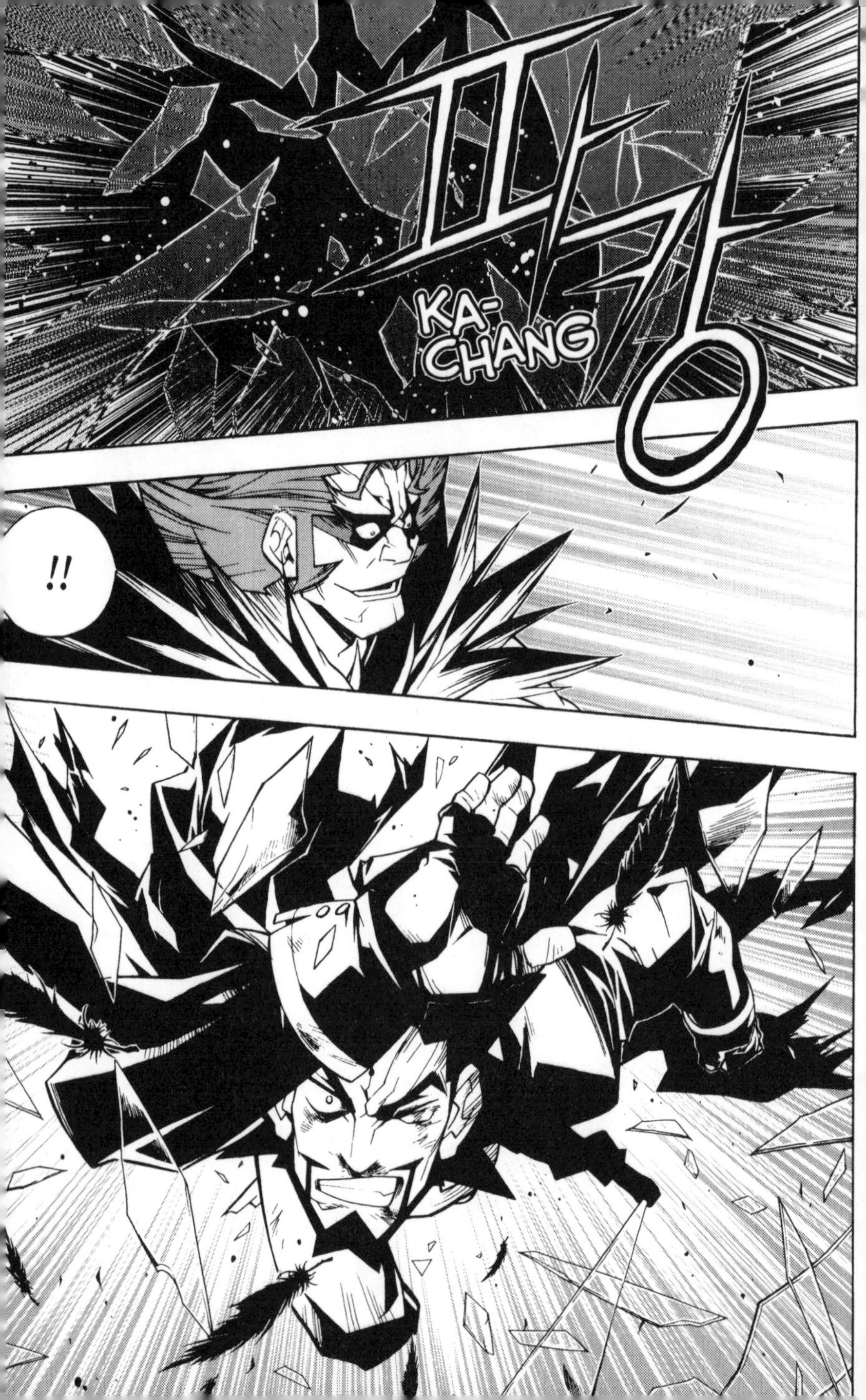
KA-CHANG
!!

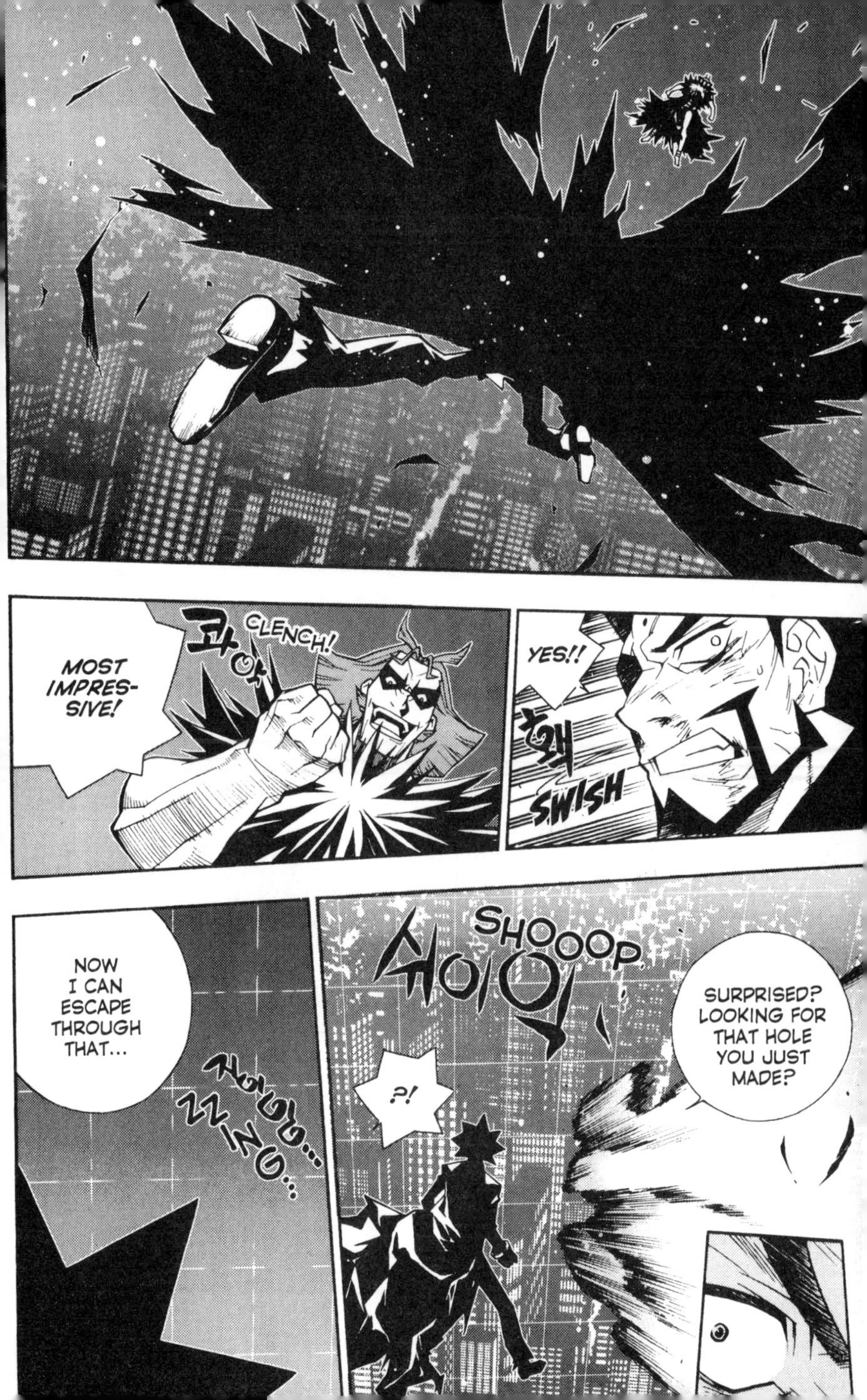
MOST IMPRESSIVE!
CLENCH!
YES!!
SWISH
NOW I CAN ESCAPE THROUGH THAT...
ZZING...
SHOOOP
?!
SURPRISED? LOOKING FOR THAT HOLE YOU JUST MADE?

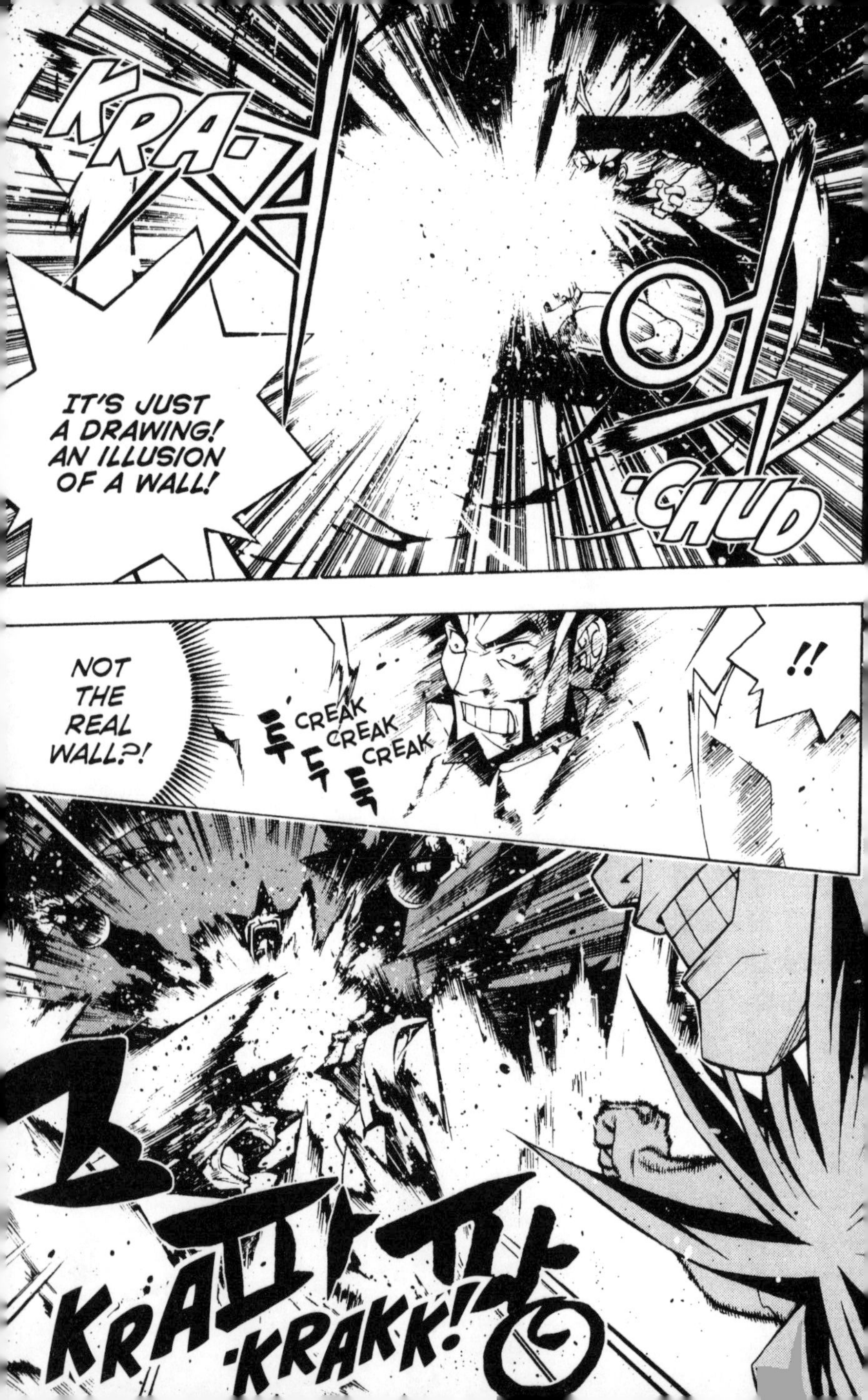
KRA-
IT'S JUST A DRAWING! AN ILLUSION OF A WALL!
-CHUD
NOT THE REAL WALL?!
CREAK CREAK CREAK
!!
KRAK-KRAKK!

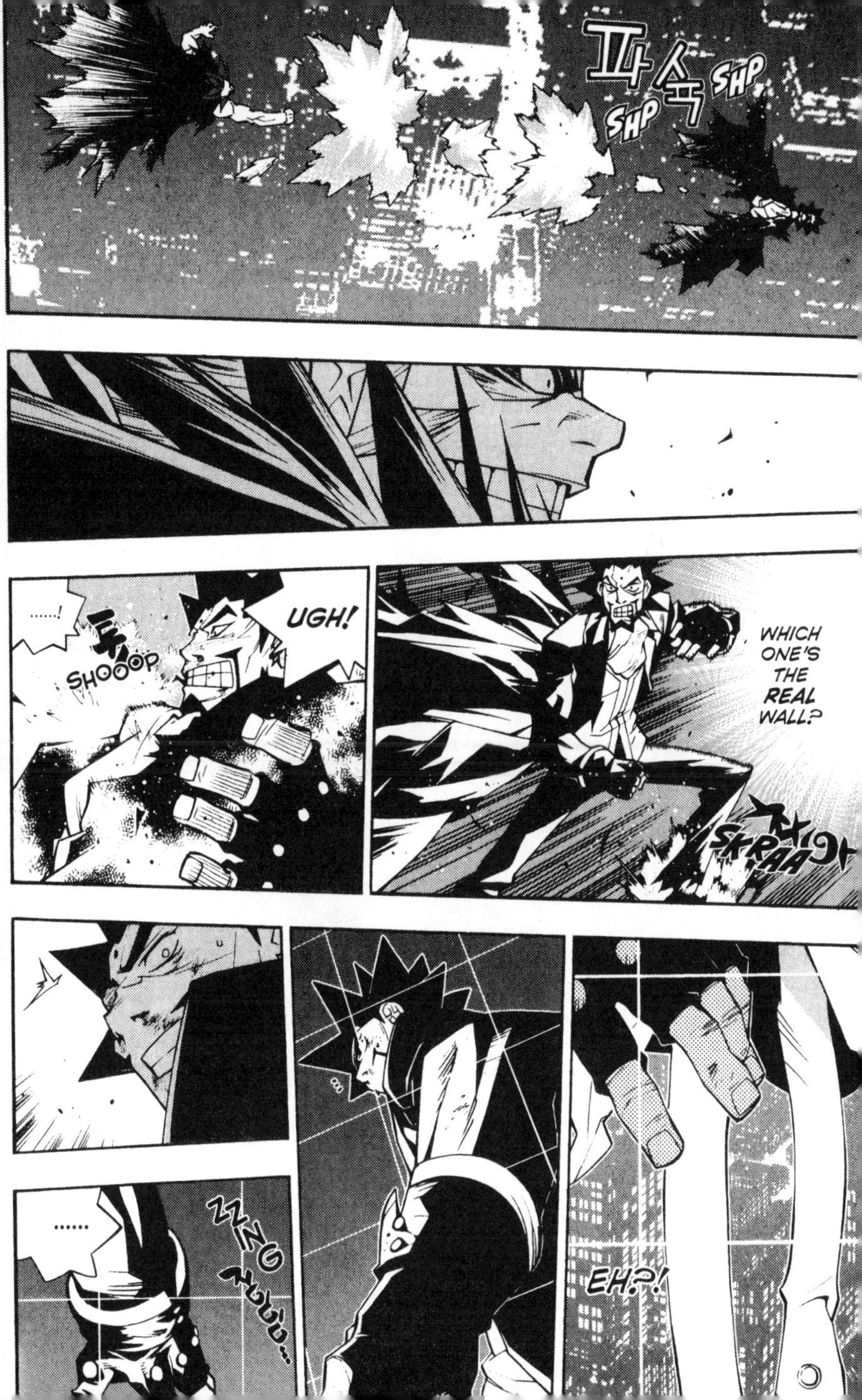

SHP SHP
......!
SHOOOP
UGH!
WHICH ONE'S THE REAL WALL?
SKRAA
......
ZZING
EH?!

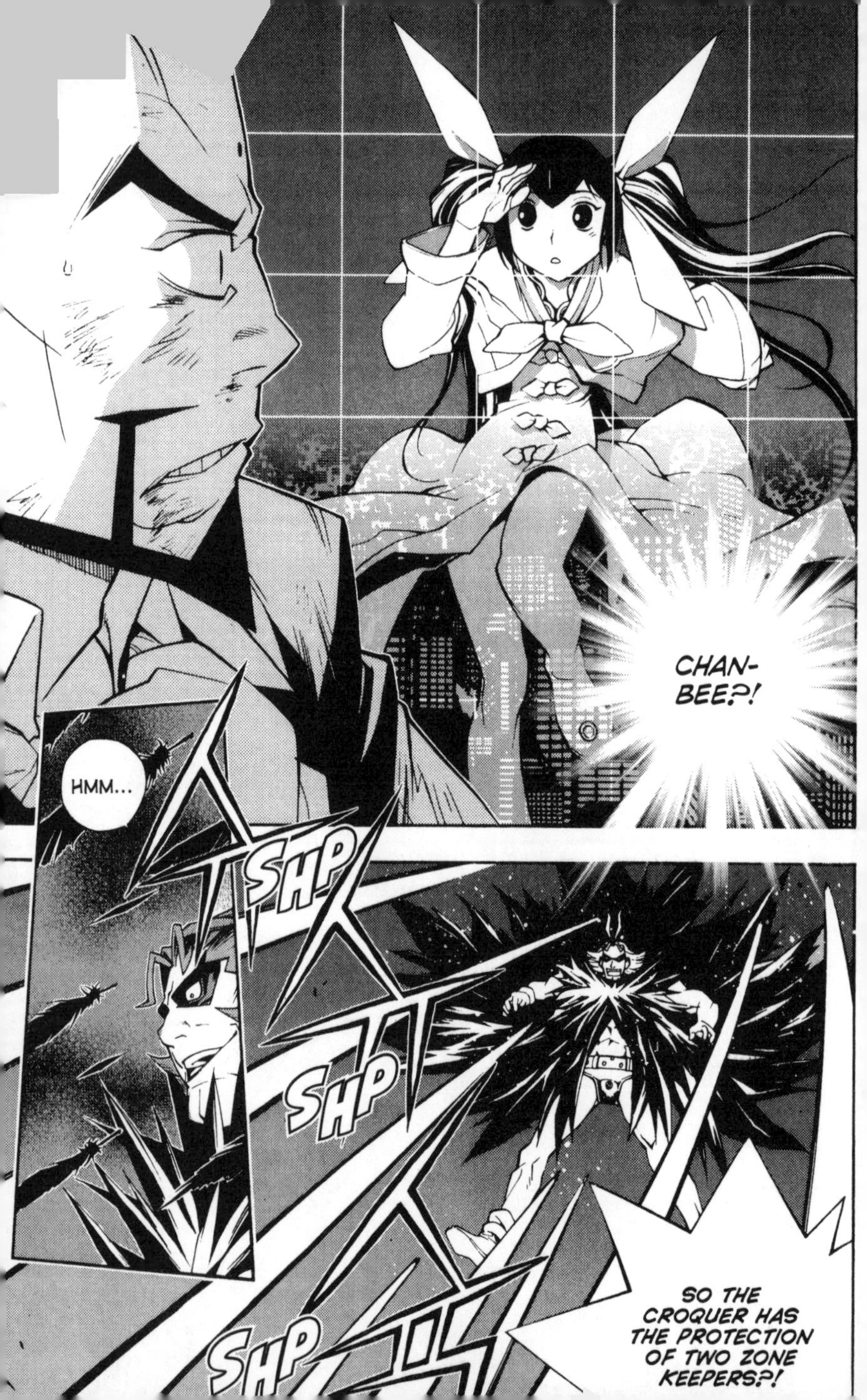
CHAN-
BEE?!
HMM...
SHP
SHP
SHP
SO THE
CROQUER HAS
THE PROTECTION
OF TWO ZONE
KEEPERS?!

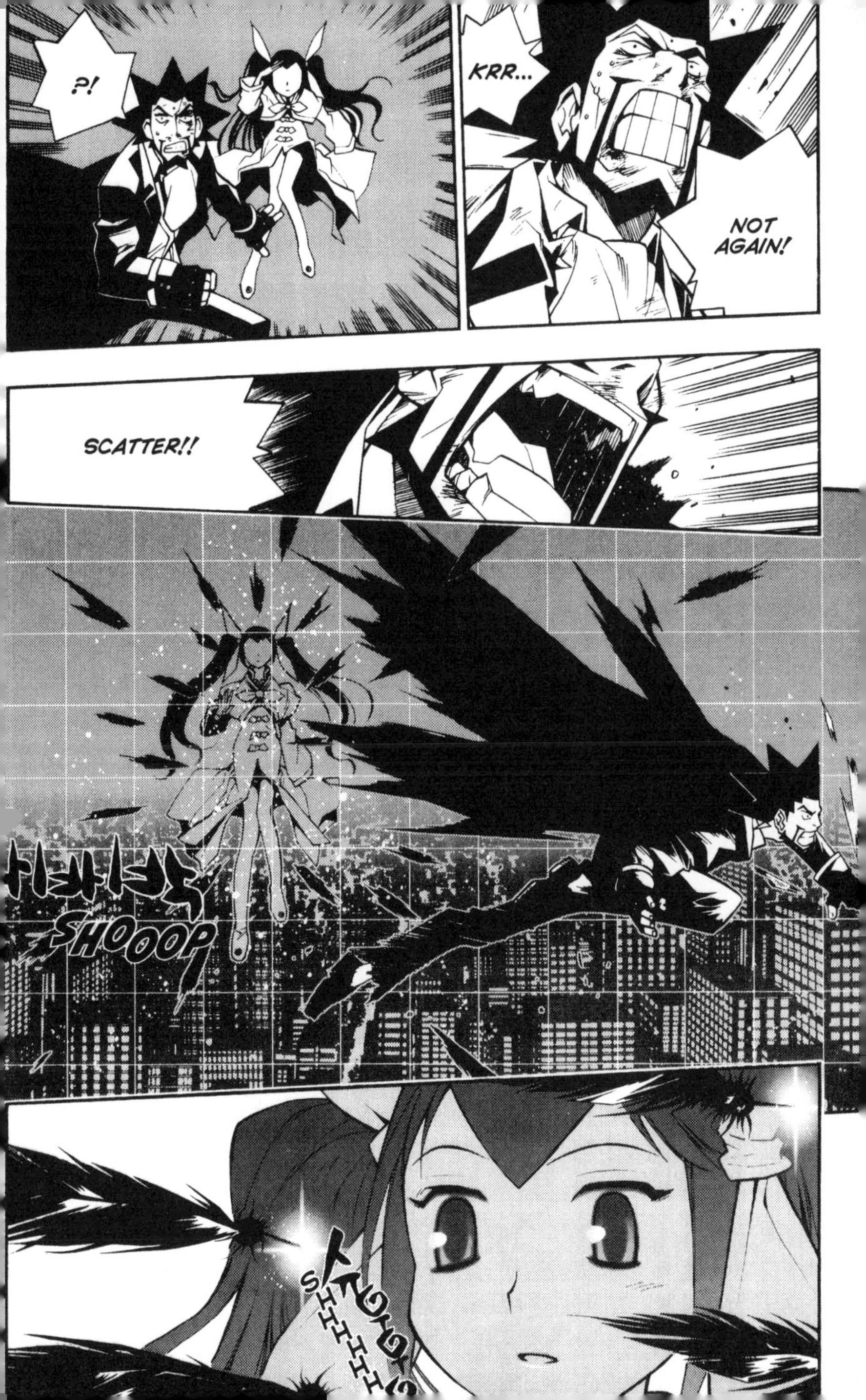
?!
KRR...
NOT AGAIN!
SCATTER!!
SHOOOP

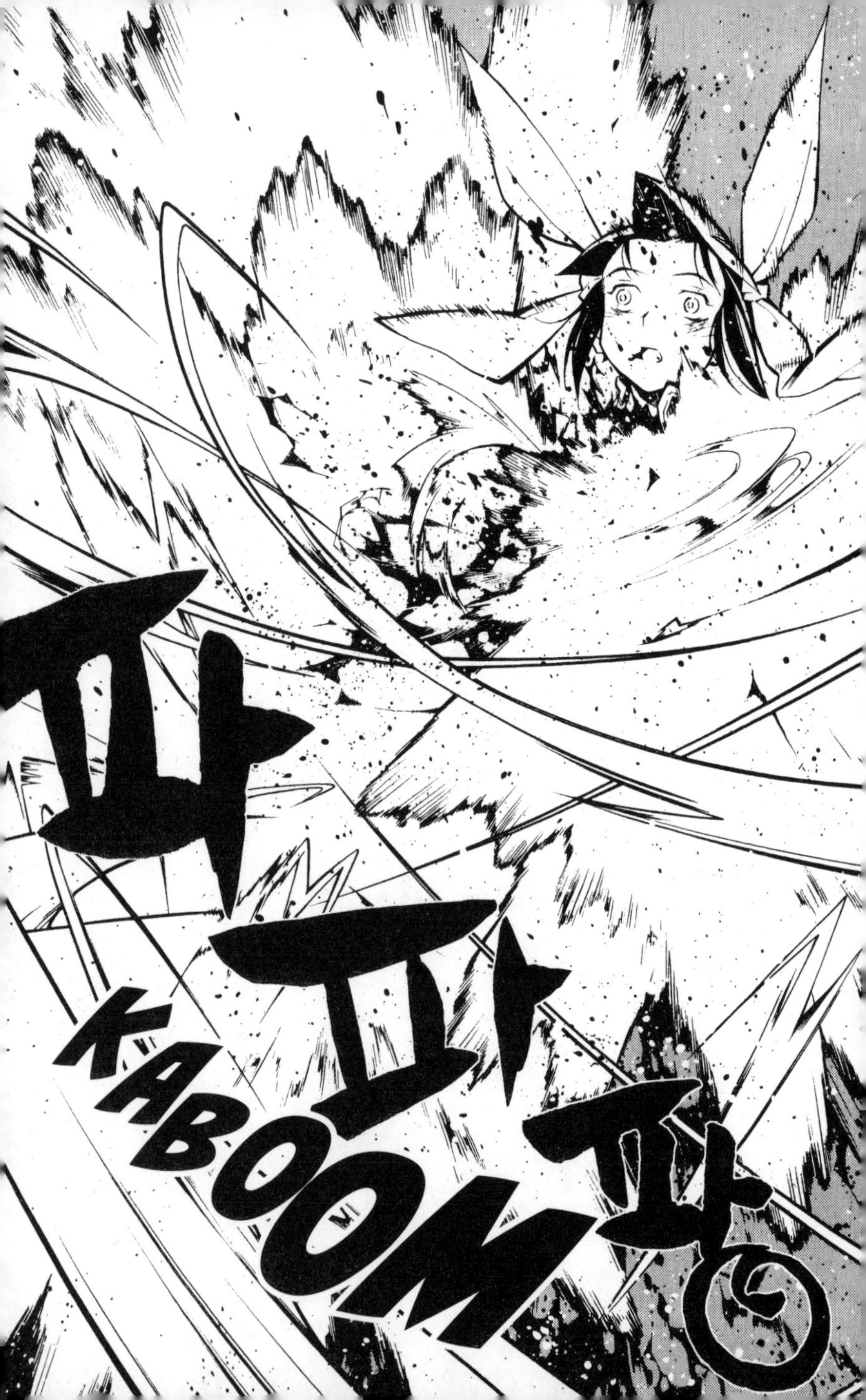
KABOOM

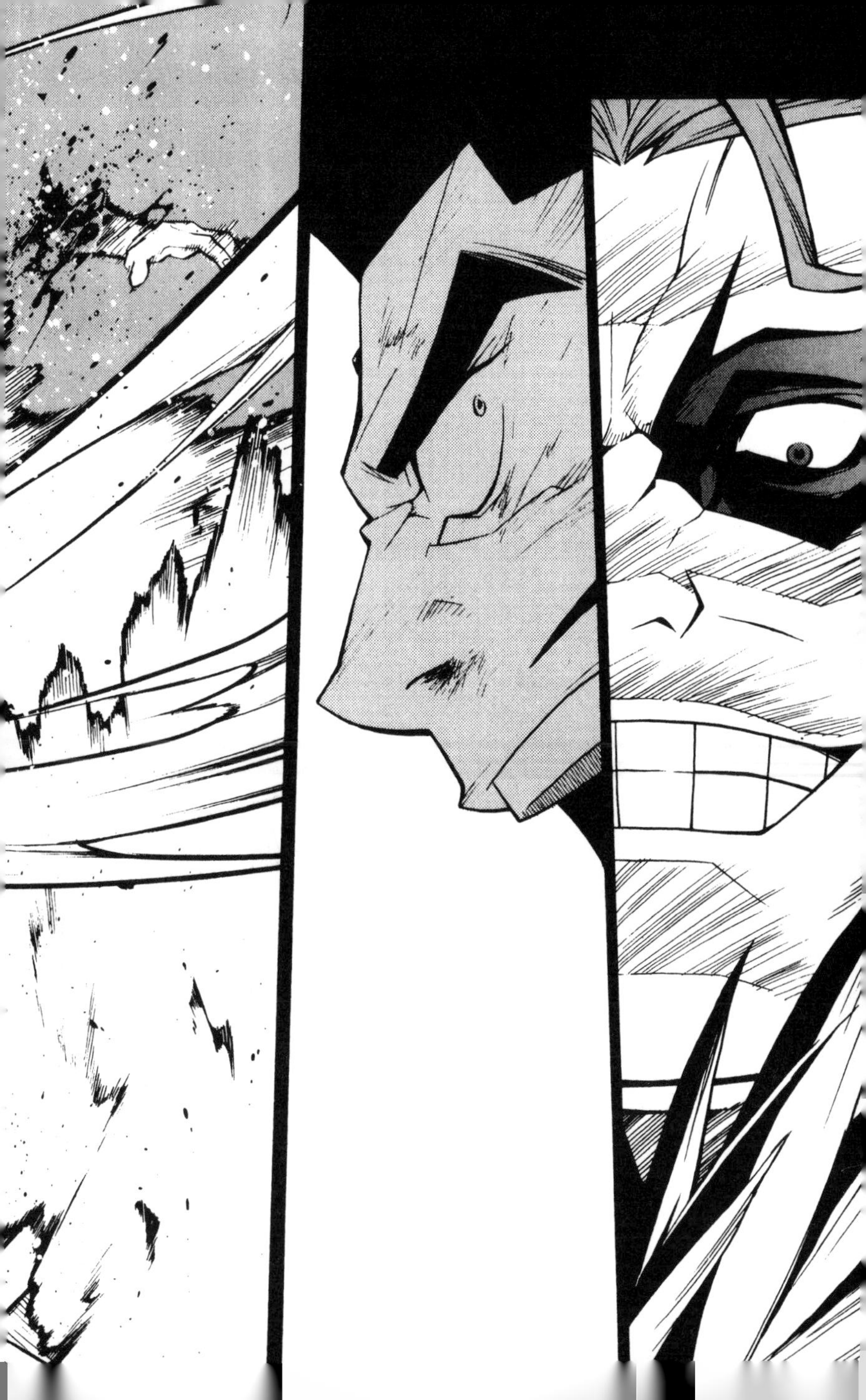

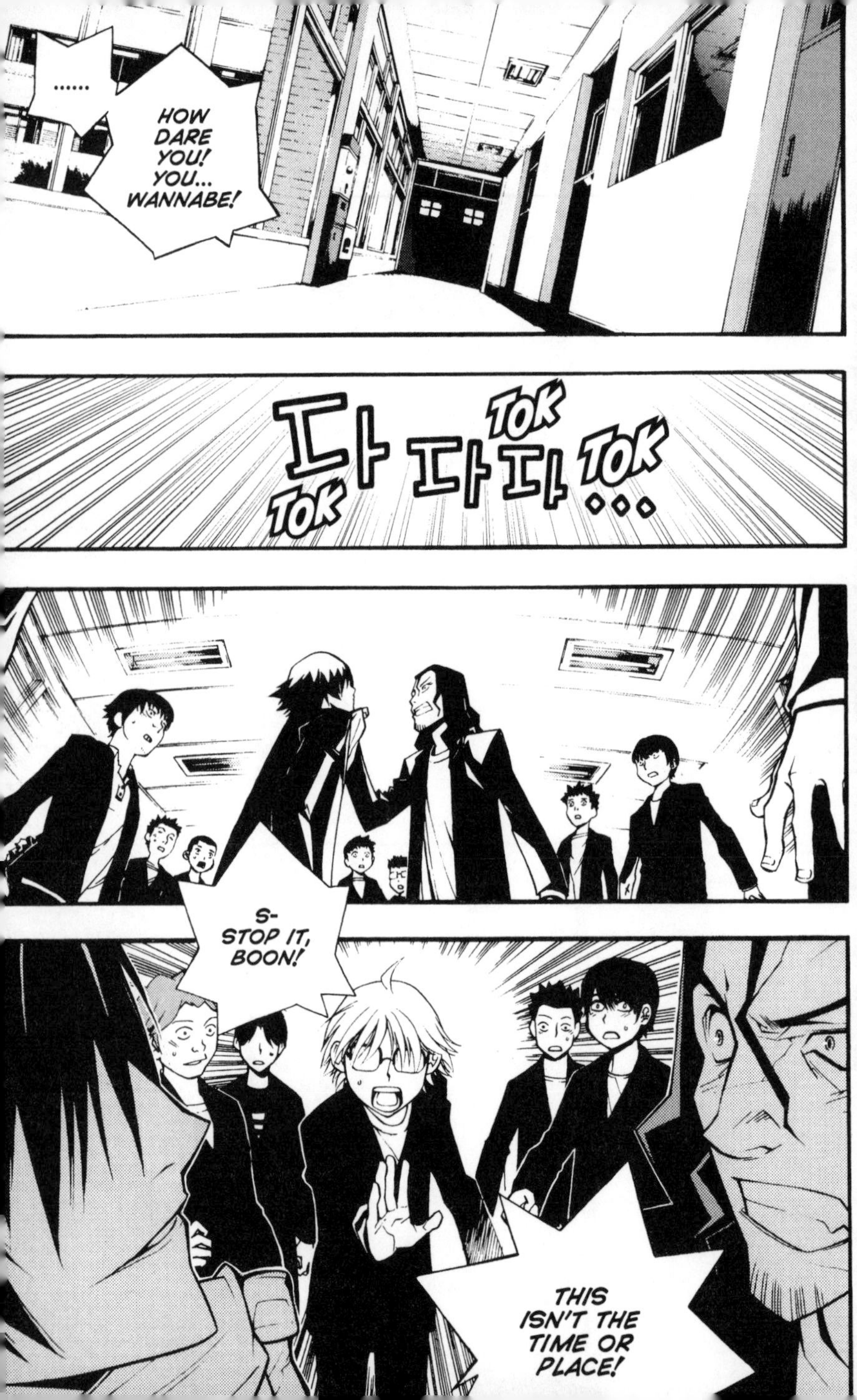
......
HOW DARE YOU! YOU... WANNABE!
TOK TOK TOK TOK
S- STOP IT, BOON!
THIS ISN'T THE TIME OR PLACE!

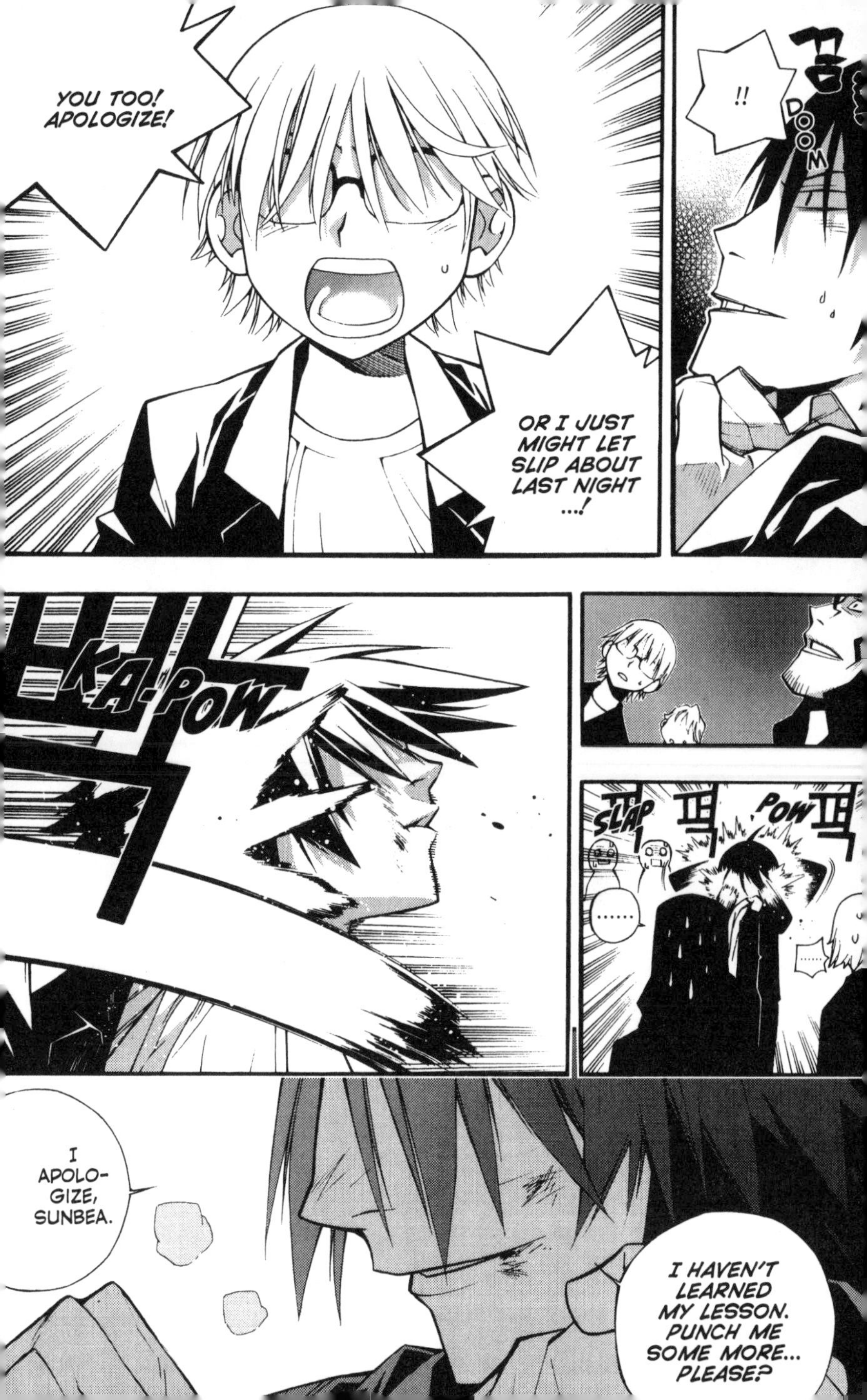
YOU TOO! APOLOGIZE!
OR I JUST MIGHT LET SLIP ABOUT LAST NIGHT ...!
!!
DOOM
KA-POW
SLAP 퍽
POW 퍽
......
......
I APOLO-GIZE, SUNBEA.
I HAVEN'T LEARNED MY LESSON. PUNCH ME SOME MORE... PLEASE?

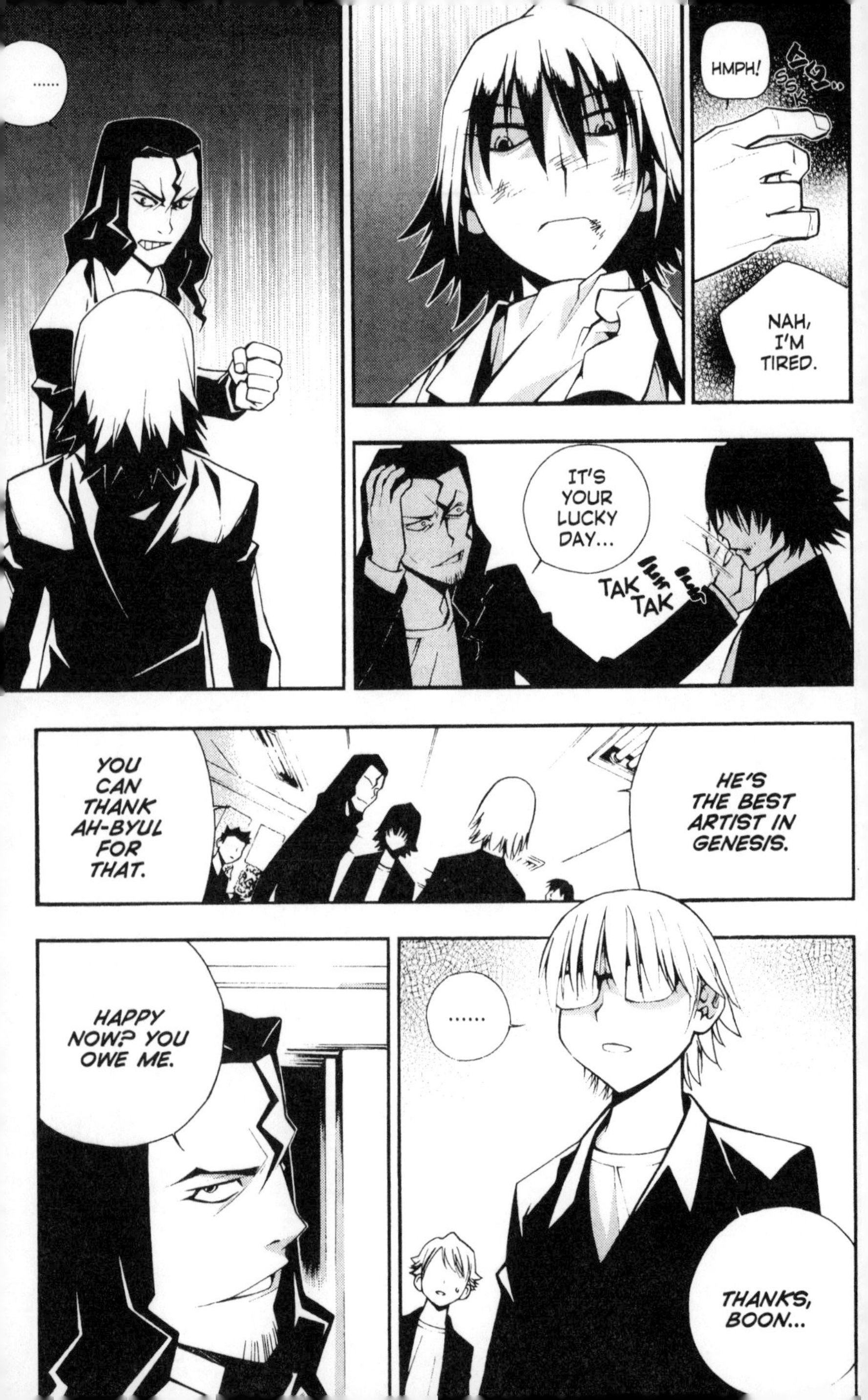
......
HMPH!
SSSK
NAH, I'M TIRED.
IT'S YOUR LUCKY DAY...
TAK TAK
YOU CAN THANK AH-BYUL FOR THAT.
HE'S THE BEST ARTIST IN GENESIS.
HAPPY NOW? YOU OWE ME.
......
THANKS, BOON...

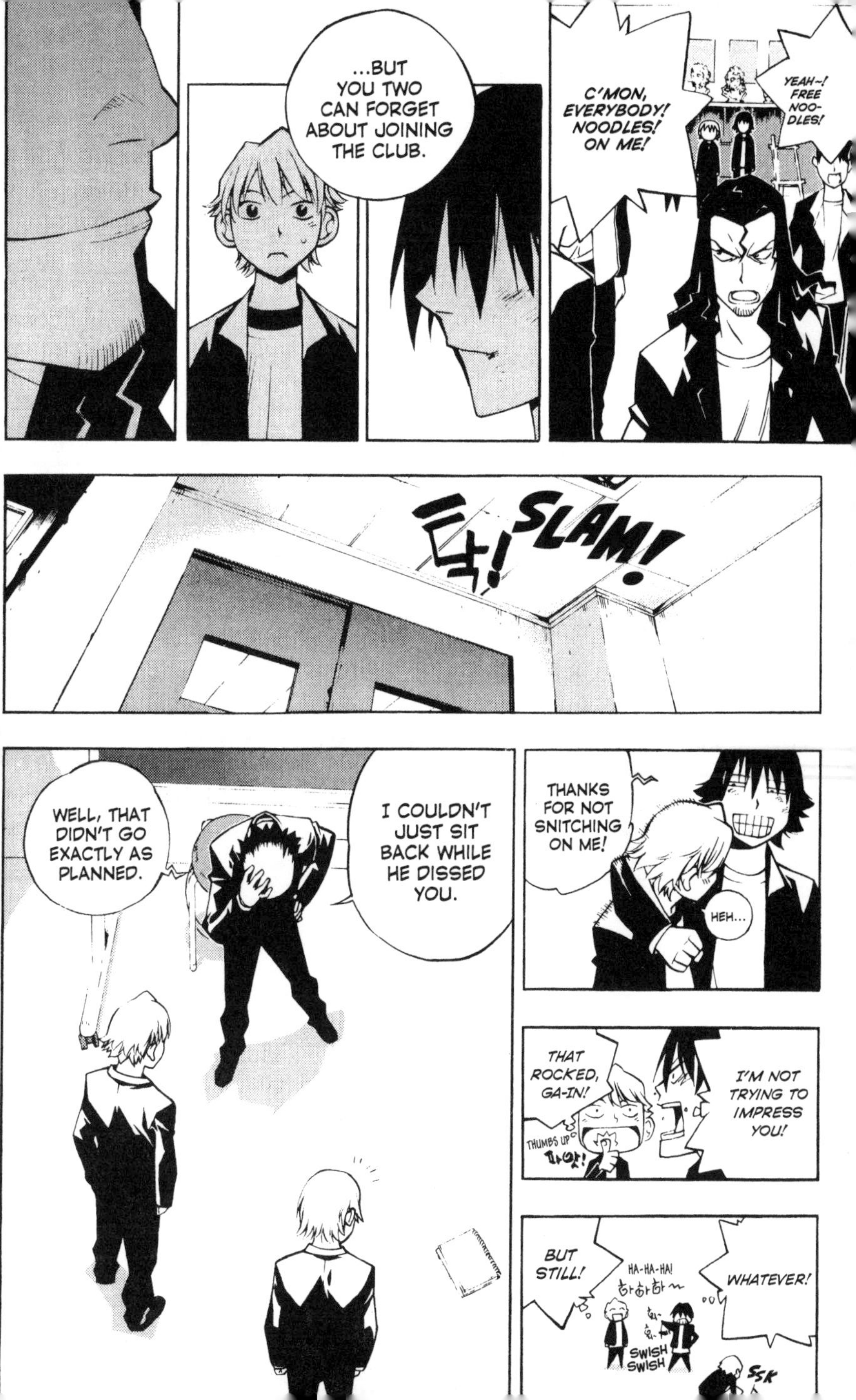

...BUT YOU TWO CAN FORGET ABOUT JOINING THE CLUB.
C'MON, EVERYBODY! NOODLES! ON ME!
YEAH~! FREE NOO-DLES!
SLAM!
WELL, THAT DIDN'T GO EXACTLY AS PLANNED.
I COULDN'T JUST SIT BACK WHILE HE DISSED YOU.
THANKS FOR NOT SNITCHING ON ME!
HEH...
THAT ROCKED, GA-IN!
THUMBS UP
I'M NOT TRYING TO IMPRESS YOU!
BUT STILL!
HA-HA-HA!
WHATEVER!
SWISH SWISH
SSK

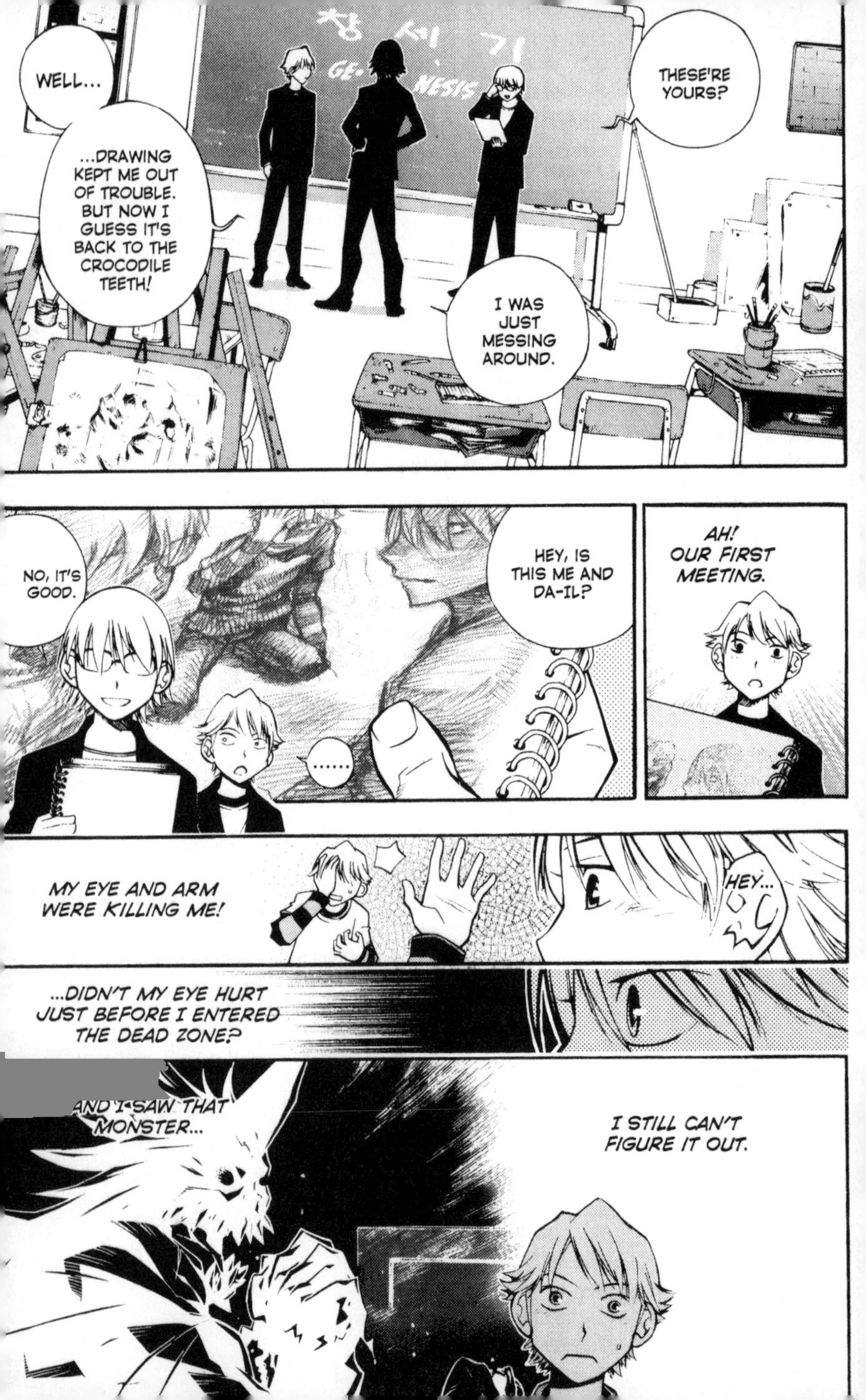

WELL...
THESE'RE YOURS?
...DRAWING KEPT ME OUT OF TROUBLE. BUT NOW I GUESS IT'S BACK TO THE CROCODILE TEETH!
I WAS JUST MESSING AROUND.
NO, IT'S GOOD.
HEY, IS THIS ME AND DA-IL?
......
AH! OUR FIRST MEETING.
MY EYE AND ARM WERE KILLING ME!
HEY...
...DIDN'T MY EYE HURT JUST BEFORE I ENTERED THE DEAD ZONE?
AND I SAW THAT MONSTER...
I STILL CAN'T FIGURE IT OUT.

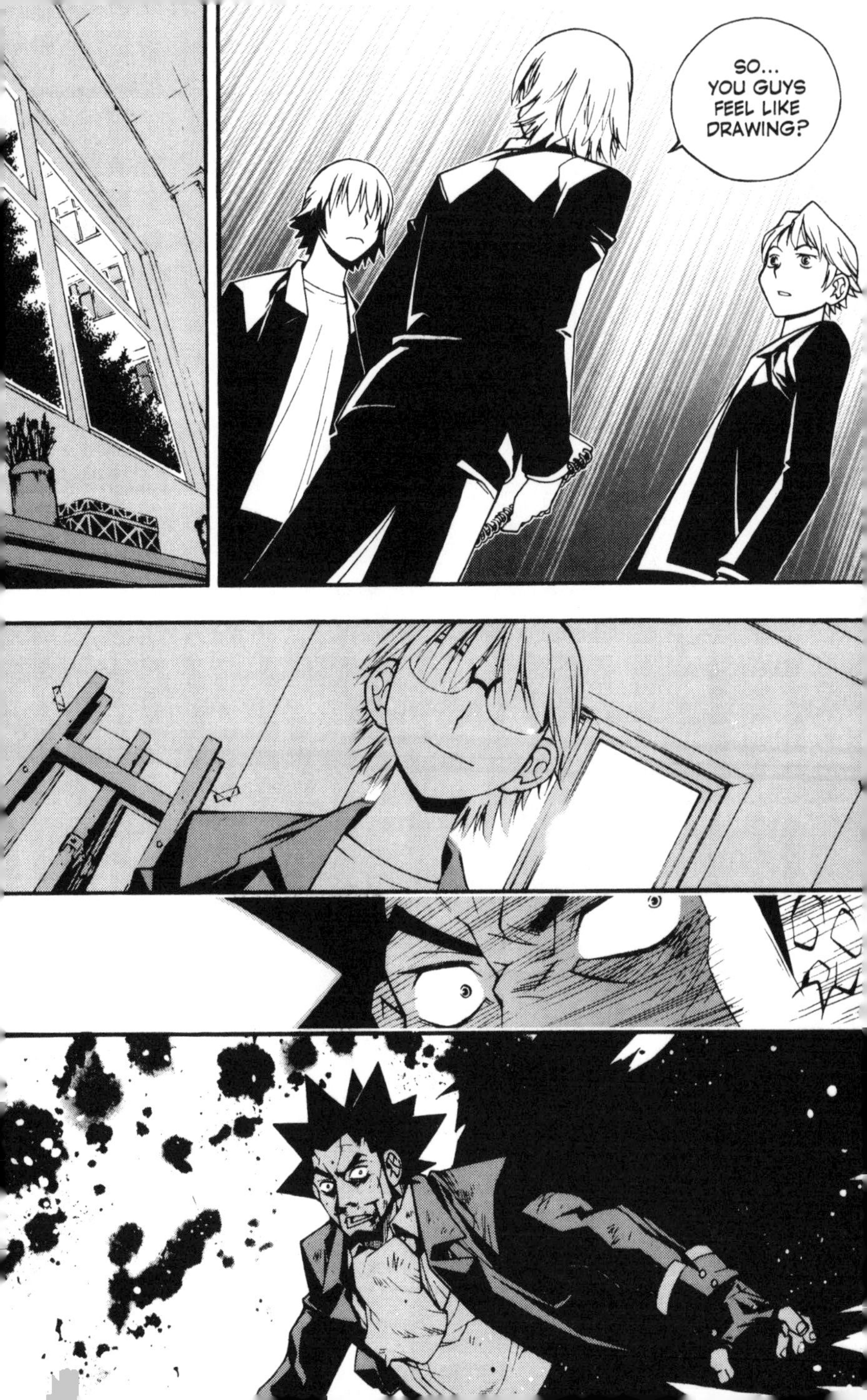
SO... YOU GUYS FEEL LIKE DRAWING?

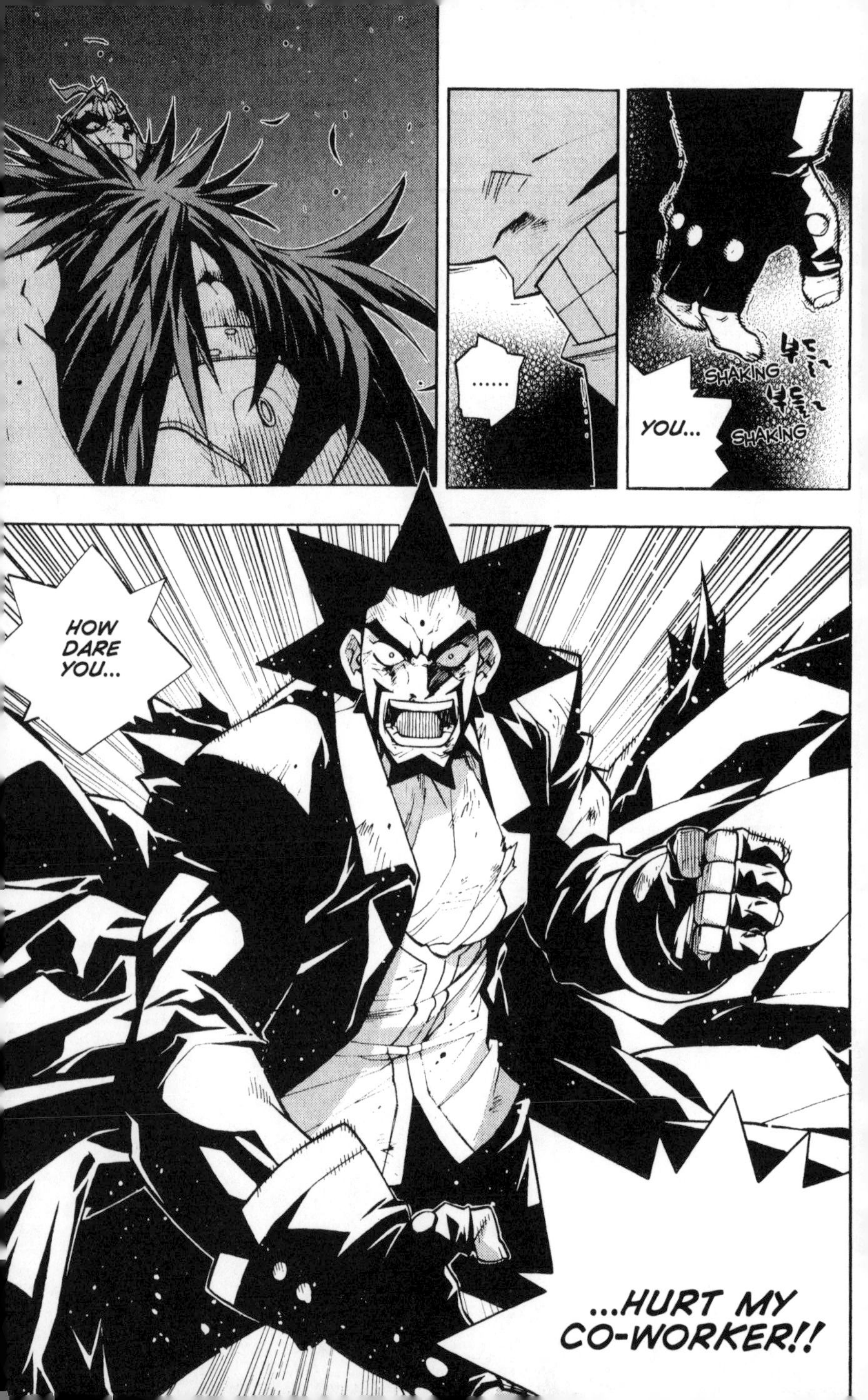

......
YOU...
SHAKING
SHAKING
HOW DARE YOU...
...HURT MY CO-WORKER!!

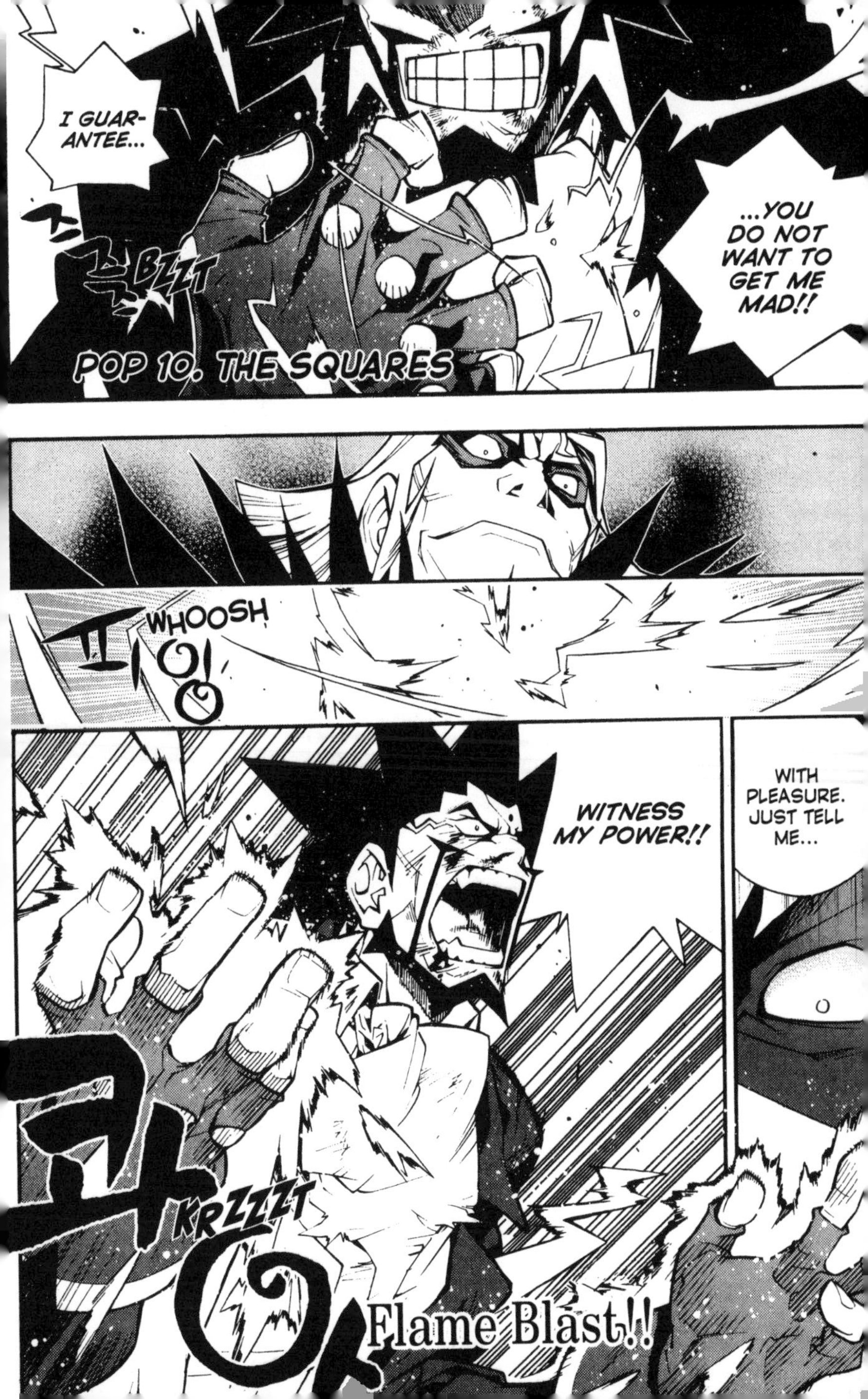
I GUAR-ANTEE...
BZZT
...YOU DO NOT WANT TO GET ME MAD!!
POP 10. THE SQUARES
WHOOSH
WITNESS MY POWER!!
KRZZZT
Flame Blast!!
WITH PLEASURE. JUST TELL ME...

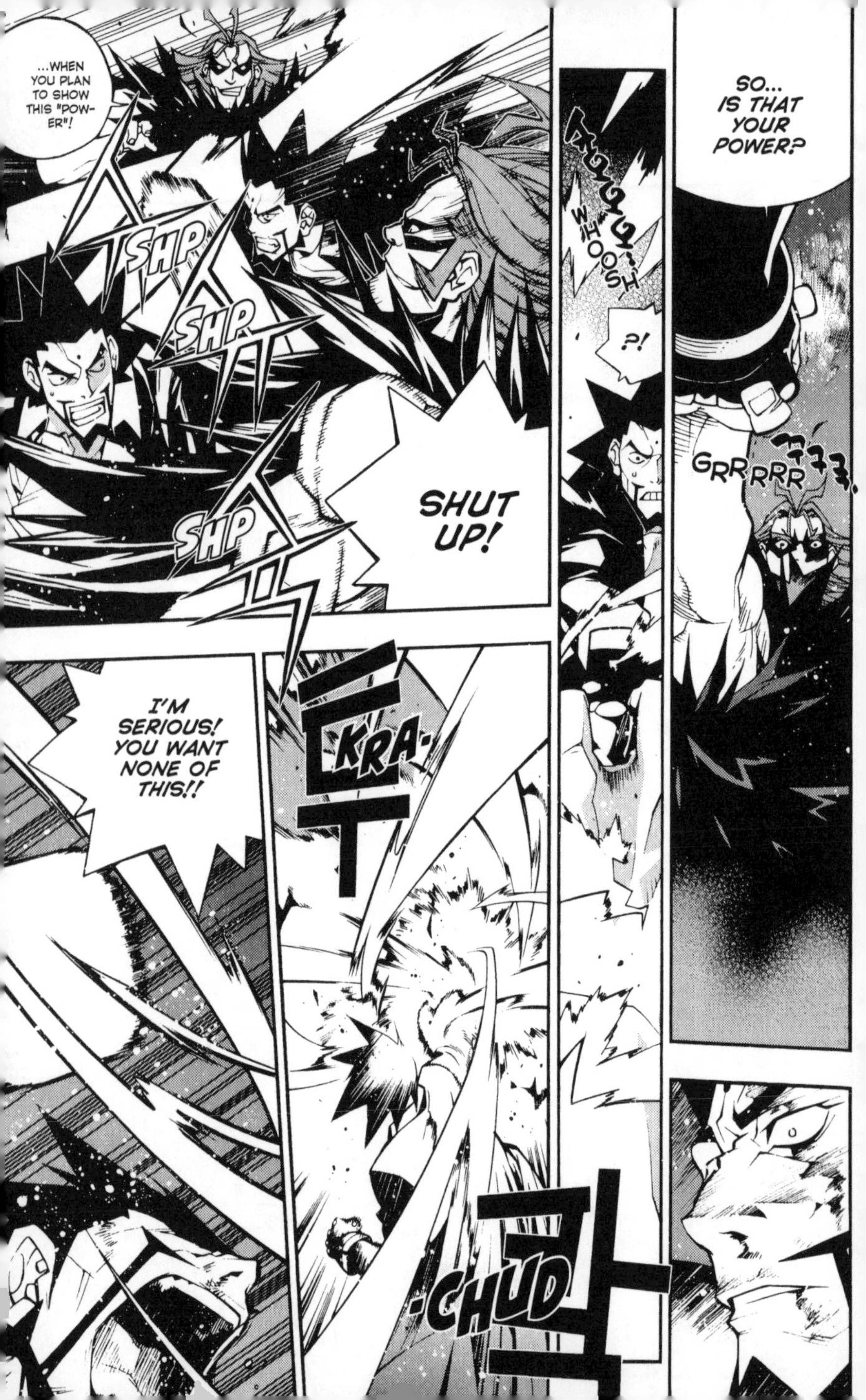
...WHEN YOU PLAN TO SHOW THIS "POW-ER"!
SHP
SHP
SHP
SHUT UP!
I'M SERIOUS! YOU WANT NONE OF THIS!!
KRA-T
-CHUD
WHOOSH
?!
SO... IS THAT YOUR POWER?
GRRRRR

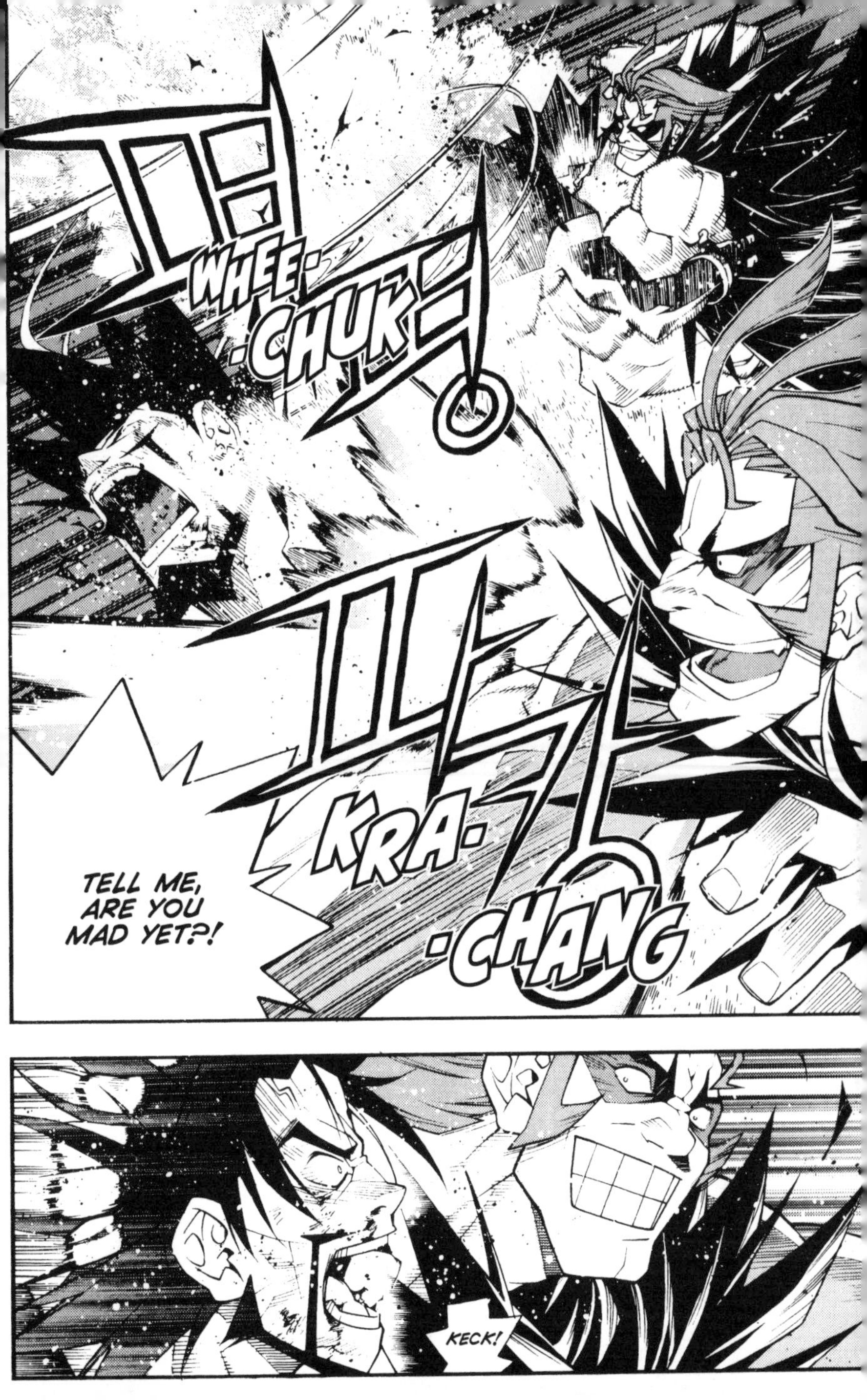
WHEE-
-CHUK
KRA-
-CHANG
TELL ME, ARE YOU MAD YET?!
KECK!

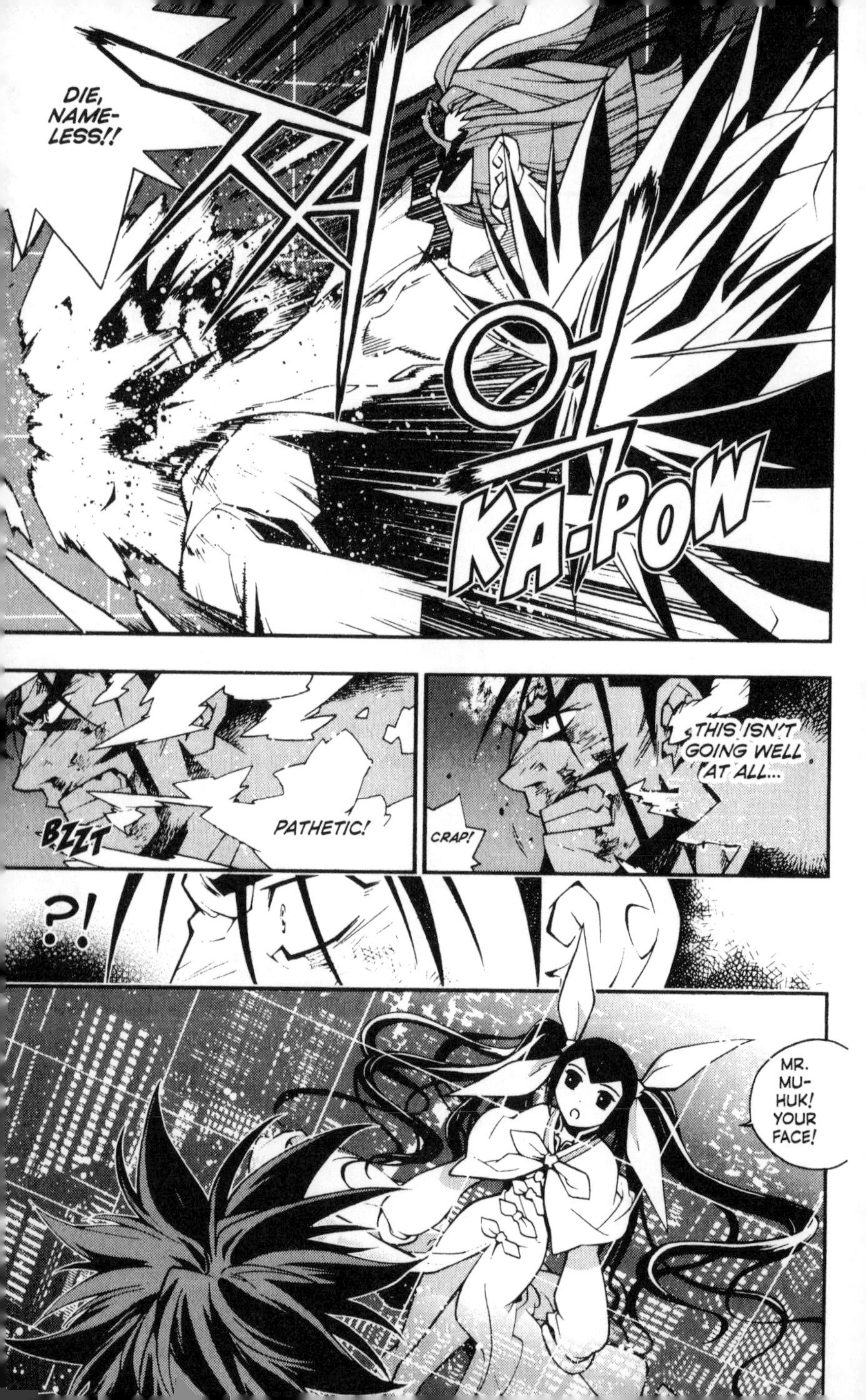
DIE, NAME-LESS!!
KA-POW
BZZT
PATHETIC!
THIS ISN'T GOING WELL AT ALL...
CRAP!
?!
MR. MU-HUK! YOUR FACE!

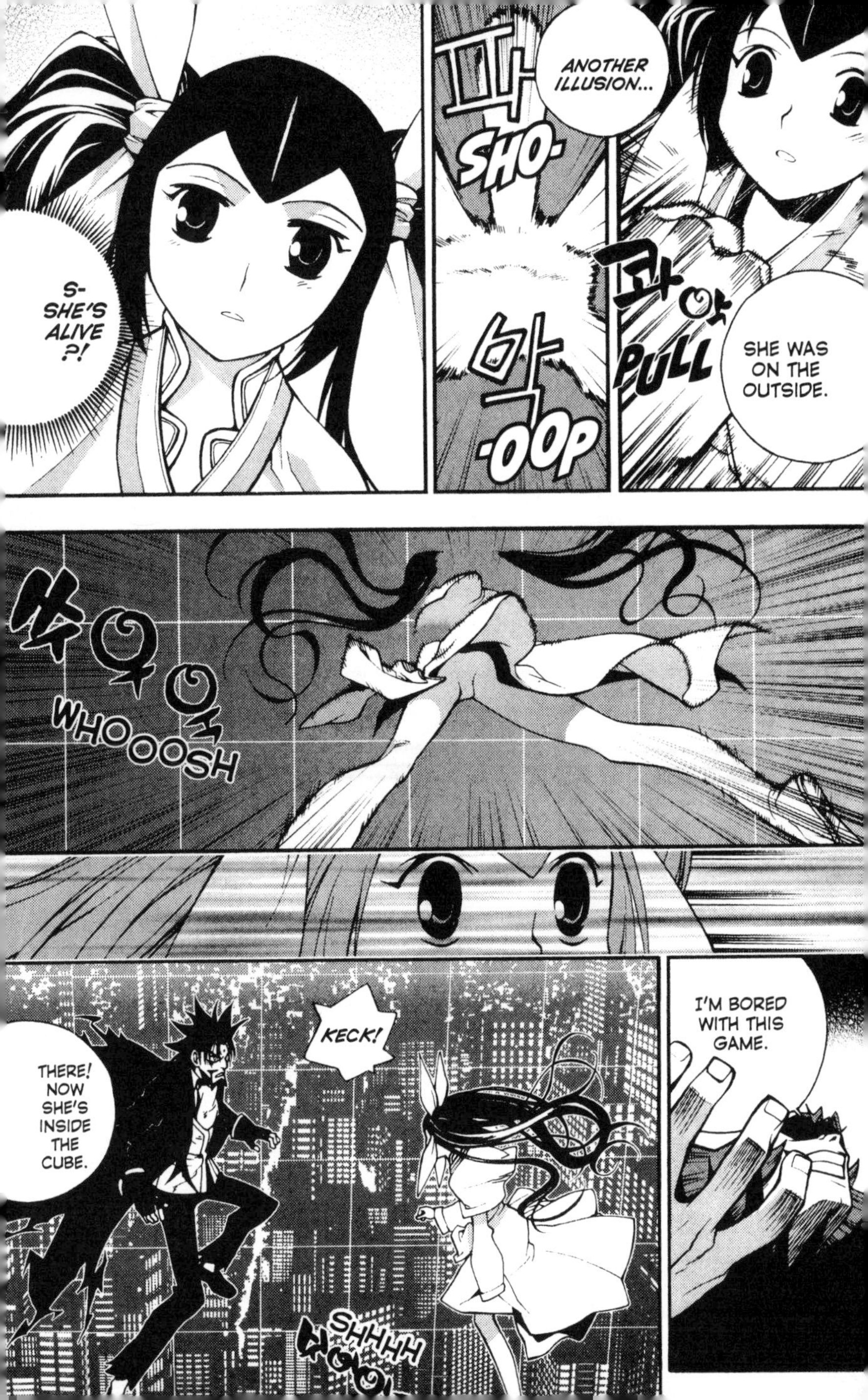
S-SHE'S ALIVE?!
ANOTHER ILLUSION...
SHO-
-OOP
PULL
SHE WAS ON THE OUTSIDE.
WHOOOSH
THERE! NOW SHE'S INSIDE THE CUBE.
KECK!
SHHHH
I'M BORED WITH THIS GAME.

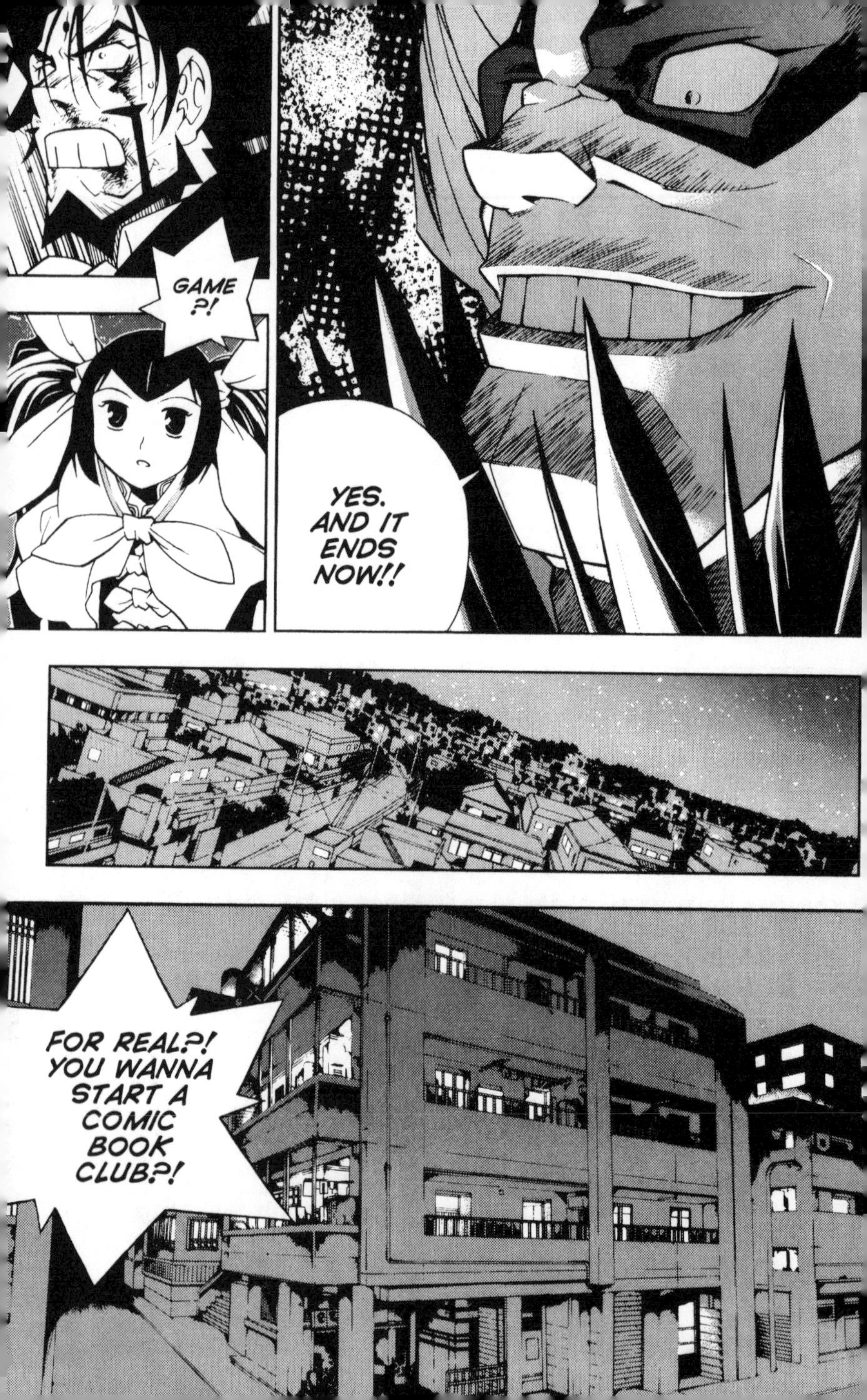
GAME ?!
YES. AND IT ENDS NOW!!
FOR REAL?! YOU WANNA START A COMIC BOOK CLUB?!

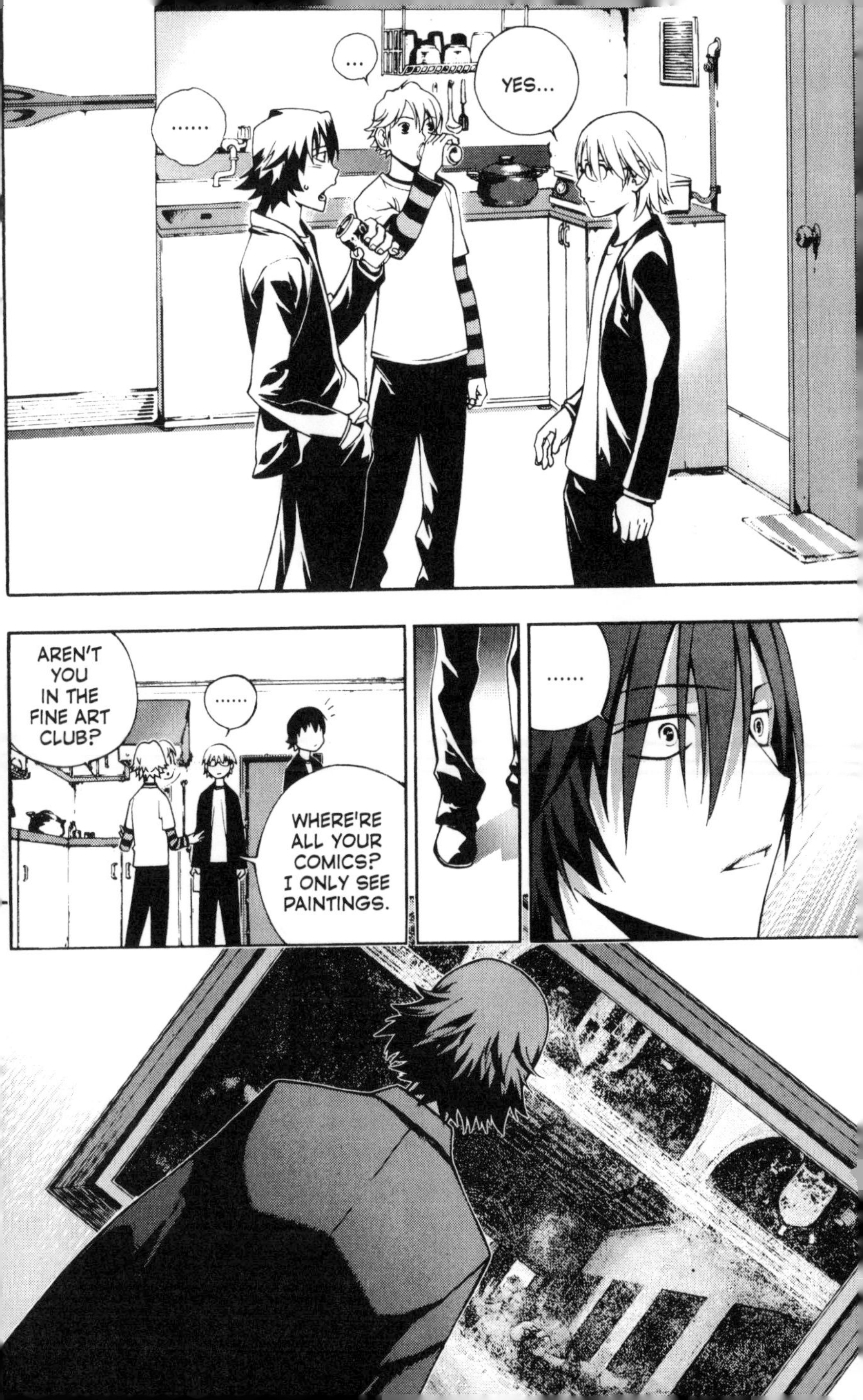
......
...
YES...
AREN'T YOU IN THE FINE ART CLUB?
......
WHERE'RE ALL YOUR COMICS? I ONLY SEE PAINTINGS.
......

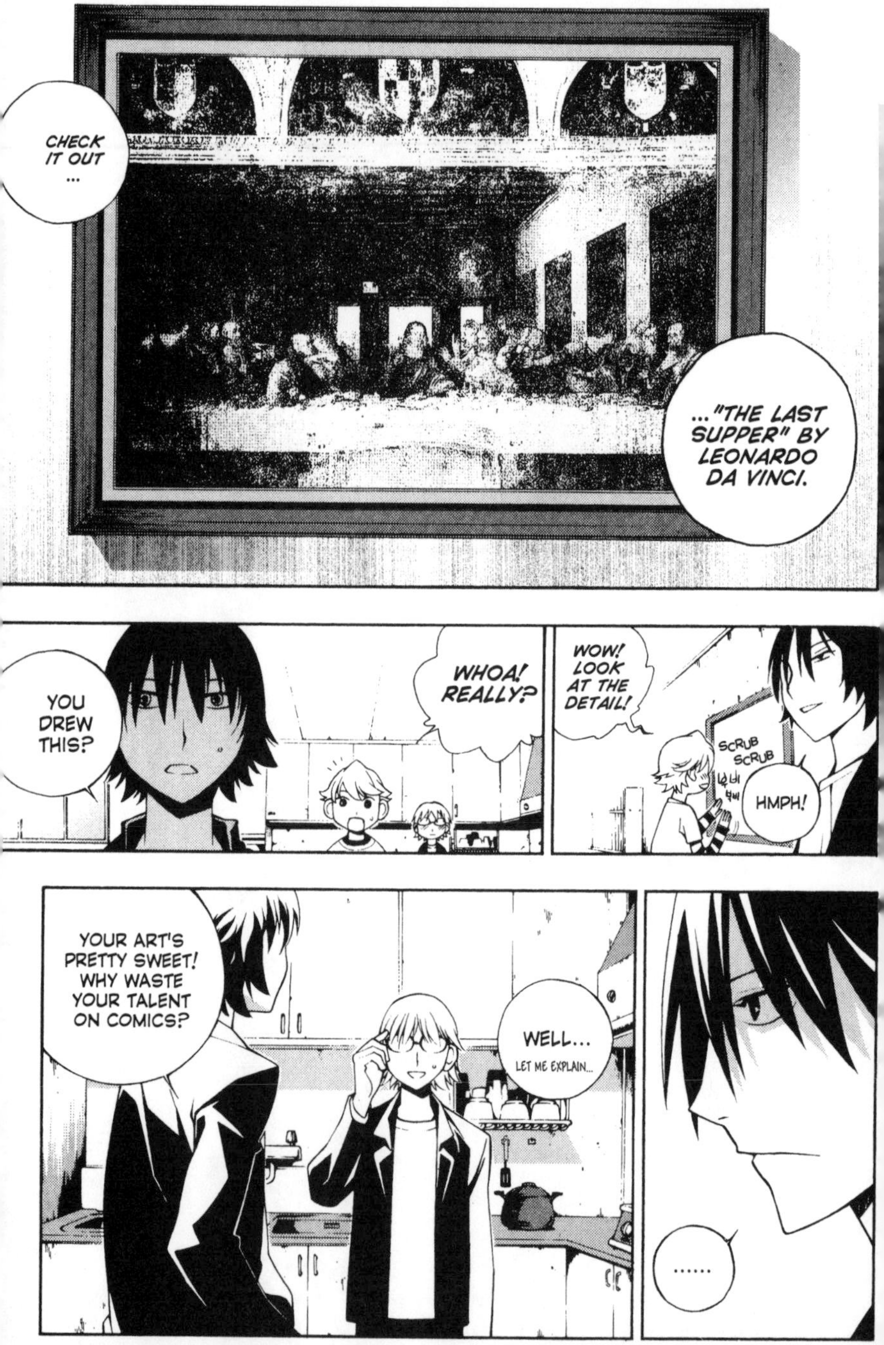
CHECK IT OUT ...
..."THE LAST SUPPER" BY LEONARDO DA VINCI.
YOU DREW THIS?
WHOA! REALLY?
WOW! LOOK AT THE DETAIL!
SCRUB SCRUB
HMPH!
YOUR ART'S PRETTY SWEET! WHY WASTE YOUR TALENT ON COMICS?
WELL...
LET ME EXPLAIN...
......

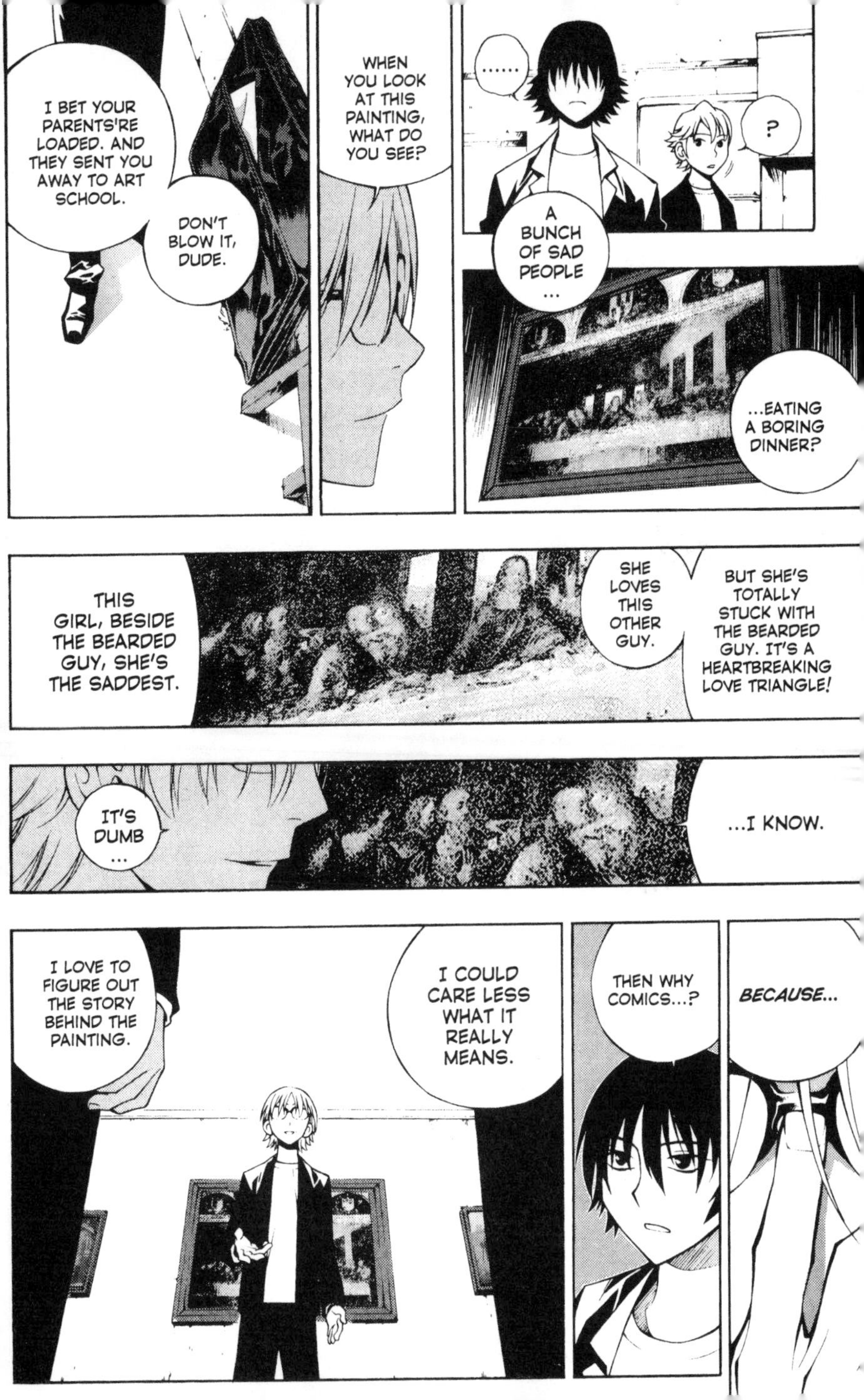
I BET YOUR PARENTS'RE LOADED. AND THEY SENT YOU AWAY TO ART SCHOOL.
DON'T BLOW IT, DUDE.
WHEN YOU LOOK AT THIS PAINTING, WHAT DO YOU SEE?
......
?
A BUNCH OF SAD PEOPLE ...
...EATING A BORING DINNER?
THIS GIRL, BESIDE THE BEARDED GUY, SHE'S THE SADDEST.
SHE LOVES THIS OTHER GUY.
BUT SHE'S TOTALLY STUCK WITH THE BEARDED GUY. IT'S A HEARTBREAKING LOVE TRIANGLE!
IT'S DUMB ...
...I KNOW.
I LOVE TO FIGURE OUT THE STORY BEHIND THE PAINTING.
I COULD CARE LESS WHAT IT REALLY MEANS.
THEN WHY COMICS...?
BECAUSE...

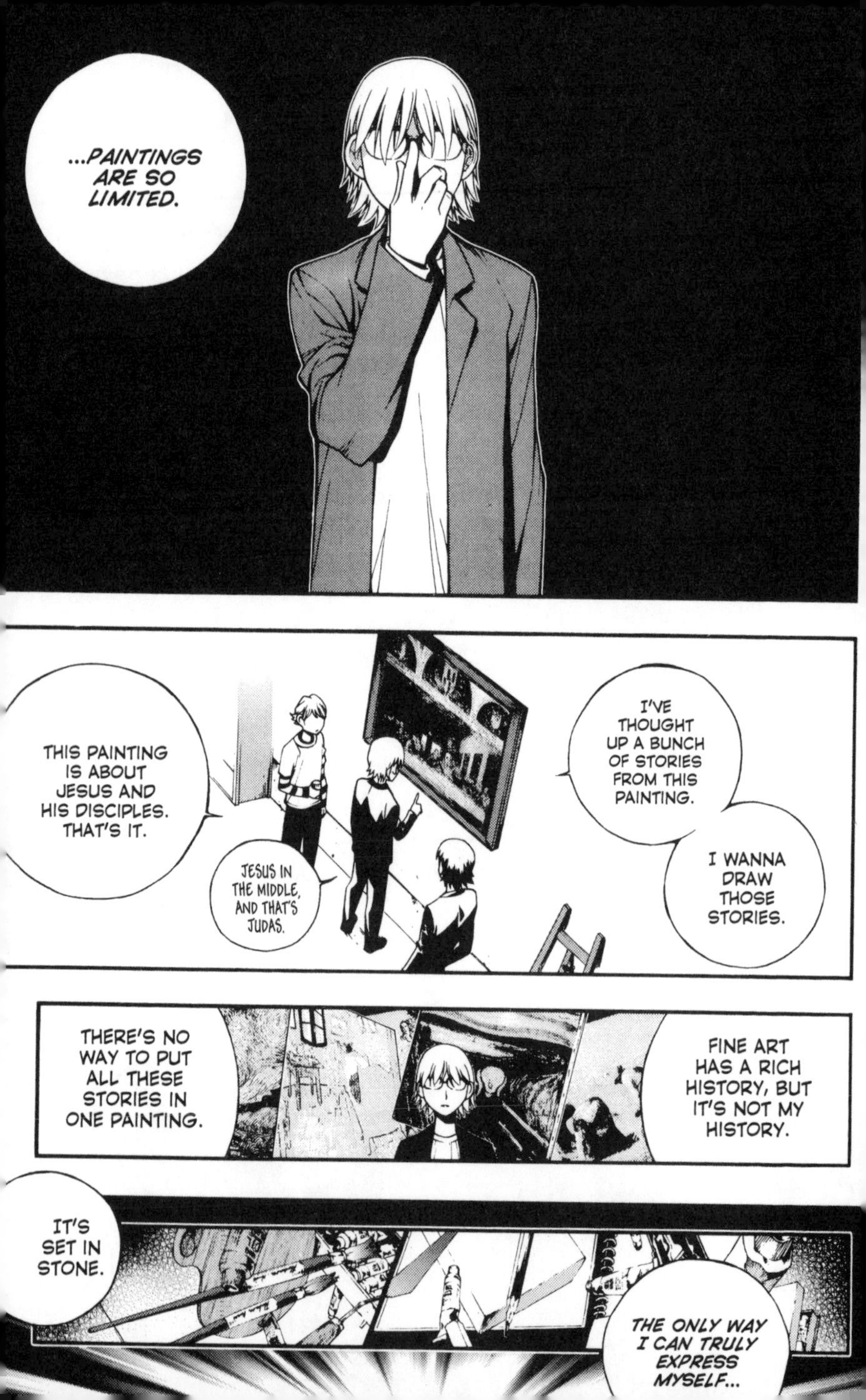
...PAINTINGS ARE SO LIMITED.
THIS PAINTING IS ABOUT JESUS AND HIS DISCIPLES. THAT'S IT.
JESUS IN THE MIDDLE, AND THAT'S JUDAS.
I'VE THOUGHT UP A BUNCH OF STORIES FROM THIS PAINTING.
I WANNA DRAW THOSE STORIES.
THERE'S NO WAY TO PUT ALL THESE STORIES IN ONE PAINTING.
FINE ART HAS A RICH HISTORY, BUT IT'S NOT MY HISTORY.
IT'S SET IN STONE.
THE ONLY WAY I CAN TRULY EXPRESS MYSELF...

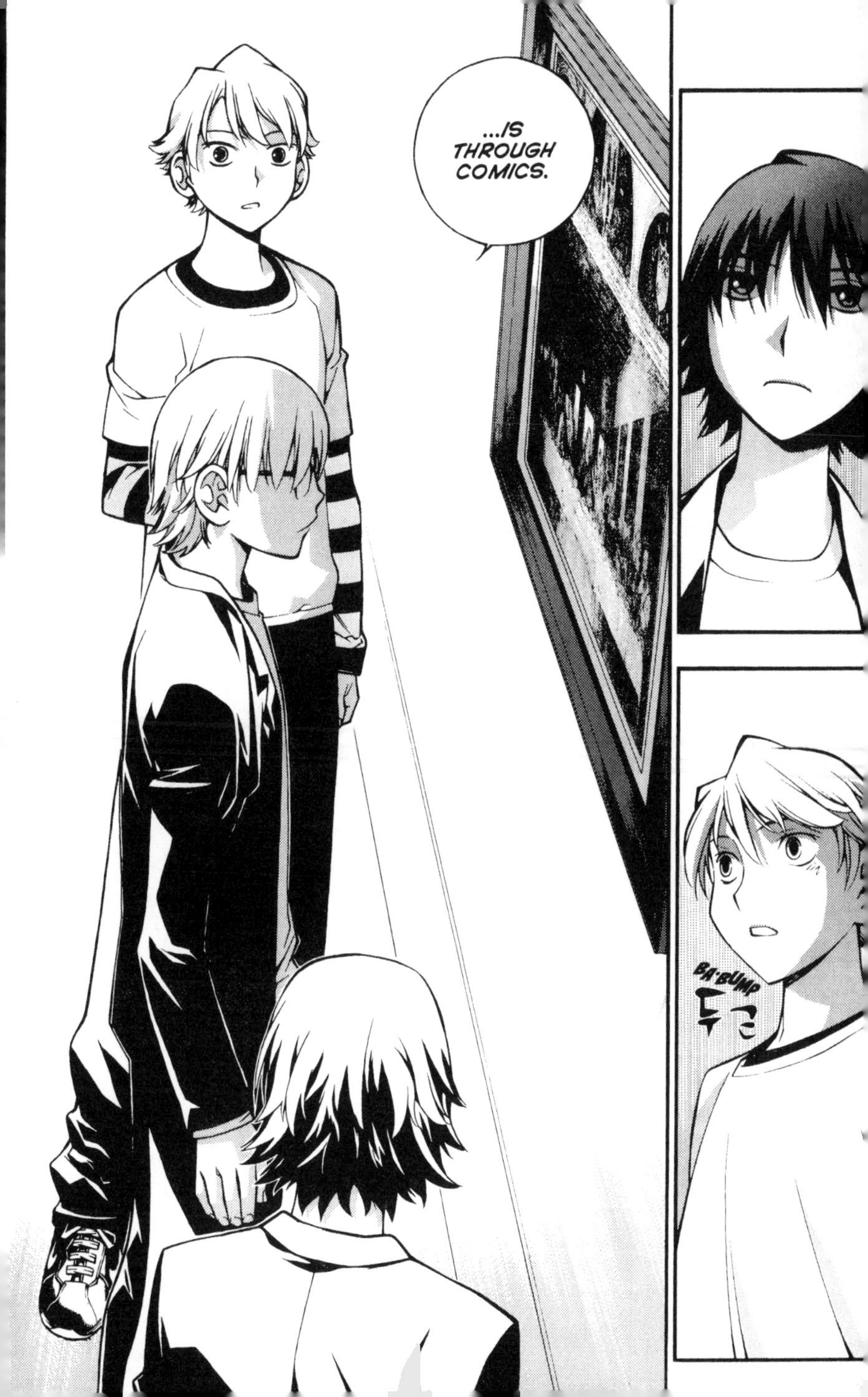
...IS THROUGH COMICS.
BA-BUMP

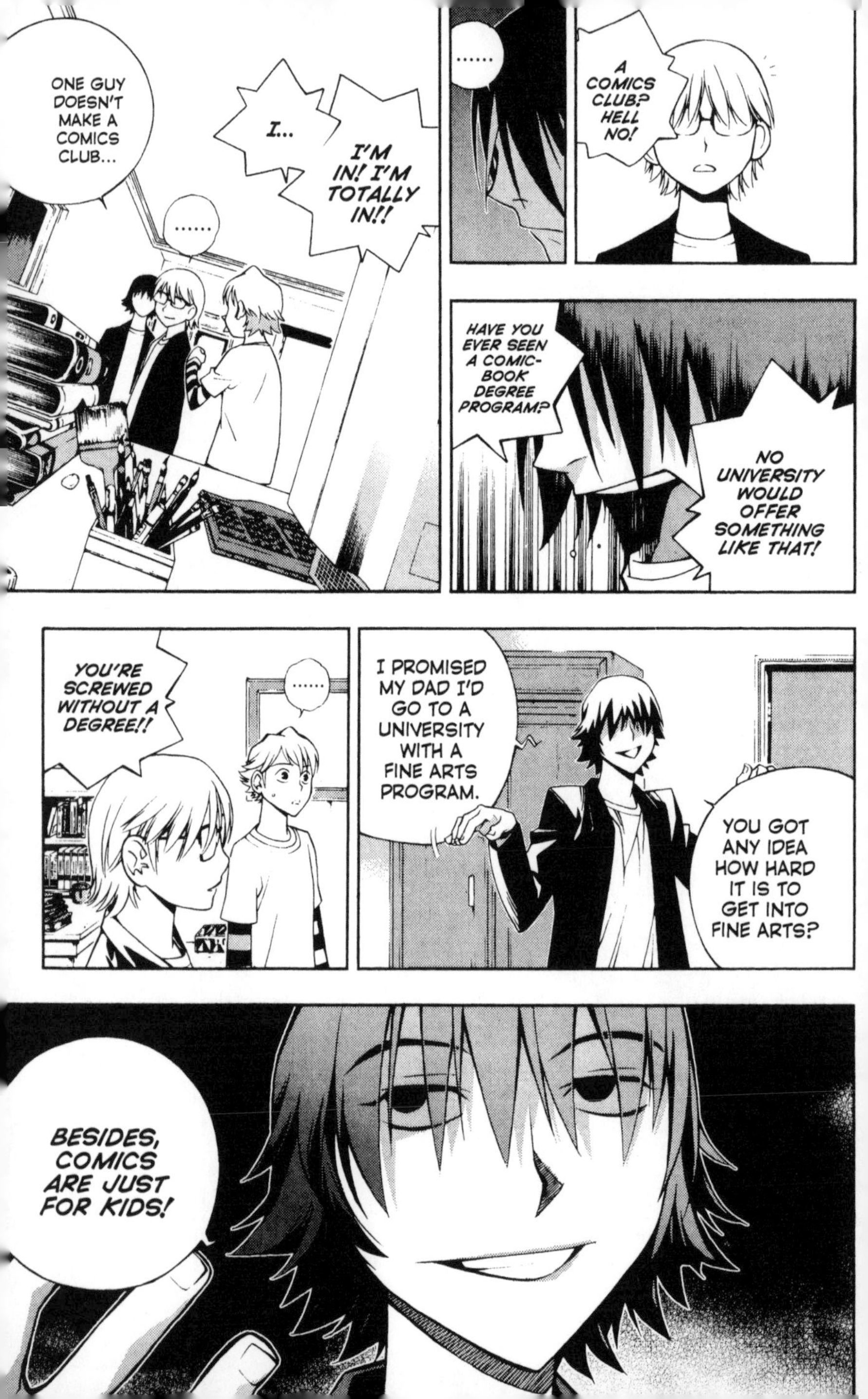
ONE GUY DOESN'T MAKE A COMICS CLUB...
I...
I'M IN! I'M TOTALLY IN!!
......
......
A COMICS CLUB? HELL NO!
HAVE YOU EVER SEEN A COMIC-BOOK DEGREE PROGRAM?
NO UNIVERSITY WOULD OFFER SOMETHING LIKE THAT!
YOU'RE SCREWED WITHOUT A DEGREE!!
......
I PROMISED MY DAD I'D GO TO A UNIVERSITY WITH A FINE ARTS PROGRAM.
YOU GOT ANY IDEA HOW HARD IT IS TO GET INTO FINE ARTS?
BESIDES, COMICS ARE JUST FOR KIDS!

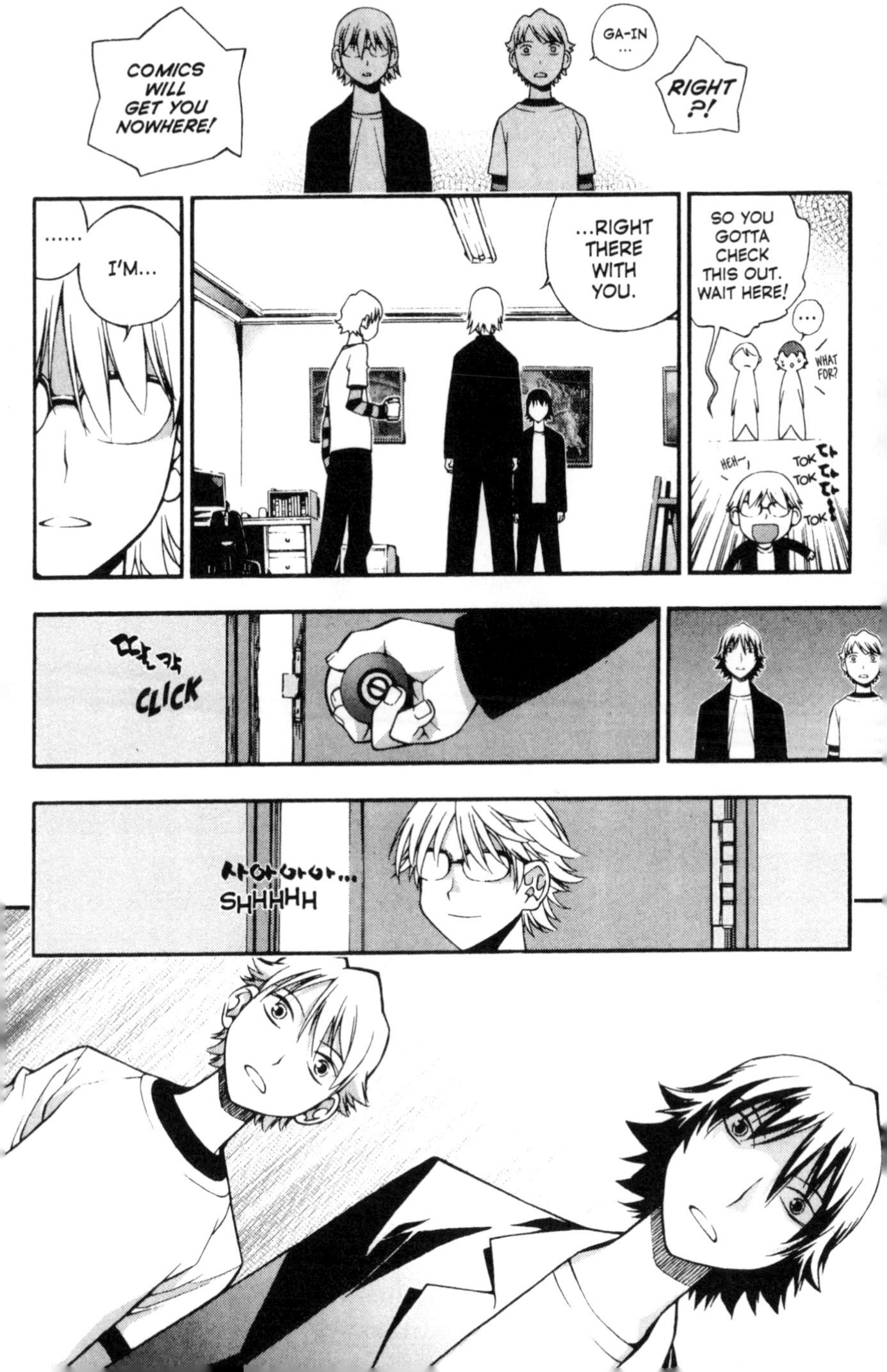
COMICS WILL GET YOU NOWHERE!
GA-IN ...
RIGHT ?!
......
I'M...
...RIGHT THERE WITH YOU.
SO YOU GOTTA CHECK THIS OUT. WAIT HERE!
...
WHAT FOR?
HEH—
TOK TOK TOK
CLICK
SHHHHH

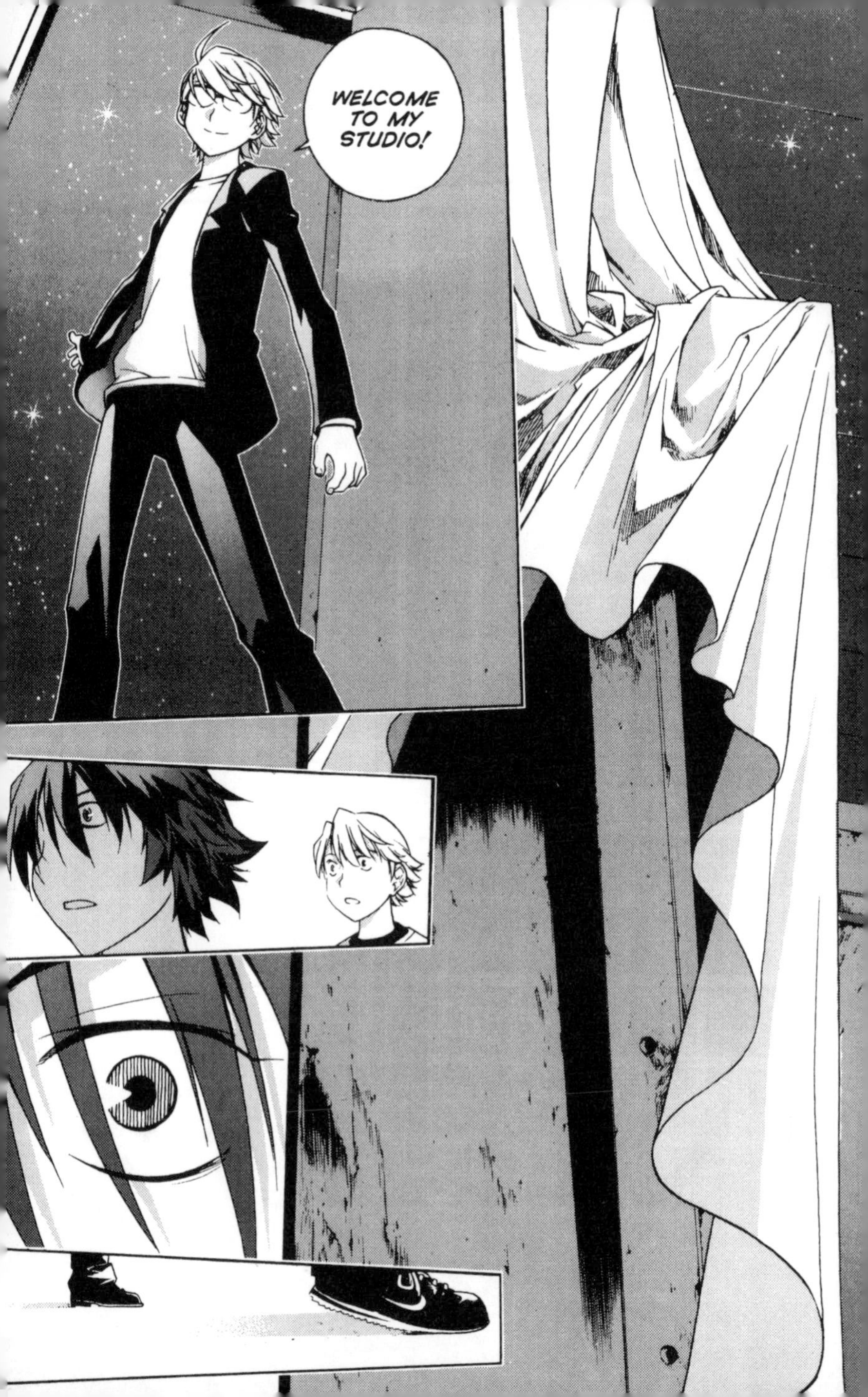
WELCOME TO MY STUDIO!

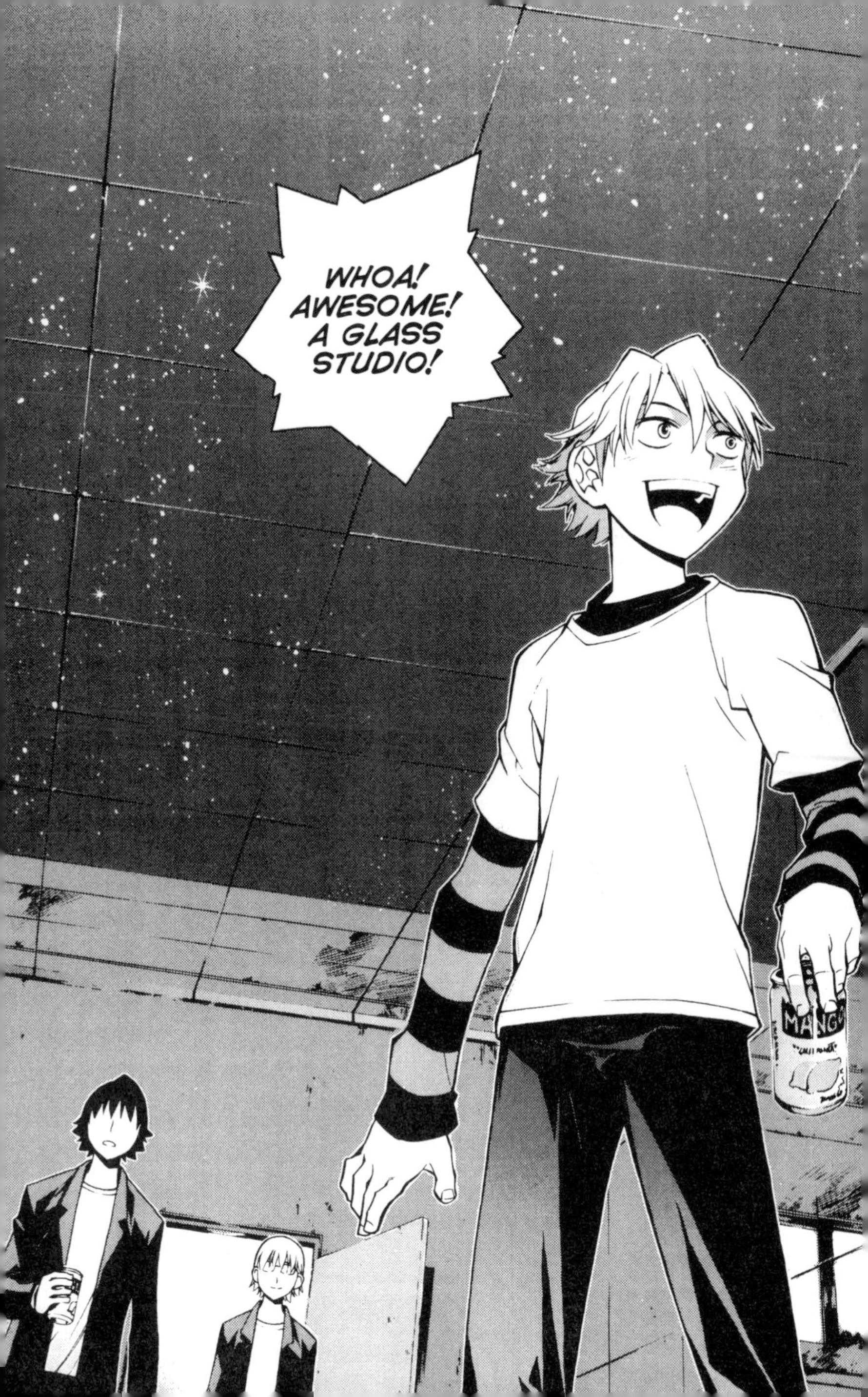
WHOA! AWESOME! A GLASS STUDIO!
MANGO

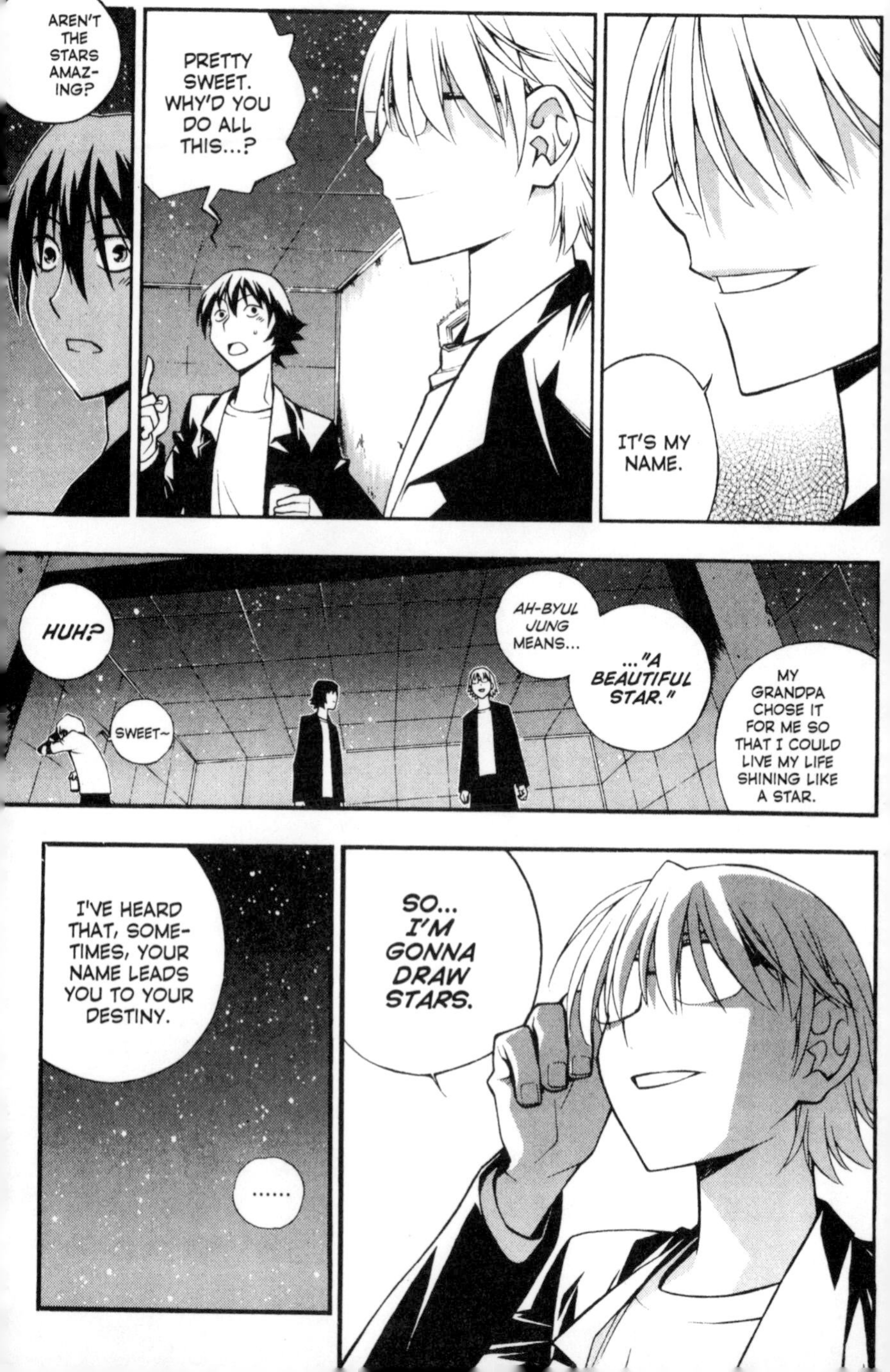
AREN'T THE STARS AMAZ-ING?
PRETTY SWEET. WHY'D YOU DO ALL THIS...?
IT'S MY NAME.
HUH?
SWEET~
AH-BYUL JUNG MEANS...
..."A BEAUTIFUL STAR."
MY GRANDPA CHOSE IT FOR ME SO THAT I COULD LIVE MY LIFE SHINING LIKE A STAR.
I'VE HEARD THAT, SOME-TIMES, YOUR NAME LEADS YOU TO YOUR DESTINY.
......
SO... I'M GONNA DRAW STARS.

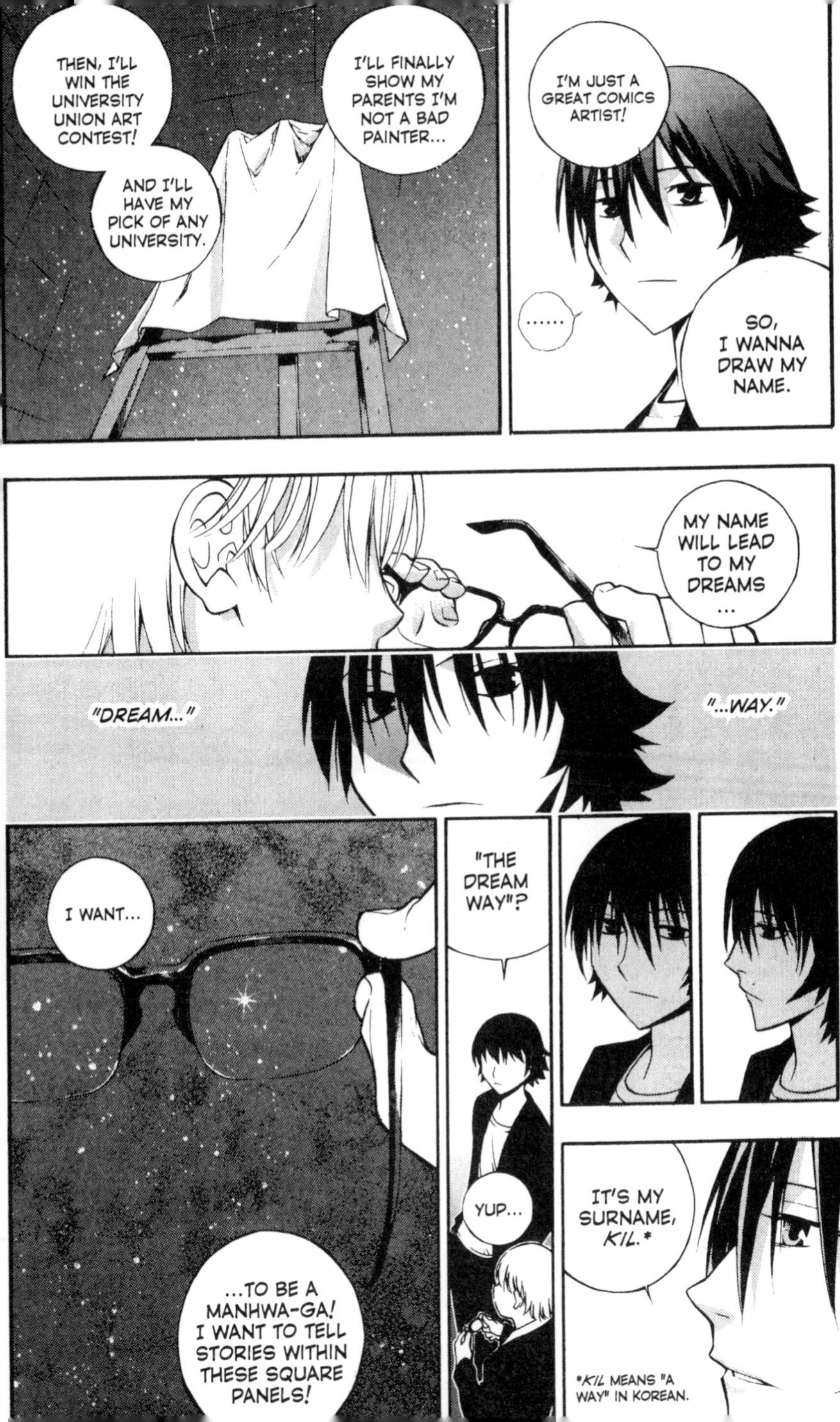
THEN, I'LL WIN THE UNIVERSITY UNION ART CONTEST!
AND I'LL HAVE MY PICK OF ANY UNIVERSITY.
I'LL FINALLY SHOW MY PARENTS I'M NOT A BAD PAINTER...
I'M JUST A GREAT COMICS ARTIST!
......
SO, I WANNA DRAW MY NAME.
MY NAME WILL LEAD TO MY DREAMS ...
"DREAM..."
"...WAY."
I WANT...
...TO BE A MANHWA-GA! I WANT TO TELL STORIES WITHIN THESE SQUARE PANELS!
"THE DREAM WAY"?
YUP...
IT'S MY SURNAME, KIL.*
*KIL MEANS "A WAY" IN KOREAN.

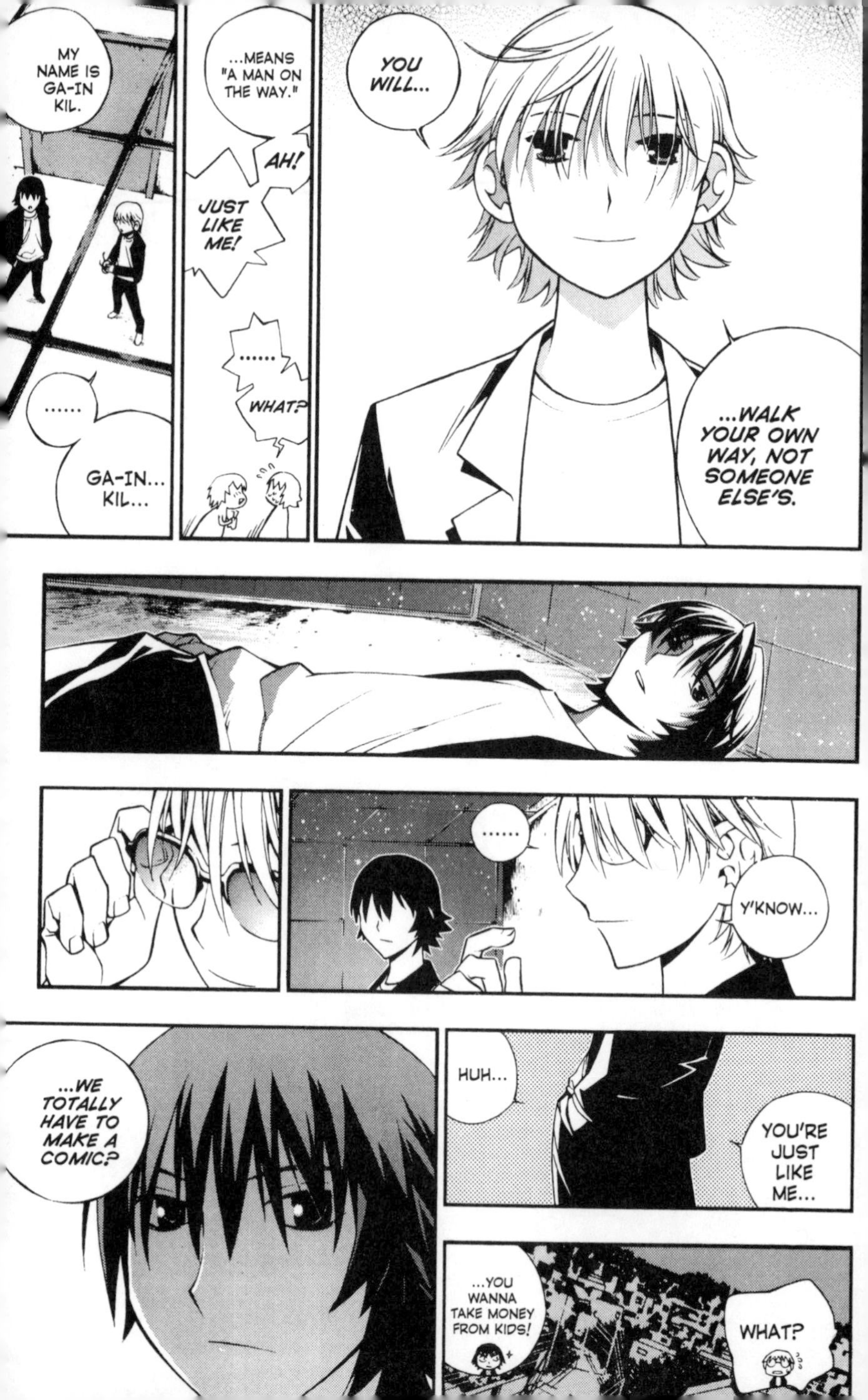
MY NAME IS GA-IN KIL.
......
GA-IN... KIL...
...MEANS "A MAN ON THE WAY."
AH!
JUST LIKE ME!
......
WHAT?
YOU WILL...
...WALK YOUR OWN WAY, NOT SOMEONE ELSE'S.
......
Y'KNOW...
...WE TOTALLY HAVE TO MAKE A COMIC?
HUH...
YOU'RE JUST LIKE ME...
...YOU WANNA TAKE MONEY FROM KIDS!
WHAT?

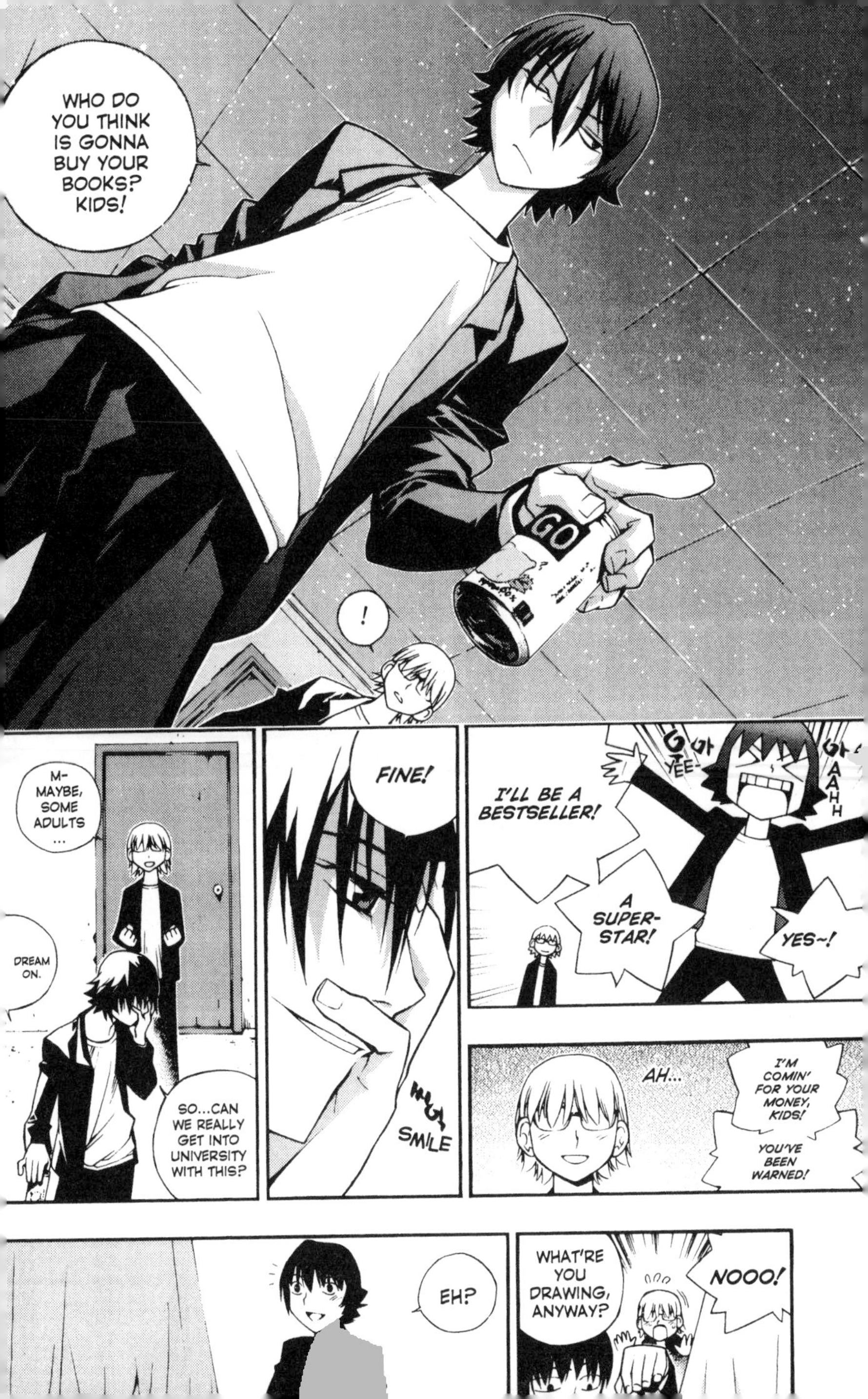
WHO DO YOU THINK IS GONNA BUY YOUR BOOKS? KIDS!
!
M-MAYBE, SOME ADULTS ...
DREAM ON.
SO...CAN WE REALLY GET INTO UNIVERSITY WITH THIS?
FINE!
SMILE
YEE-
AAAHH
I'LL BE A BESTSELLER!
A SUPER-STAR!
YES~!
AH...
I'M COMIN' FOR YOUR MONEY, KIDS!
YOU'VE BEEN WARNED!
EH?
WHAT'RE YOU DRAWING, ANYWAY?
NOOO!

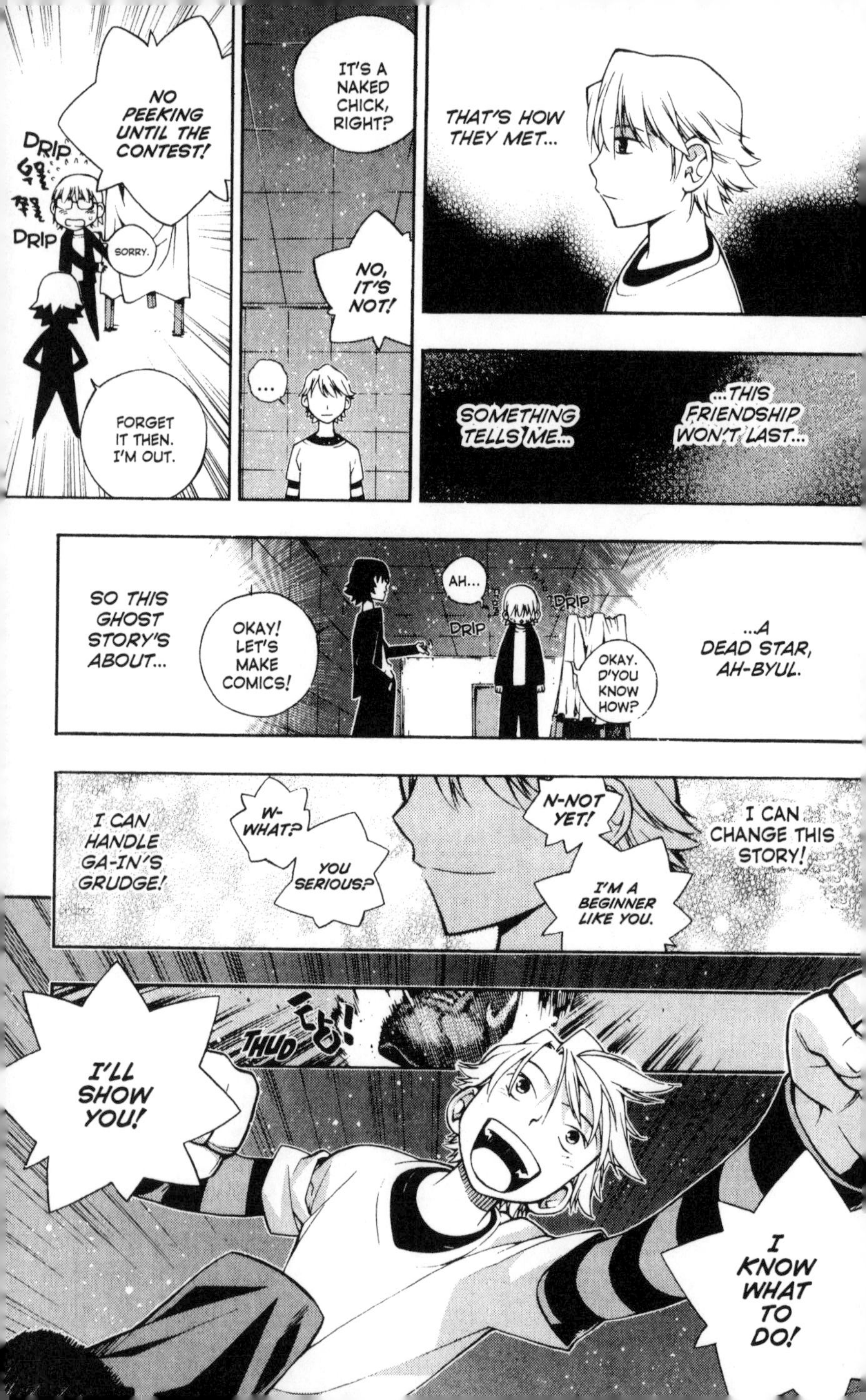
NO PEEKING UNTIL THE CONTEST!
DRIP
DRIP
SORRY.
FORGET IT THEN. I'M OUT.
IT'S A NAKED CHICK, RIGHT?
NO, IT'S NOT!
...
THAT'S HOW THEY MET...
SOMETHING TELLS ME...
...THIS FRIENDSHIP WON'T LAST...
SO THIS GHOST STORY'S ABOUT...
OKAY! LET'S MAKE COMICS!
AH...
DRIP
DRIP
OKAY. D'YOU KNOW HOW?
...A DEAD STAR, AH-BYUL.
I CAN HANDLE GA-IN'S GRUDGE!
W-WHAT?
YOU SERIOUS?
N-NOT YET!
I'M A BEGINNER LIKE YOU.
I CAN CHANGE THIS STORY!
I'LL SHOW YOU!
THUD
I KNOW WHAT TO DO!

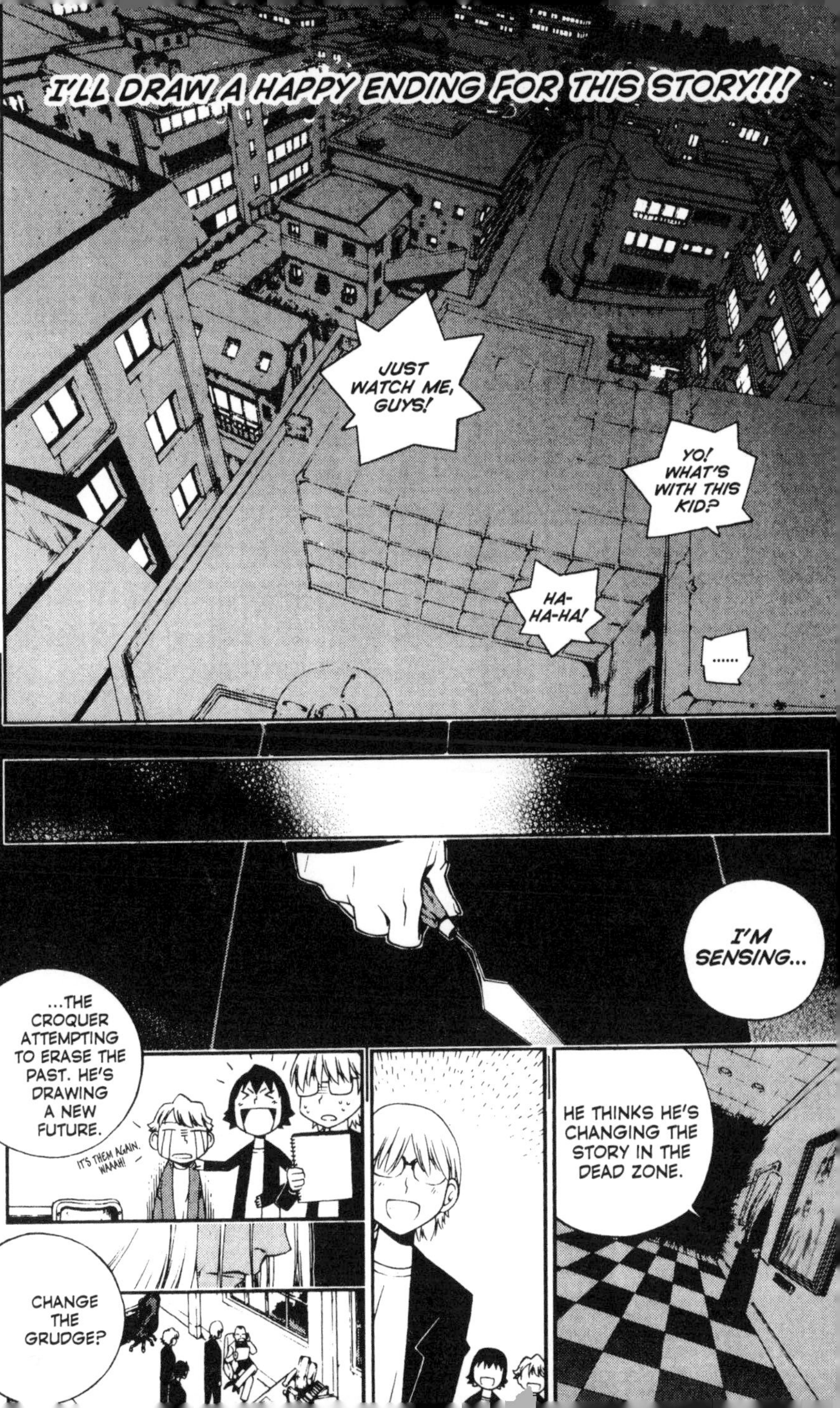
I'LL DRAW A HAPPY ENDING FOR THIS STORY!!!
JUST WATCH ME, GUYS!
YO! WHAT'S WITH THIS KID?
HA-HA-HA!
......
I'M SENSING...
...THE CROQUER ATTEMPTING TO ERASE THE PAST. HE'S DRAWING A NEW FUTURE.
HE THINKS HE'S CHANGING THE STORY IN THE DEAD ZONE.
IT'S THEM AGAIN. WAAAH!
CHANGE THE GRUDGE?

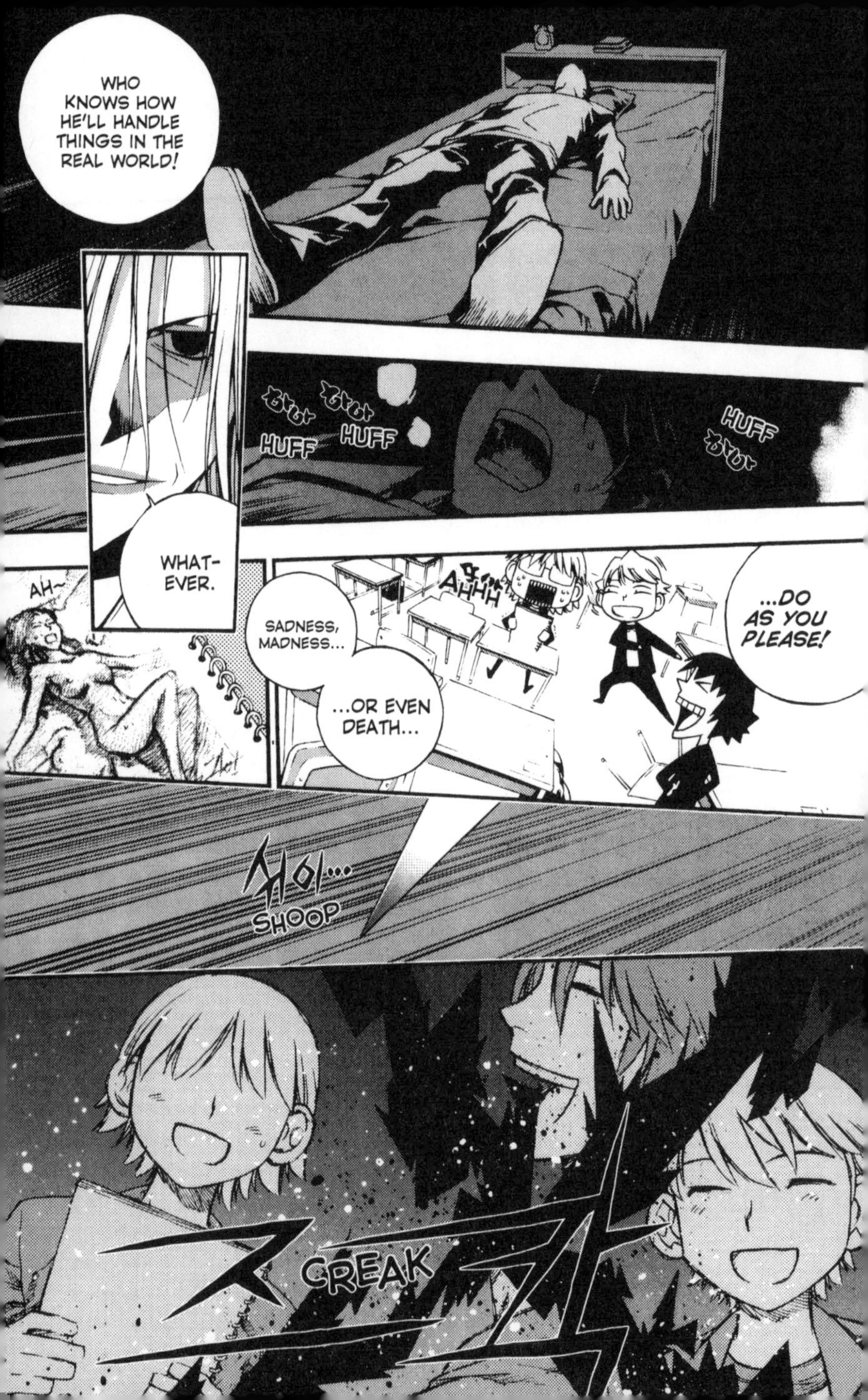
WHO KNOWS HOW HE'LL HANDLE THINGS IN THE REAL WORLD!
WHAT-EVER.
HUFF
HUFF
HUFF
AH~
SADNESS, MADNESS...
...OR EVEN DEATH...
AHHH
...DO AS YOU PLEASE!
SHOOP
CREAK

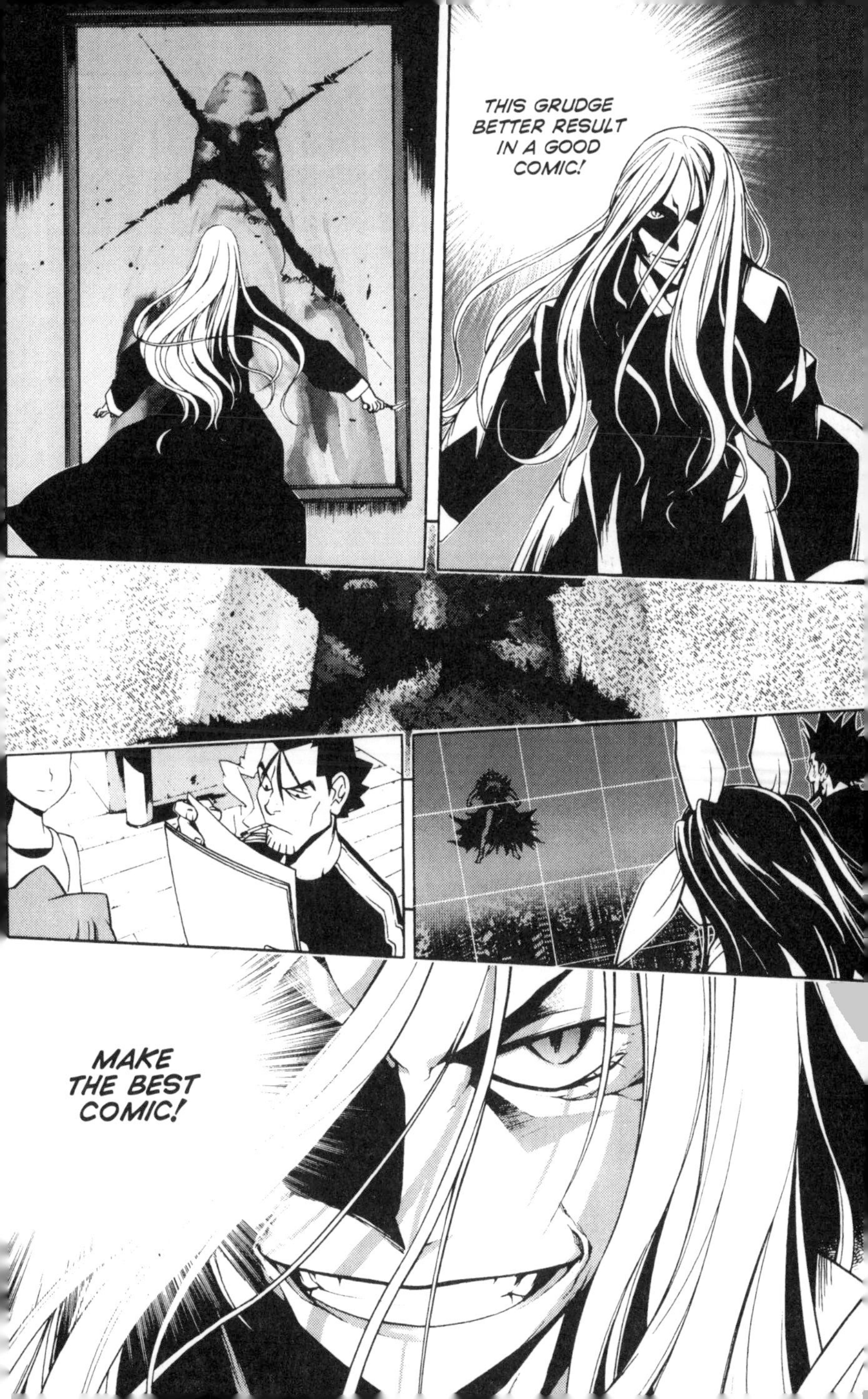
THIS GRUDGE BETTER RESULT IN A GOOD COMIC!
MAKE THE BEST COMIC!

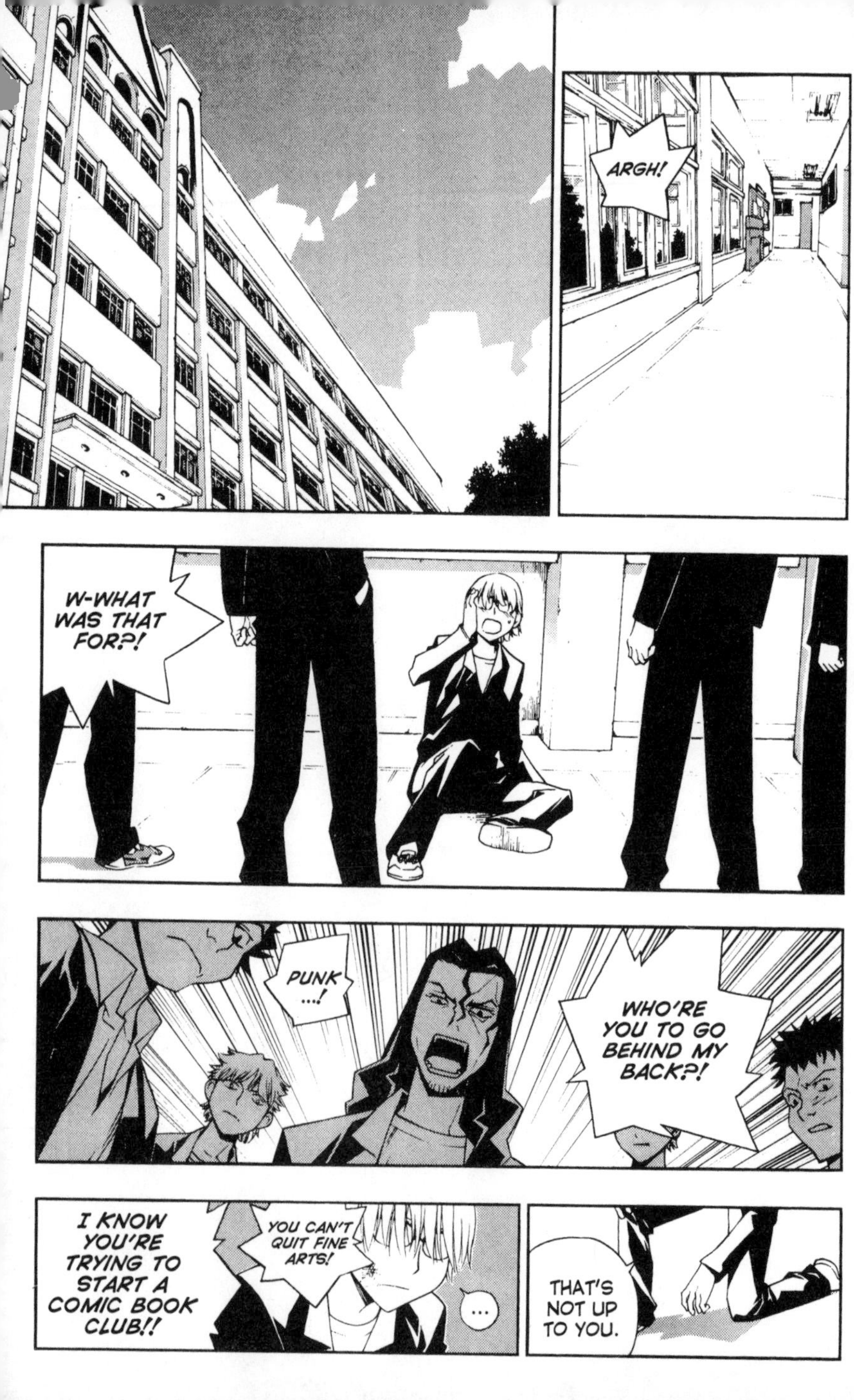
ARGH!
W-WHAT WAS THAT FOR?!
PUNK ...!
WHO'RE YOU TO GO BEHIND MY BACK?!
I KNOW YOU'RE TRYING TO START A COMIC BOOK CLUB!!
YOU CAN'T QUIT FINE ARTS!
...
THAT'S NOT UP TO YOU.

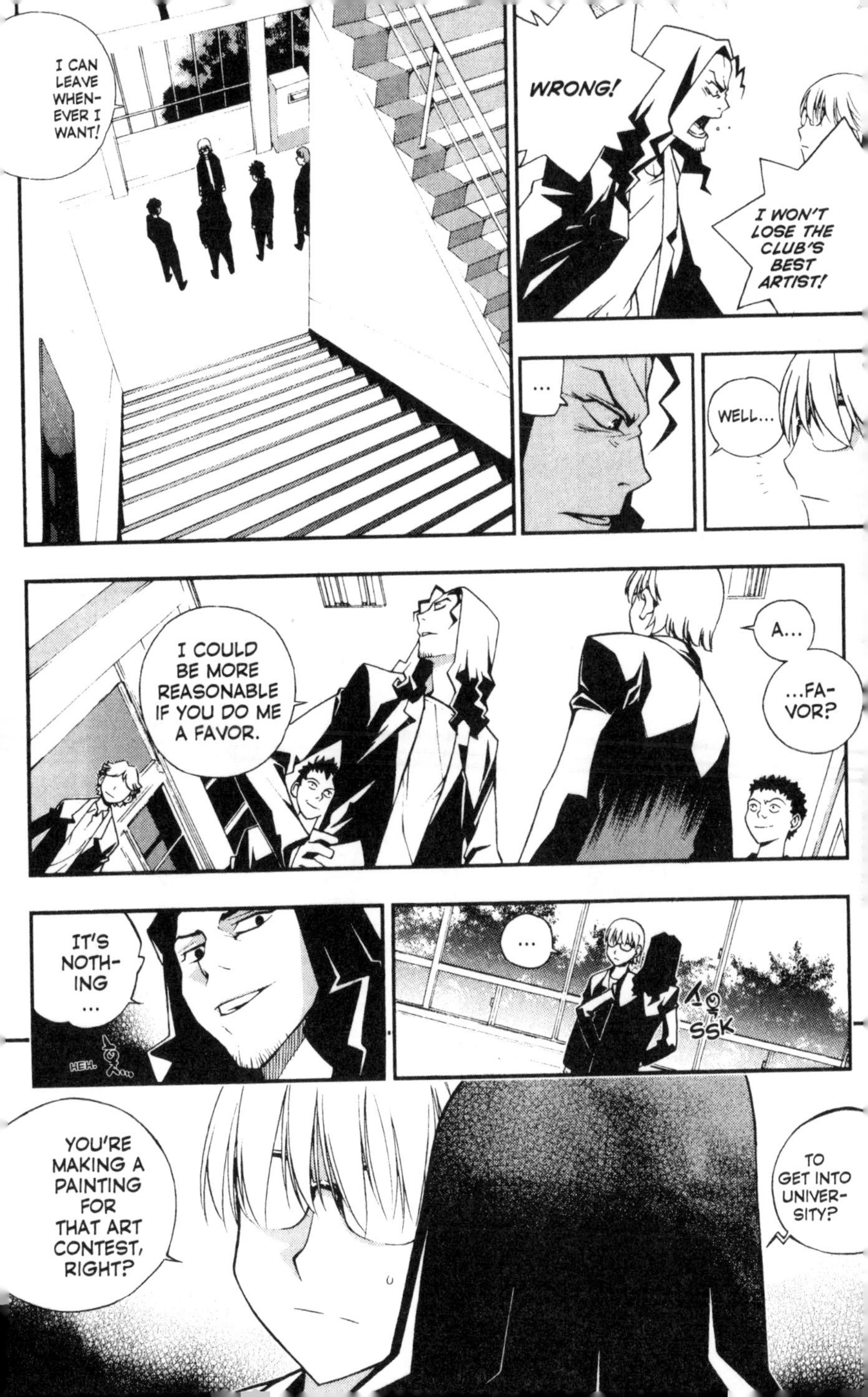
I CAN LEAVE WHENEVER I WANT!
WRONG!
I WON'T LOSE THE CLUB'S BEST ARTIST!
...
WELL...
I COULD BE MORE REASONABLE IF YOU DO ME A FAVOR.
A...
...FAVOR?
IT'S NOTHING...
HEH.
...
SSK
YOU'RE MAKING A PAINTING FOR THAT ART CONTEST, RIGHT?
TO GET INTO UNIVERSITY?

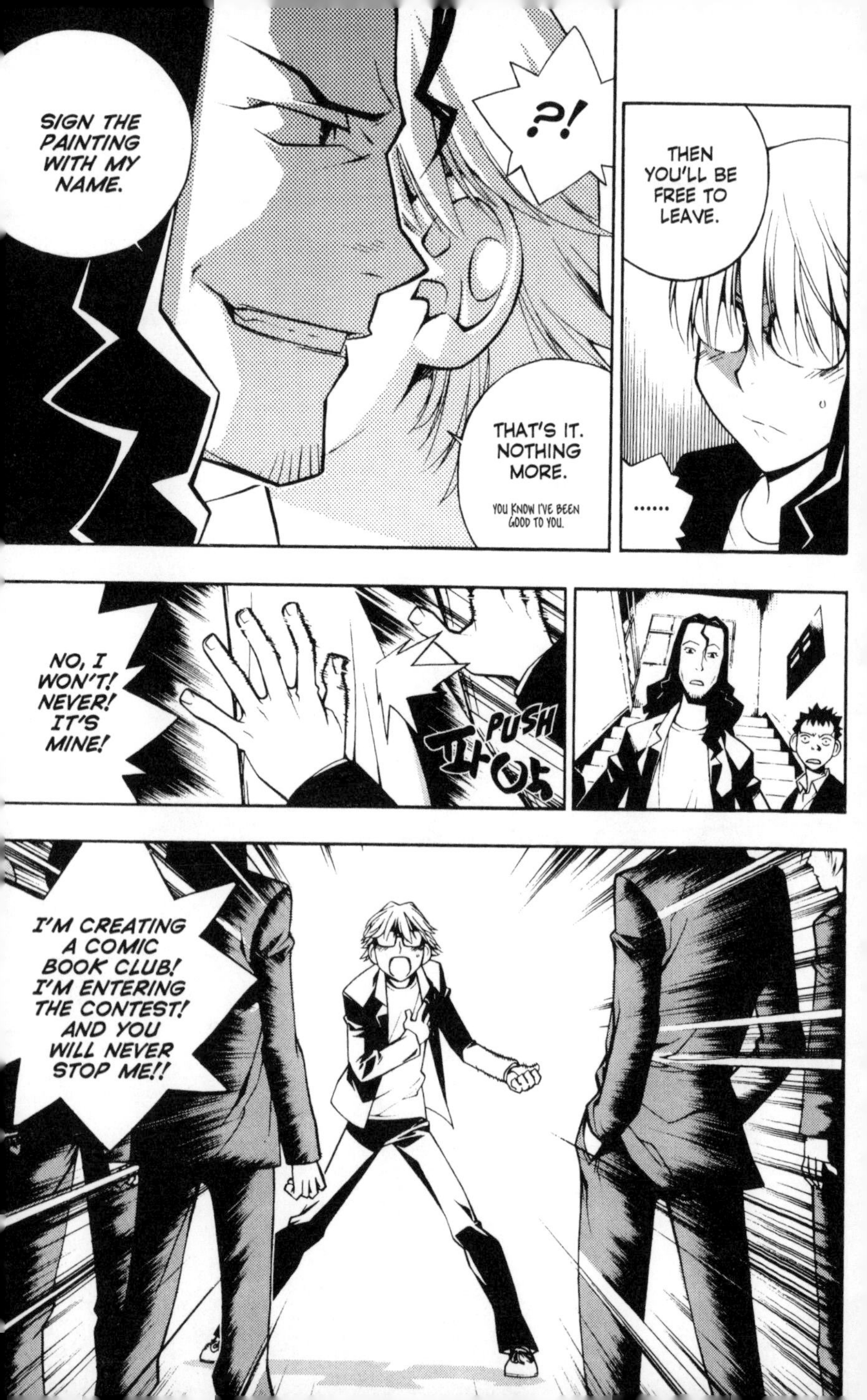
SIGN THE PAINTING WITH MY NAME.
?!
THAT'S IT. NOTHING MORE.
YOU KNOW I'VE BEEN GOOD TO YOU.
THEN YOU'LL BE FREE TO LEAVE.
......
NO, I WON'T! NEVER! IT'S MINE!
PUSH
파앗
I'M CREATING A COMIC BOOK CLUB! I'M ENTERING THE CONTEST! AND YOU WILL NEVER STOP ME!!

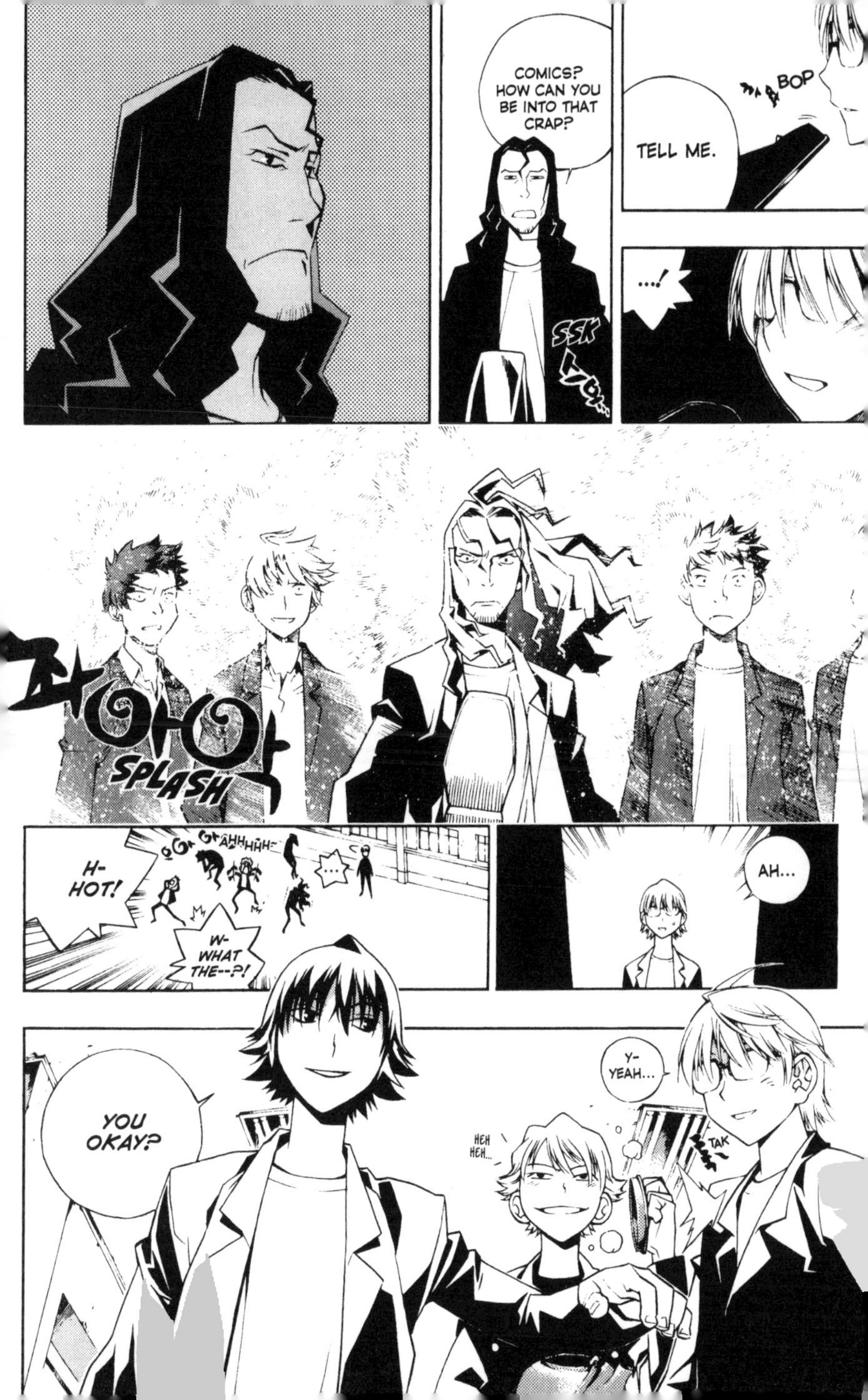

COMICS? HOW CAN YOU BE INTO THAT CRAP?
SSK
BOP
TELL ME.
...!
SPLASH
H-HOT!
...
W-WHAT THE--?!
AH...
YOU OKAY?
HEH HEH...
Y-YEAH...
TAK

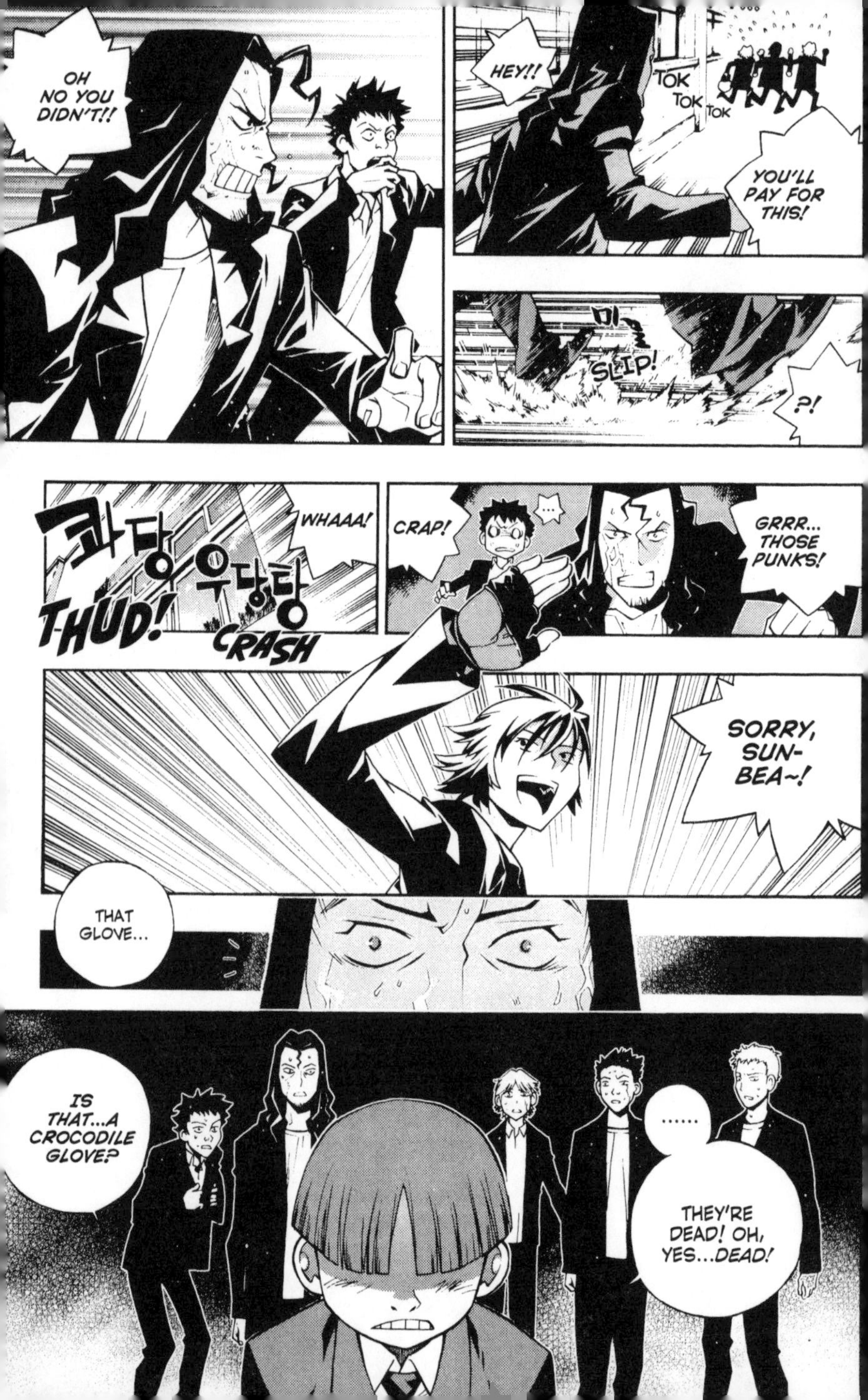
OH NO YOU DIDN'T!!
HEY!!
TOK TOK TOK
YOU'LL PAY FOR THIS!
SLIP!
?!
콰당 우당탕
THUD!
CRASH
WHAAA!
CRAP!
...
GRRR... THOSE PUNKS!
SORRY, SUN-BEA~!
THAT GLOVE...
IS THAT...A CROCODILE GLOVE?
......
THEY'RE DEAD! OH, YES...DEAD!

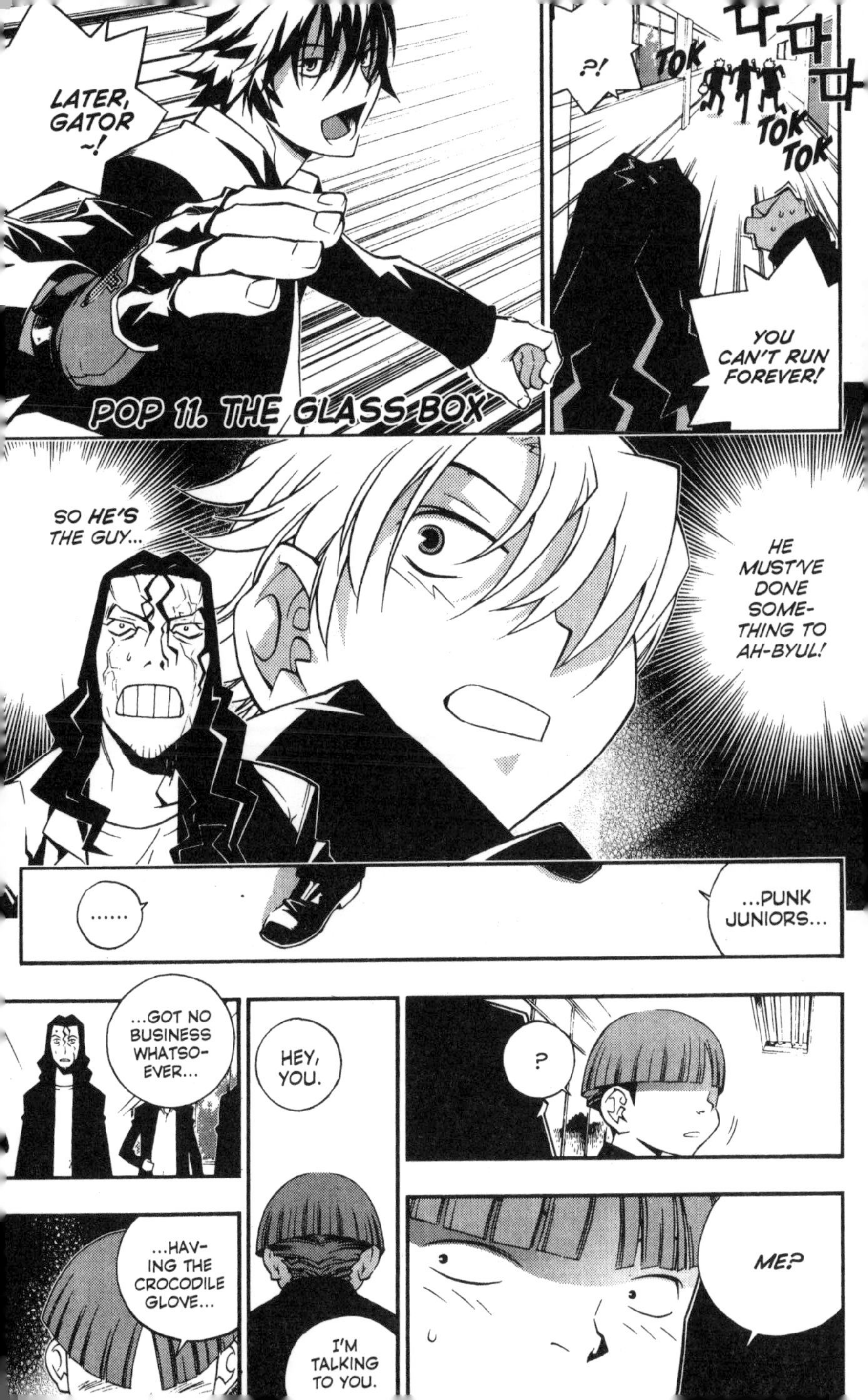
LATER, GATOR ~!
POP 11. THE GLASS BOX
?!
TOK
TOK TOK
YOU CAN'T RUN FOREVER!
SO HE'S THE GUY...
HE MUST'VE DONE SOME-THING TO AH-BYUL!
......
...PUNK JUNIORS...
...GOT NO BUSINESS WHATSO-EVER...
HEY, YOU.
?
...HAV-ING THE CROCODILE GLOVE...
I'M TALKING TO YOU.
ME?

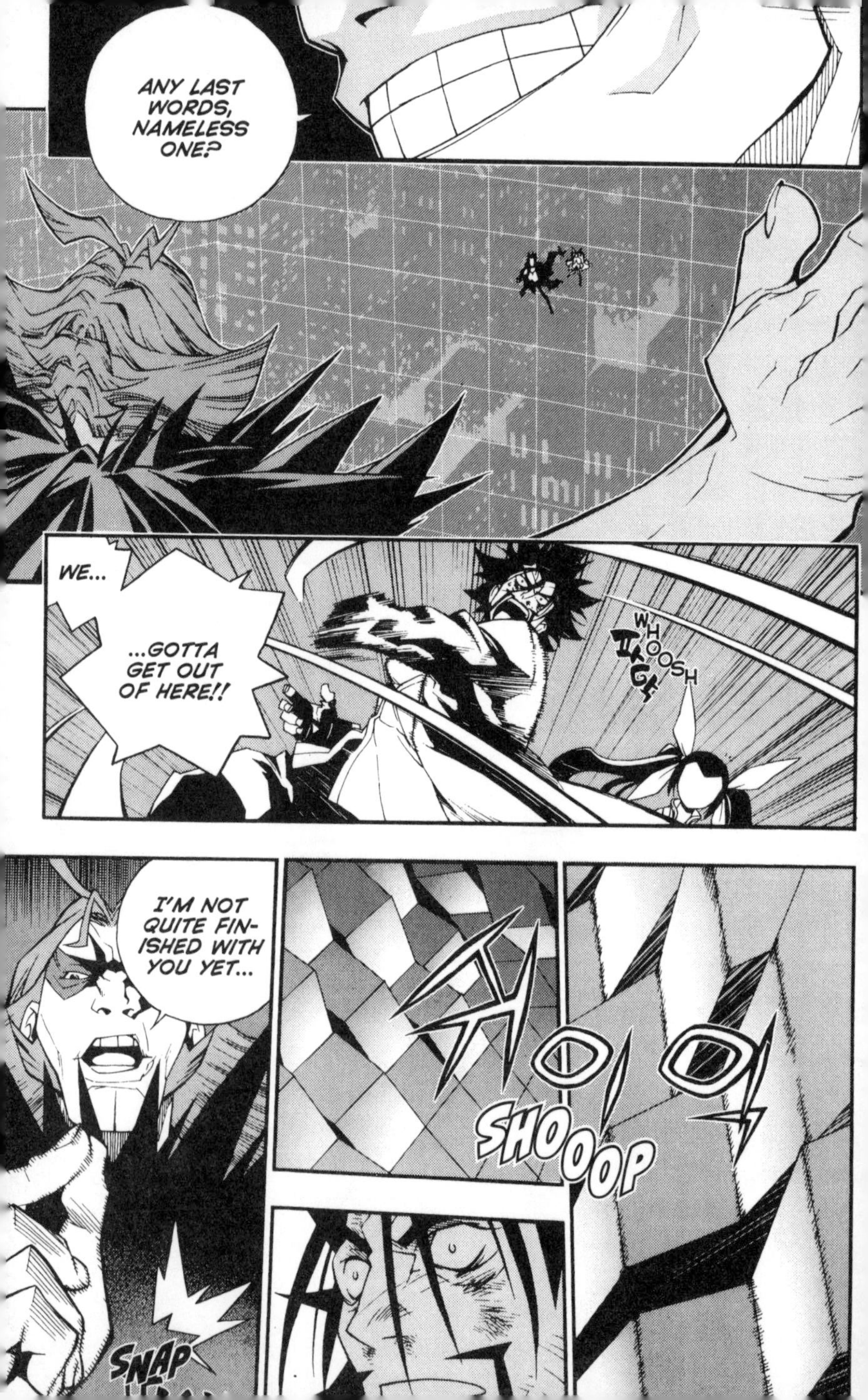
ANY LAST WORDS, NAMELESS ONE?
WE...
...GOTTA GET OUT OF HERE!!
WHOOSH
I'M NOT QUITE FIN-ISHED WITH YOU YET...
SHOOOP
SNAP

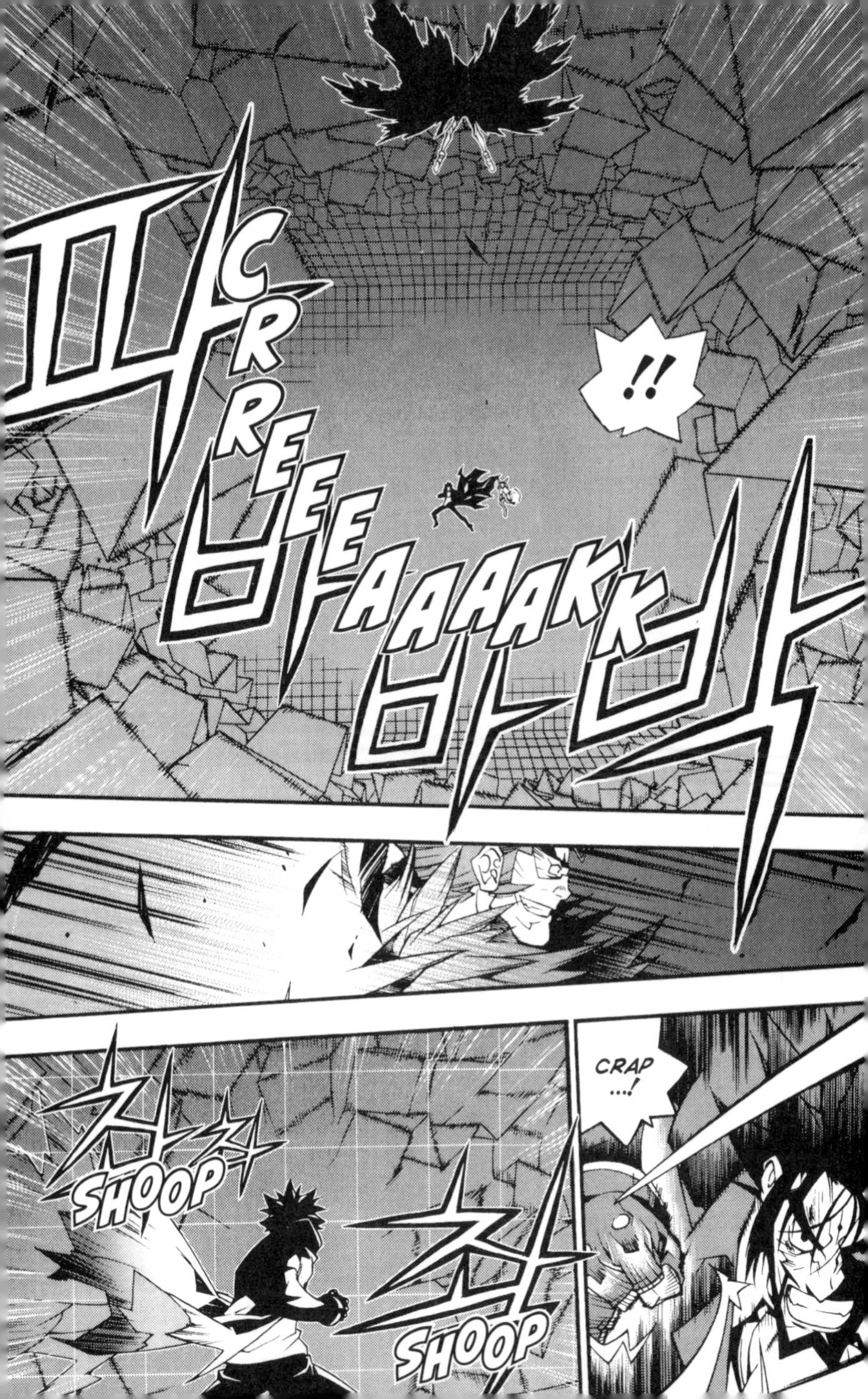
CREEEAAAAKK
!!
SHOOP
SHOOP
CRAP ...!

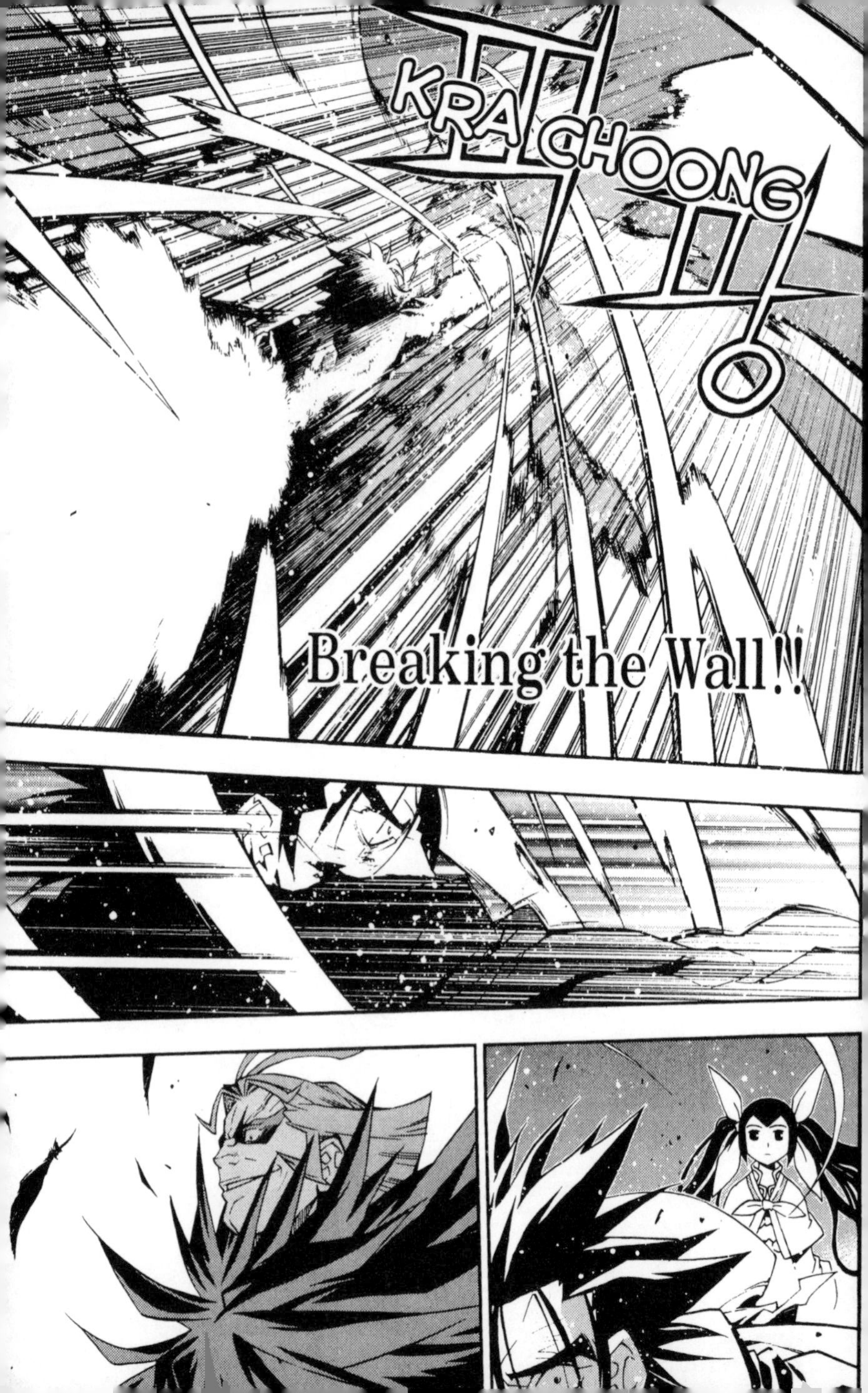
KRA CHOONG
Breaking the Wall!!

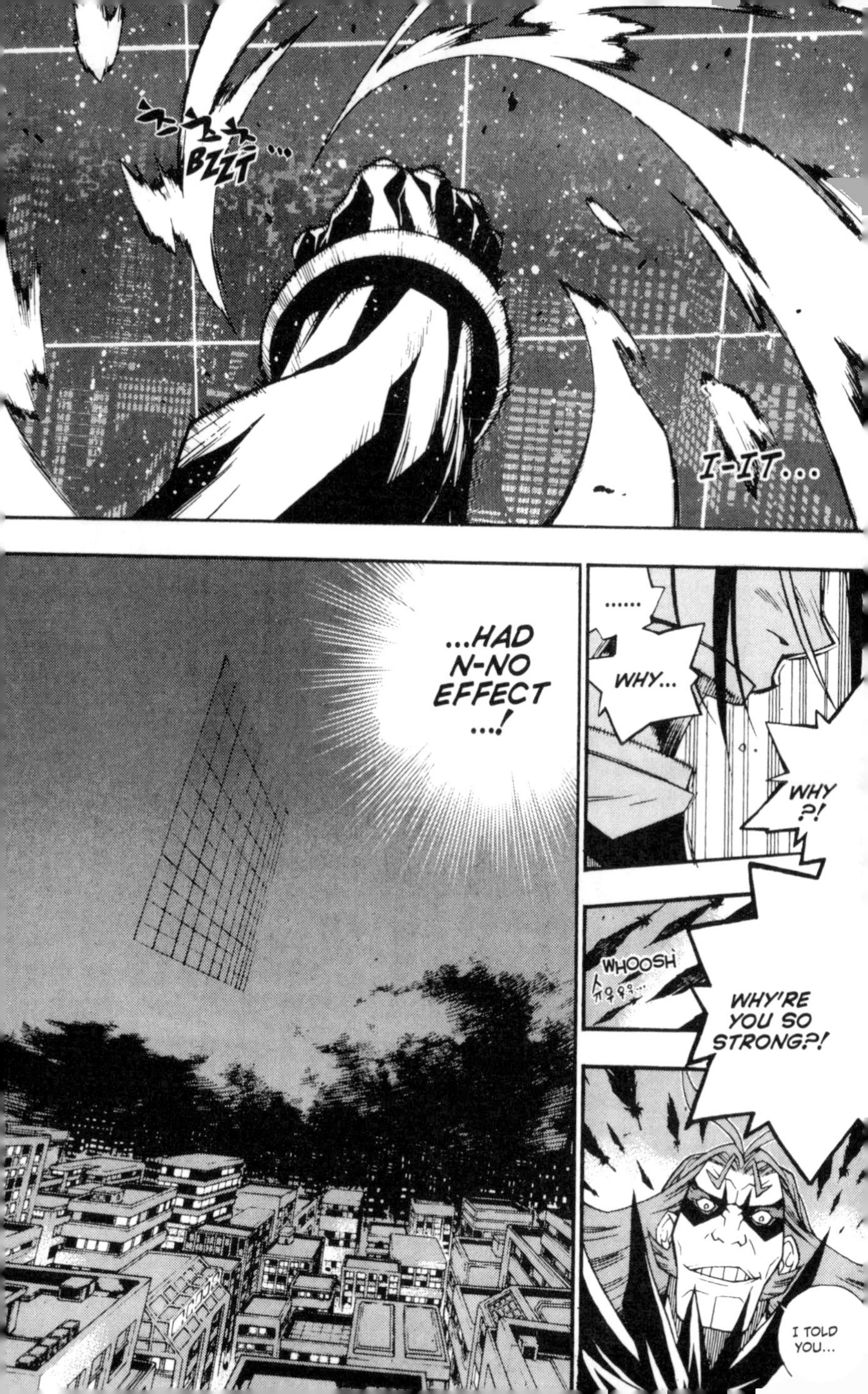
BZZT...
I-IT...
...HAD N-NO EFFECT ...!
......
WHY...
WHY ?!
WHOOSH
WHY'RE YOU SO STRONG?!
I TOLD YOU...

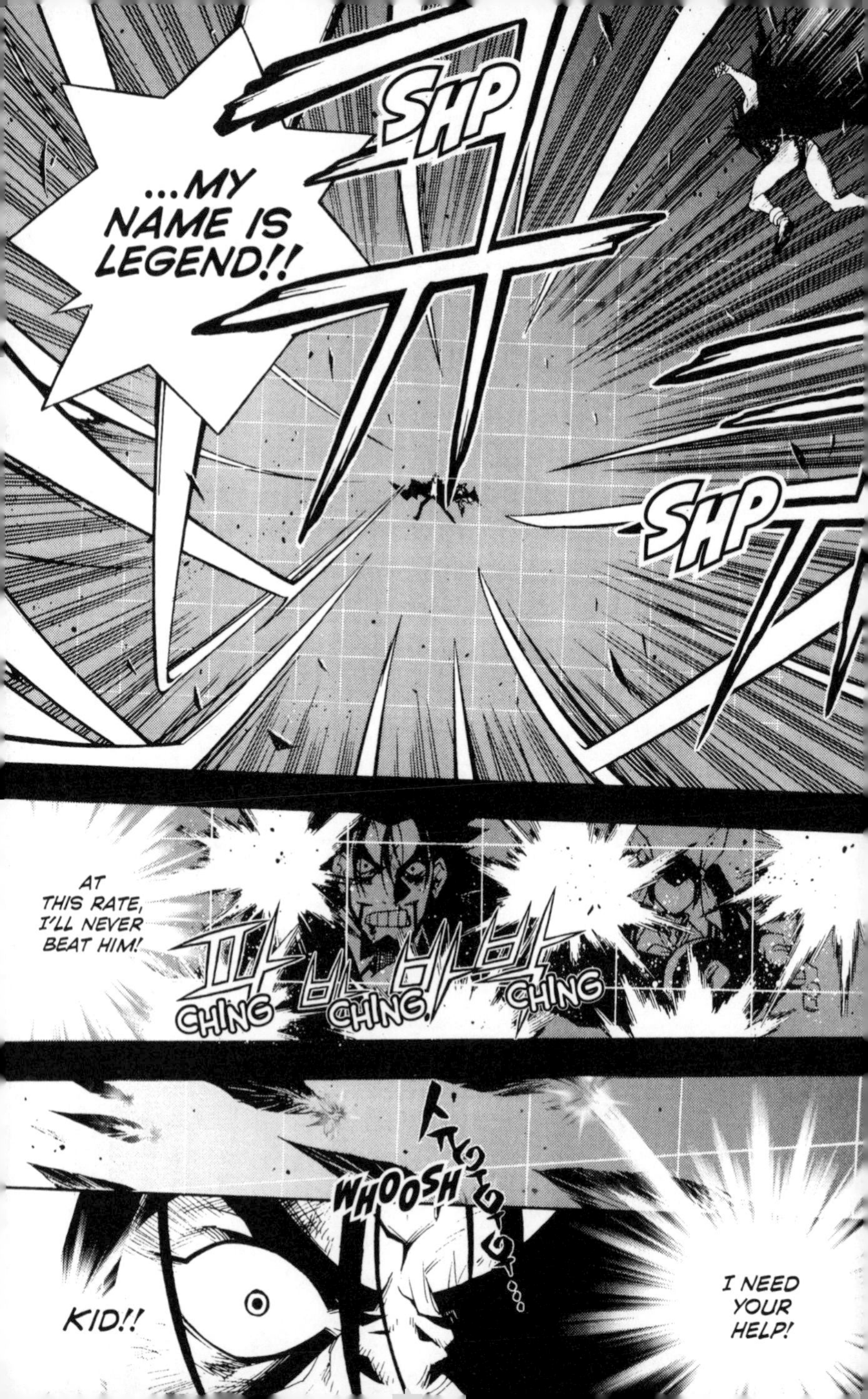
...MY NAME IS LEGEND!!
SHP
SHP
AT THIS RATE, I'LL NEVER BEAT HIM!
CHING
CHING
CHING
WHOOSH
KID!!
I NEED YOUR HELP!

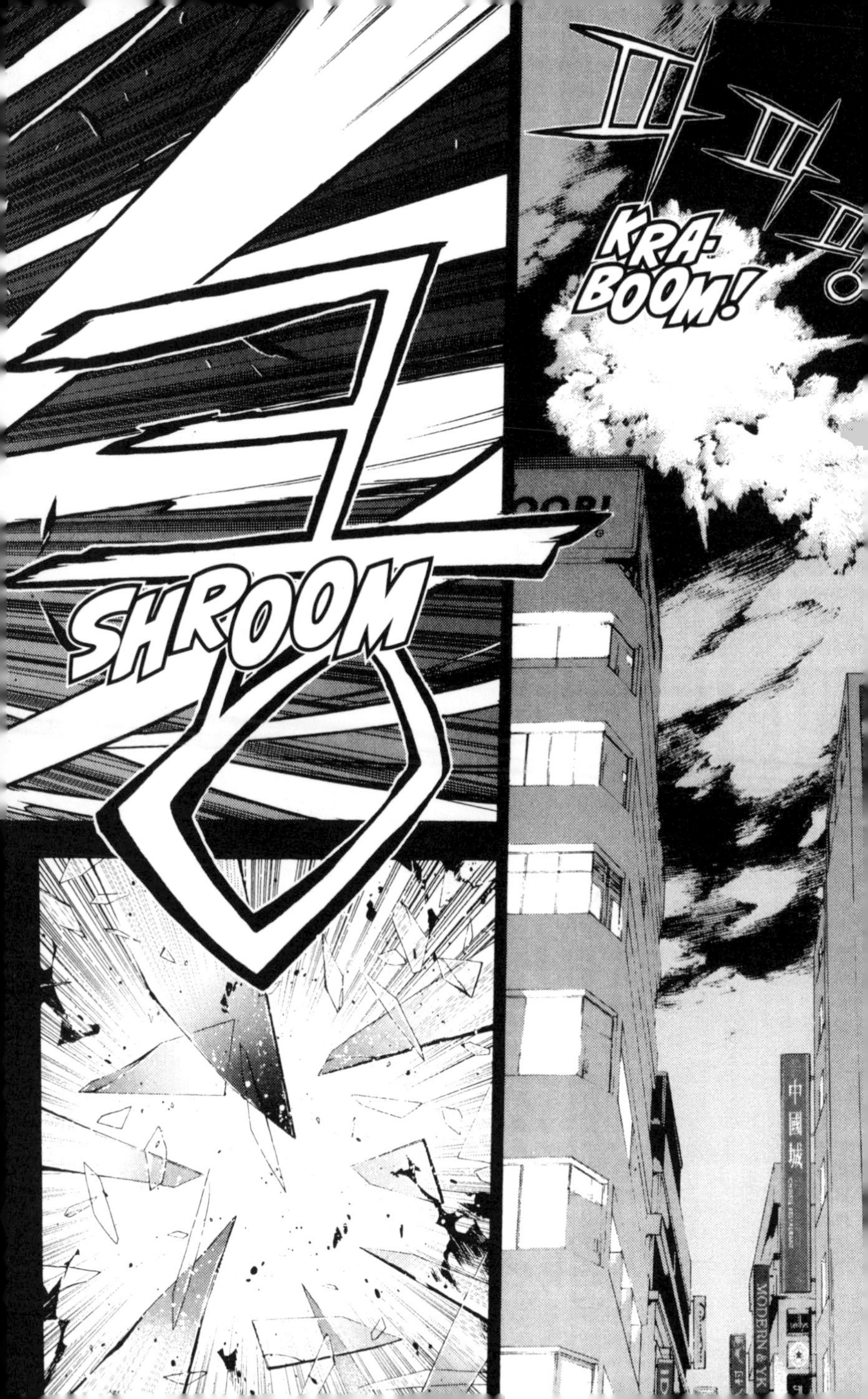
SHROOM
KRA-BOOM!
中國城

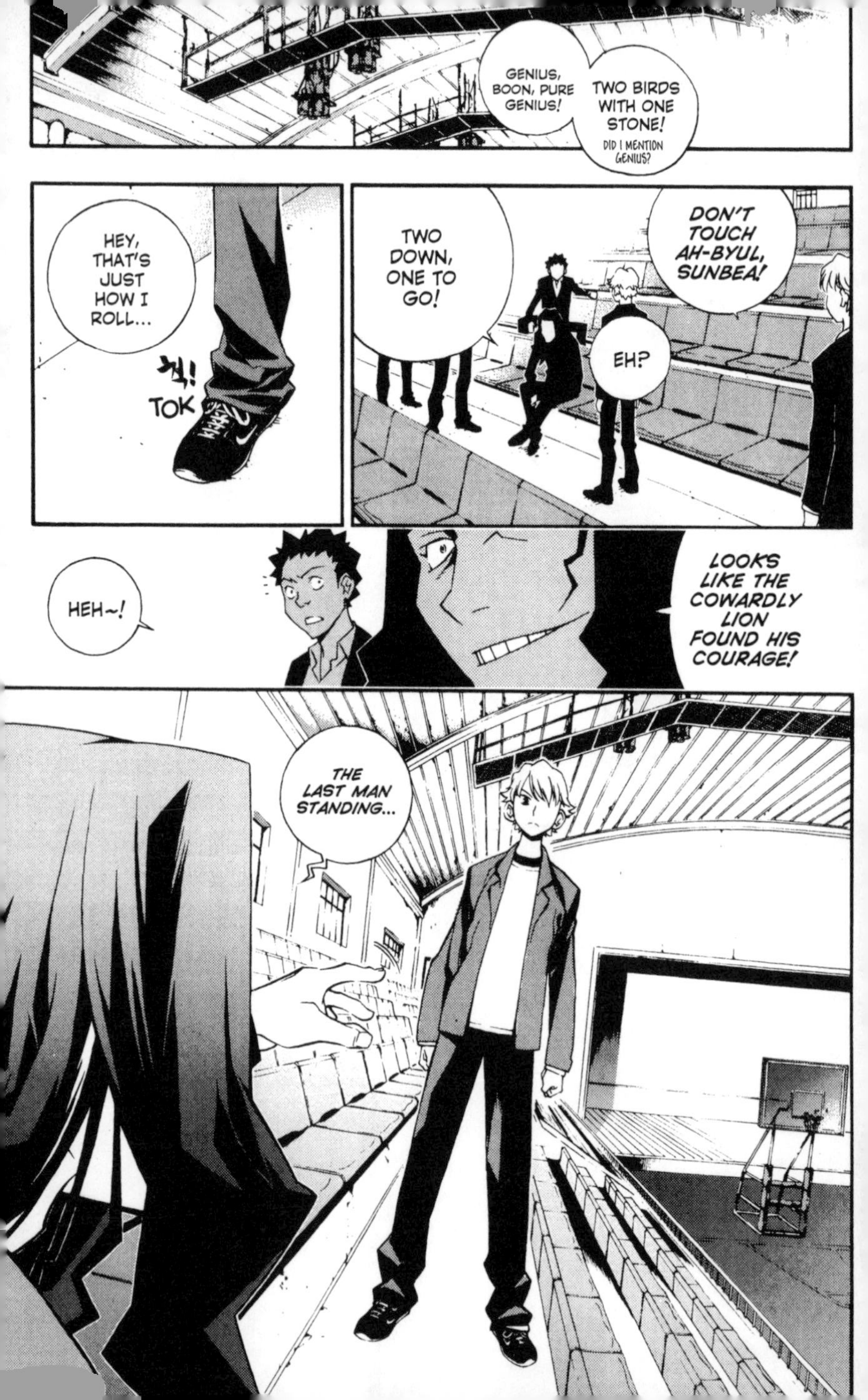
GENIUS, BOON, PURE GENIUS!
TWO BIRDS WITH ONE STONE!
DID I MENTION GENIUS?
HEY, THAT'S JUST HOW I ROLL...
TOK
TWO DOWN, ONE TO GO!
DON'T TOUCH AH-BYUL, SUNBEA!
EH?
HEH~!
LOOKS LIKE THE COWARDLY LION FOUND HIS COURAGE!
THE LAST MAN STANDING...

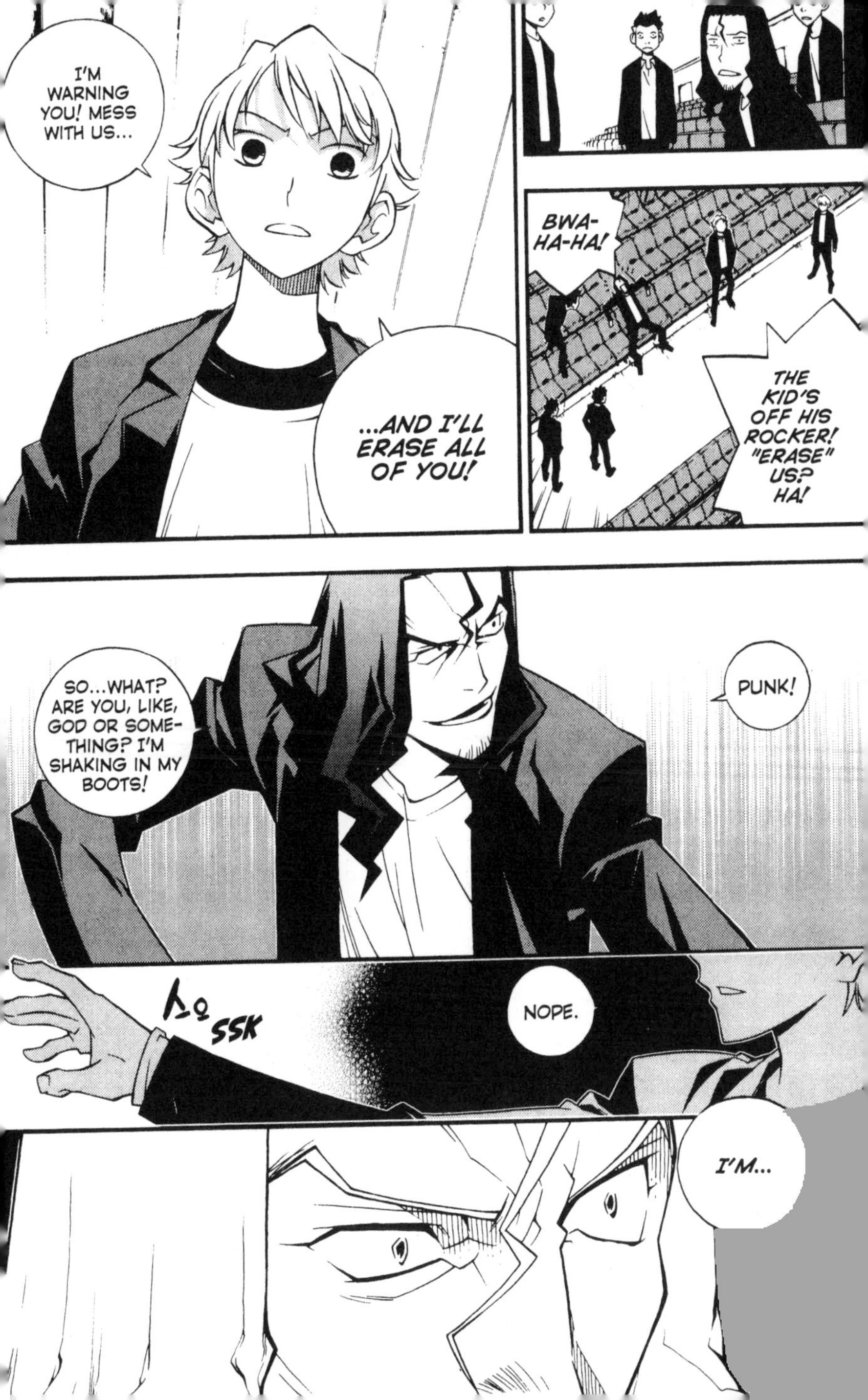
I'M WARNING YOU! MESS WITH US...
...AND I'LL ERASE ALL OF YOU!
BWA-HA-HA!
THE KID'S OFF HIS ROCKER! "ERASE" US? HA!
SO...WHAT? ARE YOU, LIKE, GOD OR SOME-THING? I'M SHAKING IN MY BOOTS!
PUNK!
SSK
NOPE.
I'M...

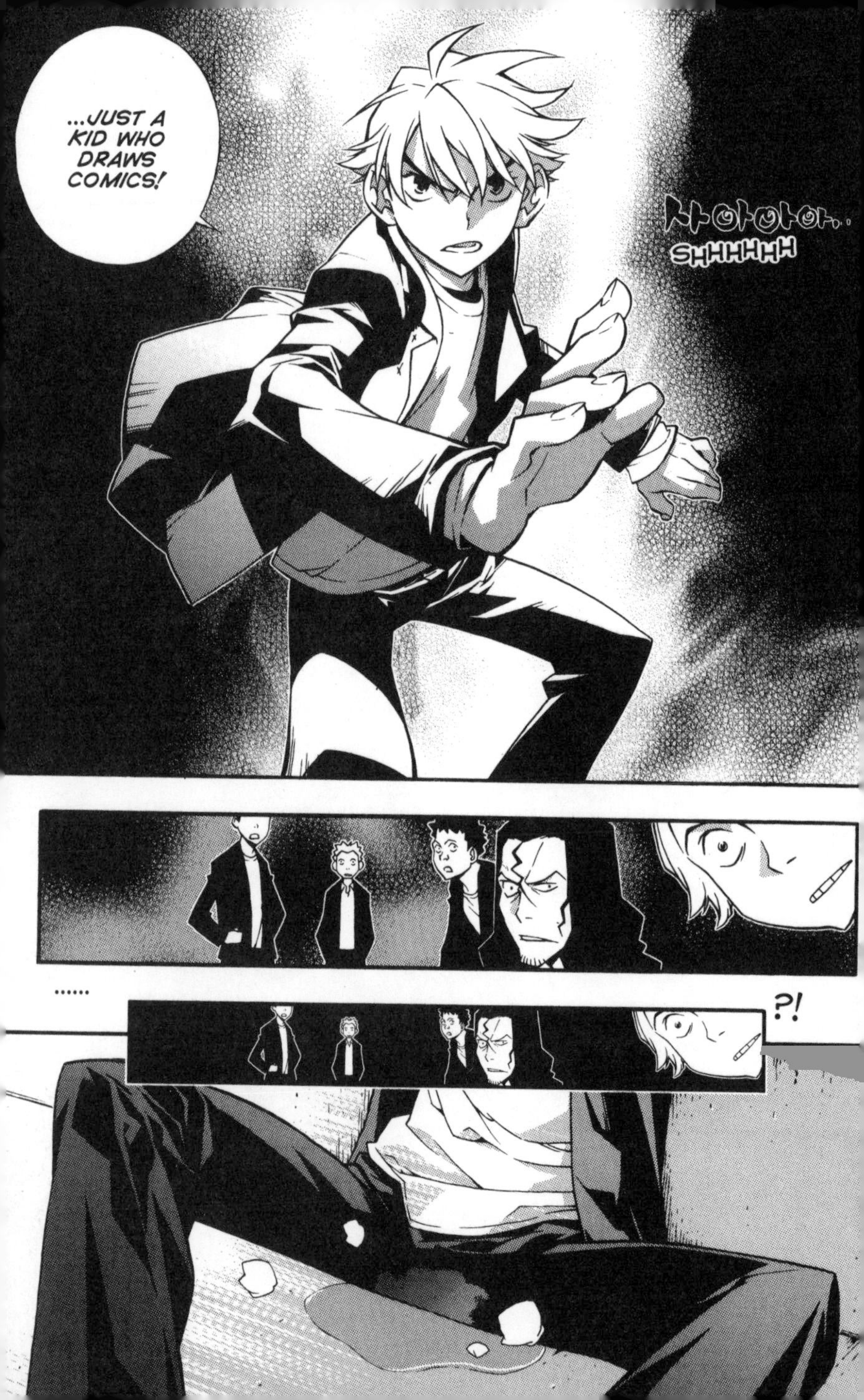
...JUST A KID WHO DRAWS COMICS!
사아아아아..
SHHHHHH
......
?!

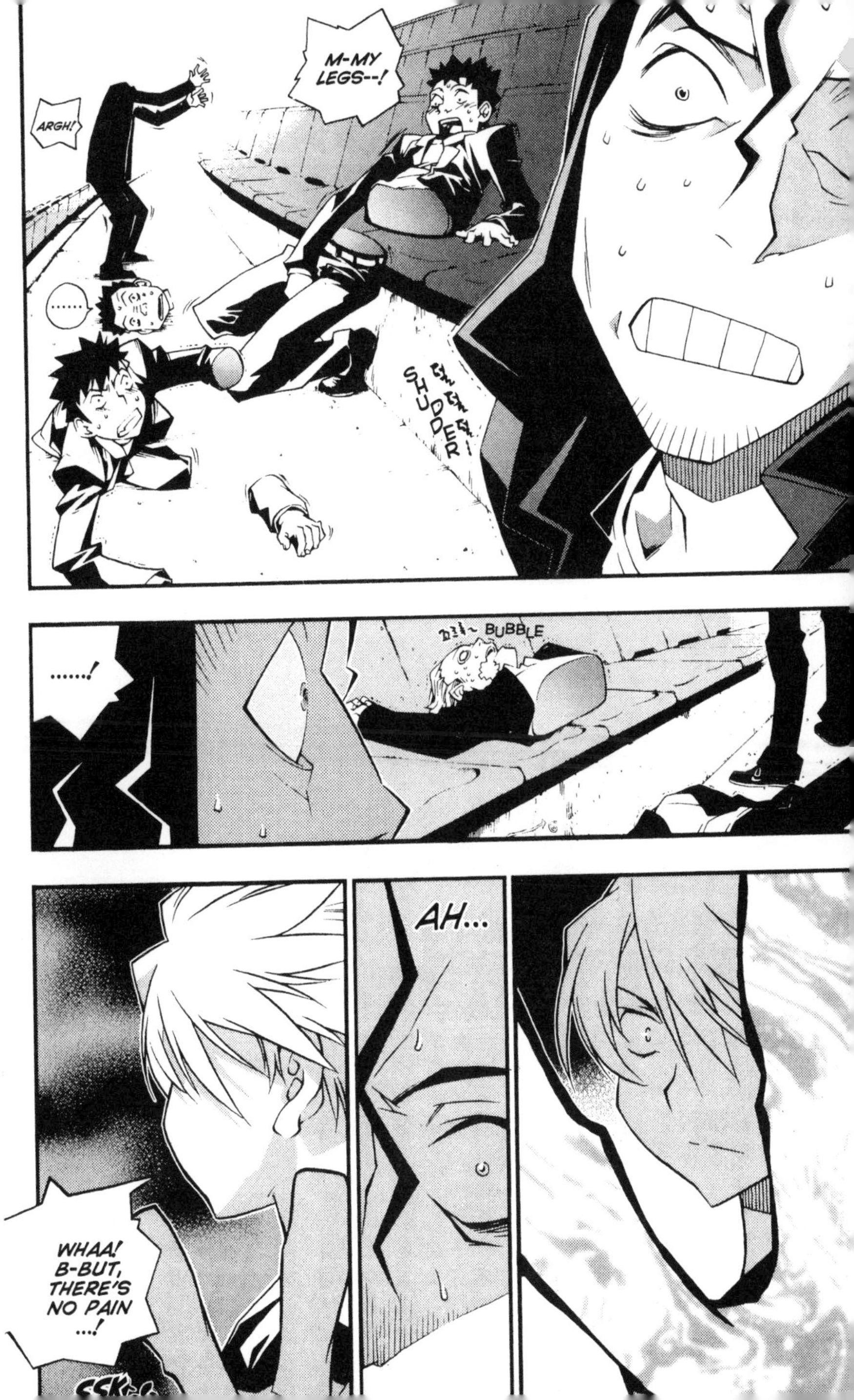
ARGH!
M-MY LEGS--!
......
SHUDDER!
......!
BUBBLE
WHAA! B-BUT, THERE'S NO PAIN ...!
AH...

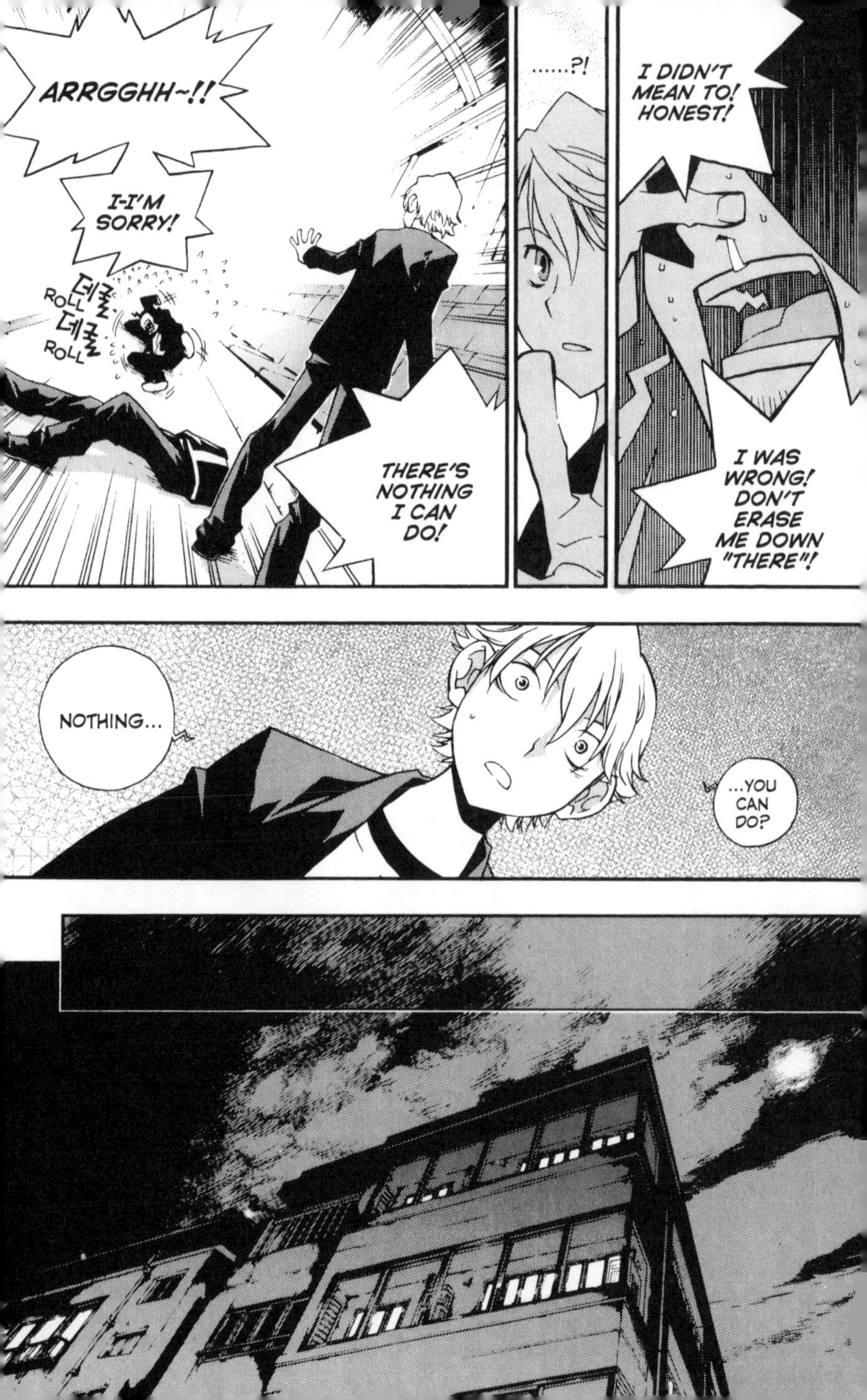
ARRGGHH~!!
I-I'M SORRY!
데굴 ROLL
데굴 ROLL
THERE'S NOTHING I CAN DO!
......?!
I DIDN'T MEAN TO! HONEST!
I WAS WRONG! DON'T ERASE ME DOWN "THERE"!
NOTHING...
...YOU CAN DO?

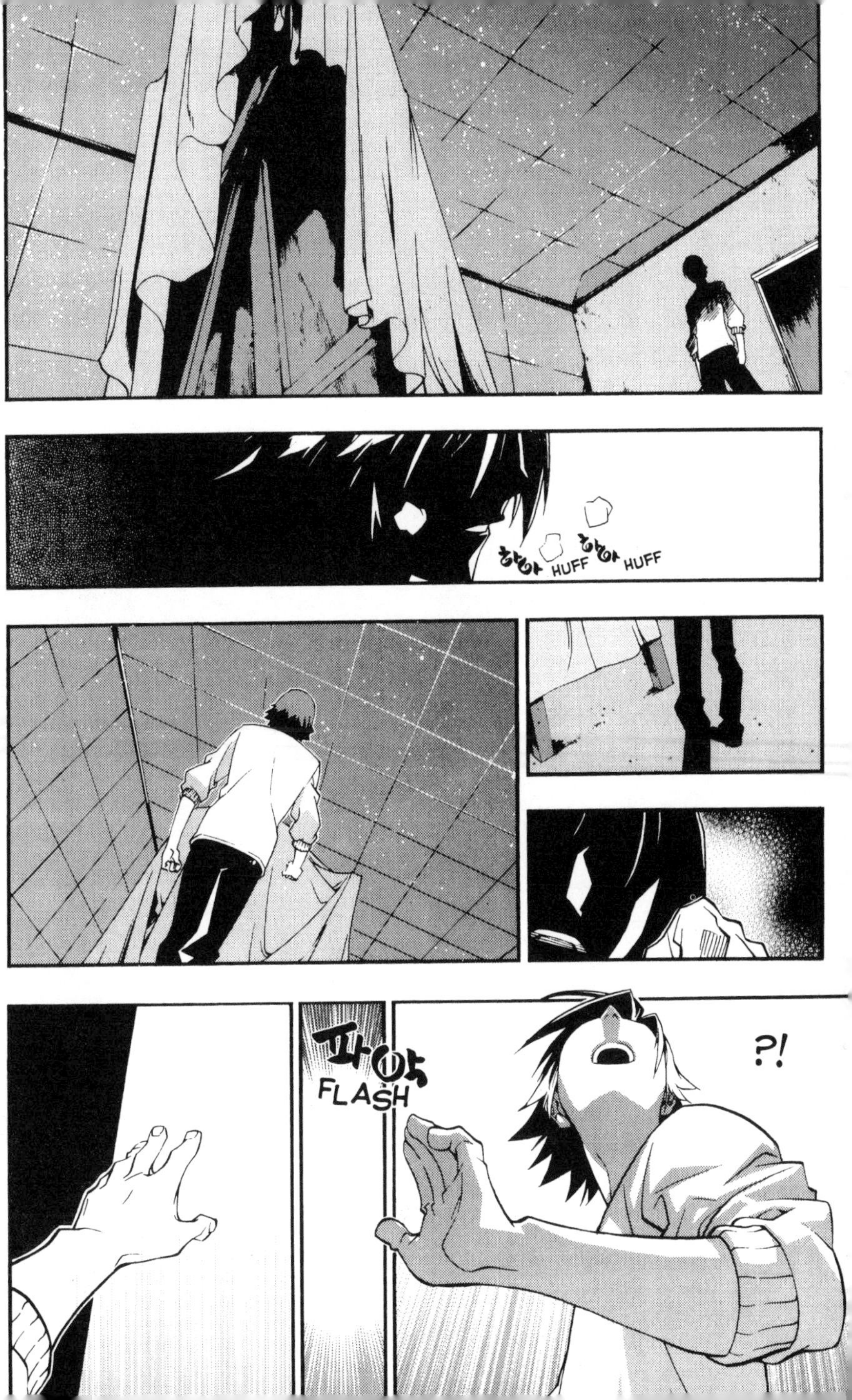

헉헉 HUFF
헉헉 HUFF
파앗
FLASH
?!

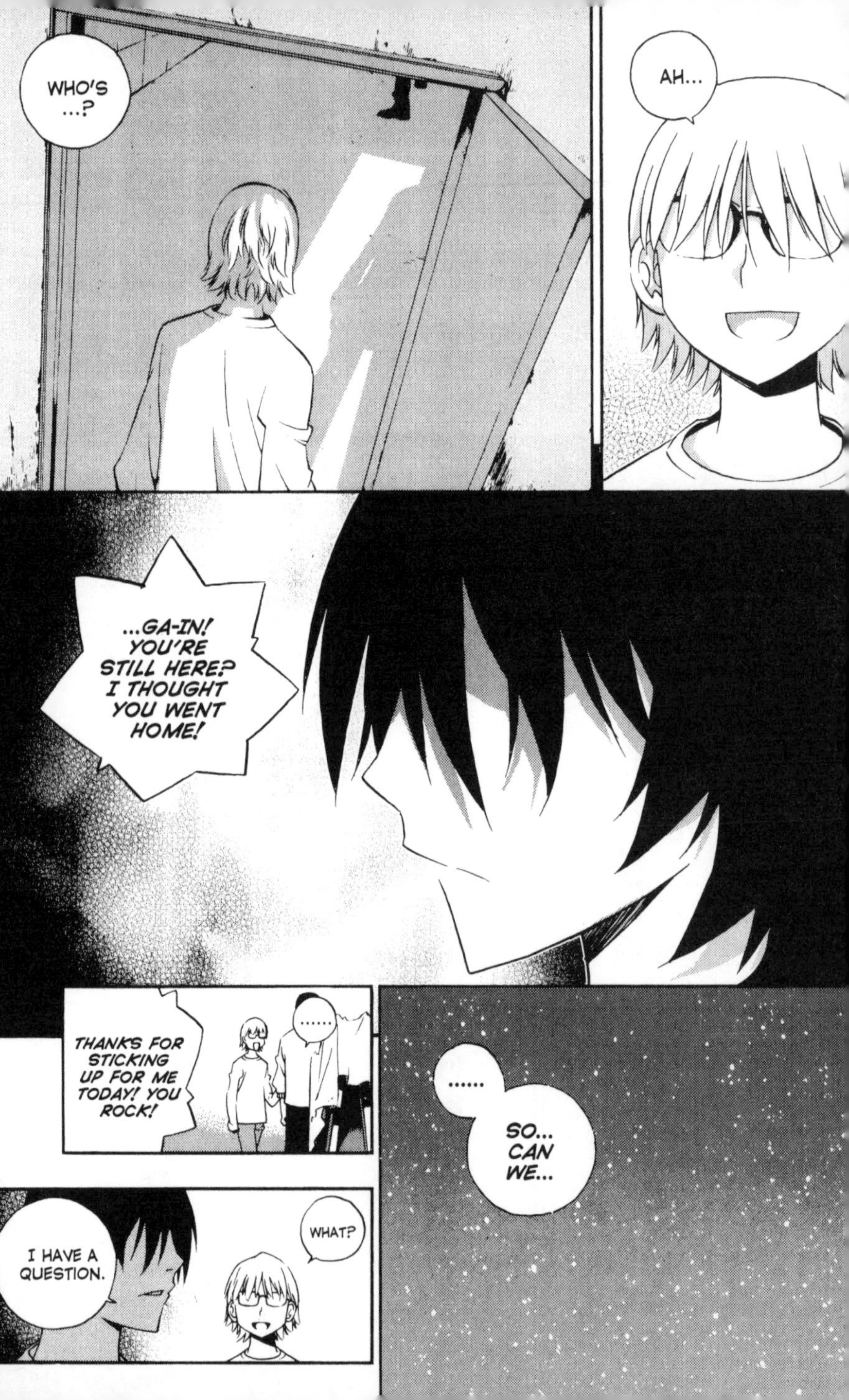
WHO'S ...?
AH...
...GA-IN! YOU'RE STILL HERE? I THOUGHT YOU WENT HOME!
THANKS FOR STICKING UP FOR ME TODAY! YOU ROCK!
......
I HAVE A QUESTION.
WHAT?
......
SO... CAN WE...

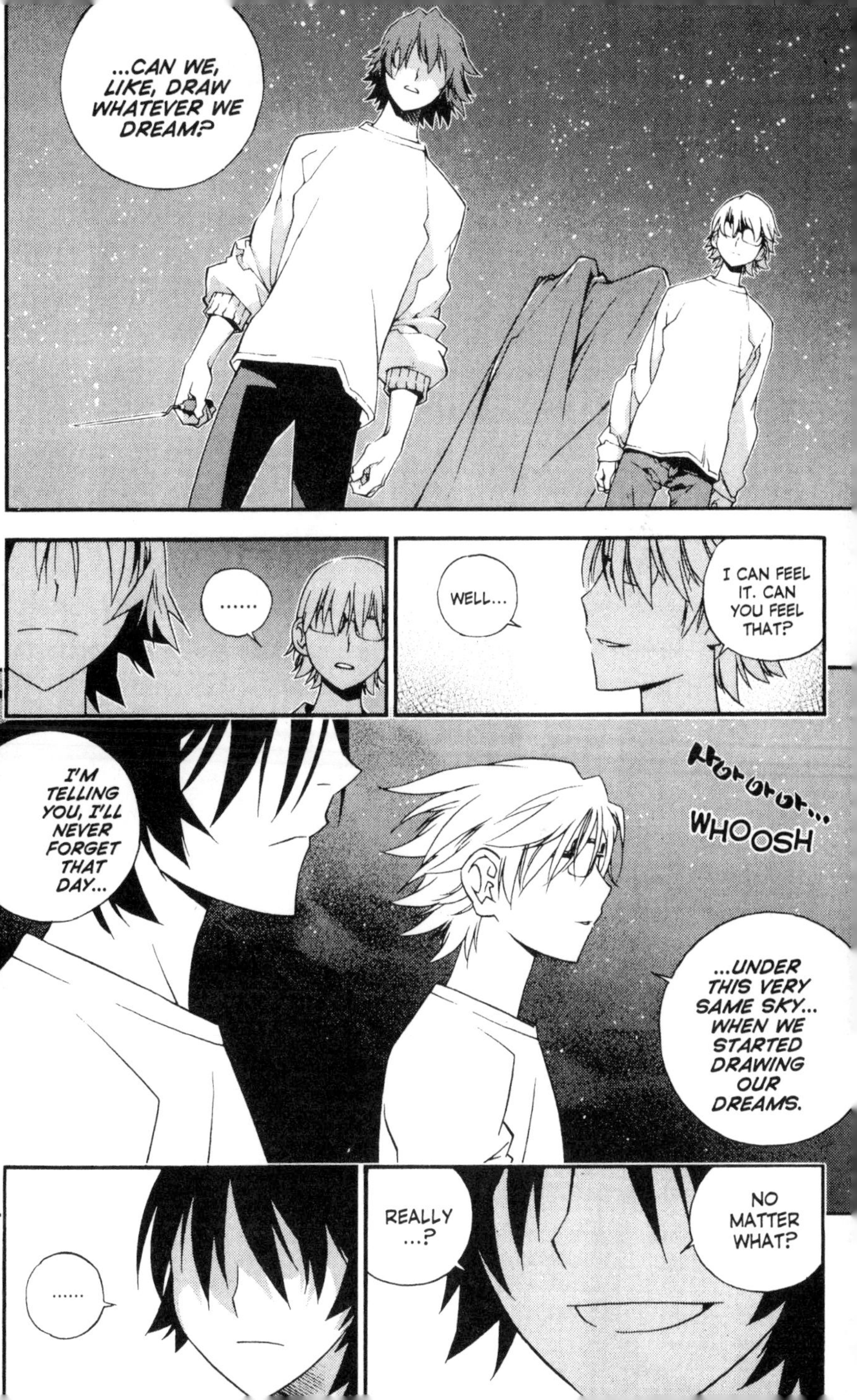
...CAN WE, LIKE, DRAW WHATEVER WE DREAM?
......
WELL...
I CAN FEEL IT. CAN YOU FEEL THAT?
I'M TELLING YOU, I'LL NEVER FORGET THAT DAY...
WHOOSH
...UNDER THIS VERY SAME SKY... WHEN WE STARTED DRAWING OUR DREAMS.
......
REALLY ...?
NO MATTER WHAT?

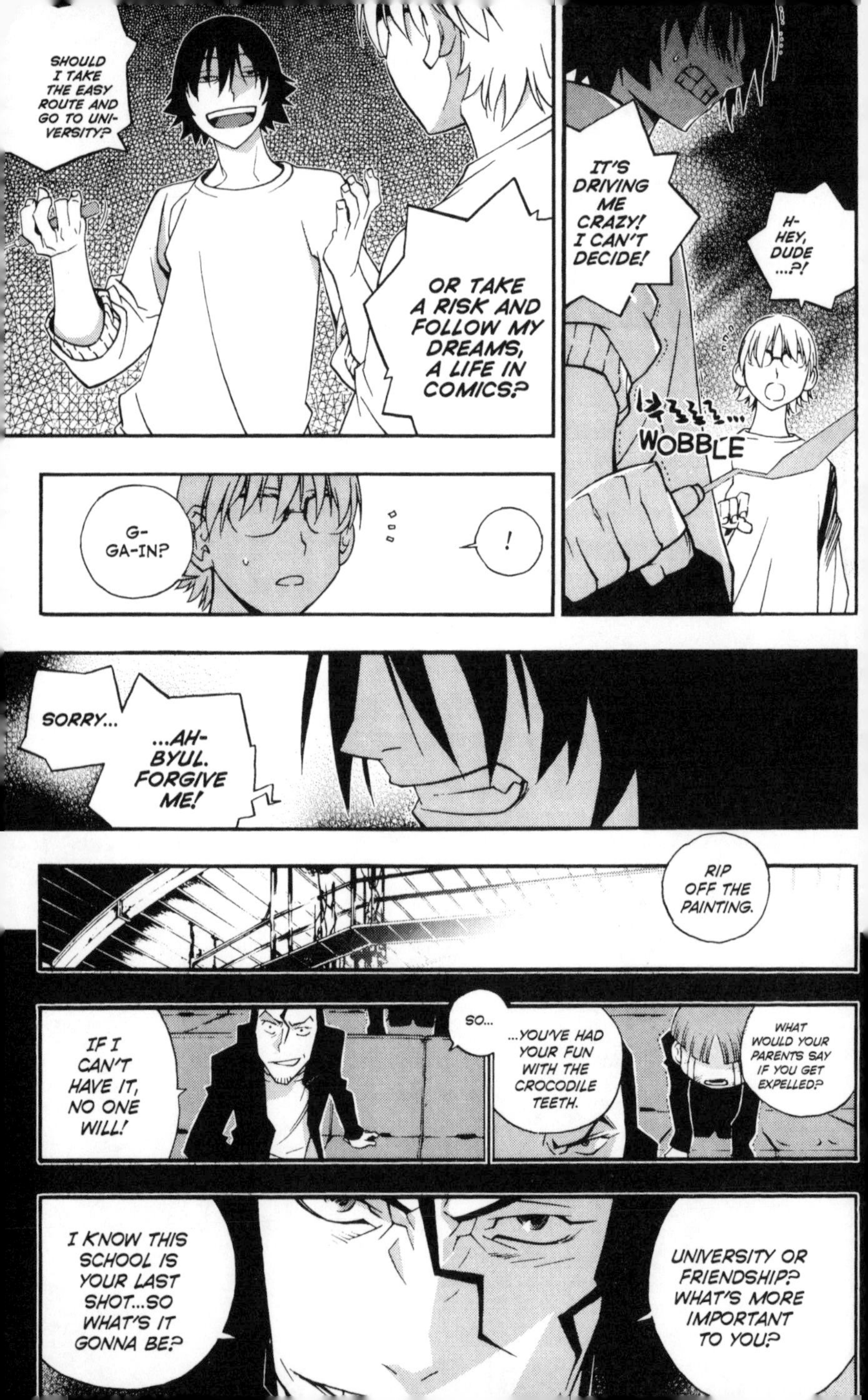
SHOULD I TAKE THE EASY ROUTE AND GO TO UNIVERSITY?
OR TAKE A RISK AND FOLLOW MY DREAMS, A LIFE IN COMICS?
G-GA-IN?
...
!
IT'S DRIVING ME CRAZY! I CAN'T DECIDE!
H-HEY, DUDE ...?!
WOBBLE
SORRY...
...AH-BYUL. FORGIVE ME!
RIP OFF THE PAINTING.
IF I CAN'T HAVE IT, NO ONE WILL!
SO...
...YOU'VE HAD YOUR FUN WITH THE CROCODILE TEETH.
WHAT WOULD YOUR PARENTS SAY IF YOU GET EXPELLED?
I KNOW THIS SCHOOL IS YOUR LAST SHOT...SO WHAT'S IT GONNA BE?
UNIVERSITY OR FRIENDSHIP? WHAT'S MORE IMPORTANT TO YOU?

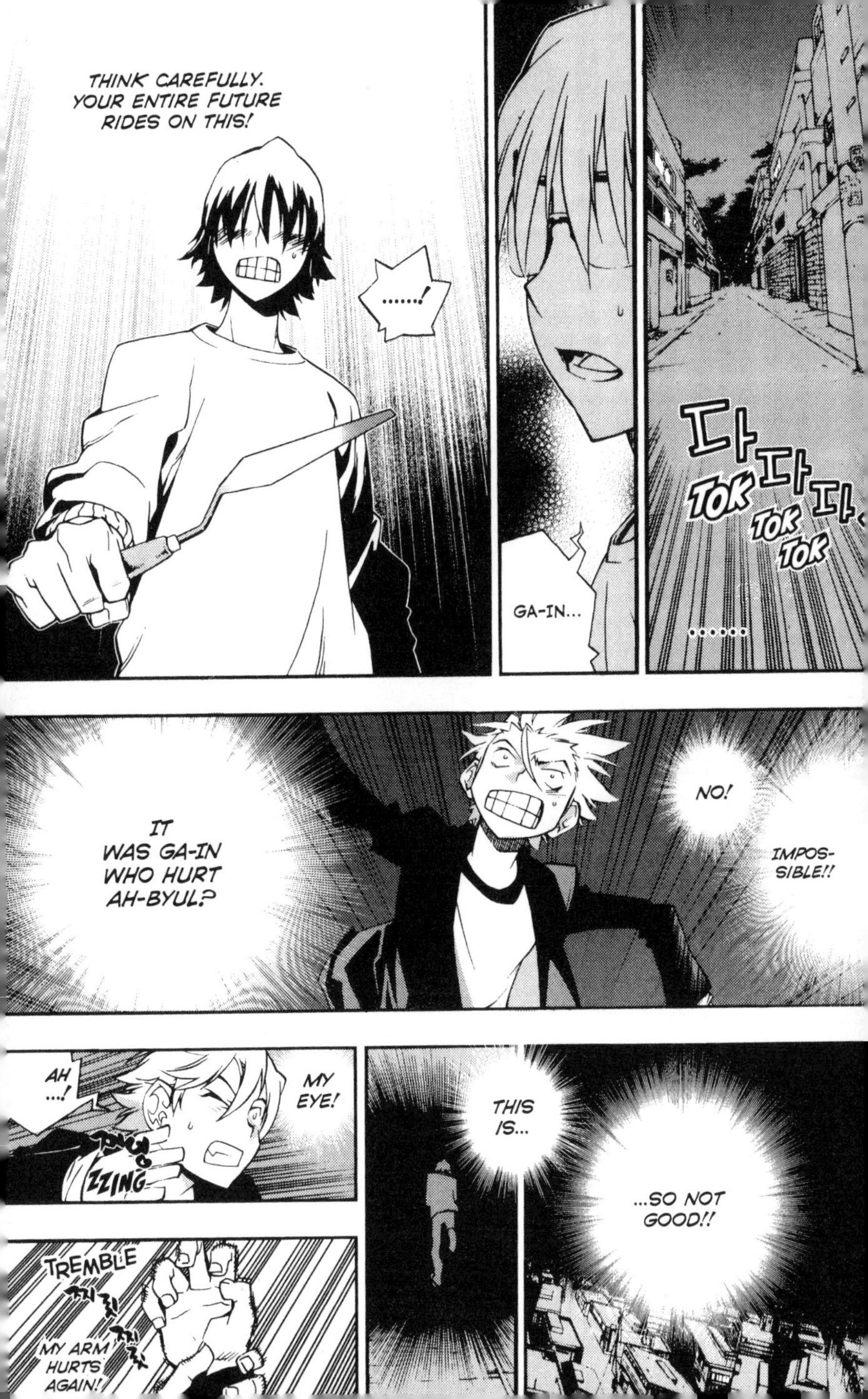
THINK CAREFULLY. YOUR ENTIRE FUTURE RIDES ON THIS!
.......!
GA-IN...
TOK TOK TOK
......
IT WAS GA-IN WHO HURT AH-BYUL?
NO!
IMPOS-SIBLE!!
AH ...!
MY EYE!
ZZING
TREMBLE
MY ARM HURTS AGAIN!
THIS IS...
...SO NOT GOOD!!

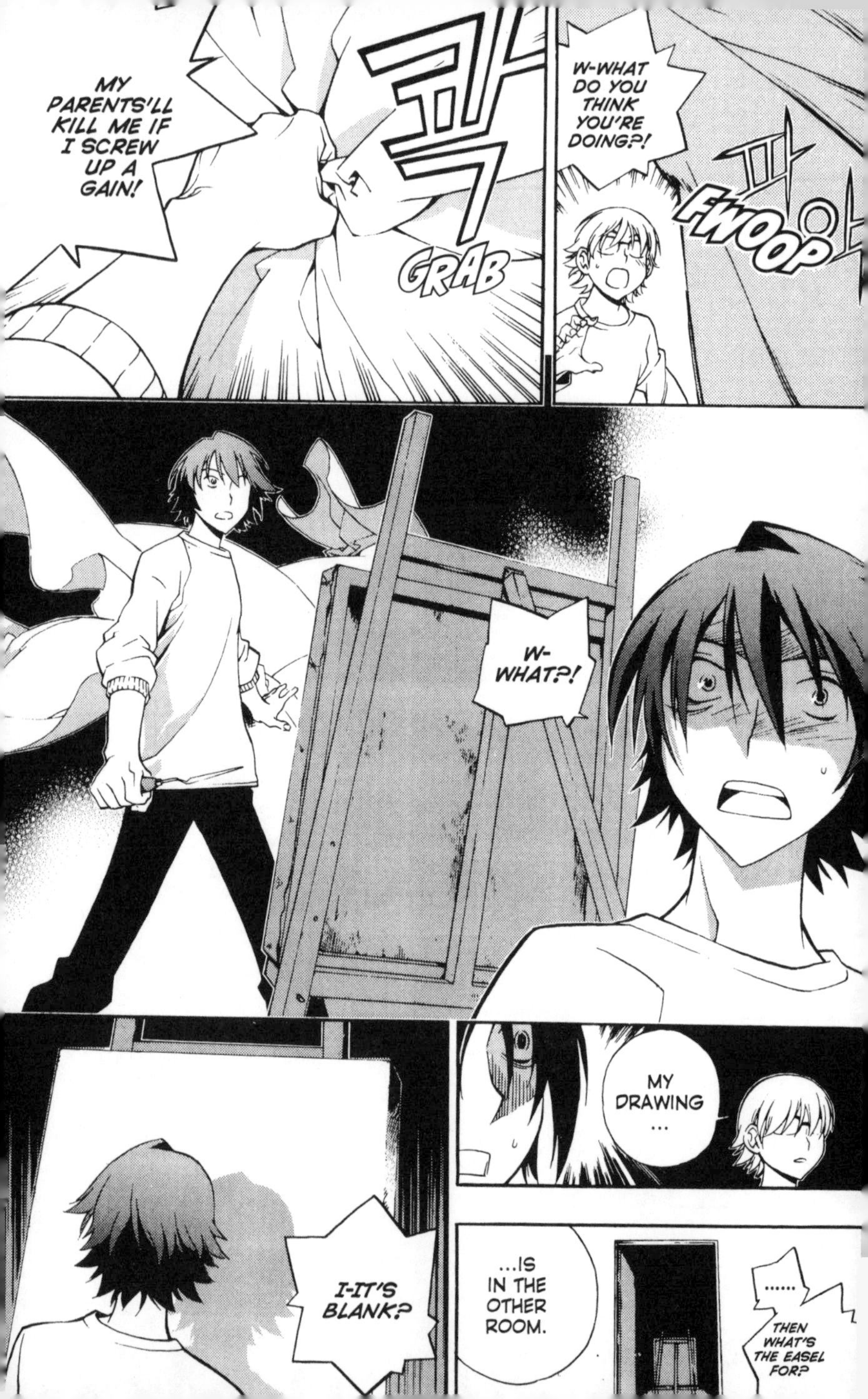
MY PARENTS'LL KILL ME IF I SCREW UP A GAIN!
GRAB
W-WHAT DO YOU THINK YOU'RE DOING?!
FWOOP
W- WHAT?!
I-IT'S BLANK?
MY DRAWING ...
...IS IN THE OTHER ROOM.
......
THEN WHAT'S THE EASEL FOR?

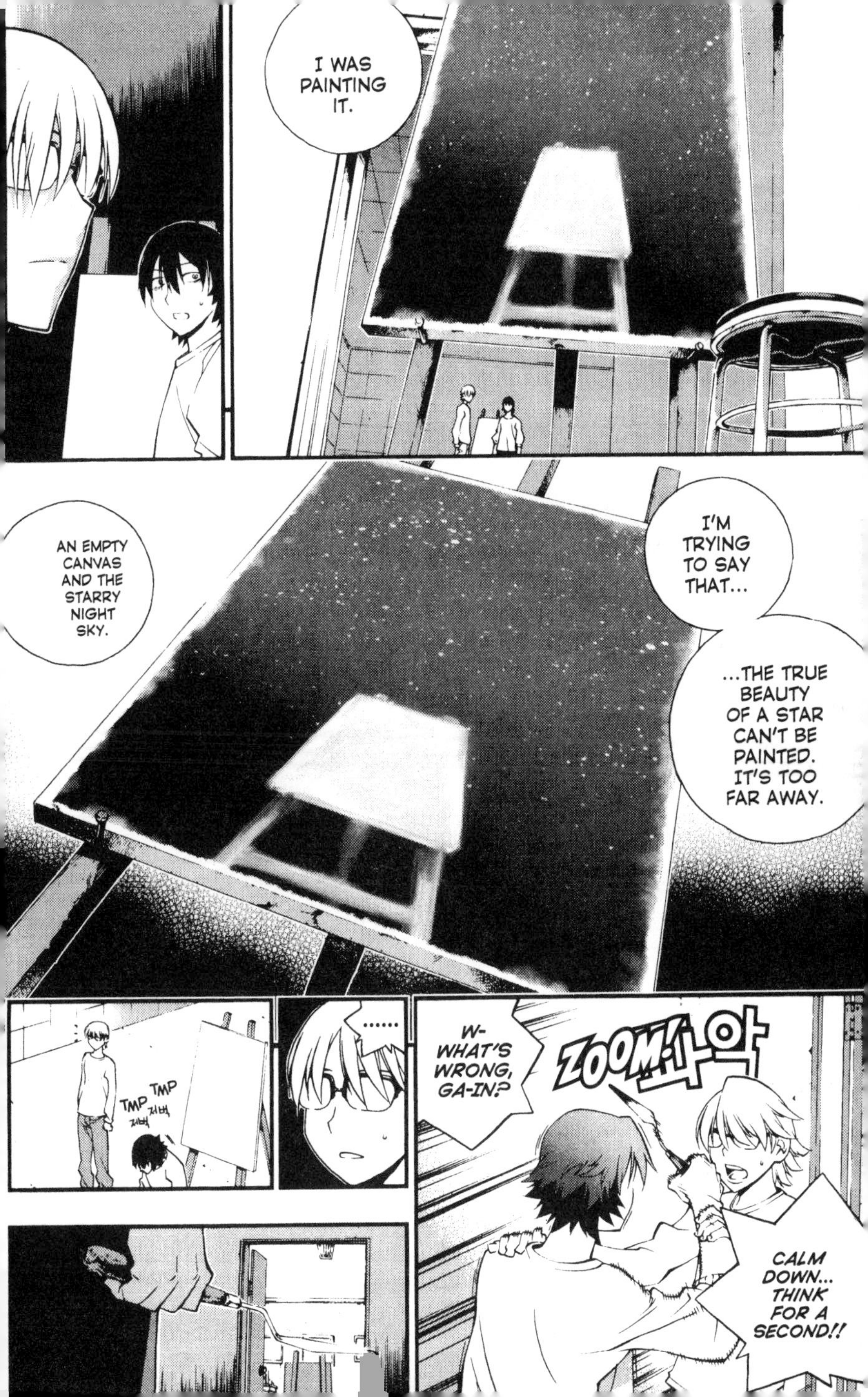
I WAS PAINTING IT.
AN EMPTY CANVAS AND THE STARRY NIGHT SKY.
I'M TRYING TO SAY THAT...
...THE TRUE BEAUTY OF A STAR CAN'T BE PAINTED. IT'S TOO FAR AWAY.
TMP TMP
저벅 저벅
......
W-WHAT'S WRONG, GA-IN?
ZOOM 파악
CALM DOWN... THINK FOR A SECOND!!

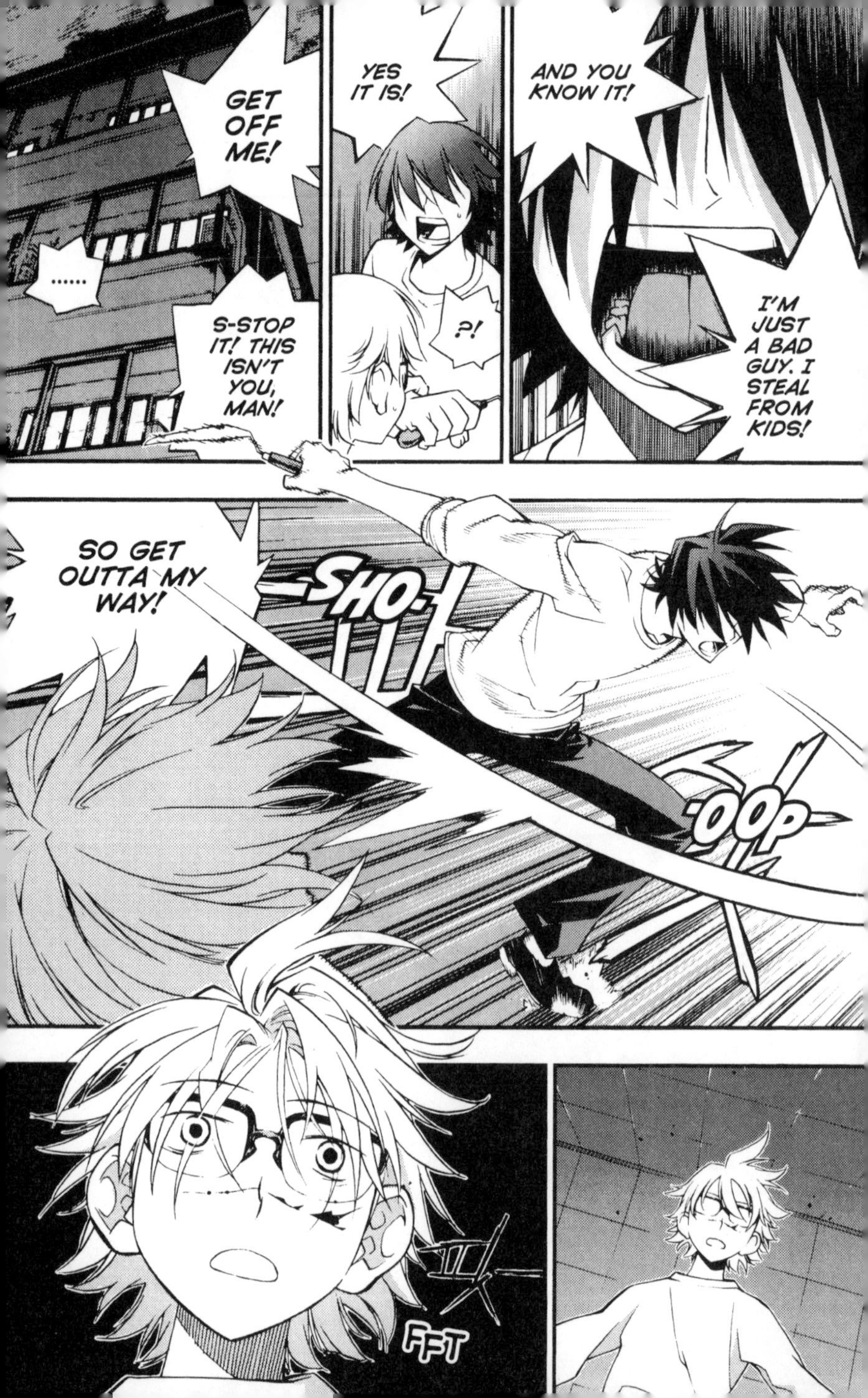
GET OFF ME!
......
S-STOP IT! THIS ISN'T YOU, MAN!
YES IT IS!
?!
AND YOU KNOW IT!
I'M JUST A BAD GUY. I STEAL FROM KIDS!
SO GET OUTTA MY WAY!
-SHO-
-OOP
FFT

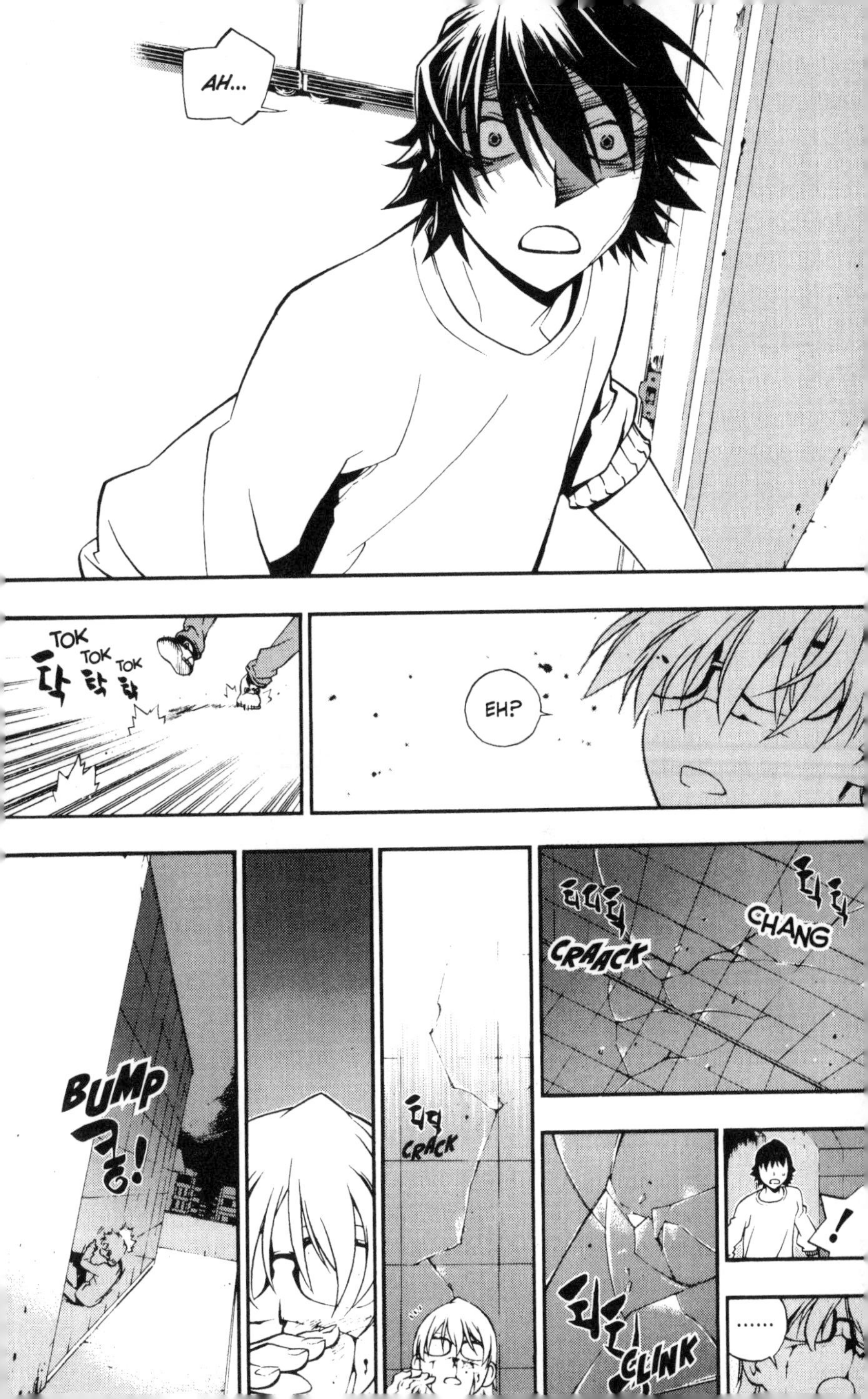
AH...
TOK
TOK
TOK
EH?
BUMP
CRACK
CRAACK
CHANG
CLINK
!
......

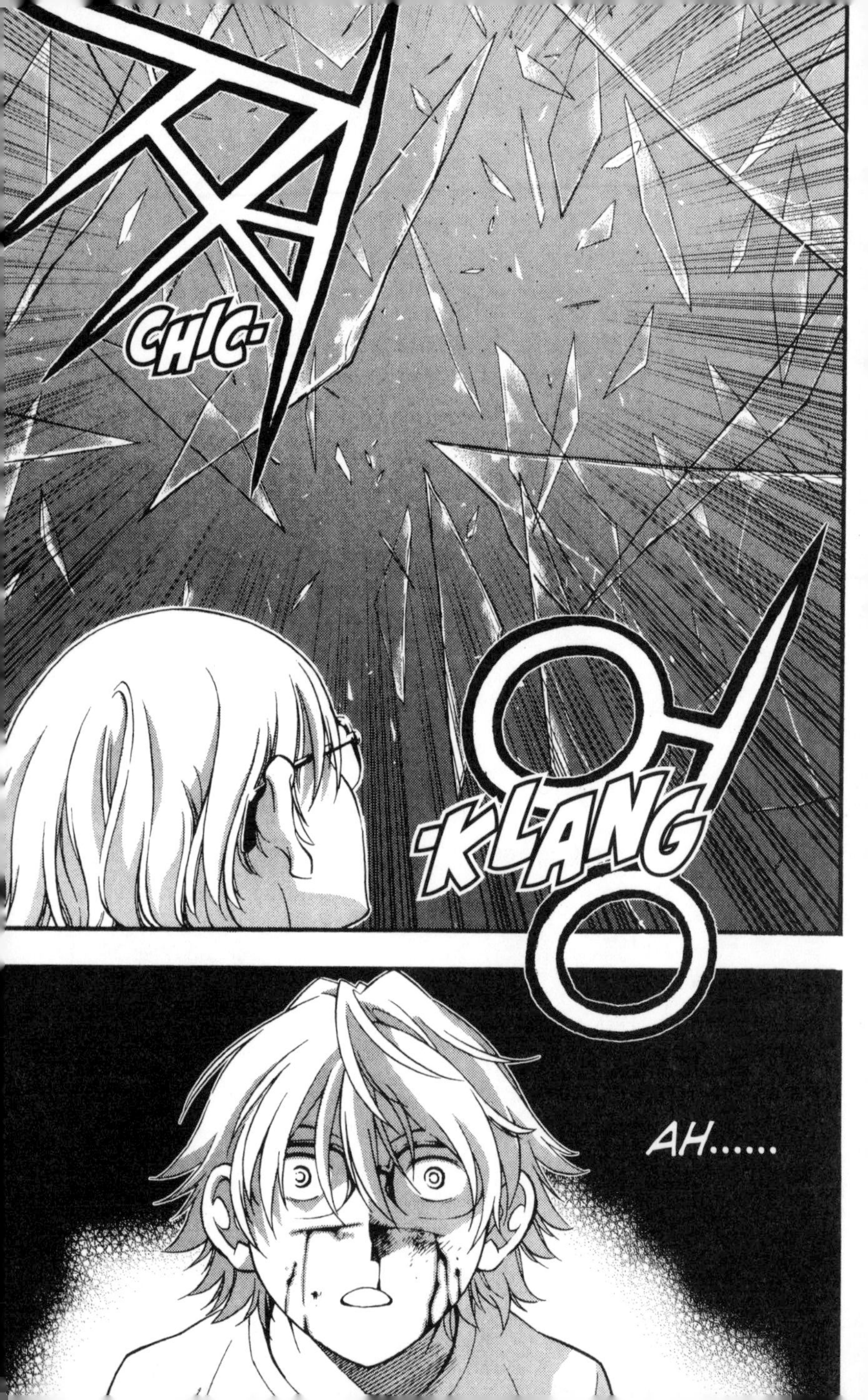
CHIC-
-KLANG
AH......

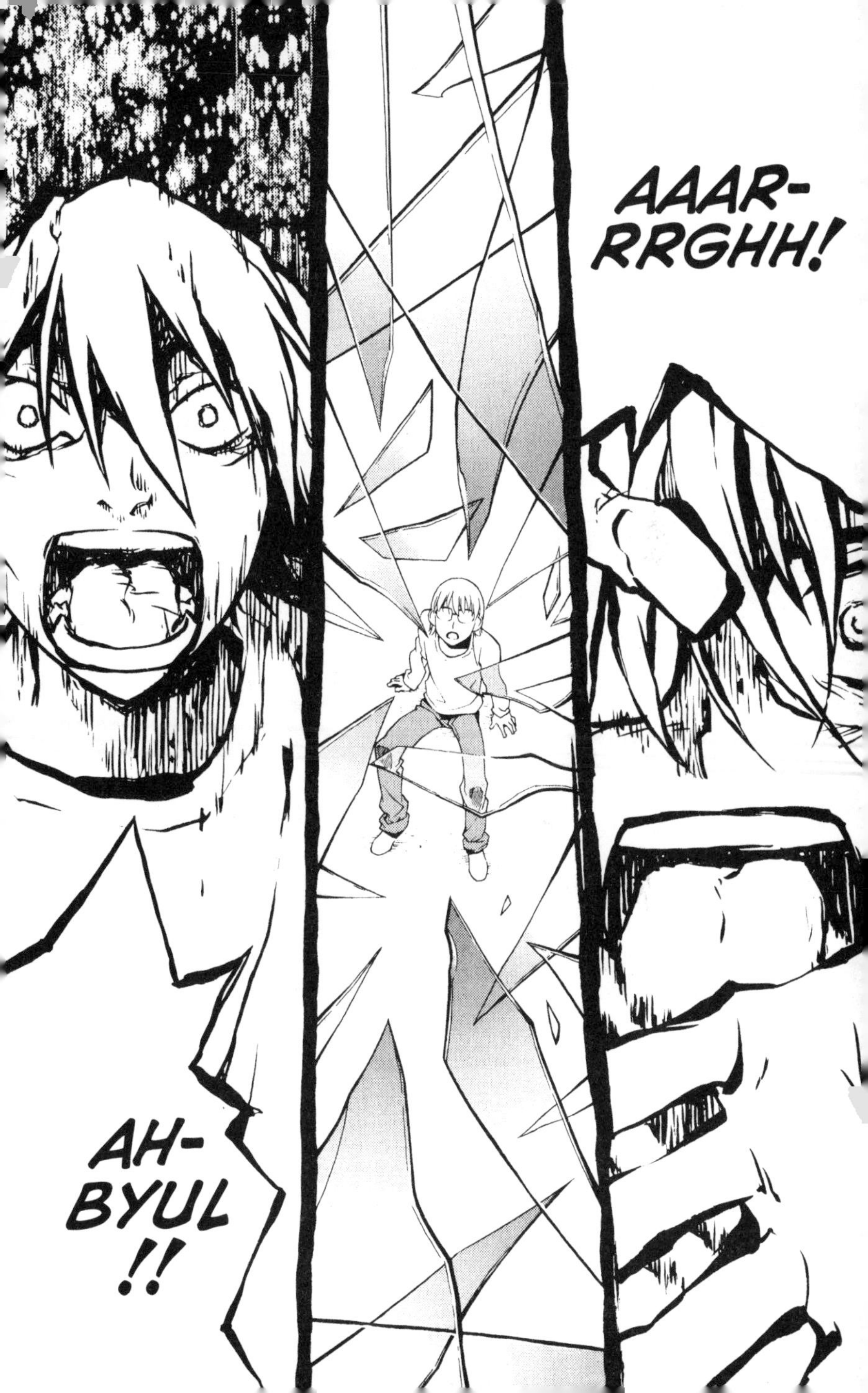
AH-
BYUL
!!
AAAR-
RRGHH!

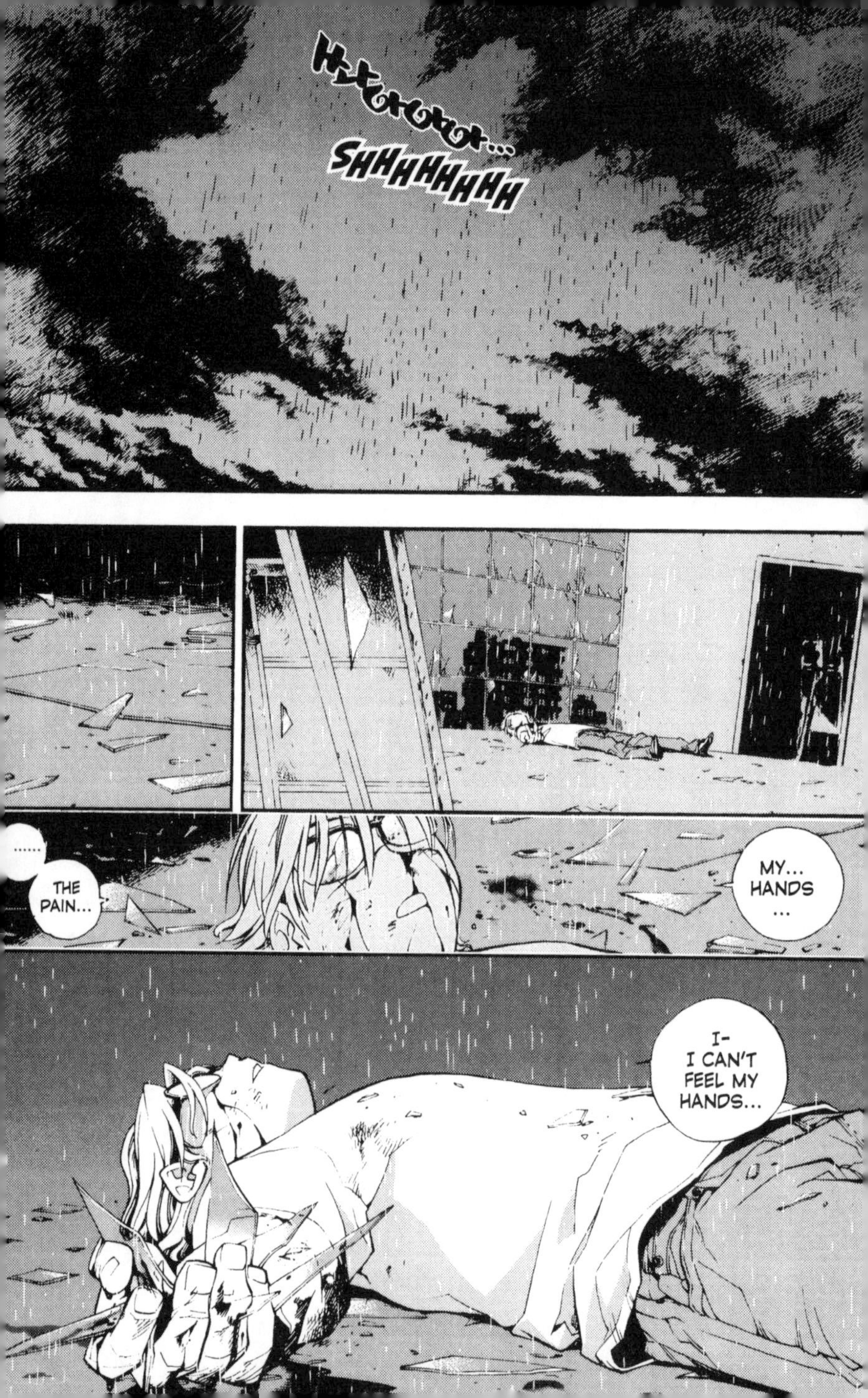
SHHHHHHHH
......
THE PAIN...
MY... HANDS ...
I- I CAN'T FEEL MY HANDS...

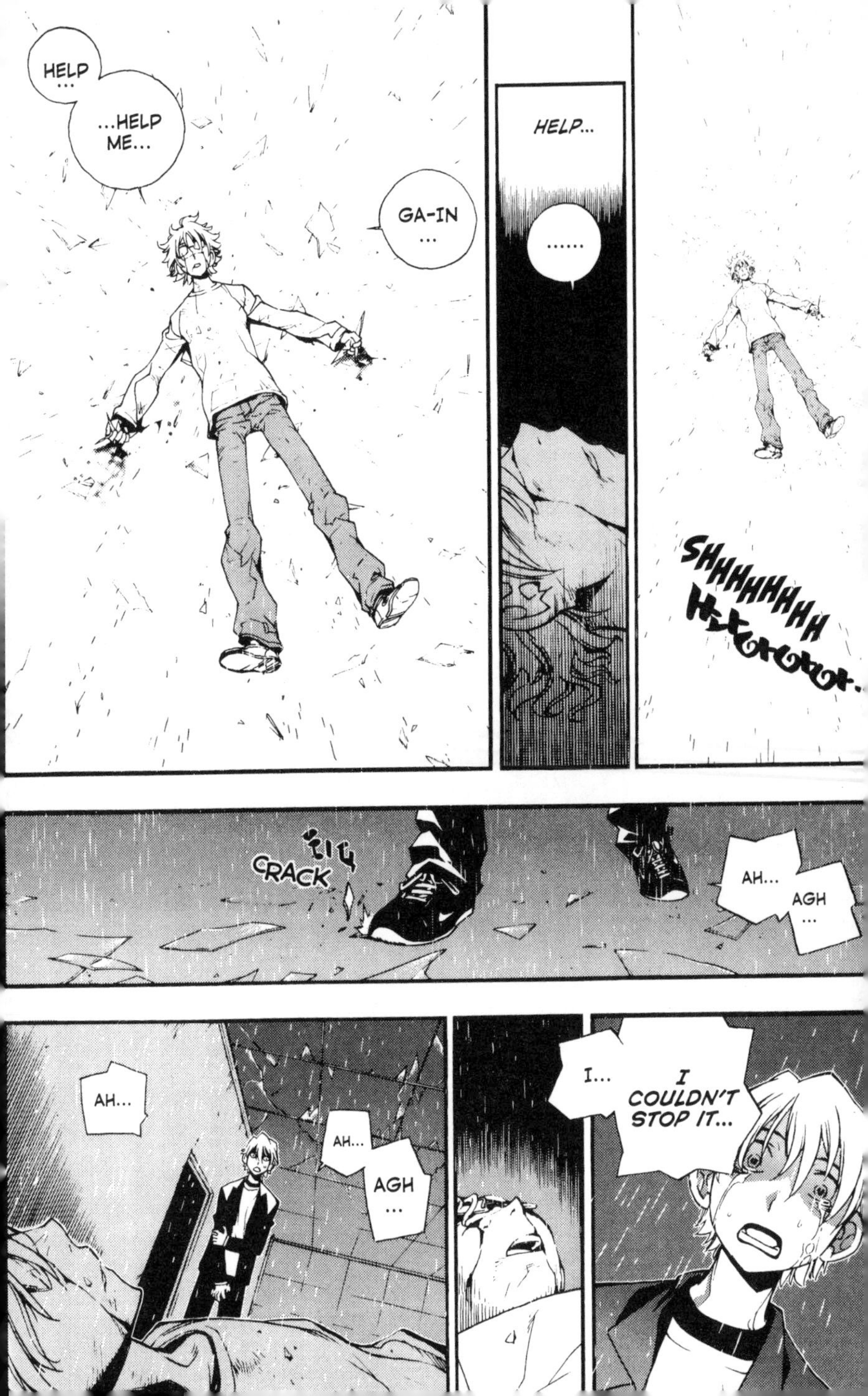
HELP ...
...HELP ME...
GA-IN ...
HELP...
......
CRACK
AH...
AGH ...
AH...
AH...
AGH ...
I...
I COULDN'T STOP IT...

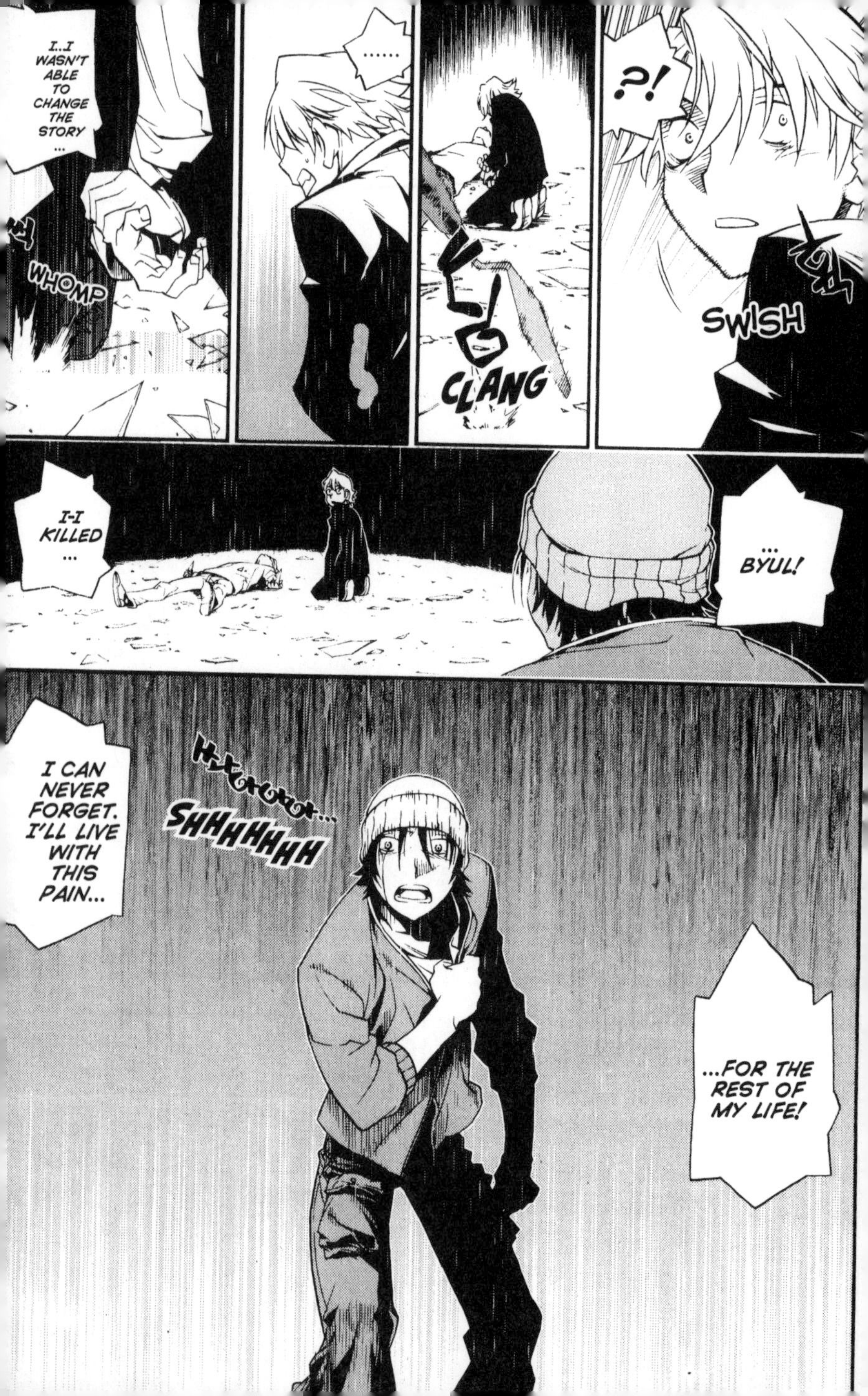
I..I WASN'T ABLE TO CHANGE THE STORY ...
WHOMP
......
CLANG
?!
SWISH
I-I KILLED ...
... BYUL!
I CAN NEVER FORGET. I'LL LIVE WITH THIS PAIN...
SHHHHHHH
...FOR THE REST OF MY LIFE!

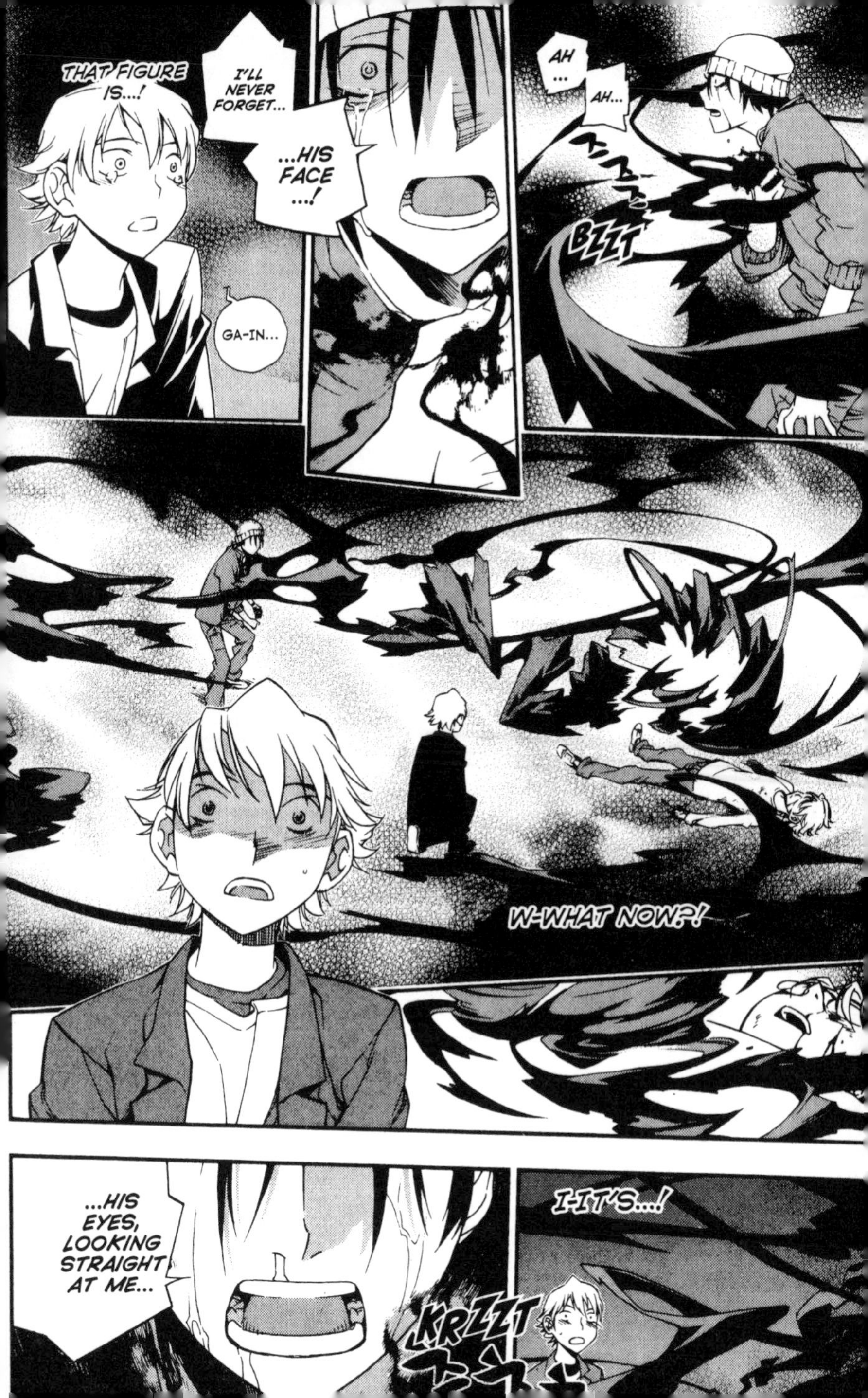
THAT FIGURE IS...!
GA-IN...
I'LL NEVER FORGET...
...HIS FACE ...!
AH ...
AH...
BZZT
W-WHAT NOW?!
...HIS EYES, LOOKING STRAIGHT AT ME...
I-IT'S...!
KRZZT

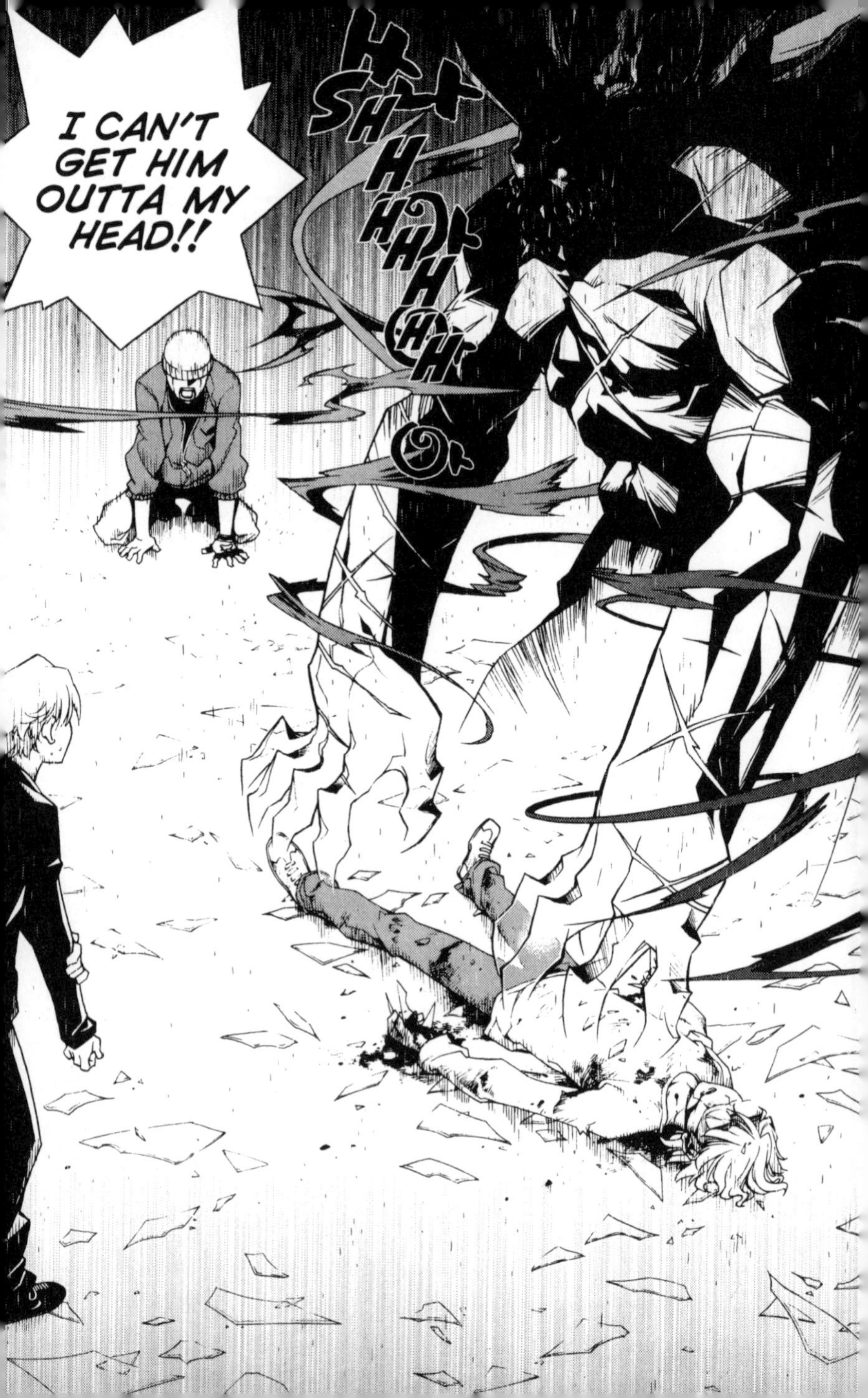
I CAN'T GET HIM OUTTA MY HEAD!!
HH SHHHHHHH

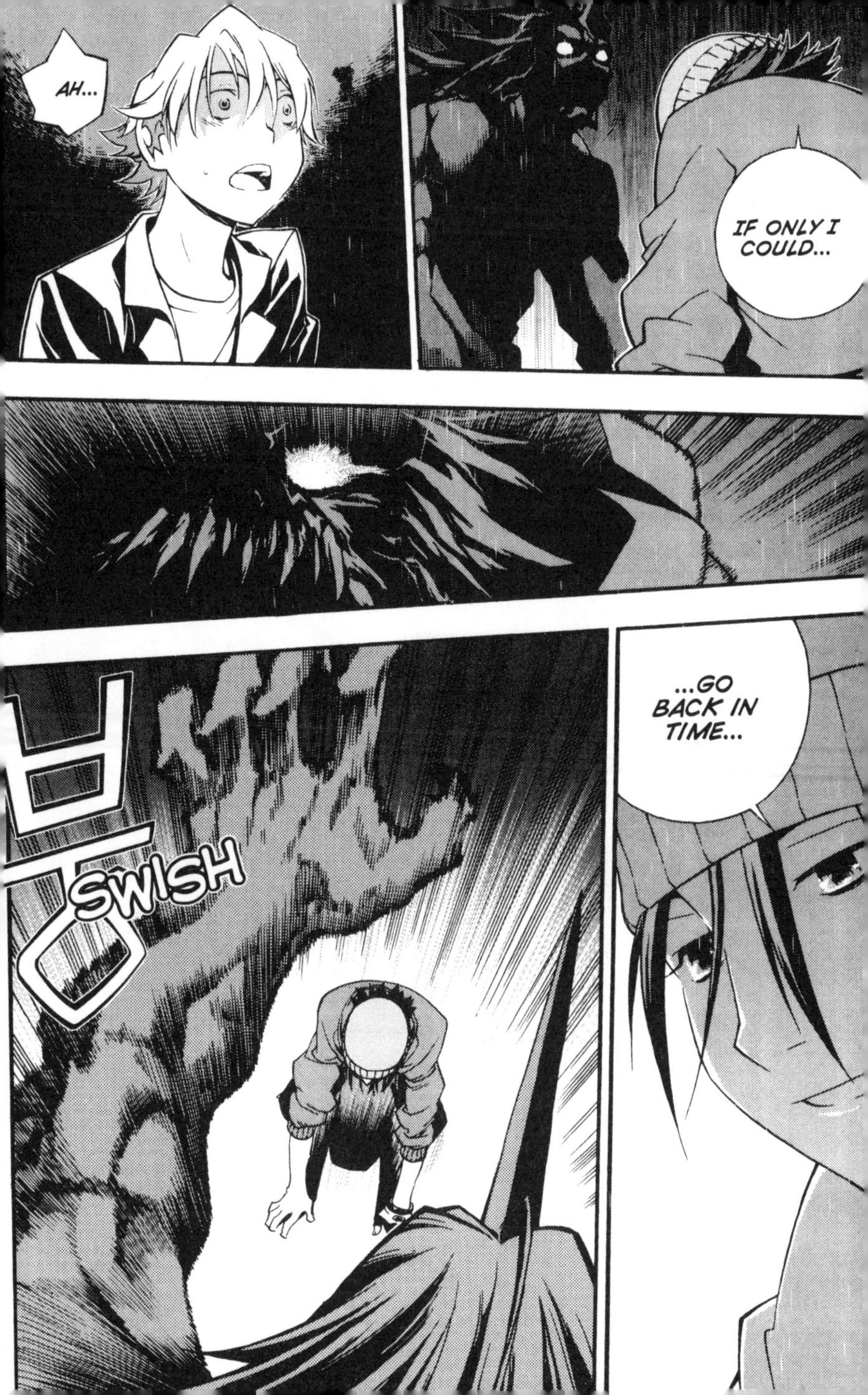
AH...
IF ONLY I COULD...
SWISH
...GO BACK IN TIME...

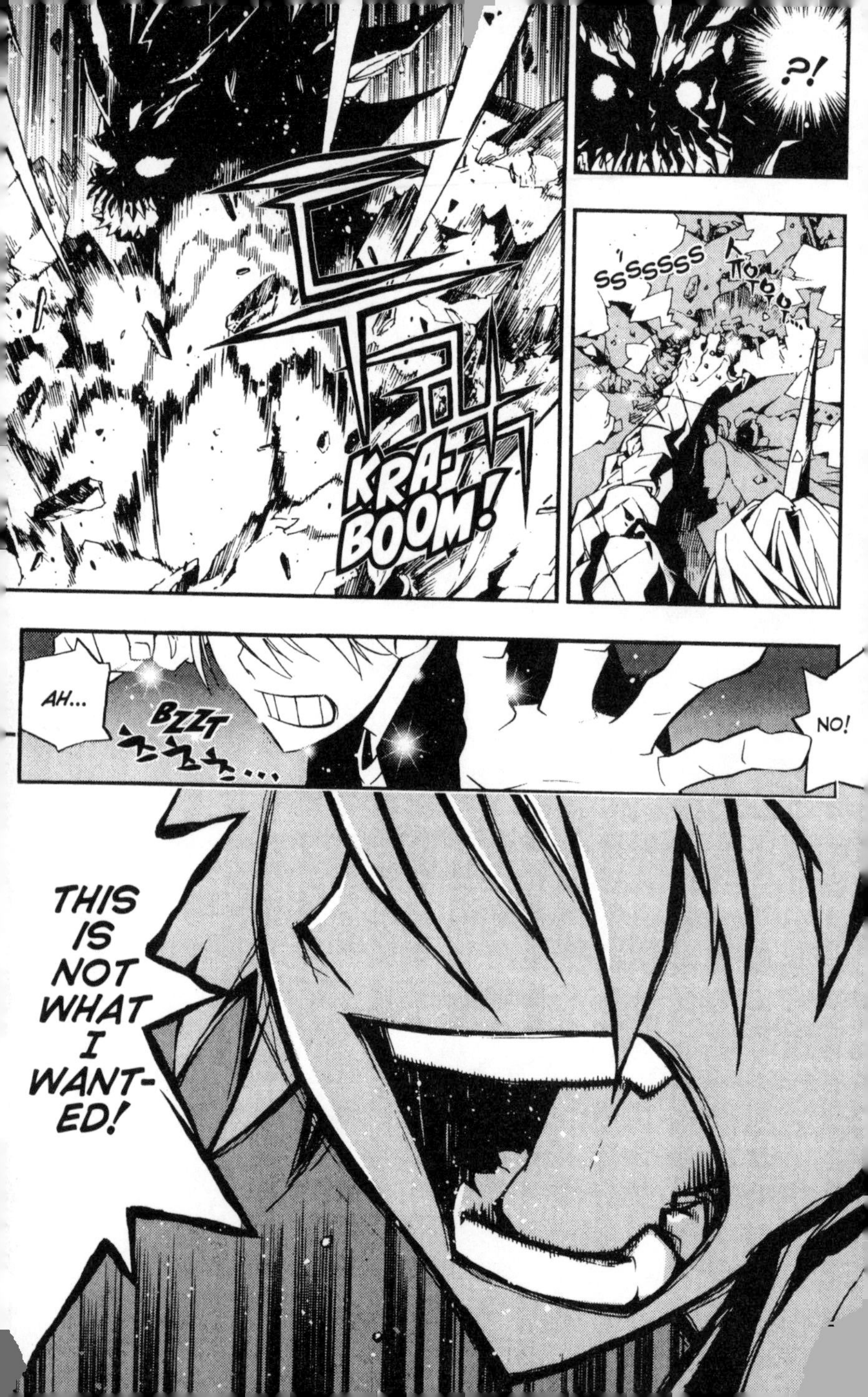

KRA-BOOM!
?!
SSSSSSS
AH...
BZZT
NO!
THIS IS NOT WHAT I WANTED!

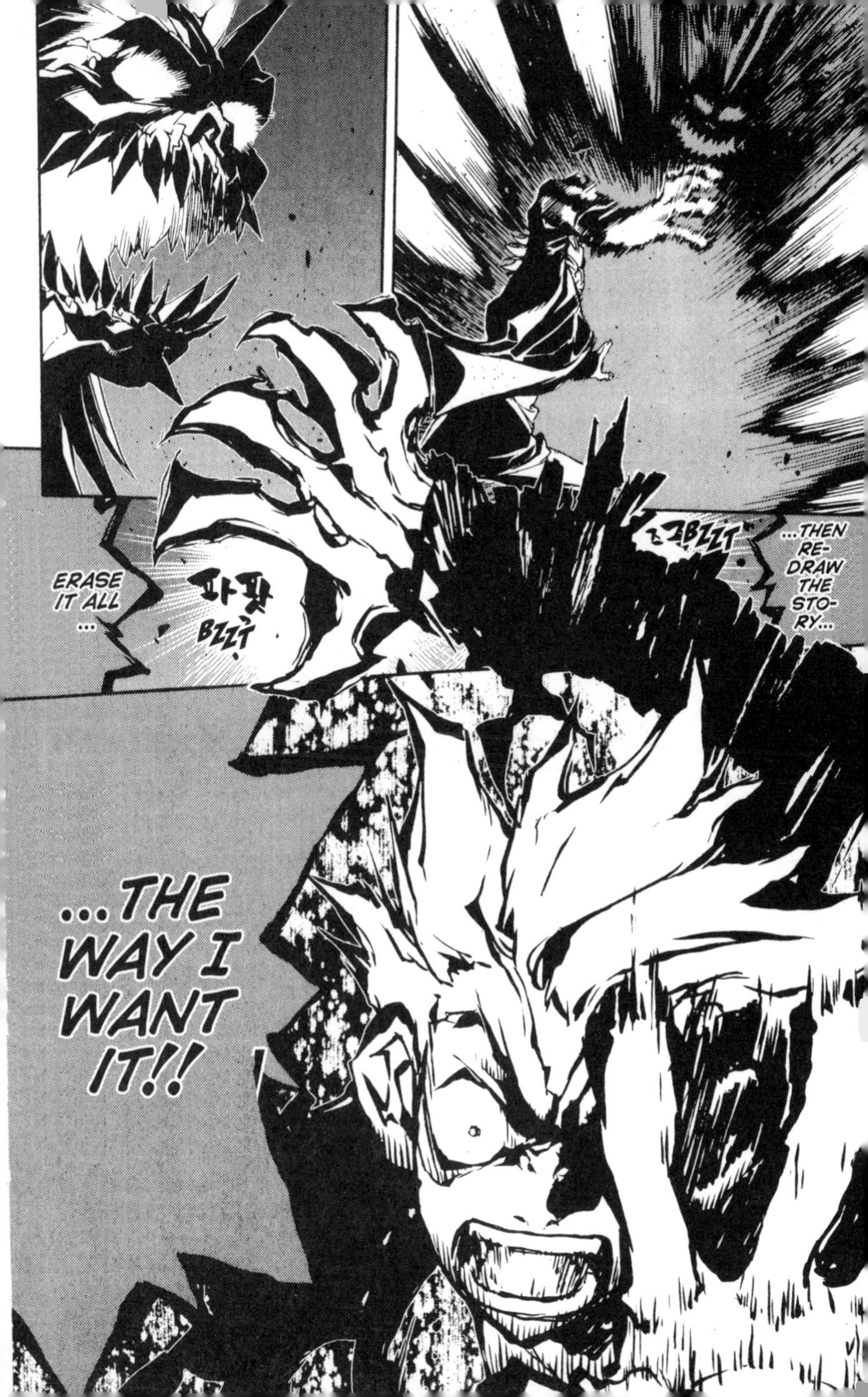
ERASE IT ALL ...
파팟
BZZT!
BZZT
...THEN RE-DRAW THE STO-RY...
...THE WAY I WANT IT!!

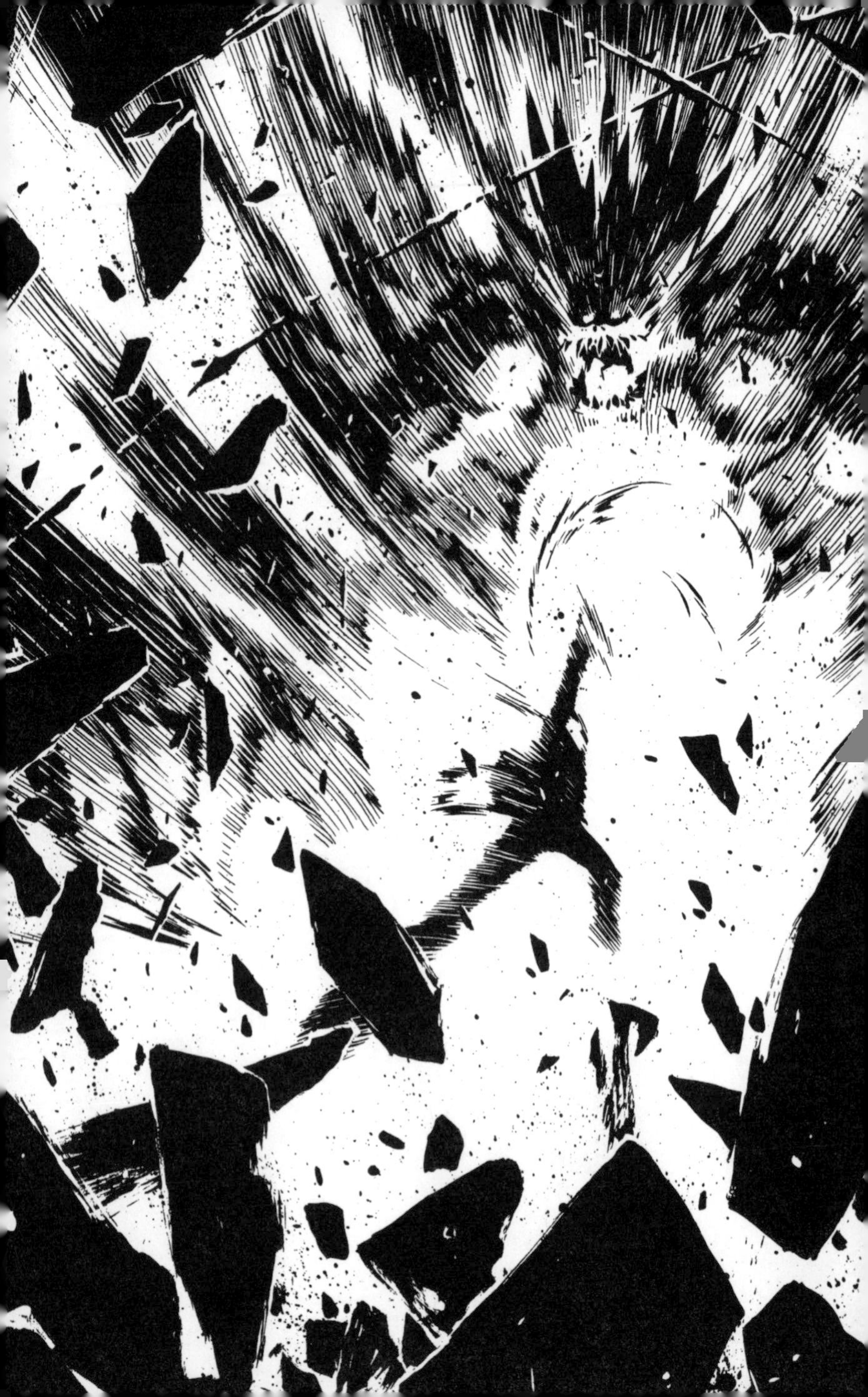

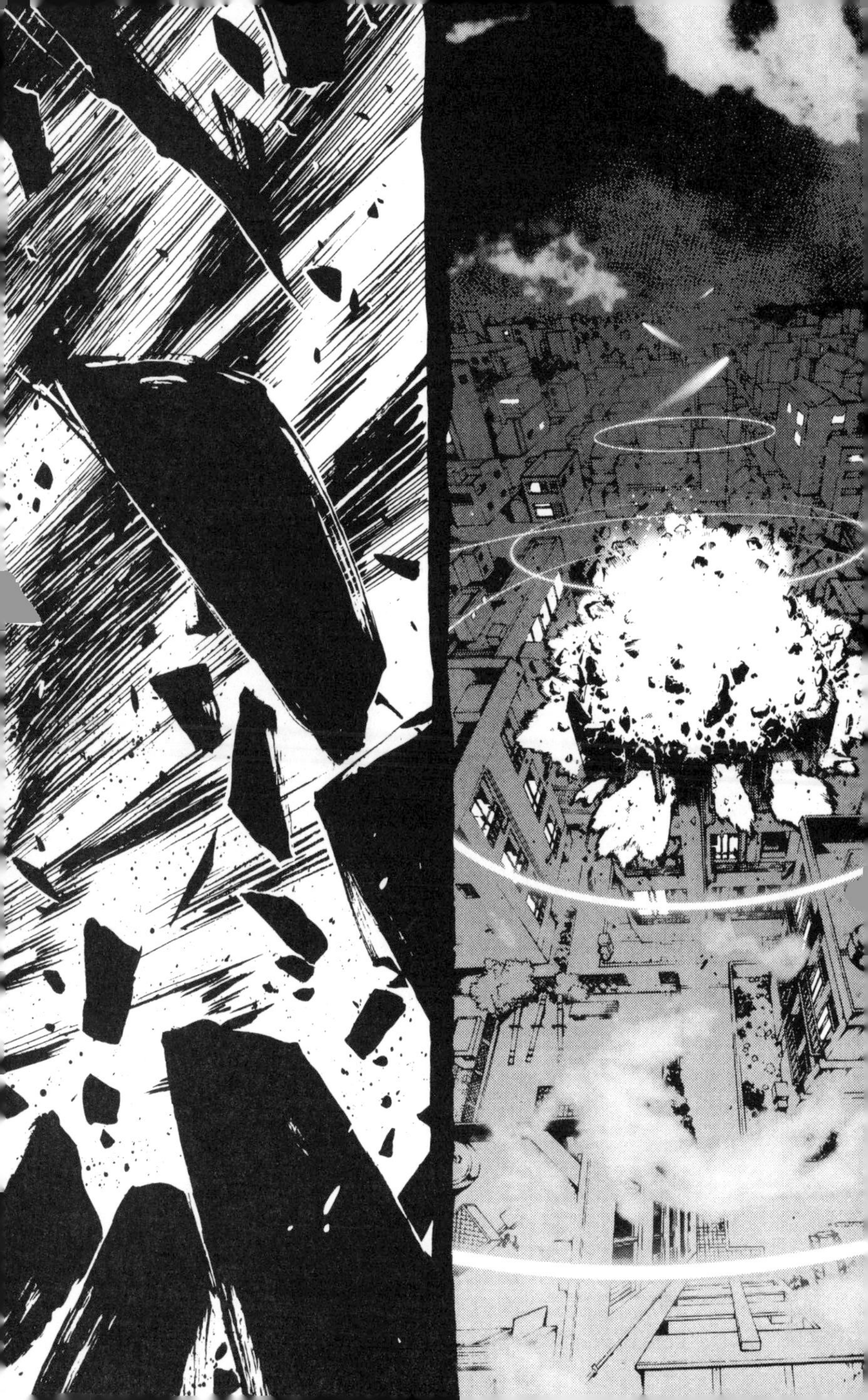

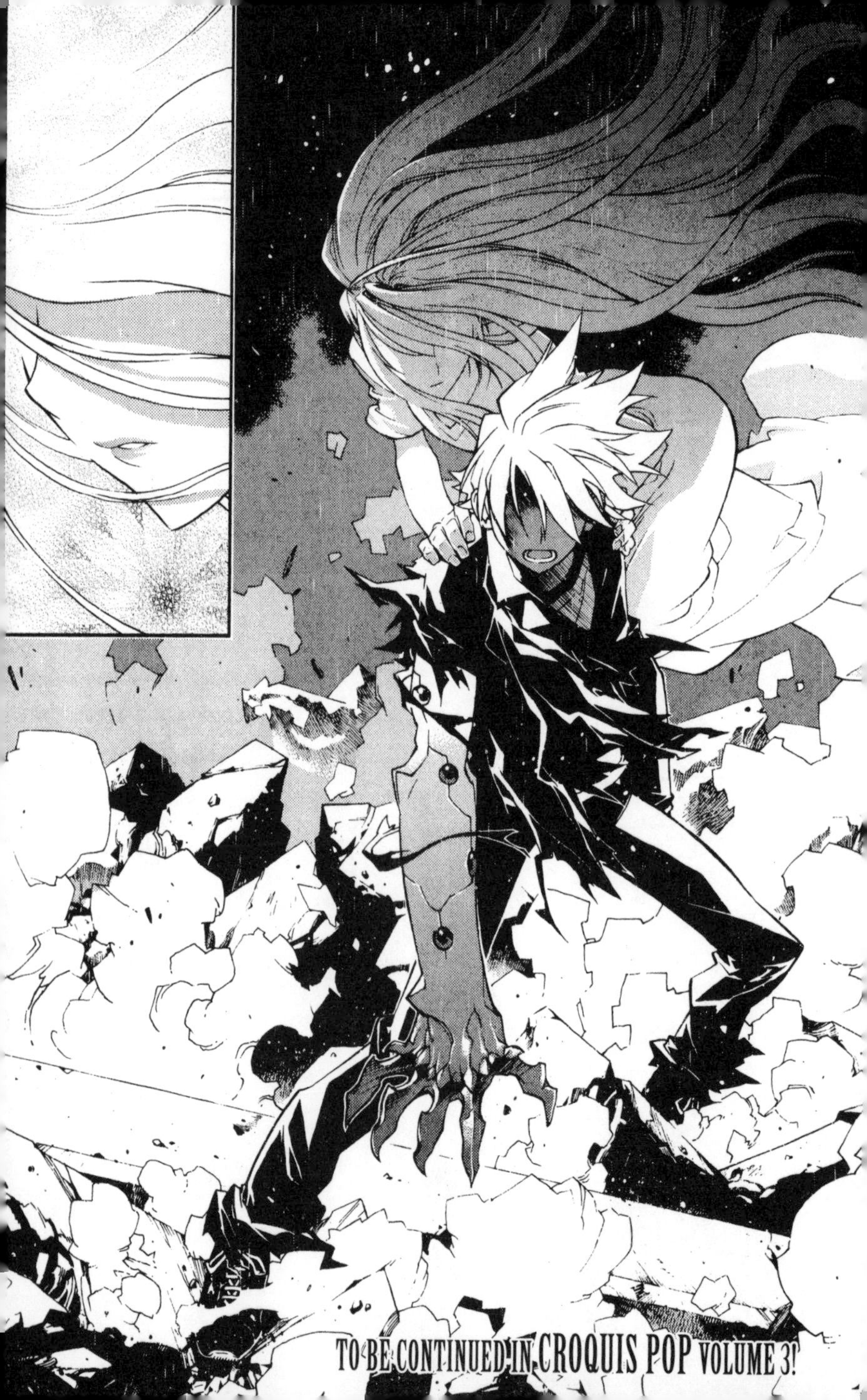
TO BE CONTINUED IN CROQUIS POP VOLUME 3!

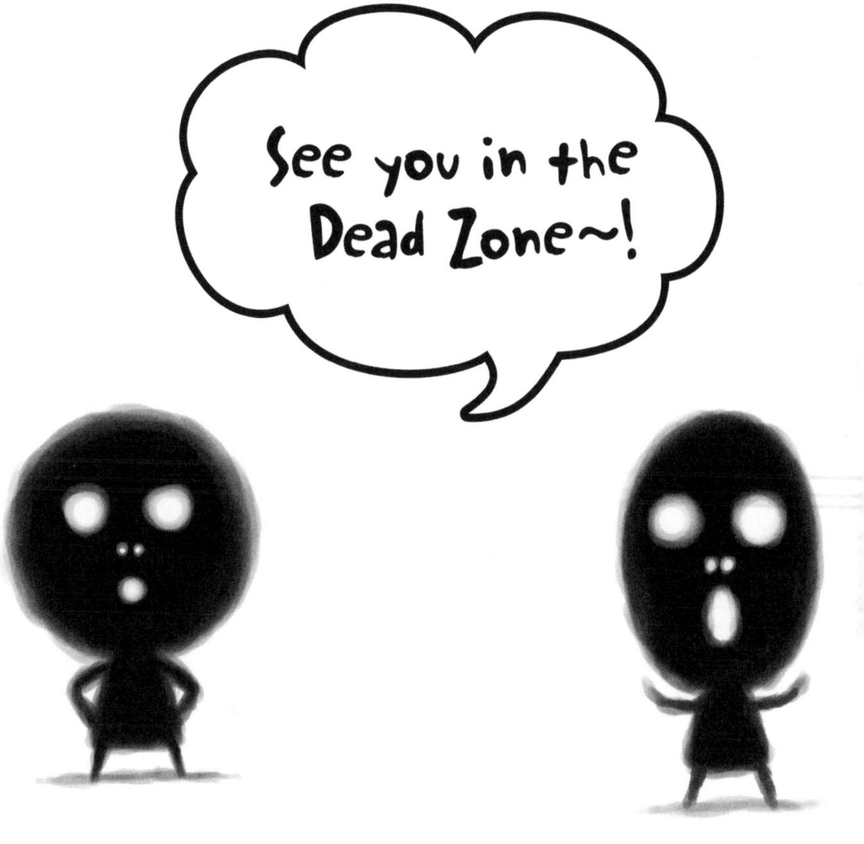
See you in the Dead Zone~!

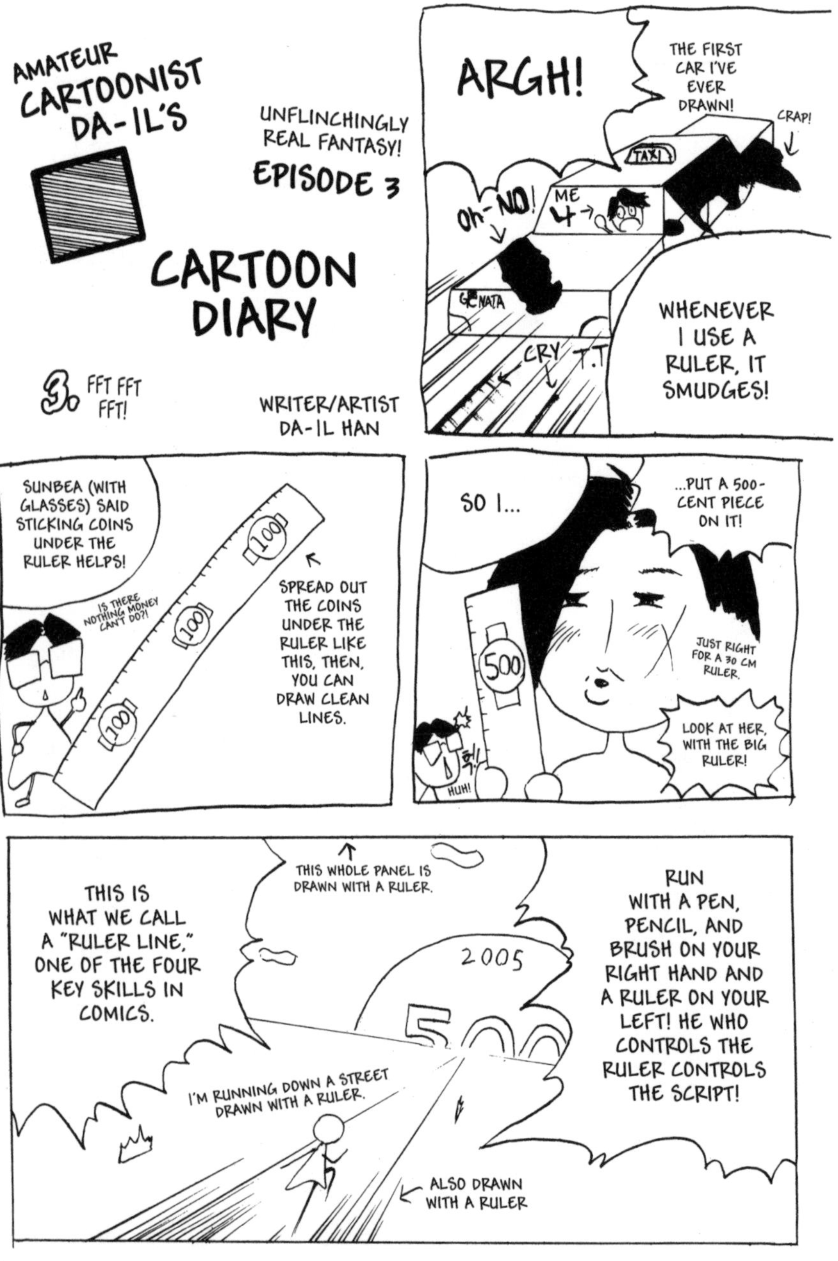
AMATEUR CARTOONIST DA-IL'S
CARTOON DIARY
UNFLINCHINGLY REAL FANTASY!
EPISODE 3
FFT FFT FFT!
WRITER/ARTIST DA-IL HAN
ARGH!
THE FIRST CAR I'VE EVER DRAWN!
CRAP!
TAXI
ME
Oh-NO!
NATA
CRY
T.T
WHENEVER I USE A RULER, IT SMUDGES!
SUNBEA (WITH GLASSES) SAID STICKING COINS UNDER THE RULER HELPS!
IS THERE NOTHING MONEY CAN'T DO?!
100
100
100
SPREAD OUT THE COINS UNDER THE RULER LIKE THIS, THEN, YOU CAN DRAW CLEAN LINES.
SO I...
...PUT A 500-CENT PIECE ON IT!
500
JUST RIGHT FOR A 30 CM RULER.
LOOK AT HER, WITH THE BIG RULER!
HUH!
THIS IS WHAT WE CALL A "RULER LINE," ONE OF THE FOUR KEY SKILLS IN COMICS.
THIS WHOLE PANEL IS DRAWN WITH A RULER.
2005
500
I'M RUNNING DOWN A STREET DRAWN WITH A RULER.
ALSO DRAWN WITH A RULER
RUN WITH A PEN, PENCIL, AND BRUSH ON YOUR RIGHT HAND AND A RULER ON YOUR LEFT! HE WHO CONTROLS THE RULER CONTROLS THE SCRIPT!

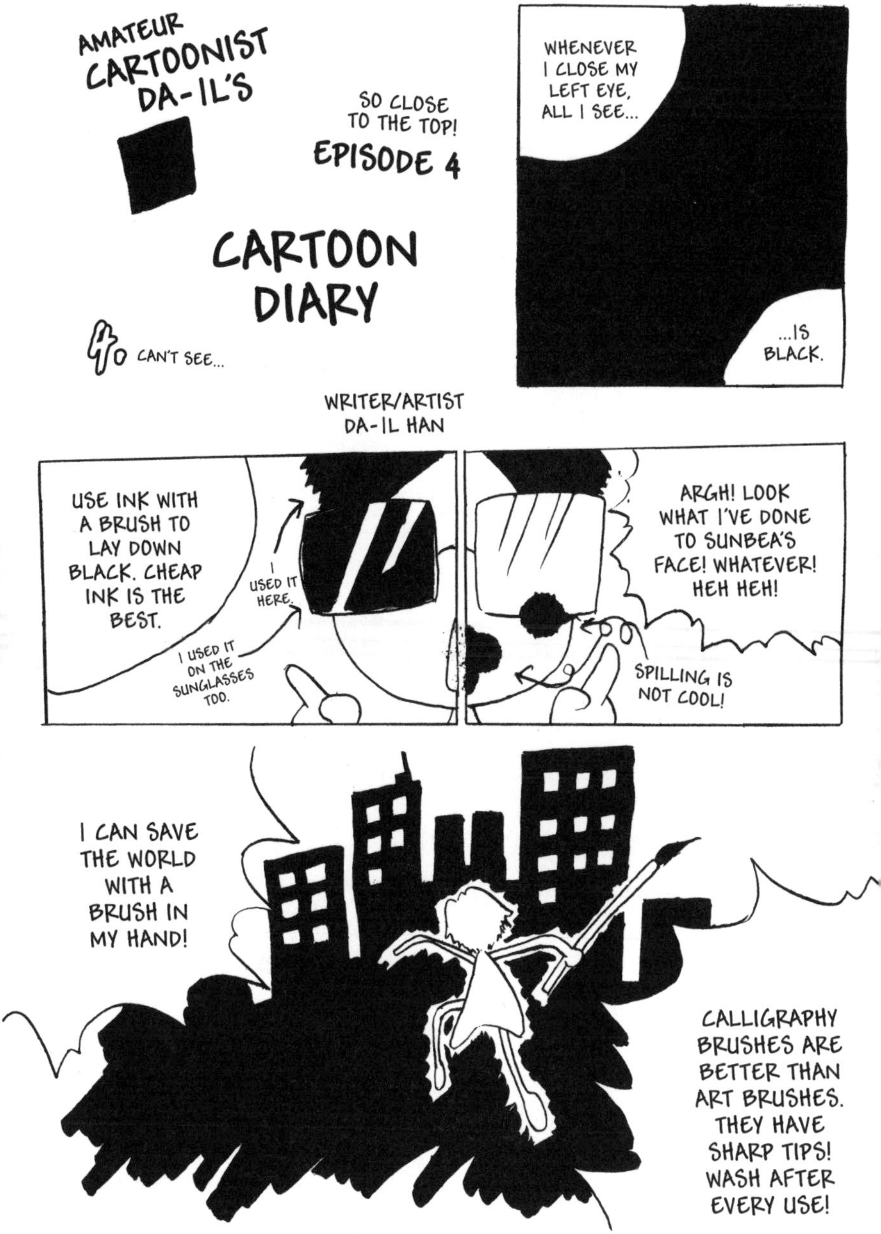
AMATEUR CARTOONIST DA-IL'S
SO CLOSE TO THE TOP!
EPISODE 4
CARTOON DIARY
4O CAN'T SEE...
WRITER/ARTIST DA-IL HAN
WHENEVER I CLOSE MY LEFT EYE, ALL I SEE...
...IS BLACK.
USE INK WITH A BRUSH TO LAY DOWN BLACK. CHEAP INK IS THE BEST.
I USED IT HERE.
I USED IT ON THE SUNGLASSES TOO.
ARGH! LOOK WHAT I'VE DONE TO SUNBEA'S FACE! WHATEVER! HEH HEH!
SPILLING IS NOT COOL!
I CAN SAVE THE WORLD WITH A BRUSH IN MY HAND!
CALLIGRAPHY BRUSHES ARE BETTER THAN ART BRUSHES. THEY HAVE SHARP TIPS! WASH AFTER EVERY USE!

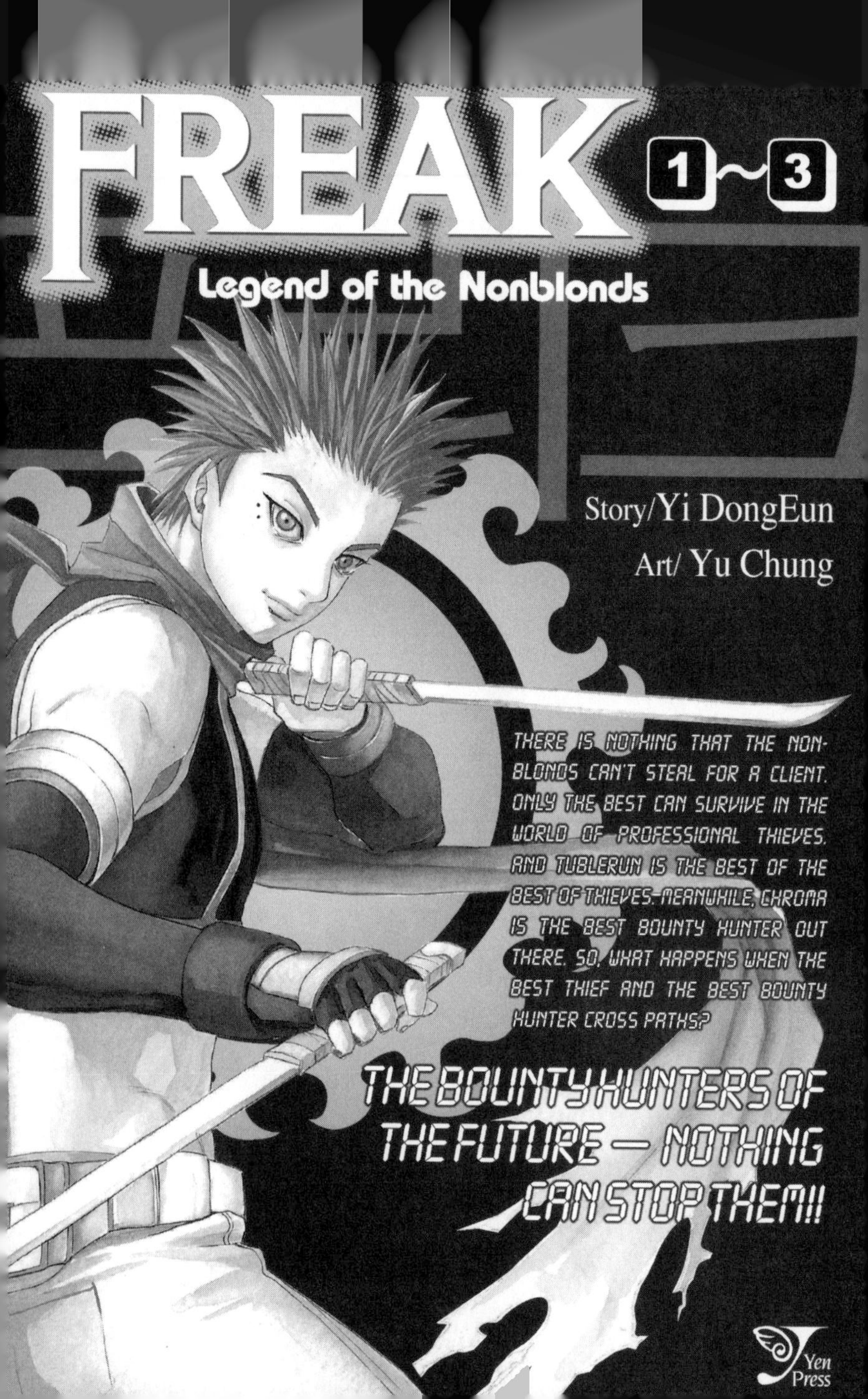
FREAK 1~3
Legend of the Nonblonds
Story/Yi DongEun
Art/ Yu Chung
THERE IS NOTHING THAT THE NON-BLONDS CAN'T STEAL FOR A CLIENT. ONLY THE BEST CAN SURVIVE IN THE WORLD OF PROFESSIONAL THIEVES. AND TUBLERUN IS THE BEST OF THE BEST OF THIEVES. MEANWHILE, CHROMA IS THE BEST BOUNTY HUNTER OUT THERE. SO, WHAT HAPPENS WHEN THE BEST THIEF AND THE BEST BOUNTY HUNTER CROSS PATHS?
THE BOUNTY HUNTERS OF THE FUTURE — NOTHING CAN STOP THEM!!
Yen Press

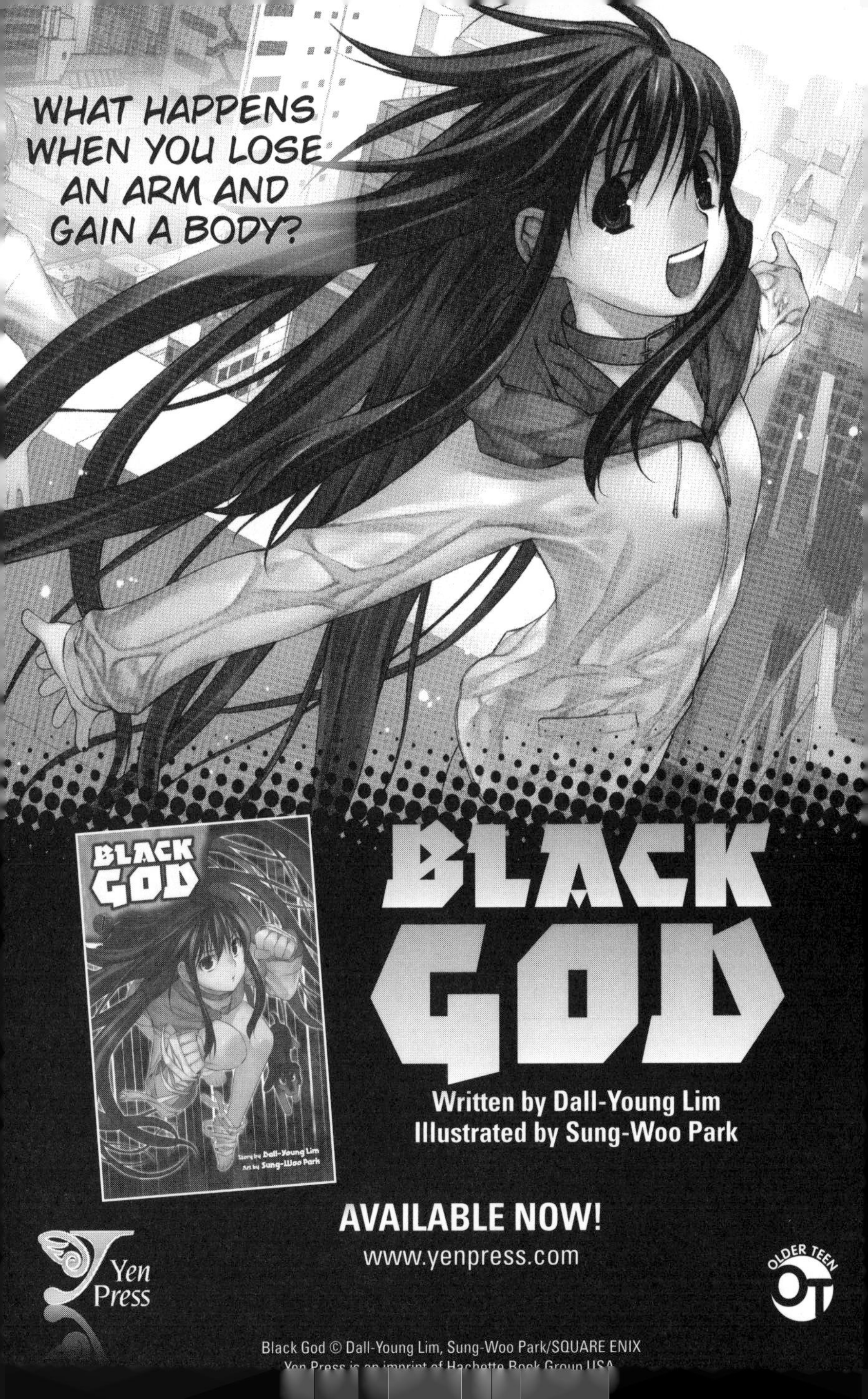
WHAT HAPPENS WHEN YOU LOSE AN ARM AND GAIN A BODY?
BLACK GOD
Story by Dall-Young Lim
Art by Sung-Woo Park
BLACK GOD
Written by Dall-Young Lim
Illustrated by Sung-Woo Park
AVAILABLE NOW!
www.yenpress.com
Yen Press
OLDER TEEN
OT
Black God © Dall-Young Lim, Sung-Woo Park/SQUARE ENIX
Yen Press is an imprint of Hachette Book Group USA